SACRAMENTO PUBLIC LIBRARY

D0175006

14

6/2009

BOOKS BY IVO H. DAALDER

Beyond Preemption: Force and Legitimacy in a Changing World

America Unbound: The Bush Revolution in Foreign Policy
(with James M. Lindsay)

Getting to Dayton: The Making of America's Bosnia Policy

BOOKS BY I. M. DESTLER

*Presidents, Bureaucrats, and Foreign Policy: The Politics of
Organizational Reform*

Our Own Worst Enemy: The Unmaking of American Foreign Policy
(with Leslie H. Gelb and Anthony Lake)

American Trade Politics

In the
the Oval

Profiles of the National Security Advisers

and the Presidents They Served—

From JFK to George W. Bush

Simon & Schuster

Shadow of Office

Ivo H. Daalder
and
I. M. Destler

NEW YORK   LONDON   TORONTO   SYDNEY

Simon & Schuster
1230 Avenue of the Americas
New York, NY 10020

Copyright © 2009 by Ivo H. Daalder and I. M. Destler

All rights reserved, including the right to reproduce this book or
portions thereof in any form whatsoever. For information address
Simon & Schuster Subsidiary Rights Department,
1230 Avenue of the Americas, New York, NY 10020.

First Simon & Schuster hardcover edition February 2009

SIMON & SCHUSTER and colophon are registered trademarks of Simon & Schuster, Inc.

For information about special discounts for bulk purchases,
please contact Simon & Schuster Special Sales at
1-800-456-6798 or business@simonandschuster.com.

Designed by Paul Dippolito

Manufactured in the United States of America

1   3   5   7   9   10   8   6   4   2

Library of Congress Cataloging-in-Publication Data
Daalder, Ivo H.
In the shadow of the Oval Office : profiles of the national security advisers and
the presidents they served—from JFK to George W. Bush / Ivo H. Daalder and I. M. Destler.
p.   cm.
Includes bibliographical references and index.
1. United States. Special Assistant to the President for National Security Affairs—History.
2. Presidents—United States—Staff. 3. United States—Foreign relations.
4. National security—United States. I. Destler, I. M. II. Title.
JK552.D33 2009
355'.0330730922—dc22   2008040699

ISBN-13: 978-1-4165-5319-9
ISBN-10:   1-4165-5319-3

To Elisa and Harriett

Contents

———

In the Shadow of
the Oval Office

1

"The President Needs Help"

S ome say it all began with "Colonel" Edward M. House, a man "neither elected nor appointed to any office," who operated as Woodrow Wilson's *de facto* secretary of state during the Paris Peace Conference of 1919. Others point to Harry Hopkins, who also held no foreign policy position but who served as Franklin Roosevelt's primary diplomat during World War II. Or perhaps it was Brigadier General Andrew Jackson Goodpaster, "staff secretary" to Dwight Eisenhower, "tending the door and handling urgent messages silently." There were other precursors to the fourteen men and one woman who have held, since 1961, the modern position of "assistant to the president for national security affairs," aka "national security adviser." John F. Kennedy was not the first president who needed and empowered an aide, responsible to him alone, to handle critical foreign policy business. But with the coming of the Cold War, requiring the United States to pursue a global foreign policy and maintain a huge national security establishment, pressures on presidents grew. It was only a matter of time before they organized the White House so they could respond to this leadership challenge.

The American presidency is the most demanding job in the world. What presidents do can decide the fate of millions—even of the earth itself. It is also the most lonely job—since presidents cannot share their ultimate responsibility—and yet it is one they cannot do on their own. Presidents need help. They need aides to help them understand the issues they must address, and to manage everything from their daily schedules to their most consequential policy deliberations. In earlier times, these aides were often members of the cabinet, the heads of various government departments and agencies. But as government grew larger, presidents learned that people who were designated to be the White House's representative to their agency often became their agency's representative to the White House, offering advice that reflected interests of the agency but not necessarily of the president. Charles G. Dawes, the first U.S. budget director, concluded in the early 1920s that cabinet members were "the natural enemies of the President," because they were, functionally, "Vice-Presidents in charge of spending." Presidents often found their cabinet members unresponsive on non-budget matters as well. Increasingly, presidents discovered that they needed advisers who were beholden to no person, institution, or interest other than the president and his office.

Colonel House, Harry Hopkins, Andy Goodpaster—their roles were ad hoc responses to presidential needs. Beginning with Roosevelt, however, Congress and the president also moved to build durable, White House–based staff institutions. Faced with overseeing the enlarged range of government programs established under his New Deal, FDR established the President's Committee on Administrative Management, chaired by Louis Brownlow, which summarized its findings with a memorable sentence: "The President needs help." To provide some of this help, Congress in 1939 established the Executive Office of the President. Additional support was offered by the designation of general purpose "administrative assistants to the president," who—the Brownlow group urged—should combine a "passion for anonymity" with devoted service to their chief. FDR's successor, Harry S. Truman, relied on White House special counsel Clark Clifford to handle a broad range of policy and political matters. Truman's successor, Dwight David Eisenhower, added a chief of staff, former New Hampshire governor Sherman Adams, and special aides for congressional relations. By 1963, leading presidency scholar Richard E. Neustadt could write that, due to their key policy and operational roles, "presidential aides outrank in all but protocol the heads of most executive departments."

As impressive was the development of separate staff units within the Executive Office of the President, which became known as the "institutional presidency." At its core was the Bureau of the Budget (Office of Management and Budget after 1970), which enhanced the chief executive's authority over government spending and domestic policy. Others were added over time to deal with a broad range of subjects—from economic policy to the environment, from science policy to drugs. Today, the president's Executive Office totals eighteen hundred employees, working across seventeen separate entities. Central to the story here, though, is the institution that would provide the organizational base for presidential national security advisers: the National Security Council (NSC), established by the National Security Act of 1947.

The creation of the NSC did not generate many headlines. The big story in the July 27, 1947, *New York Times* was President Truman signing on the previous day "the history-making legislation unifying the nation's armed forces," and the naming of James Forrestal as America's first secretary of defense. Only on page two did the *Times* get around to reporting that the legislation "further provides for a National Security Council, consisting of the heads of the units making up the new national military establishments. Its meetings will be presided over by the President."

This second-order treatment of the NSC was hardly surprising. "The Council," David Hall noted in his study of its early years, "seemed a marginal proposal in the context of the momentous debate over the unification of the Army and Navy into a single Defense Department." This bruising battle had been mediated at Truman's behest by Clark Clifford, who later remarked that the NSC was born "almost as a byproduct to military reorganization." Nor was the NSC intended by its original designers to enhance the power of the president. Roosevelt's "intimate, personalized, *ad hoc*, 'disorderly'" conduct of World War II decision making had "caused great pain at the Pentagon and State." In his position as secretary of the Navy, Forrestal had been one of those who felt that pain most acutely. Contrasting the operations of FDR's White House with the British War Cabinet, Forrestal saw much to recommend in the latter. He became the foremost advocate of the NSC concept because he wanted to regularize presidential decision making, and hence constrain the chief executive, by establishing a formal, top-level group with which he would be obligated to meet regularly.

But Truman had his own ideas. Though he was a passionate supporter of unifying the military, he resisted creation of the NSC until the statutory language was toned down to make it clear that this would be an advisory, not a decision-making body. He also insisted that the title of its chief of staff be changed from the powerful-sounding "director" to the more reassuring "executive secretary," perhaps to mollify Secretary of State George C. Marshall, who worried that with the president as its chair and senior cabinet officials as its members, the Council could "markedly diminish the responsibility of the Secretary of State."

Once the Council was established, Truman moved to underscore his independence from it: after presiding over its inaugural session, "he did not attend a council meeting for another ten months," though he encouraged it to meet without him. Truman also put Forrestal in his place. He rebuffed the new defense secretary's bid to locate the Council staff in the Pentagon, and he ordered the secretary of state, not defense, to preside over it in his absence. He did, however, welcome the executive secretary of the NSC as an "enlargement of the Presidential staff," choosing for the position Rear Admiral Sidney Souers, an experienced national security hand and St. Louis business executive. Souers defined his role as that of "a non-political confidant of the President," who would "subordinate his personal views on policy to the task of coordinating [and] forego publicity and personal aggrandizement." With Truman's approval, Souers recruited a staff of civil servants who, Truman intended, "should serve as a continuing organization regardless of what administration was in power."

The NSC got off to an active start, but its main role was to foster interagency cooperation on emerging policy issues rather than to address current presidential choices. For ongoing policy decisions, Truman relied heavily on his secretaries of state—first General Marshall, who he considered "the greatest living American," and then Dean Acheson. And while Truman employed NSC meetings to help him manage the Korean War that followed the North's invasion of the South in 1950, he did so by working with his chief cabinet advisers. James Lay, who succeeded Souers as executive secretary, was a competent careerist who sat at least two notches below them in the bureaucratic pecking order.

When Eisenhower became president, he upgraded the National Security Council. He decided that it needed to be managed by a presidential aide with senior rank, so he created, on top of Lay and the career staff, the position of special assistant to the president for national security affairs. Its first occupant, Robert (Bobby) Cutler, organized an elaborate interagency process featuring detailed policy papers covering essentially all significant national security issues. To review and debate these papers, the NSC met weekly—a total of 346 times during the eight years Ike was president—and he himself presided about 90 percent of the time. The aim, in the words of one close Eisenhower aide, was "to establish a fabric of policy that would reflect the security interests of the United States." And Cutler lovingly described the NSC process as "policy hill," with papers marching upward to the Council and decisions flowing downward for implementation. Under him and his successors, the NSC became a substantial institution, its several dozen career aides now reinforced by a five-person "special staff" tasked with providing independent analysis and review. At the very least, the Eisenhower NSC's "process of coordinating, planning, discussing [and] educating" created, in the words of a senior staff member, "a network of relationships which constituted a national security community" within the U.S. government. (Eisenhower liked to quote the Prussian general Von Moltke's aphorism that "plans are nothing, but planning is everything.")

Even with this heightened visibility and activity, however, the NSC did not challenge the authority of the secretary of state. John Foster Dulles, who as a junior aide had watched his uncle, Secretary of State Robert Lansing, be humiliated by Woodrow Wilson and Colonel House at the Paris Peace Conference, combined assiduous cultivation of the president with fierce and relentless defense of the prerogatives of his office. And Eisenhower, the most organization-minded of all American presidents, believed in delegating authority to his cabinet members. So his administration, like Truman's before, relied on the secretary of state to develop and implement the main lines of its foreign policy.

Beyond State and the NSC, Ike also had a third resource for foreign policy management: his staff secretary Andrew Goodpaster. The formal job was created in 1954 when Eisenhower lost his temper over mismanagement of White House paperwork—"Andy's" initial task was to be sure it flowed smoothly, to the right people. But once Goodpaster solved that problem, he was available to do much more. Quietly and efficiently, he handled much of Eisenhower's most critical national security and intelligence business. He sat in the West Wing, down the hall from the Oval Office. He organized and took notes for the president's many informal meetings with senior advisers on international matters. He smoothed communications between Eisenhower and Dulles, and perhaps even more between the president and Dulles's successor, Christian Herter. He watched over the sensitive U-2 surveillance aircraft flights that flew over the Soviet Union, and over the nascent Cuba operation that became Kennedy's Bay of Pigs. He did not provide independent substantive advice, nor was his stature equal to that of Eisenhower's formal national security assistants, Bobby Cutler and later Gordon Gray. But he played a key operational coordination role. And Eisenhower trusted him totally—he would remark that every man would want his son to be like Andy Goodpaster.

It was this day-to-day policy support, in fact, that John F. Kennedy and subsequent presidents would find essential. But Eisenhower and his people never publicized the Goodpaster role or the importance the president attached to it, choosing instead to highlight their formal NSC-based process. This invited, in turn, a withering attack from skeptics of the process, above all from the arguably partisan but intellectually credible reports of the Senate Subcommittee on National Policy Machinery, chaired by Senator Henry M. Jackson. Their negative take was buttressed by expert outsiders asking questions like, "Can We Entrust Defense to a Committee?" The general picture they painted was one of thick papers reviewed at long, sterile meetings, producing mushy compromise formulations for a passive president while John Foster Dulles ran the show.

Subsequent evidence has demonstrated that this picture was, at best, oversimplified. But as the historian Anna Kasten Nelson put it, Eisenhower and his NSC associates "unwittingly . . . supported the conclusions of their critics" by the way they responded to the system's detractors. "The role of the council was so greatly overstated that its real usefulness as a policy mechanism was completely denigrated." And, as two of the Eisenhower system's staunchest defenders noted, "Eisenhower's . . . procedures [for organized policy planning] did not outlast his terms in office." In a December 1960 Oval Office meeting to discuss the presidential transition, Eisenhower urged Kennedy "to avoid any reorganization until he himself could become well acquainted with the problem." Kennedy asked Eisenhower to postpone Goodpaster's follow-on military assignment so that he could stay on for the new administration's first month; but he had no intention of keeping the elaborate NSC machinery in place. He was determined to start anew.

The modern National Security Council dates back to that Eisenhower-Kennedy transition. Since then, presidents have given less priority to making the overall government function with maximum effectiveness, and more to having a White House staff that is loyal to them alone. Over time, the size of the president's staff has gradually increased—and so has the distance between the president and the rest of the federal government. The action—the real locus of decision making—moved from the cabinet to the White House. This has sometimes brought greater presidential control over policy and execution, but it has also encouraged greater secrecy and threatened accountability. These dangers have been particularly acute at various points in our history of national security policymaking, notably in the 1970s, the mid-1980s, and since 9/11.

The process began in earnest with the Kennedy administration. There, for the first time, Americans could see in practice what General Marshall had warned against fourteen years earlier—the potential, inherent in the NSC, to "markedly diminish the responsibility of the Secretary of State." But it came not from the Council per se, but from the staff position that Eisenhower had created, that of presidential assistant for national security affairs. Kennedy gave broad, day-to-day responsibility for coordinating foreign policy to a senior aide he had chosen personally for this position and would work with intimately. McGeorge Bundy was the first national security adviser to have an office in the West Wing. And he was the first to bring a coterie of men into the White House to serve as the president's own national security staff.

Subsequent presidents followed this model, leaning heavily on a man (Condoleezza Rice was the lone woman) and staff that was responsible to them—and them alone. They were often very influential. In August 1990, for example, Brent Scowcroft was appalled by the initial NSC discussion of the Iraqi conquest of Kuwait. His colleagues had been concerned about rising oil prices and the impact on the U.S. economy, not about reversing aggression in the world's most volatile region. Later that day, Scowcroft conveyed his distress to President George H. W. Bush. At the next day's NSC meeting, he proposed to Bush, he would argue that the Iraqi invasion was intolerable and needed to be reversed—by force, if necessary. The president agreed. "This will not stand, this aggression against Kuwait," the president subsequently declared. There ensued in six short months the assembling of an international coalition of 540,000 troops, which ousted Saddam Hussein's forces. Scowcroft was the man who first made the case for this action to the president and his most senior officials. And in the months that followed he supported the president in the numerous actions, large and small, through which his administration implemented this initial August decision.

Not all national security advisers have had such influence, and few have played the role with Scowcroft's deftness. Their relationships with successive presidents have varied, shaped by how each chief executive operated and what problems he confronted. Some presidents (Kennedy, Nixon, Carter, and Bush the elder) engaged deeply in policymaking; others (Reagan, early Clinton, and Bush the younger) were happy to leave the details to their subordinates. Some preferred regular and formal processes, while others worked better informally. Some advisers gave priority to running a good policy process (Bundy, Scowcroft, Stephen Hadley) and others were more focused on making and explaining policy (Henry Kissinger, Zbigniew Brzezinski, Rice). Some administrations have operated in wartime, when there was a clear focus in policy (Johnson, Bush the son); others came to office when priorities were less settled (Carter, Clinton). Each of these variables helped to shape the relationship between the president and his national security adviser, and the role and responsibility of the advisers and their staffs within the administration as a whole.

None of these advisers had held a top government position outside the White House prior to their appointment. The most prominent were distinguished academics, and most had significant foreign policy background. But their overriding qualification was that their president wanted them to do this job in his White House. Cabinet members might have to serve multiple constituencies—the advisers could concentrate on serving just one. Indeed, the fact that the president can choose pretty much whomever he wants to fill this post increases the odds that their relationship will prosper and that the national security adviser will come to wield enormous power. In every transition between presidencies, reporters speculate obsessively on who will be named to the cabinet, above all who will be chosen for its most senior position, that of secretary of state. But it is typically the adviser, not the secretary, who sits at the crossroads of policy.

America's capacity for wise and effective foreign policy has come to depend on the capacity of the national security adviser not just to do what the president wants, but also to make the broader U.S. foreign policymaking system work. Never has this been more important than in today's increasingly complex and interconnected world. The White House has become the locus of effective policymaking—both for foreign and national security matters and for economic and domestic policy—and all the more so as the distinctions between these disparate policy spheres have increasingly blurred. Presidents have come to rely on the national security adviser as their point person to integrate the many different policy dimensions—defense and diplomacy, international and homeland security—into a coherent whole. Indeed, though presidents have other senior aides for economics and the environment, they often rely on their national security advisers to coordinate these issues as well—because of the overlap with traditional security concerns and because presidents work more closely with, and hence have more trust in, this unique individual. And they expect the adviser to work with the many different agencies, departments, and interests that necessarily need to be involved in addressing these different policy issues. It's an extraordinary set of responsibilities for one person to have.

The job exists because presidents want it to exist. And the person occupying it has power and influence over policy because the president wants him or her to have that power and influence. In the following chapters, we tell the story of how presidents from John F. Kennedy to George W. Bush have relied on their national security advisers to manage America's engagements overseas. It's a story about different personalities, their power and their principles, as they confront a complex and dangerous world. It's a story of how chief executives, to enhance their own control over government, have empowered aides accountable to no one but themselves. It's a story that begins with the Cold War confrontation with the Soviet Union, and continues to the problems of today, from combating terrorism to countering weapons proliferation to coping with the turmoil in the Middle East. It's not a story about national security policy per se, but about how presidents and their aides have made that policy.

The primary focus is on the advisers themselves—the fifteen people who have held this position over the past forty-eight years. Their ambitions, operating styles, and policy views were critical in shaping America's response to the Cold War and post–Cold War worlds. Even more important to their performance, however, were the presidents they worked for: how those presidents governed, what they wanted from their aides, their relationships with their national security advisers and the other senior members of their foreign policy teams. Therefore, this historical examination of how these national security assistants operated provides a rare window into the Oval Office—its occupants and the policies they pursued. And drawing upon that history, we conclude with suggestions of how future national security advisers might best assist their presidents—and the nation—that they serve.

2

"You Can't Beat Brains"

There's this job in the White House as the president's Special Assistant for National Security Affairs." It was late December 1960, and the voice on the phone was that of John F. Kennedy. He was speaking to McGeorge Bundy, dean of the faculty at Harvard University. The president-elect was offering Bundy a job that would do much to shape his administration, and all those that followed. Neither man knew this at the time. But Kennedy wanted Bundy, and Bundy wanted a policy position in his administration. So he said yes, took a brief vacation in Antigua, and reported for duty the second week of January 1961.

After his narrow electoral victory over Richard M. Nixon, Eisenhower's vice president, Kennedy had spent most of November and December sorting out appointments. He was particularly focused on foreign policy: that was what mattered to the nation, he believed, and that was what interested him (he had served four years on the Senate Foreign Relations Committee). He anguished for weeks over who to choose for secretary of state. Senior Democratic Party figures like Adlai Stevenson, party standard-bearer in 1952 and 1956, and Representative Chester Bowles, a leading foreign policy spokesman, could have won the job had they offered Kennedy full support at crucial stages in his campaign for the Democratic nomination. But they hadn't, and now Kennedy saw them as likely to prove too independent. Other highly qualified candidates had different disqualifications. Senator J. William Fulbright, chairman of the Committee on Foreign Relations, had a negative record on civil rights. Former Defense Secretary Robert Lovett was unavailable for health reasons. Veteran diplomat David Bruce seemed past his prime. Bundy, just forty-one, looked too young when paired with a forty-three-year-old chief executive.

Kennedy resolved the problem in his typical *ad hoc* fashion. He made Bowles under secretary of state, the number two position. He appointed Stevenson to the position of U.S. Ambassador to the United Nations. Only then did he offer the secretaryship to the solid, likable Dean Rusk, president of the Rockefeller Foundation, who had served competently, if invisibly, as assistant secretary of state for the Far East under Truman and Acheson, and whom Kennedy first met a day before he gave Rusk the job. The contrast with Defense was telling. JFK quickly settled on the dynamic new president of the Ford Motor Company, Robert S. McNamara, to head the Pentagon. And he had no problem accepting McNamara's condition that the defense secretary be free to name his own subordinates.

It was only after all his cabinet-level appointments had been made that Kennedy turned to Bundy, with whom he had been acquainted since their Boston childhood. Bundy was a liberal establishment Republican who had worked in Thomas E. Dewey's 1948 presidential campaign and voted twice for Dwight D. Eisenhower. He had, however, gotten to know Kennedy through the senator's service on Harvard's Board of Overseers, had endorsed Kennedy over Nixon, and had helped organize academic advice for his campaign. Kennedy, in turn, was impressed with the dean's virtuosity in running the university, and the strong endorsements from Walter Lippmann, the preeminent Washington columnist of the day, and JFK's historian supporter, Arthur M. Schlesinger, Jr. Bundy was the sort of bright, pragmatic man that Kennedy wanted in his administration—and with the White House national security job, he found a place to put him.

Kennedy and Bundy would end up revolutionizing White House

foreign policymaking. They made three enduring changes. First, the special assistant to the president for national security affairs was made responsible for handling the chief executive's day-to-day action agenda, including the most urgent foreign policy issues. In performing this role, he became an influential and oft-prominent player in decisions on current issues, on a par in importance (if not yet in rank) with the secretaries of state and defense. Second, the NSC staff was transformed from a planning operation, with slots filled by career civil servants, into an action arm of the presidency, with its members recruited to serve the current incumbent. And finally, Bundy and his staff created the Situation Room to give the White House a capacity to oversee and coordinate governmentwide foreign policy operations—those of the State Department, in particular—by monitoring communications to and from overseas posts.

No earlier president had had such strong, close-in foreign policy support. Few if any subsequent presidents would want to do without it. Thus was born the modern national security adviser.

But who was this McGeorge Bundy? Why did Kennedy turn to him? "Mac" Bundy was a product of the Boston aristocracy. His mother's mother was a Lowell. ("And this is good old Boston; / The home of the bean and the cod; / Where the Lowells talk only to Cabots; / And the Cabots talk only to God.") His father, Harvey Bundy, had been number one in his class at Harvard Law School and served as special assistant to Secretary of War Henry Stimson during World War II. Mac followed his enormously competent older brother Bill at Groton Academy, doing even better there, and then entered Yale as the first applicant ever to earn perfect scores on all three entrance exams. He excelled academically and engaged passionately in the debates of the day, a liberal internationalist denouncing the Munich agreement in his column in the *Yale Daily News*. Upon graduation with a major in mathematics, he was named a junior fellow at Harvard—a rare status allowing him to study anything he wanted, with any professor.

In fact, Bundy postponed going to Cambridge in order to serve in

World War II: first as a civilian, then as a code-breaking naval aide to the ranking admiral at the Normandy invasion. (First rejected for poor vision, he secured entry into the officer corps by "memorizing the eye chart.") Thereafter, his postwar time at Harvard as junior fellow, and then instructor, won him in 1951 a tenured appointment as an associate professor in government, even though he had never taken an undergraduate or graduate course in the field. Upon approving the department's recommendation, university president James B. Conant remarked that something like this would never happen in chemistry, his own department.

Bundy's public service commitment and centrist political orientation were reflected in his singular postwar achievement: co-authoring the memoirs of Stimson, the ultimate bipartisan statesman, who had been secretary of state for Herbert Hoover and twice secretary of war—to William Howard Taft before World War I and to Franklin Roosevelt during World War II. Then, after working for Dewey's unsuccessful presidential campaign in 1948, Bundy made himself a visible defender of Truman's secretary of state, Dean Acheson, who was under virulent attack from the Republican right as an "appeaser," by publishing an edited volume of his speeches under the title *The Pattern of Responsibility.*

Within four years of his appointment as a Harvard instructor, Bundy was given serious consideration to succeed Conant as president (*sic transit gloria Bundy,* quipped the classics scholar John Finley, when Nathan Pusey of Wisconsin got the job). In the summer of 1953, Pusey named Bundy to be dean of the faculty. In that position of intellectual and operational leadership, he flourished. The rap on Bundy was that he was too smart, bordering on arrogant, too quick with the put-down, not always willing to listen to those who couldn't match his pungency of expression. But this was balanced by a fluidity of mind and lack of a strong ideology: "Gray is the color of truth," he would later declare. The Harvard faculty loved him, and he brought new strength and breadth to its ranks. When he left for Washington in 1961, Pusey delayed appointment of his successor, thinking he might like to run the university himself for a while!

There was between Kennedy and Bundy a remarkable convergence of character and style that boded well for their working relationship. On the surface, to be sure, they seemed very different. One was a politician; the other an academic. Bundy, the Boston Brahmin, was "a confirmed but unconvinced Episcopalian." Kennedy was an Irish Catholic, whose ancestors had formed the underclass in eastern Massachusetts; but his father Joe was an enormously successful (if unscrupulous) businessman, and he handed down to his sons money and high expectations. Both the president and his new assistant saw their advantages as something to build on, not rest with. Both were ambitious—even driven—smart, impatient, and easily bored. Both were intellectual but not doctrinaire. Both were doers. Both had lifetime commitments to public service. Both "delighted in the play of minds, not of emotions," as the leading presidential scholar wrote retrospectively of JFK. Both were highly informal, and prone to speak in shorthand, preferring the quick word or phrase, preferably with a twist, to the long-windup, structured presentations that would come from a Chester Bowles. Both saw themselves as liberal, but also as pragmatic, skeptical.

Bundy came to Washington, however, with only a vague job description: his task was, in the president-elect's words, "to strengthen and to simplify the operations of the National Security Council." Kennedy had no detailed plans for organizing the White House or managing the government. Indeed, he had never run anything larger than the staff of his Senate office. He had, however, one overriding operating principle: not to be captured by any one source of information, or any one instrument for action. He therefore wanted to be free to deal with advisers as he liked—whoever, whenever, on whatever. And he knew what he didn't want: elaborate, Eisenhower-type procedures that would constrain him and waste his time.

This personal preference for informality was consistent with the received organizational wisdom of the day. Senator Henry Jackson's Subcommittee on National Policy Machinery had urged that the incoming president "deinstitutionalize" and "humanize" the NSC. Columbia professor Richard E. Neustadt had just published a path-breaking book, *Presidential Power,* arguing that the chief executive must actively maintain his power to decide, must make his aides serve him and not be encumbered by them. When engaged by Kennedy as transition adviser, Neustadt highlighted the role of Ike's staff secretary, Brigadier General Andrew Goodpaster, who handled much of the president's day-to-day foreign policy and intelligence business, and urged that the job of "special assistant for national security affairs be avoided by all means." Bundy assumed the title, but not the planning role that had been central under Eisenhower and which the incoming administration quickly eliminated.

It wasn't clear, in the beginning, just how influential Bundy would become within the administration. By the time of his appointment, other Kennedy assistants had gobbled up all the decent White House offices, so he began work not there but in the Executive Office Building next door. He didn't get to choose his first deputy, MIT economics professor Walt Whitman Rostow (Kennedy owed Rostow a position, and Rusk had resisted his placement at State). A glitch in transition planning meant that Bundy did not even initially take on the crucial role of briefing the president on each day's new intelligence—a role most of his successors would take for granted. And he was far from the sole channel for presidential foreign policymaking. Kennedy had very little organizational discipline: if he had a question, he would reach out to anyone who might supply the answer. Thus he famously telephoned the startled State Department desk officer for the tiny Southeast Asian nation of Laos, whose government was at risk from Communist rebels, to ask him about recent developments there. Within the White House there were other men who engaged with the president on foreign policy: Ralph Dungan, Richard Goodwin, and Arthur Schlesinger all got themselves involved in Latin America issues, for example.

An early Bundy priority was process and personnel. One of his first tasks was to carry out the Jackson-Neustadt recommendation and dismantle the formal Eisenhower policymaking system. The frequency of National Security Council meetings dropped from once a week under Eisenhower to fifteen in Kennedy's first nine months. The interagency

Operations Coordinating Board (Ike's vehicle for policy implementation) was abolished, as were dozens of other interagency committees. Members of the career NSC staff were encouraged to find other government employment. In their place, Bundy gradually brought on board a small number of aggressive action intellectuals committed specifically to the Kennedy administration. First to join was Robert Komer, who Mac's brother Bill had recommended as the best operator in the analytic wing of the Central Intelligence Agency. Three months later came Carl Kaysen, a Harvard political economist, who was lured with a Mac Bundy phone call: "Come on down, we're having a lot of fun."

The new administration was a curious blend of pessimism about the situation its members had inherited and confidence about their capacity to cope with it. Kennedy's first State of the Union address to Congress, delivered on January 30, 1961, painted the current plight of the United States in extraordinarily bleak terms:

> No man entering this office . . . could fail to be staggered upon
> learning—even in this brief 10-day period—the harsh enormity
> of the trials through which we must pass in the next 4 years.
> Each day the crises multiply. Each day their solution grows
> more difficult. Each day we draw nearer the hour of maximum
> danger, as weapons spread and hostile forces grow stronger.

There followed a detailed description of specific challenges across the globe; the military, economic, political, and diplomatic steps with which the president proposed to respond; and a foreboding conclusion: "There will be further setbacks before the tide is turned. But turn it we must."

Yet the administration conveyed also a message of vigor and hope. Its members saw themselves as a new generation, confronting a "new frontier." In its opening weeks, their dynamism overshadowed their disorganization. The president's public approval ratings were strong. McNamara, his new defense secretary, was moving actively and visibly to take charge at the Pentagon. In his revealing if hagiographic chronicle of the Kennedy presidency, in-house historian Schlesinger entitled his chapter about these weeks "The Hour of Euphoria":

> The currents of vitality radiated out of the White House, flowed through the government and created a sense of vast possibility. . . . The Presidency was suddenly the center of action: in the first three months, thirty-nine messages and letters to Congress calling for legislation, ten prominent foreign visitors . . . nine press conferences . . . and such dramatic beginnings as the Alliance for Progress and the Peace Corps. . . . Euphoria reigned; we thought for a moment that the world was plastic and the future unlimited.

The open, informal, fluid policymaking of the early Kennedy administration suited the president to a T, and the ever flexible Bundy was comfortable with it as well. McNamara operated smoothly within it, taking the initiative, dealing with JFK—and with Bundy—in the direct, positive, action-oriented manner that they valued. Thus, they had little incentive to reach below him.

Secretary of State Rusk, by contrast, was most uncomfortable with it, thinking it inappropriate for a person of his rank to argue policy in large meetings with staff aides, or to handle matters *ad hoc* with Kennedy or Bundy over the telephone. Kennedy respected Rusk and often valued his advice, but he was frustrated by the secretary's seeming passivity. This reticence had the effect of encouraging JFK and Bundy to work around Rusk, the very practice the secretary so resented. When Rusk brought in Acheson's former aide Lucius Battle as executive secretary, his chief operational aide, he told him on his first day: "For God's sake try to get the White House under control. They are all over this building, at every level."

Unfortunately, open and loosely structured policy processes can backfire on a president. For such a process can be exploited by subordinates with their own strong agendas, as they choose how issues are framed and what facts are presented. This is precisely what came about—with a vengeance. In February and March 1961, advocates of action against the radical-turned-Communist Fidel Castro in Cuba pressed their plan to deploy a Cuban exile force to overthrow him. CIA director Allen Dulles and his deputy, Richard Bissell, were in charge of the plan and determined to move it forward. And if Dulles was an aging if legendary holdover from the prior administration, Bissell was an aggressive action intellectual, admired by many on the Kennedy team; he had, in fact, taught both Bundy and Rostow economics at Yale. The new president seems to have considered Bissell to be Dulles's logical successor as director of central intelligence.

Castro's forces had overthrown the unpopular dictator, Fulgencio Batista, marching triumphantly into Havana on New Year's Day, 1959. The initial U.S. response to his revolution was cautiously positive, but it quickly turned negative as Castro staged public executions of former Batista officials, nationalized property owned by U.S. nationals, and began to work with Communists at home and abroad. In March 1960, Eisenhower secretly approved a CIA recommendation to train a force of anti-Castro Cuban exiles for possible future use. And in a memorable exchange with Vice President Nixon in the fourth and last of their history-making presidential debates, Kennedy (not knowing of this activity) urged support of such a rebel group, while Nixon (privy to and supportive of the CIA program) felt compelled to denounce the idea as "dangerously irresponsible." Kennedy was also squeezed by his predecessor. Eisenhower had stressed to Goodpaster, his national security aide, that he had only approved planning for a raid, not its execution. But he recommended to Kennedy, in their personal meeting the day before his inauguration, that the CIA's training of anti-Castro forces at a secret camp in Guatemala "be continued and accelerated."

Kennedy was innately skeptical of ventures such as that proposed for Cuba, and Bundy, in keeping with his own intellectual bent and operating style, fueled that skepticism through the month of February. Gradually, however, both men became convinced that some sort of invasion had to go forward, and that it had a fighting chance of success without overt U.S. involvement. They edged into this conclusion, driven importantly by the messiness and political humiliation that would result from disbanding the Cuban force (which would presumably go public then with cries of betrayal). But while the Joint Chiefs of Staff (JCS) gave the plan *pro forma* approval after the president asked them to review it, neither Kennedy nor Bundy demanded a thorough, serious analysis of whether it was militarily feasible, and whether it was likely to trigger the sort of strong anti-Castro action within Cuba upon which its success would ultimately depend. Nor did Bundy or his staff ask hard questions about specific details of the proposed operation. In meetings with Kennedy, Dulles and Bissell were able to dominate the discussion. At the same time, Kennedy's determination to mask U.S. involvement led to changes that further reduced the plan's already very dubious prospects.

What resulted was one of history's few pure failures. Upward of 1,000 hapless Cubans went ashore at the Bay of Pigs on a mid-April morning and were quickly surrounded by perhaps fifteen times as many troops and militia loyal to Fidel Castro. As Dean Acheson later remarked to his son-in-law Bill Bundy, it didn't take "Price-Waterhouse to discover that 1,500 Cubans weren't as good as 25,000 Cubans." The jig was up within a day.

The failure had multiple impacts on the young administration. It fueled a personal distrust of military advice that persisted through Kennedy's presidency. It triggered a wild, multifaceted, and futile covert campaign to "get" Fidel Castro by one means or another, with the president's brother, Attorney General Robert F. Kennedy, playing a lead role. On the positive side, it led to a far better, more structured decision process when Kennedy faced a far graver challenge in the Cuban missile crisis eighteen months later. Most durably, it reinforced the president's national security adviser, and led to new procedures and capabilities that buttressed his role.

In the immediate aftermath, all the Kennedy people were stunned. Neustadt remarked ruefully that in dismantling the old administration's policymaking system, "We aimed at Eisenhower and hit Kennedy." Bundy's reputation suffered along with the rest. He offered his resignation ("You know that I wish I had served you better in the Cuban episode. . . . If my departure can assist you in any way, I hope you will send me off"). The president felt he had relied too much on "experts" and too little on persons whose judgment and loyalty he trusted, like his brother Bobby and his longtime policy adviser Ted Sorensen. He took full public responsibility; partly for this reason and partly due to the tendency of Americans to rally round their president in times of crisis, a Gallup Poll of early May found that a remarkable 82 percent of the public approved of Kennedy. "It's just like Eisenhower," Kennedy remarked with his typical sardonic humor. "The worse I do, the more popular I get."

One immediate step the president took was to buttress his capacity to deal with the generals and admirals. As he told one adviser, "Mac's okay for foreign affairs, but I have to have someone who knows these military people." He brought into the White House General Maxwell Taylor, Army chief of staff under Eisenhower, who had resigned in protest against what he saw as inadequate attention to building up conventional military forces and had published a critical book in 1960 entitled *The Uncertain Trumpet*. Kennedy made Taylor a personal adviser, had him chair the "special group" overseeing covert intelligence operations in place of Bundy, and charged him, together with Robert Kennedy, with leading an informal commission of inquiry to investigate the Bay of Pigs fiasco. In the fall of 1962, he would move the general back to the Pentagon to serve as the chairman of the Joint Chiefs of Staff.

At the same time, it was clear that Kennedy needed a senior aide responsible for pulling together all the strings of foreign policy information and action. Given the intensity of the president's foreign policy engagement, and the reticence of Secretary of State Rusk, this person had to be in the White House. Bundy was the obvious choice. But to meet the increasing demands of his job, he needed to be closer to the president. So, one day shortly after the fiasco, Bundy went to Bromley K. Smith, the most senior management official remaining from the old Council staff, and said, "Come on with me. We're going across the street." Smith, who had had little direct contact with Bundy since the inauguration, thought he was being summoned to a White House meeting. He soon learned that they were moving Bundy's office to the basement of the West Wing.

As Bundy explained it later, the move was a product of short-term necessity, not long-term planning. The frequency of his presidential business had multiplied, so he needed to be one minute's walk away from the Oval Office. "I moved to the basement because that was the only space available at the time." At first, he displaced the White House records office. But later he needed more space. "We are currently extremely crowded," Bundy wrote Kenneth O'Donnell, the senior Kennedy aide responsible for such matters. "Come and see. (The President called it a pig-pen, and my pride is hurt.)" After explaining why support of the president, management of communications, and other urgent needs required that more of his immediate staff be housed in the White House proper, Bundy offered the clincher:

> In the olden days of Eisenhower, the NSC people all stayed on the other side—but I just can't do my job from over there—and so most of this trouble follows naturally on. It all comes from having a President who has taken charge of foreign affairs.
>
> So we need the space—and I can promise you we'll be crowded even after we get it.

"Nothing propinks like propinquity!" declared George W. Ball, senior State Department official under Kennedy and Johnson, pointing to the importance of physical proximity in cementing working relationships. Once in the White House, Bundy could respond immediately to his president; because he responded effectively, Kennedy kept going back to him. With his West Wing office, and the mandate to connect the chief executive to his aides across the range of national security issues, Bundy became the first senior, full-fledged, presidential foreign policy assistant.

Once in the White House proper, Bundy moved quickly to establish a communications center—to ensure that the president could have the information he needed, and to provide himself and his staff with the capacity to oversee and coordinate agency actions. To do this, he relied heavily on the man he had brought with him "across the street."

Bromley Smith was a career civil servant who had risen, in the formal Eisenhower system, to the chief staff position at the Operations Coordinating Board. Its abolition left him without obvious responsibilities, and he had busied himself initially with finding government positions for the dozens of NSC staff people that Kennedy's organizational cleansing had left redundant. He was known as a consummate and extraordinarily discreet bureaucrat, but before the Bay of Pigs fiasco he had done little for the new administration and had no real sense of what his fate would be in the new regime.

Now, suddenly, Bundy needed a man who knew government and day-to-day management processes. Bromley Smith was there and available, so Bundy used him. He later gave Smith the statutory post of executive secretary of the National Security Council, saying that if he (Bundy) didn't fill it, someone else would, and he'd get somebody he didn't like. But neither man could wait for such formalities in the spring of 1961. The president needed support "now." He was a voracious reader. He wanted "raw stuff," direct communications, as well as summaries from his staff.

So Smith used the resources at hand. He found, in the White House bomb shelter, teletype machines belonging to the military services that were apparently intended for emergency communications but went largely unused. One man with authority over them was Ted Clifton, military aide to the president, who had (through an organizational glitch) been given the role of intelligence conduit to Kennedy at the outset of the administration. Smith worked with Clifton to set up the machines so they would receive cable traffic between the State Department and overseas embassies.

Smith and his associates also needed a place where large numbers of cables could be sorted and sent quickly to the appropriate staff member. They found one in an area the U.S. Navy had controlled ever since World War II, when FDR had set up a Map Room to follow the progress of U.S. troops in the Atlantic and Pacific theaters. With the indispensable help of naval aide Tazwell Shepherd (and the budget resources he controlled), this became the Situation Room. Now, at least potentially, the president and the national security staff could get their information in real time, in raw form, just as the departments and agencies did.

They needed, of course, to work closely with State and other departments to make the system function. Fortunately, Secretary Rusk did not challenge the system, so Bundy was spared a confrontation over its establishment. There was widespread concern that the president and his staff might use it, intentionally or not, to "one-up" or embarrass the departments—if, for example, Kennedy phoned Rusk about a specific document that the secretary of state was not yet aware of. The staff sought to prevent this through close communication between Smith and Rusk's executive secretary—they would inform State about specific documents the president had, so that Rusk could read them *before* he was asked. More generally, they sold the system to the State Department with the argument that it would help regularize communications between the department and the presidency.

A bigger concern, from the White House vantage point, was how to be sure the NSC got the *important* cables without being deluged with routine communications. Michael Forrestal, who joined the staff in January 1962, recalled a time when—after learning about a JCS cable to Saigon, Vietnam, that was contrary to what the president wanted—he told Smith that he needed to get all the relevant traffic, and within a day documents were pouring out all over the floor. Eventually, Smith recalled, they found a workable solution: all cables labeled "priority" or higher would be copied to the White House. This got them almost all the really important messages—but, of course, a good number of unimportant ones as well. Still, what is impressive is how quickly the basic system was put together in the wake of the

April Bay of Pigs debacle. By June 22, 1961, Bundy could report that "the White House now has sure and rapid access to all important messages, and they all come in to one place. . . . This puts Mr. Kennedy and his people where none of his predecessors have been. It is the cable and dispatch traffic, above and beyond anything else, that gives the immediate flavor of the daily world and shows the President and his people where to look further and where to intervene."

Staff aides used the system not in isolation, but in conjunction with other means of getting information from departments and agencies. A key task was knowing what "the state of play" was on the issue at hand—who was pushing what, which players were effectively engaged, broad patterns of interagency conflict and cooperation. By playing the highly useful role of White House connection for officials much further removed from the center of power, aides could get information early, a look at cables before they were sent out, early warning of problems and issues likely to emerge. And coordination with State was enhanced with the department's parallel establishment of a twenty-four-hour-a-day Operations Center.

By summer 1961, Bundy's substantive staff numbered eight people. The senior members were his deputy Walt Rostow, Robert Komer, Bromley Smith, Carl Kaysen, and Robert H. Johnson, a holdover from the career NSC who was invited to remain and who covered East Asia. It included one in-house radical, the young Marcus Raskin, who tried to make disarmament a viable option and would frequently cross intellectual swords with his boss at the end of the day. In his June 22 report to Kennedy, Bundy declared that "the President's staff is at present about two-thirds of the way toward a sound and durable organization for his work in international affairs." But it was very much a work in progress. Bundy the terse pragmatist never meshed well with Rostow the wordy ideologue. Komer was only beginning to play an effective role. Johnson, uncomfortable with the bang-bang style of Kennedy White House discourse, would move to the State Department policy planning staff the following January. And other presidential aides continued to cause problems. In June, the State Department (regularly dubbed "unresponsive" by the Kennedy folk) drafted a high-priority statement concerning Berlin and sent it promptly to the White House for review, only to have it end up "in the safe of Ralph Dungan," one of Kennedy's special assistants, who "then went off on a two-week holiday."

More important than the staff's growing pains was the uneven overall performance of Kennedy's foreign policy team. Presidential foreign policymaking was now centered on Bundy, but Kennedy still wanted—and got—inputs from a broad range of officials across the government. The president's "plain sense of the matter," Bundy's same memo records, was "that the White House must be the center of both final authority and initiatives, <u>but</u> that the great roles of the State and Defense Secretaries must never be undermined."

Kennedy was pleased with McNamara and the aggressive team of senior civilians he had recruited for the Pentagon. Roswell Gilpatric, under secretary of the Air Force under Truman, was tapped for the key deputy slot. And to get an analytic grasp on the complex choices among weapons systems, McNamara named Charles Hitch from the RAND Corporation as comptroller. Hitch brought along a group of RAND analysts, including Alain Enthoven, and, later, Les Aspin— who were soon dubbed McNamara's "whiz kids." Paul Nitze, Dean Acheson's planning staff director, was put in charge of international security affairs. Together, this team helped McNamara mount the most serious effort yet to subordinate the Pentagon to presidential purposes. Though the military resented what it saw as heavy-handed intrusion, Kennedy was delighted.

But he was frustrated with State. As early as February 1961, before the Bay of Pigs fiasco, Bundy was suggesting that with "the developing pattern of responsibility in the Department of State," the president should move Richard Bissell from the CIA to a top position at Foggy Bottom, where he could play the role of senior "operating executive officer" and energize the department. Six months later, Kennedy's continuing dissatisfaction was illustrated by his request that Rusk "prepare a memorandum on the present assignment of responsibility within the Department of State." Rusk's deliberative style was at loggerheads with the Kennedy-Bundy *modus operandi*. His deputy, Chester Bowles, clashed with the president stylistically and, to some degree, substantively. Bowles had a rare nose for talent, and had been responsible for bringing a number of strong players onto the Kennedy team, such as Ambassador to Japan Edwin O. Reischauer. But he wore his values on his sleeve and spoke in long paragraphs. He had opposed the Bay of Pigs operation and urged thereafter a live-and-let-live attitude toward Castro that struck senior administration officials—Robert Kennedy, in particular—as far too soft. And he was not proving effective as a State Department manager. Bundy privately expressed to friends the view that a shake-up at State was necessary and, since firing the secretary would be too bald an admission of initial presidential misjudgment, Bowles would have to go. An initial summer move to make him a roving ambassador was staved off when Bowles's numerous friends flew to his defense. But his days as under secretary were clearly numbered.

Meanwhile, there was in the department a man who was exceeding expectations: the sixty-nine-year-old former governor of New York, W. Averell Harriman. In recognition of his distinguished past service (including ambassador to the Soviet Union under Roosevelt and Truman), Kennedy had made him the State Department's ambassador-at-large, on the condition that he would obtain and use a hearing aid. Harriman seized upon this seemingly token opportunity and soon took over international negotiations for compromise settlement of the war in Laos. Frustrated by the bloated size of the U.S. delegation to the Geneva talks, and the fact that many of the most senior people opposed the stated goal of neutralization for Laos, he informed the State Department that he wanted an effective but relatively junior officer, William Sullivan, to serve as his deputy. Told that this was impossible given the number of those in the delegation who outranked Sullivan, Harriman solved the problem by having them all reassigned! He then proceeded to make unexpected progress in the negotiations. Thus he enhanced his legendary reputation as a ruthless bureaucratic infighter ("The Crocodile"), and signaled his availability for advancement in the New Frontier.

Overall, however, Kennedy's foreign policy was under enormous pressure in the second half of 1961. The president had been shaken by a June confrontation with Soviet premier Nikita Khrushchev in Vienna, where his Cold War adversary had repeated threats to "normalize" the status of Germany, which would put into question the status of the pro-Western enclave of West Berlin, located in the heart of Communist East Germany. Kennedy saw his counterpart's blustering posture as reflecting a sense, engendered by the Bay of Pigs, that he was weak. Partly for this reason, Kennedy buttressed U.S. troop strength in Vietnam, and ordered "a rapid build-up of combat troops in Central Europe" in July. When the East German government erected the Berlin Wall the following month to stem the flood of refugees from east to west, the president responded by sending a contingent of 1,500 American troops down the Autobahn to reassert Western transit rights. In retrospect, the wall was clearly a defensive measure, but many saw it otherwise at the time, and Kennedy was under pressure to mount a vigorous response. Overall, the political climate strongly favored foreign policy "hawks." Both Kennedy and Bundy responded to their pressure, resisting suggestions from Lippmann and others that the time was ripe for a broad German settlement involving substantial Western concessions, though they also resisted more confrontational measures recommended by former Secretary of State Dean Acheson.

But Kennedy remained discouraged about the State Department, and in late November he carried out a substantial reshuffle there, one that the press immediately dubbed "The Thanksgiving Day Massacre." Bowles was removed as the number two man, and given the long but essentially meaningless title of Kennedy's special representative and adviser for Asian, African, and Latin-American affairs. The more operationally oriented George W. Ball was promoted from the number three spot into the deputy role he had in fact been playing for Kennedy and Rusk since the summer. Rostow was moved from his post as deputy national security adviser (where he hadn't worked well with Kennedy or Bundy) to head policy planning at State. And Harriman was named assistant secretary of state for East Asian affairs. It was a better, more congenial team. Yet Kennedy remained unhappy with the department. Indeed, in late 1962 he told his close aide Kenneth O'Donnell that he wanted to energize State by moving Bundy to the number two position there, with White House counsel Ted Sorensen assuming the national security adviser role. (O'Donnell responded that this would be "a disaster," because Sorensen had been a conscientious objector to military service and could not therefore argue credibly for the use of force. No more was heard of the idea: indeed, Sorensen did not learn of it until decades later, when he began to work on his memoirs.)

After the reshuffle at State the Bundy staff broadened its senior ranks, but in a nonhierarchical manner that was consistent with Kennedy's informality and Bundy's comfort in coexisting with strong NSC peers. Carl Kaysen was named deputy, enhancing his already significant role. In January 1962, Michael Forrestal joined the staff. And near the end of that year, Robert Komer became one of the small number of people with direct access to Kennedy.

The recruitment of Forrestal was vintage Kennedy: it built on a personal relationship and responded to a specific need. He was a New York lawyer, son of the legendary James Forrestal, the first secretary of defense. He knew both Kennedy and Harriman socially. During the transition, Kennedy had asked to speak to him privately at a reception: the attorney was somewhat deflated to learn that the president-elect's primary purpose was to secure his help in getting Averell to wear a hearing aid. But JFK also inquired about his availability, and Forrestal responded that he couldn't move then as he'd just been made a partner in his law firm—perhaps in a year. By that time, Harriman had been given State's East Asia portfolio, and there was a need for someone in the White House to work with him. So Kennedy phoned Forrestal, saying he remembered his statement about his availability, and he really needed him now. Bundy followed this up by bringing Forrestal down to Washington. When Forrestal asked what his job might be, Bundy took him to Kennedy and left the two together. The president said he really needed help on issues related to the Far East; the young lawyer replied, "I don't know it at all." Kennedy said that wasn't his problem, he had "too many experts." He wanted someone with an objective mind, who could learn quickly and who could also be his ambassador to Averell Harriman.

Forrestal was hired as a senior Bundy subordinate. But Bundy made it clear that, on important matters, he should deal directly with the president. Forrestal then learned about the two doors to the Oval Office. One was jealously guarded by Kenneth O'Donnell, protector of the president's time. The second was watched much more loosely by Evelyn Lincoln, Kennedy's personal secretary, who maintained a working list of people the president was willing to talk to one-on-one. If he had a piece of serious presidential business, he could come over, check who was talking to Kennedy, wait until that person left, and she would say, "Go on in."

Kennedy liked to deal directly with a range of people, specifically including second-tier staff aides, provided he found them useful and knew where they were coming from, what "made them tick." More surprising, perhaps, Bundy encouraged this—though he did ask that they keep him informed. Later in 1962, after a September revolution overthrew the royal government in the Persian Gulf nation of Yemen, Kennedy would ask Bundy for updates. Bundy would reply, "Don't ask me, ask Komer. Remember, he's that Harvard classmate of yours who was a dozen years with the agency [CIA]." But Kennedy hadn't yet connected to Komer and didn't follow up.

Then, one day, Komer got a call from Mrs. Lincoln saying that the president had a phone call with British Prime Minister Harold Macmillan scheduled for that evening: the main topic was Germany, but the question of recognition of the Yemeni republicans was likely to come up and JFK would like him in the room. When Komer arrived that evening, the president was alone. The phone rang. Kennedy and Macmillan resolved the German issue in five minutes, and then turned to Yemen. Kennedy made, cogently, the argument in favor of recognition that Komer had provided through Bundy—and then, after listening to his counterpart's concerns, he made it again. When Macmillan repeated his objections, Kennedy said: "I've got my expert here, and he knows a lot more about Yemen than I do, so let him explain it to you." He handed the phone to Komer, who repeated the president's words and then responded to Macmillan's specific questions. Finally, the prime minister conceded: he could "live with what he [Kennedy] wants if we handle it in a careful way."

The next morning, Komer found a pile of notes on his desk from Bundy, who asked him to "tell me the story," for Bundy had gotten a call that evening from the president asking, "Who is this guy, Komer? He really cleaned up on the prime minister!" After Komer responded, Bundy declared, "The president has now focused on you. He will now go directly to you rather than through me. Feel free to deal directly with him; but when there's time, please send your memos through me so that I can initial them and he'll know that we're connecting."

For a time Komer would become, in the words of one authority, "the dominant influence on American policy toward the Middle East." Forrestal became a persistent "soft hawk" on Vietnam, favoring aggressive pursuit of nonmilitary measures: his policy role became so important that the historian Andrew Preston devotes a full chapter to it in his recent book about Bundy, the NSC, and Vietnam. And Carl Kaysen "had a finger in almost every pie that was being cooked over the three years of the Kennedy administration," as he recalled decades later.

I turned out to be the economics person on the NSC staff, although that was not what I was recruited for nor was it Bundy's idea to have an economics person. . . .

The first two things I did were, one, write a civil defense program, two, start liberating Okinawa, from the Americans that is. But partly because I was a professor of economics at Harvard and partly because of personal relationships, and I stress this, I fell into dealing with the economic problems. . . .

There was no sense at that time that there was a bundle of problems called international economic policy.

Kaysen noted that although there were jurisdictional lines between Bundy's national security aides, they were loose and fluid. People were brought on as needed and as the budget allowed. Bundy was clearly *primus inter pares*, and more. But as Komer described it in 1964, "Kennedy made very clear we were his men, we operated for him, we had direct contact with him. This gave us the power to command the kind of results that he wanted—a fascinating exercise in a presidential staff technique, which, insofar as I know, has been unique in the history of the Presidency." The press came to call the staff the "Little State Department."

Bundy liked others to handle issues like Vietnam or economics or Yemen, because it broadened service to the president, relieved some of the enormous daily pressure on him, and helped him to keep focused on what he saw as central—above all, Europe and the Soviet Union. There were also tasks that he could not delegate, such as chairing the administration's "special group" on covert intelligence operations, a responsibility he regained after Taylor's move to the Pentagon. This was a matter on which Congress gave administrations wide leeway from the 1940s through the early 1970s. The Kennedy administration exploited this leeway, as had its predecessor.

Most of all, however, Bundy worked the issues that preoccupied Kennedy. This included providing documents and information to feed the voracious presidential appetite for relevant reading material. The "Week End Papers for Hyannis Port," dispatched on September 8, 1961, for example, contained ten items, including "the Berlin negotiating papers presented by the Secretary of State on Friday morning"; "a report from General Taylor on the disagreement about intelligence on nuclear testing"; an "important paper from Henry Kissinger" arguing "against the call-up of reserves" being considered to show strength concerning Berlin; and "a release from Senator Jackson of a letter which I wrote him about the process and use of the NSC," in which Bundy "tried to leave your hands as free as possible." A "Week End Reading" package dispatched two years later included "A fascinating but somewhat implausible account of [Chancellor Adenauer's] tergiversation on the test ban treaty"; the "latest Gallup Poll on the Conservatives" in

Britain; a "private cable from Bowles"; "Joseph Alsop's views on Diem and Nhu"; and an "interesting memorandum on our relative economic leverage with South Africa." Bundy thus conveyed to the president both a range of others' analyses and views and his own acerbic take on them—all this to Kennedy's enormous satisfaction. "I only hope he leaves a few residual functions to me," JFK quipped to his longtime friend, *Newsweek* bureau chief Ben Bradlee. "You can't beat brains."

Kennedy and Bundy faced their greatest test in October 1962, triggered on the day when, as Bundy wrote twenty-six years later, "photoanalysts in Washington concluded firmly that the Soviet Union was installing in Cuba nuclear missiles that could reach the United States." Kennedy had declared the previous month that should such an "offensive" deployment take place, "the gravest issues would arise." Bundy had urged him to make just such a statement, in order to justify administration acquiescence in lesser Soviet deployments on the island (such as weapons for coastal defense). Bundy, like most of his colleagues, was convinced that Khrushchev would never deploy missiles with nuclear warheads in Cuba. When the Soviet leader did so, Kennedy felt he had to take strong action—yet a military response posed a real risk of triggering escalation to nuclear war.

The U.S. response began with a decision reflecting Bundy's self-confidence, operational sense, and strong presidential mandate: he opted *not* to tell Kennedy when he (Bundy) learned about the deployment on the evening of October 15, but instead to wait until the following morning, when Kennedy would be able to see the evidence. "I decided," he later wrote the president, "that a quiet evening and a night of sleep were the best preparation you could have in the light of what would face you in the next days."

Policy was then shaped in a series of long, daily meetings involving the president and his senior advisers, beginning on Tuesday, October 16, and continuing until Sunday, October 28, when Khrushchev sent a public message to Kennedy promising to remove the missiles in return for a commitment not to invade Cuba. Two early decisions guided the initial debate: that the United States had to *act* (a protest was not enough) and force removal of the missiles; and that the discovery of the missiles had to be kept secret until the president was ready to announce his response. A third implicit decision was revealed by Kennedy's persistent leaning against any response that risked triggering a nuclear war.

The secrecy held, even though no fewer than thirty-three officials were involved in these deliberations, and fifteen policy officials attended all or almost all of the crisis meetings. The group became known as "Ex Comm," for the Executive Committee of the National Security Council, established officially on October 22, and that label is typically applied to all of the Cuban missile crisis meetings. Bundy's role has been the subject of substantial controversy. Given the range of players, the enormous stakes, and the intense involvement of Bobby Kennedy, Bundy could not manage the process directly in the way he did for lesser issues. Instead, he worked within it to ensure that Kennedy heard the broadest range of views, and that no option was prematurely rejected. Within two days, the options with serious support had narrowed down to two: an air strike to destroy the missiles before they became operational; and a blockade (soon relabeled a "quarantine") to prevent further material from reaching the island, and to signal American seriousness and readiness to go further.

Bundy found neither very satisfactory, and between Thursday evening and Friday morning, the 18th and 19th, he seemed to endorse, sequentially, three separate positions: a low-key diplomatic response (which no one supported); the quarantine; and a surprise air strike. He then stuck with the last, believing that both of the serious options needed refinement by people the president trusted, and knowing that McNamara, Sorensen, and Robert Kennedy were all backers of the quarantine. Bundy served as "straw boss" of the group working on that air strike option, which he and General Taylor presented to the president on Saturday afternoon. By then, JFK had pretty much decided on the quarantine as a first step. Both Robert Kennedy and Sorensen expressed unhappiness with Bundy's behavior: the former thought he "did some strange flipflops"; the latter would recall it as "not one of Bundy's best weeks." But the president wanted the air strike option kept open—because he had doubts the blockade would work, and perhaps also because he wanted the military to believe that their preferred course of action was receiving full consideration. "I almost deliberately stayed in the minority," Bundy recalled later. "I felt that it was very important to keep the President's choices open."

Ernest May and Philip Zelikow, after years of listening to and summarizing tape recordings of Ex Comm sessions, found Bundy "unsettled during the first week about what to do, offering many questions but fewer answers," but becoming "stronger and more focused as the crisis develops." Such behavior, they do not add, was however fully consistent with the role of protecting the president's choices. (Of course, few officials stuck with one option throughout the extraordinarily lengthy, sophisticated, and intense discussion. The attorney general's condemnation of a sudden air strike as a "Pearl Harbor" would make him remembered as a constant advocate of the quarantine. "But there is no evidence that Robert Kennedy knew which option he favored from the start," and the final Ex Comm choice that his brother adopted included the threat of an air strike should the blockade prove insufficient.)

Bundy played additional critical staff roles during the crisis. As David Hall notes, he "encouraged others to be completely uninhibited in their views," ensured that those outside the Ex Comm—Lovett, Acheson, and McCloy—"were fully conversant with all relevant information," did the same for the CIA's Soviet experts, prepared "the checklist of topics to be taken up at each Ex Comm session," and even took time to console one second-tier participant, State Department intelligence director Roger Hilsman, whom Kennedy had given "a tongue lashing" for allowing the leak of sensitive information.

The entire Ex Comm process has been widely heralded as an example of collegial decision making at its best. The president encouraged his advisers to argue and analyze their way to a consensus on what his choices were, and to present them to him, warts and all. Bundy worked in multiple ways to facilitate this exemplary process. But not all the relevant players were consistently at the table. Astonishing in retrospect is the limited participation of the uniformed military, as the president, in Bundy's words, "kept all of [the Joint Chiefs] but Max Taylor at a distance from ExComm." Kennedy, though, did meet with the chiefs, separately and at a formal NSC session, and their pro-invasion views were conveyed regularly and forcefully in person and through the chairman, General Taylor.

Moreover, in the harrowing final days between Kennedy's speech on the evening of Monday, October 22, announcing the blockade and Khrushchev's Sunday morning, October 28, promise to withdraw the missiles, Kennedy went outside the group's parameters, substantively and procedurally, to minimize the danger of nuclear war. The United States had nuclear-armed missiles deployed in Turkey, a NATO ally, that neither Kennedy nor Eisenhower had wanted or thought America needed. Ex Comm members had agreed, though, that to offer to trade them for the missiles in Cuba would show weakness and undermine NATO. On the final Saturday, however, Kennedy spoke persistently in the Ex Comm discussion of how he could hardly justify an invasion of Cuba if removal of the missiles in Turkey could get the Soviet missiles out of Cuba. He then invited a "smaller group" of eight to join him in the Oval Office, and this group crafted, at Secretary Rusk's recommendation, a message that the president's brother would deliver personally to Soviet ambassador Anatoly Dobrynin: that Khrushchev had to decide to withdraw the missiles "within the next 12 or possibly 24 hours," and that no explicit trade-off with the missiles in Turkey was possible. However, Robert Kennedy added, the president had previously intended to remove those missiles, and planned to do so quietly a few months after the missiles in Cuba were removed.

So anxious was JFK to avoid nuclear war that he went even further: he also approved that Saturday a secret proposal by Rusk that in the event Khrushchev rejected the terms proffered by his brother, a Columbia University professor (former UN official Andrew Cordier) would recommend to UN Secretary-General U Thant that he make a public proposal for a Turkey-for-Cuban-missiles trade. The president made no promise to accept such a proposal, but the fact that he was willing to have Rusk create this possibility was testament to his determination to walk at least two extra miles. And Khrushchev's posture was similar. As Allison and Zelikow summarized the matter, "to end this crisis, Kennedy was prepared to pay more, and Khrushchev to accept less, than the other required or understood." Or as John Lewis Gaddis concludes in the light of post–Cold War revelations, "far from opposing a compromise, [JFK] pushed for one more strongly than anyone else in his administration."

The denouement came on Sunday morning, when the Soviet government broadcast its leader's answer. It had "given a new order to dismantle the arms which you described as offensive, and to crate and return them to the Soviet Union," and the Soviet premier accepted "with respect and trust" Kennedy's assurances against an invasion of Cuba. It was Bundy's "happy task," as he later recounted, "to give this news to the president over the telephone. He was pleased." As the crisis wound down, Kennedy admonished his aides not to gloat, not to declare victory. But victory is how it was widely perceived.

Kennedy's success in the stark missile confrontation opened the way for a more conciliatory Cold War policy. Despite his poor relations with the military (save for General Taylor), Kennedy's reputation was buttressed sufficiently for him to give a memorable speech at American University in June 1963 that paved the way for the signing in July of a Limited Test Ban Treaty in Moscow. Averell Harriman, now number three in the State Department, led the American delegation to the test ban talks. Carl Kaysen, deputy to Bundy, played an important role in Harriman's selection for this task, worked to get pro–test ban witnesses on the list for a preliminary hearing at the Senate Armed Services Committee, and served, according to one respected journalist, as "a key member, perhaps the key member, of the Harriman mission."

Less salutary was policymaking on Vietnam. Here the Kennedy-Bundy *ad hoc* mode of operation generated a series of incremental decisions that coped with the present but piled up problems for the future. After the French defeat and withdrawal from Vietnam, and the division of the country, the Eisenhower administration provided substantial economic and military aid to the South against the Viet Cong insurgency supported by the Communist North. Kennedy reluctantly expanded the American commitment, with the active support of McNamara, Taylor, and (more skeptically) Rusk, and amid the active questioning of more junior officials—notably Forrestal, Harriman, and Roger Hilsman (who had taken over the East Asia portfolio at State from Harriman). Bundy facilitated both the escalation and the skepticism, as his president wanted. In the short run, this tension worked: it kept Kennedy informed of competing views and options, while allowing incremental new deployments of military advisers to go forward. But the goal of the skeptics was Vietnamese reform, not U.S. withdrawal.

A crisis came in late August 1963, when the South Vietnamese dictator Ngo Dinh Diem, urged on by his brother and chief political adviser Ngo Dinh Nhu, responded to rising Buddhist opposition by ordering brutal raids on pagodas across the country. In response, Hilsman drafted a cable declaring, essentially, that Diem must rid himself of Nhu or lose American support. With Kennedy away vacationing on Cape Cod and McNamara, Rusk, Bundy, Taylor, and CIA director John McCone also off for the weekend, Forrestal got the cable cleared by subcabinet officials (and by Kennedy and Rusk on the telephone). He then sent it forward on August 24 as official policy, exploiting the Kennedy-Bundy pattern of informality and delegation of power within the Bundy staff. McNamara and Taylor were livid, and Rusk cabled Saigon rescinding the August 24 directive. But with the newly arrived ambassador to Vietnam, Henry Cabot Lodge, sympathetic to the original message, it "set the administration on a new course that would result in the overthrow of Diem and Nhu and the Americanization of the war." This was despite the fact that, as McNamara would later say, "U.S. officials in both Washington and Saigon remained deeply divided about the wisdom of [Diem's] removal." "My God! My government is coming apart," Kennedy declared.

Yet this "coming apart" on Vietnam was a symptom of the Bundy system's larger strength. The president wanted options kept open. For an ongoing, multifaceted enterprise like the Vietnam War, the only way to keep them open was to nurture and reinforce a competing group of advocates, and that meant giving White House backing to those in weaker positions institutionally who were willing to press their critical views if given the chance. More generally, working for a president with a strong sense for people and virtually no organizational instincts, Bundy brought far more order to his administration's foreign policymaking than Kennedy had a right to expect. And as a traditionalist believer in established institutions, he worked to protect Rusk even as the Kennedy process, and Bundy's own dynamism, undercut the secretary of state. Martin Hillenbrand, who from his vantage point at State's German desk saw frequent "confusion" at the White House, noted that the situation was often saved by "the extraordinary ability of McGeorge Bundy to synthesize cabinet room discussions, and to get the president to sign off on skillfully drafted action memorandums."

On balance, Bundy's fluid, informal system worked well under Kennedy. He was strong in managing issues for the president, yet trusted as an "honest broker" and conduit for the views of other officials. He went out of his way to bring other strong people into the process. He respected—and sometimes highlighted—intelligent viewpoints that differed from his own. In his fast-paced, informal way, he imposed substantially more structure and regularity on the policy process than the president himself would have done. He was, in many respects, a model for future national security advisers, and for Kennedy, as close to the ideal national security adviser as humanity was likely to produce. Bundy would continue in the position under Lyndon B. Johnson. But the new president was very different. The process changed, and so did Bundy's role, in ways that were not always in the best interest of Johnson or the nation.

———

Bundy was at the Pentagon, meeting with McNamara, when John F. Kennedy was shot on November 22, 1963. He returned immediately to the White House. He was one of those whom Lyndon Johnson had asked to meet Air Force One when it completed its tragic journey from Dallas to Andrews Air Force Base outside Washington, D.C., that day. The new president asked Bundy and several other senior officials to join him and Jacqueline Kennedy with the coffin on the helicopter ride from there to the White House. As they were landing, McNamara and Bundy were among those who heard Johnson's urgent words: Kennedy had "gathered around him the ablest people I've seen. . . . I want you to stay. I need you." As Bundy's biographer noted, "No other words could have better appealed to Bundy's sense of himself and his duty to the presidency."

It is impossible today to recapture the shock, the anxiety, the uncertainty that gripped Americans in the hours and days following the Kennedy assassination. It was Johnson's first task to reassure a shaken and stricken nation. He did so by embracing his predecessor's legacy. Echoing Kennedy's inaugural phrase, "Let us begin," Johnson made his theme, "Let us continue." Substantively, he endorsed the landmark Kennedy legislative proposals on civil rights and economic stimulus, both of which became law the following year. Continuity extended to people also: Rusk and McNamara ended up serving Johnson longer than they had his predecessor. LBJ's efforts to ensure that Bundy would stay on included inviting Bundy's mother for a one-on-one conversation in the Oval Office when he learned that she was in town visiting her son. And he quickly recognized the value of the substantive and operational policy support that the national security adviser was providing.

Continuity in form masked a jarring shift in the reality. Johnson urged second-tier foreign policy aides to remain, even inviting Kaysen, Komer, Forrestal, and Ralph Dungan to a swim in the White House pool and lunch in the presidential living quarters, where Kennedy had never had them. But in contrast to Kennedy, LBJ showed little interest in the substance of their work. Bundy, too, found Johnson's appetite for foreign policy information at best a fraction of his predecessor's. So he brought fewer issues to him. LBJ, in turn, was less inclined than JFK to rely on staff aides, more disposed to delegate decisions to his cabinet secretaries, notably Dean Rusk, the fellow southerner who the Kennedy people had generally found wanting.

The new president's forte was domestic policy. During his extraordinarily effective service as Senate majority leader from 1955 through 1960, LBJ had developed enormous understanding and feel for the nuances of domestic issues. He possessed a towering ability to convince his fellow politicians to see the issues his way. And those who had gotten "the full Johnson"—arm around the shoulder, face thrust close, pushing the argument in a charming, steady southern drawl—usually did. He would apply his skills masterfully as president: winning enactment of landmark civil rights, tax, and "War on Poverty" laws in 1964, and an unprecedented harvest of liberal legislation the year after. But his confidence did not extend to foreign policy. Whereas Kennedy had grown increasingly comfortable in this sphere, this was the area where Johnson was most insecure.

There was also a deep cultural gap—a chasm, really—between the new president and the "Harvards" who held sway under the old. Kennedy's was, at bottom, an elitist administration, taking its color and much of its staff from the Ivy League (Harvard and Yale in particular) and the New York legal, financial, media, and cultural institutions populated by their graduates. Its aura evoked a mix of discomfort, envy, resentment, and contempt in LBJ, the graduate of Southeast Texas State Teachers' College. And it fed his warring impulses simultaneously to defer to them and to put them in their place. "Johnson was a rough person," McNamara later observed. "He took every person's measure. He sought to find a person's weakness, and once he found it, he tried to play on it." He was arbitrary and uneven in his dealings with subordinates—sometimes overly solicitous, sometimes brutal in using his power and rubbing in their weaknesses. On Bundy, he imposed what Schlesinger labeled "a brutal and characteristic Johnson loyalty test" by having him convey to Attorney General Robert Kennedy his request that Kennedy withdraw from consideration as Johnson's vice-presidential running mate in 1964. (RFK, in turn, saw Bundy's delivery of this message as "an act of inexplicable disloyalty" to *him*.) Johnson would occasionally insist on aides briefing him while he sat on the toilet, and speak contemptuously of their discomfort. This contrasted sharply with Kennedy's consistent, cool, arm's-length courtesy. And yet, Johnson felt he needed these people—because he knew they brought exceptional qualities to government, and because he could ill afford to have them leave and turn against him.

Bundy the patriot knew he had to stay. Bundy the elitist found the going hard. The Johnson style was ebullience, overstatement, passion, wearing his emotions on his sleeve, a sharp contrast to Kennedy's style and a poor fit with Bundy's. Bundy realized, of course, that it was mainly he who would have to adjust, and he made considerable efforts to do so. But it was never easy. The discomfort could only fuel resentment on both sides, and ultimately a lessening of mutual confidence and respect.

Given his druthers, this accidental president would have subordinated foreign policy to his ambitious domestic agenda—as he indeed seemed to do in 1964 and early 1965. Yet Johnson remembered how Republicans had pilloried Truman and Acheson for the "loss of China" fifteen years before, and he was determined not to put his administration and his party in that position again. So, while he minimized international engagement in 1964, his response to his biggest foreign policy challenge that year reflected this determination to protect himself politically.

On August 2, 1964, North Vietnamese PT boats attacked the destroyer USS *Maddox* in broad daylight during its patrol in the Gulf of Tonkin off the North Vietnamese coast. No damage was done to the U.S. vessel, and its retaliatory fire drove the attackers away. The Johnson administration (knowing that CIA-instigated raids on North Vietnamese territory were ongoing in the area) limited its response to a letter of warning.

Two days later, though, the captain of the *Maddox* reported evidence of a second attack—this time in the dead of night, hence midmorning Washington time. Almost immediately, the captain began questioning his own reports. Less than three hours after the first report, he sent a flash message stating that "freak weather effects on radar and overeager sonarmen" had apparently misled him. "Many reported contacts and torpedoes fired appear doubtful." Since there had been "no actual visual sightings," he suggested "complete evaluation before further action taken." McNamara checked with the admiral in charge of the Pacific Fleet, who first said there was a "slight possibility" there had been no attack at all, but on further investigation conveyed his conclusion that the attack had occurred, though initial reports had exaggerated its scope. (It is now the general consensus of analysts and participants, including McNamara, that the second "attack" never happened, though administration decision makers did, apparently, sincerely conclude that August day that it had.)

Several hours earlier, however, Lyndon Johnson had decided to act. After hearing the first reports, he "had come storming over to Bundy's office" that morning and "announced that he had decided to retaliate." "I interrupted," Bundy recalled thirty-one years later, "and said I thought we ought to think it over." Johnson snapped back, "I didn't ask you that. I told you to help me get organized." Bundy realized his place. "I was just a messenger boy," he recalled, "and he made sure I stayed that way." Bundy then behaved in the same way with his White House colleagues, announcing at a staff meeting that Johnson had decided to ask for a broad congressional resolution. When domestic aide Douglass Cater asked, "Do we have all the information?" Bundy said that the president's mind was made up. When Cater persisted, saying, "he hadn't really thought it through," Bundy responded, "Don't."

By the time the captain's second thoughts were cabled in, Johnson was meeting with the National Security Council ostensibly to ask his advisers' views, but in essence demanding their concurrence. Doubts were cast aside, retaliation was set in motion, and Congress passed the famous Gulf of Tonkin resolution in support of the president (and an open-ended war) with only two dissenters. Procedurally, this was highly unusual for Johnson. He rarely decided without the advance counsel—and the moral and political support—of his senior advisers. (They did unanimously endorse the action early that evening, with the president's preference already made clear.) Politically, however, it was a master stroke—for election year 1964. The United States was making, the president declared, a "measured" response to a "deliberate" pattern of "naked aggression." How better could he show his own determination to defend U.S. interests, while contrasting himself with his presumably trigger-happy election opponent, Republican Senator Barry Goldwater? The Arizonan was never able to shake the image of recklessness, and Johnson rode to an overwhelming election victory in November.

Shortly thereafter, Bundy played a central role in Johnson's shelving of a long-simmering proposal to develop a multinational nuclear force (MLF) within NATO. Advocates saw this force as essential to head off future German efforts to acquire nuclear weapons unilaterally, but Bundy brought in presidential scholar Neustadt to assess British attitudes toward the MLF, which were lukewarm at best. With the Germans not pressing the issue, and Bundy assuring Johnson that JFK had never endorsed the idea, LBJ effectively rejected it on the eve of a summit meeting with British Prime Minister Harold Wilson. At a December 1964 White House reception in Wilson's honor, Dean Acheson—a staunch MLF supporter—declared to Neustadt, "I know your theory. You think Presidents should be warned. You're wrong. Presidents should be given confidence."

Warning was what Bundy provided on the MLF: This group is selling you something, Mr. President, and you ought to know the reasons why you might not wish to buy it. He had played this role regularly with Kennedy, whose skeptical mind and style meshed well with his own. On Vietnam, however, Bundy under Johnson began to warn less and less and urge strong action more and more, very much in the Achesonian manner. By early 1965, by Andrew Preston's detailed analysis, Bundy "had undergone the transformation from adviser to advocate." The basic reason was "the serious and deteriorating situation" in that country, and Bundy's sense that the president needed to be pushed to make a sufficiently strong response. He withheld from Johnson a lengthy October 1964 memo by Under Secretary of State George Ball arguing that the war could only get worse and should be abandoned. Though Bundy discussed the memo with Ball, Rusk, and McNamara in November, the president only saw it four months later when Ball sent it through Johnson's longtime adviser Bill Moyers. Before then, on January 27, 1965, Bundy had sent the president a pivotal message, which became known as "the fork-in-the-road memo," expressing the view of himself and Secretary McNamara ("Dean Rusk does not agree with us") that "the worst course of action" would be to continue the current American advisory role, and that the best course was, essentially, escalation: "to use our military power in the Far East and to force a change of Communist policy."

The president responded by sending Bundy to Vietnam in early February. As the national security adviser and his team were moving toward recommending strong action, Viet Cong forces attacked a U.S. military outpost in the town of Pleiku, killing eight U.S. servicemen and wounding 126. Bundy recommended—and Johnson ordered— an immediate retaliatory response, and in less than a day, over one hundred U.S. jets were bombing targets in North Vietnam.

A program of "sustained reprisal" followed in the days thereafter. Its purposes were to buttress the deteriorating political situation in Saigon and compel Hanoi to seek relief; when it failed to accomplish either, the only remaining option (save negotiation and withdrawal) was deployment of ground troops. This began in earnest in the spring of 1965, and by summer, successive Johnson decisions had brought the number in the country to around 75,000. Bundy was unhappy about this, and when McNamara on July 1 presented a massive military program calling for 200,000 ground troops and a tripling of the bombing rate, the national security adviser initially labeled it "rash to the point of folly." But before the end of the month, with Johnson pretty much committed, Bundy had acquiesced. Among government officials only George Ball, invited by the president to express his views, offered serious dissent. By this time, the national security assistant was once again ambivalent about the means the United States was employing to win in Vietnam. But he, like his president, could not abide losing. Johnson found himself in an excruciating bind: he was worried about being trapped in a land war in Asia that would drain resources from the domestic programs he had launched so brilliantly, but he was unwilling to take the risk of withdrawal. And Bundy did nothing to make the withdrawal option more viable.

Bundy did, on July 7 and 8, convene a group of senior advisers that became known as "the wise men." Established originally to lend gravitas to Johnson's 1964 election campaign, it included such august personages as former Secretary of State Dean Acheson and Council on Foreign Relations chairman John J. McCloy. After extensive briefings from McNamara, Bundy, and others, six of them met with the president and conveyed their view that escalation was the only answer. Indeed, Acheson—impatient at how the discussion was going—chastised the president for whining about his plight: presidents were supposed to make hard decisions and stick with them! Not included in this meeting was Johnson's longtime confidant Clark Clifford, who had conveyed a dissenting view in April.

Later in July, Johnson did invite Clifford to share his skeptical views—first at the White House, then at Camp David. LBJ also received cautionary counsel from Senate Armed Services chair Richard Russell, his longtime mentor. But there was no effort to bring all the senior critics and advocates together for extended debate before the president, along the model of Kennedy's Ex Comm for Cuba. Johnson did not like such meetings; he wanted to control the environment, and prevent leaks. Bundy was certainly not disposed to push him into one. So, notwithstanding his deep anxieties, LBJ plunged ahead.

Bundy still accommodated dissent within his staff: his junior aide, East Asia expert James C. Thomson, Jr., would write a laudatory op-ed upon Bundy's sudden death in 1996, highlighting how his boss "tolerated and even encouraged" his Vietnam skepticism at the very time Bundy himself was pressing for escalation. Chester Cooper, a former CIA analyst serving at the Johnson-Bundy NSC, was similarly doubtful about what American ground troops could accomplish against a guerrilla army. But Bundy no longer nurtured skeptical subcabinet officials at State, as he had under Kennedy. Johnson wasn't much interested in the views of people at that level (aside from Ball, who combined serious internal dissent with relatively senior rank and absolute personal loyalty to the president).

Bundy also departed from his established role in another way—he became a negotiator. Johnson sent him to the Dominican Republic in May 1965 to try to broker a political deal between feuding politicians there. Johnson had made a precipitate decision to send U.S. troops to the island in late April, in response to the collapse of the ruling junta and shaky reports of a potential Communist takeover. What was "the first armed U.S. intervention in a Latin American country in thirty years," one close student of this decision concluded, was decided upon "with amazingly little discussion of the full range of options and their associated risks." Bundy was surprised by the negotiating assignment, and his ten-day effort in the Caribbean nation was serious, though unsuccessful.

By this time, though, significant tension was developing between Johnson and his NSC adviser. Bundy supported—indeed, encouraged—Johnson's escalation decisions, but believed that the president should be speaking out loud and clear about how and why he was expanding the American involvement in Vietnam, both the reasons for the policy and the costs that would be incurred. He saw this as essential to build public support and sustain the policy in the years ahead. Johnson was determined instead to proceed by stealth, partly because he hadn't yet persuaded himself of the irrevocability of the choices he was making, and partly because he wanted to maintain as long as possible the enormous spring and summer 1965 momentum behind his domestic "Great Society" program. As Larry Berman notes in his analysis of Vietnam decision making, "Medicare and the Civil Rights Bill were at crucial stages in conference committee" during the very July week that Johnson made his decision to have U.S. troops take over the ground war. So he represented what he was doing on Vietnam as essentially a continuation of previous policy, which over time helped create an enormous credibility gap.

Johnson, moreover, didn't want a loud public controversy, or any activity that would elevate the status of critics of the Vietnam War. In fact, Bundy later concluded that the president had dispatched him to the Dominican Republic on such short notice in order to prevent his national security adviser from participating in a scheduled debate with the Cornell University Asia scholar George McT. Kahin at a Washington, D.C., "teach-in" on the war. Bundy's withdrawal just three hours before that event was to take place had embarrassed his academic supporters, and when he returned, he acted to fulfill his commitment to debate the war—in the full knowledge that he was going against LBJ's wishes. Insisting on a "non-partisan" forum, with none of the teach-in's potential for domination by a crowd of critical students, he arranged to appear in June on *CBS* with war critic (and leading international relations scholar) Hans Morgenthau. Network veteran Eric Sevareid served as moderator.

Bundy was relentless and, by debating standards, demolished his hesitant academic opponent: one war critic who had pressed for such a debate concluded that "we pursued McGeorge Bundy until he caught us." But Johnson was livid—he viewed it as rank insubordination and vented his anger to Bill Moyers: "He didn't tell me because he knew I didn't want him to do it. Bill, I want you to go to Bundy and tell him the president would be pleased, mighty pleased, to accept his resignation."

Moyers did not do so, and Johnson never spoke to Bundy about the debate. But the assistant knew he had incurred the president's wrath: "He didn't want me to do it," he recalled twenty-nine years later. "And he knew that I knew he didn't want me to do it—and I did it anyway." Moreover, Bundy's triumphal debate performance was featured in a *Time* cover story, which glorified the adviser as "Ambassador to the Academe" and highlighted the president's dependence on him. Bundy knew he had crossed a line: one way he could tell the president was unhappy with him, he said later, was that LBJ's wife, Lady Bird Johnson, was going out of her way to be kind to him. Another was that the president would increasingly "forget" or mispronounce his name. By summer, he was phoning the president of Harvard to ask if the university would have him back. Then, in early November, without prior discussion, Bundy was offered the presidency of the Ford Foundation. Within two weeks, he decided to accept. It was a good, new challenge. He could go there without breaking openly with Johnson over policy. His wife Mary liked the idea of living in New York. And he felt the president needed a more compatible national security adviser.

Bundy told the president of his decision; they agreed that he would leave by the end of February 1966. Johnson was not at all gracious about the matter, but he did ask Bundy to confirm with the Ford Foundation that he would be available thereafter for special presidential assignments.

Though Johnson never shared Kennedy's attitude toward the Bundy staff, he did rely on it. He promoted two of Bundy's aides to the rank of deputy: Robert Komer as across-the-board number two man; and Francis Bator, who had assumed the international economic policy portfolio after Carl Kaysen returned to Cambridge. Both handled certain issues face-to-face with Johnson. And he honored NSC executive secretary Bromley Smith with the President's Award for Distinguished Federal Civilian Service for having "revolutionized the communications system supporting Presidential decision-making and action in foreign affairs."

Still, the fate of the NSC staff and the post of adviser was uncertain when Bundy departed as scheduled on February 28, 1966. He had recommended at least twice that Bill Moyers, then White House press secretary, be named his replacement: Moyers was smart, effective, policy-sensitive, and a Texan who had a long relationship with Johnson. But even with over three months' advance warning, the president had not acted. He told Komer to act as his special assistant and to do everything that Bundy had done, but not tell anybody he was doing so—if it got in the newspapers, it would be all over between them. Komer never figured out how he would accomplish this, but he did the best he could, and a month or so thereafter Johnson named him to head a special new White House office that "coordinated and supervised Washington support for pacification and other nonmilitary campaigns" in Vietnam.

Meanwhile, two days after Bundy's departure, Johnson issued an order, National Security Action Memorandum 341, aimed at enhancing State Department authority over foreign policy. Following the recommendations of General Maxwell Taylor and Deputy Under Secretary of State U. Alexis Johnson, it established two levels of committees: the Senior Interdepartmental Group (SIG) and the Interdepartmental Regional Groups (IRGs), chaired, respectively, by the under secretary and assistant secretaries of state. Their task was to assist the secretary of state in carrying out his presidentially delegated "authority and responsibility . . . for the overall direction, coordination and supervision of interdepartmental activities of the United States Government overseas."

Finally, Johnson held what he called "a White House impromptu news conference" on March 31, 1966, to announce the naming of two new "Special Assistants," Robert Kintner and Walt Whitman Rostow. Both would "earn $30,000 annually." Rostow (mentioned second) would "work principally, but not necessarily exclusively, in the field of foreign policy." A reporter asked: "Mr. President, could it be said that as your new Special Assistant, Mr. Rostow will take over all or many of the duties and assignments handled by McGeorge Bundy?" Johnson replied: "It could be, but that would be inaccurate. It would not be true." Bundy's work was being distributed among a number of aides, and the president expected his men to "play any position here." He underscored the point by not including "for National Security Affairs" in Rostow's title.

Rostow had been a socialist at Yale, from which he graduated at age nineteen. By the 1950s, when he became professor of economic history at the Massachusetts Institute of Technology, he had become an activist anti-Communist liberal—urging expanded aid to developing countries and commitment to counterinsurgency. Rostow was a brilliant and facile thinker across a range of issues: his policy-relevant publications dwarfed those of Bundy in quantity and substantive scope. His *Stages of Economic Growth*—published first in *The Economist* and later in book form—refuted the widely held belief that the Soviet Union was gaining economically on the West and was likely to surpass it in the years ahead. He saw Communists as "scavengers of the modernization process" in developing countries, and urged active U.S. resistance to revolutions which they sponsored. Consistent with this approach, Rostow was a true believer in the Vietnam War: he had advocated bombing the North, and sending in American ground troops, as early as 1961.

Rostow had been advising Johnson intermittently since 1964 from his post as State Department director of policy planning. The president had told him in February 1966 that he wanted him to move to the White House, but swore him to secrecy. "It was not until a few moments before the announcement of my appointment," Rostow later recalled, "that the matter was firm." Among his Kennedy-Johnson administration colleagues, he had earned a reputation as an ideologue—enamored of his own positions and lacking Bundy's flexibility and intellectual skepticism. This was one reason Kennedy had moved him away from the NSC in late 1961, and why none of Johnson's senior advisers had recommended him as Bundy's replacement. Johnson was aware of these concerns. In a phone conversation with McNamara (who, like Bundy, favored Moyers), the president worried that choosing Rostow would "get everybody to thinking we're going back to war and a hard-liner." But precisely because nobody else wanted him, he could be, in words attributed to Johnson, "my goddamned intellectual," chosen by the president and owing the job only to him. And the president was kinder to Rostow, more respectful, than was typical of his relationships with aides.

In saying Rostow would not have the same job, Johnson was putting down his old national security assistant, not his new one. As Bundy remarked to colleagues a few years later, the tacit explanation for his departure was typical: "Someone who hasn't been doing anything useful here is leaving, and we're all getting along just fine!" Combined with the issuance of the memorandum on the new interagency groups, though, the president's press conference language could only cause problems for Rostow and the staff in reestablishing their authority over the foreign affairs agencies.

That said, it was not long before it became clear that Rostow was Bundy's *de facto* successor. He headed the staff. He reviewed and channeled departmental communications to the president. He replaced Bundy at key advisory meetings. He met the president's needs for foreign policy information and staff support. Under him, the staff underwent modest expansion—to about sixteen members. But the process remained informal, and the staff's character did not change. Moreover, the State Department never seized the leadership opportunity proffered by Johnson's March 1966 directive.

But the assistant and staff were less important to Johnson than they had been to Kennedy. For JFK, they were the central mechanism (though by no means the only one) for reviewing and managing foreign policy. For LBJ, that role was played by his senior cabinet officials, Rusk and McNamara, above all. It was made manifest by what became his most important instrument for policymaking, the "Tuesday Lunch." Beginning sporadically in February 1964, continuing regularly in 1965 after Vietnam gained center stage, the president hosted (in his private dining room) "more than 150 Tuesday lunch meetings" with the secretaries of state and defense and the national security adviser. Over time, participation was expanded to include the director of Central Intelligence, the chairman of the Joint Chiefs of Staff, and certain senior White House aides (initially Bill Moyers).

When notes were taken, it was "done for historical rather than operational purposes." For this reason, Johnson felt that he could explore issues freely, get the feel of his advisers, and protect himself from press leaks. Sometimes, the forum served its stated purpose. But when LBJ was depressed, as was often the case, "he reduced the Tuesday lunch to a stage on which to vent his emotions," in Doris Kearns's words, "holding forth at great length with a diatribe against the critics or calling out in a self-pitying way for understanding of his plight." And even when the discussion was constructive, there were serious communication problems with subcabinet officials, who had difficulty determining what was decided and what the action implications were.

Such follow-up was, to some degree, Rostow's responsibility; he developed the Tuesday lunch agendas, in consultation with Rusk and McNamara (and later Clifford), and watched over the implementation of decisions reached. But here his limitations got in the way, for Rostow was not regarded—as Bundy generally had been—as a reliable policy broker. On Vietnam policy in particular he was the perennial booster, seeing the silver lining where others perceived mainly clouds. And his reputation spilled over into other issues. Rostow had substantially greater intrinsic interest in the developing world than Bundy. Yet William Gaud, director of the U.S. Agency for International Development, trusted Bundy to convey his messages to the president, but feared that Rostow would give them his own spin. Other officials made the same comparison. Bundy could be rough intellectually and would sometimes wound with words, but he was an honest and accurate transmitter of others' views. Rostow was not as demanding, and perhaps "nicer" in ordinary personal relations, but his strong views undercut his capacity as process manager. As one academic analyst put it, "despite prodigious skills as a writer and social analyst, Rostow lacked the emotional control and detachment necessary for maintaining impartiality. He was, instead, a highly opinionated and self-confident individual who 'knew what he thought about everything' since he was a 15-year-old undergraduate at Yale and who was benignly impervious to others' criticism."

An interesting if minor illustration of this insensitivity came to one of the authors early in his career when, as a staff aide to a senator, he sat in on a late 1966 panel at a conference of editors of college newspapers. The topic was Vietnam; the panelists included Rostow and Richard Goodwin, the early 1961 Kennedy aide who had been "exiled" to the State Department, returned to the White House under Johnson, then left to become a prominent critic of administration Vietnam policy. Rostow centered his presentation on the assertion that, as a member of the Southeast Asia Treaty Organization (SEATO), the United States was obligated to come to Vietnam's aid. Goodwin followed by declaring that he had been at the White House when the portentous 1965 decisions were made, and no one had ever mentioned the SEATO Treaty. When it came his time to rebut, Rostow repeated the same statement, without changing a word. A Bundy would have responded to Goodwin with a wicked substantive or personal rejoinder. Rostow seemingly felt no need to respond at all. He lost that "debate," but didn't seem to know or care.

By early 1968, the president knew that his policy had failed. Two years to the day after he announced Rostow's appointment, Lyndon Johnson reversed course on Vietnam and withdrew his candidacy for reelection. The enemy's Tet Offensive, launched in January 1968, had demolished administration credibility, even though it was rebuffed militarily. Clark Clifford, who replaced McNamara as secretary of defense, pressed hard for a policy reversal. He was backed in March by key members of the "wise men" group, including Dean Acheson (who abandoned his earlier support) and one of its newer members, McGeorge Bundy, who wrote Johnson: "I just don't think the country can be held together much longer by determination and patriotism alone." Bundy had previously opposed a bombing halt, "but no longer . . . I think nothing less will do."

Until March 1968, the operative issue had been how many more troops to send. And Rostow, committed to the end, favored a further increase beyond the 500,000-plus troops already deployed. But Johnson understood that public support for escalation had evaporated. From then on, the questions would be how fast troops could be withdrawn and how best to pursue the peace negotiations that Johnson also launched on March 31, 1968. Rostow, however, used his position as national security adviser to minimize conciliatory steps toward Hanoi, effectively delaying a full halt to the bombing of the North for seven full months. As recalled by Richard Holbrooke, a member of Ambassador Harriman's negotiating delegation at the Paris peace talks, "This eliminated any prospect that Johnson could achieve the peace agreement he sought in his final months in office."

Kennedy and Bundy had created the modern position of national security adviser. For it to survive, subsequent presidents would have to adopt it and make it their own. Lyndon Johnson did so—first as part of his larger commitment to continuity; thereafter because he found useful the staff support that the assistant provided. He did so ambivalently. He was never personally comfortable with Bundy, and when he named Walt Rostow as Bundy's successor, he denied that he was replacing Bundy at all. Indeed, in important respects, Rostow didn't "replace" Bundy, because he was less effective and trusted as a broker, and because his president relied much more on his secretary of state than Kennedy ever had.

Nonetheless, Johnson and Rostow maintained the three core elements of the Kennedy-Bundy innovations: the adviser handling the president's day-to-day foreign affairs business; the staff recruited to serve the current administration; and the communications and information system centered in the Situation Room. All subsequent presidents would build on this foundation. Johnson's immediate successor, Richard Nixon, would use it as a base for unrivaled White House foreign policy dominance.

But personality mattered. The same Bundy who meshed so well with one president was clearly out of sync with his successor. As a fellow Ivy Leaguer, Kennedy was compatible culturally with Bundy, and no doubt felt empowered by what Bundy did on his behalf. With Johnson, the culture clash was acute. For most of two years, the two men swallowed their discomfort and got along—there was urgent business to do, and they needed each other to do it. But Bundy seems to have trusted LBJ less than he had JFK, one reason perhaps why he became an unvarnished advocate pressing for the Vietnam escalation which Johnson both resisted and saw no way around. Ultimately, the Texan came to see Bundy as threatening his capacity to govern as he wished to. Bundy left, and Johnson brought in an intellectual he could call his own. The president no doubt realized that Rostow lacked some of Bundy's strengths. But he wholeheartedly supported the president and his policies, and adapted to his way of doing business. And that suited Johnson just fine.

3

"You Don't Tell Anybody"

O
n the afternoon of January 20, 1969, senior foreign and defense policy officials returning from the presidential inauguration of Richard M. Nixon found on their desks four documents. The most important was entitled "Reorganization of the National Security Council System," and signed by the president himself. It declared that the NSC "shall be the principal forum for consideration of policy issues," and established a network of interagency committees to support the NSC's work. Central was the National Security Council Review Group, chaired by the new national security adviser, Henry Kissinger, which would "examine papers prior to their submission to the NSC" and ensure that "all realistic alternatives are presented."

Cognoscenti of such documents noted that this new system placed the Department of State's top regional officials, responsible for preparing most policy papers, under the direct authority of the national security adviser. And these directives were quickly followed by a series of National Security Study Memoranda (NSSMs or "Nissims") tasking the bureaucracy with developing analyses and options on issues ranging from the ongoing Vietnam War to U.S. relations with Japan.

Nixon presented the new system as a repudiation of Kennedy-Johnson informality: as a candidate, he had "attribute[d] most of our serious reverses abroad since 1960" to the replacement of Eisenhower's structured NSC by "catch-as-catch-can talkfests between the President, his staff assistants, and various others." He would therefore "restore the National Security Council to its pre-eminent role in national security planning." To underscore the change, he held his first Council meeting on the afternoon of January 21, 1969. Taken together, these initial acts sent a clear message: A new president was in charge, and he was determined to manage policy his own way, from the White House.

In fact, however, Nixon was not repudiating what Kennedy had established and Johnson had maintained. Rather, he was building on it. He retained and reinforced the national security assistant responsible for current presidential foreign policy business, backed by an independently recruited staff and the Situation Room, which would now be used not just to monitor intragovernmental communications but also to create "back channels," enabling Nixon and Kissinger to deal directly with foreign governments without the knowledge of the State Department or others. With Nixon's support, Kissinger would become the dominant foreign policy official, short of the president himself, as adviser, negotiator, and (ultimately) public spokesman. But due to the peculiarities of their relationship, the incapacity of either man to trust and share power with colleagues, and their obsession with "leaks," policymaking became highly secretive. Conflict with established departments became persistent and raw. And the process became far more informal, personal, and unstructured than the one Nixon had condemned in his Democratic predecessors.

Heinz Alfred Kissinger was born in Bavaria in 1923. His father was a teacher; he was a bookish boy, with a strong attachment to soccer. He entered his teens as the Nazi repression was closing in on German Jews, and his family reluctantly emigrated to New York City in August 1938. In America, he changed his first name to Henry, and excelled in high school and at City College. He became a naturalized citizen when he was drafted into the Army in 1943. There his exceptional intelligence (and language facility) led to his being named to administer (while still a private) a newly conquered German city of 200,000 inhabitants, where he impressed all with his exceptional competence and fairness. After further service in the occupation, he left the Army as a sergeant and enrolled at Harvard in 1947 as a twenty-four-year-old undergraduate. He wrote his honors thesis on "The Meaning of History," and by 1954 had completed a notable PhD dissertation on the reestablishment of the balance of power after the Napoleonic Wars. Remaining at Harvard as a teacher, he won tenure in 1959 thanks in part to the "maneuverings" of the dean of the faculty, one McGeorge Bundy.

By that time, Kissinger was on his way to becoming one of the world's leading scholars of foreign policy and international relations. His *Nuclear Weapons and Foreign Policy* had made a seminal contribution to the strategic debates of the 1950s. He had watched as Bundy, his much less published Harvard colleague, moved to a front-and-center position in the Kennedy White House. He had hoped to do the same in a Nelson Rockefeller presidency, but the New York governor fell far short in his quest for the Republican nomination in the 1968 elections. So, during the presidential campaign, Kissinger kept lines of communication open to the camps of both Nixon and his Democratic rival, Vice President Hubert Humphrey. And while he asserts in his memoirs that a late November invitation to meet with the president-elect "filled me with neither expectation nor enthusiasm," he had been told that he was high on Nixon's list as possible NSC adviser by two credible sources: campaign national security adviser Richard Allen and leading Washington journalist Joseph Kraft.

Still, for anyone but a diffident, socially awkward president, the choice of a man he had barely met for such a critical post would have been inconceivable. Even Nixon labeled it "uncharacteristically impulsive." When "the grocer's son from Whittier and the refugee from Hitler's Germany" had their first substantive conversation at the Hotel Pierre in New York, Nixon's transition headquarters, Kissinger quickly learned what his boss-to-be already knew: that they shared a "realist" perspective, and that Nixon had a sophisticated grasp of international politics. At their second meeting, Nixon offered him the job, and the appointment was made public on December 2, 1968, nine days before the president-elect announced the choice of Secretary of State William P. Rogers and the rest of his cabinet.

Nixon asked Kissinger to develop a formal, White House–based policy process with the NSC at its core. For this, and as part of his broader effort to hit the ground running, Kissinger immediately began assembling a staff. Prominent among its initial members was Morton H. Halperin, a thirty-year-old former Harvard colleague who had been serving with formidable effectiveness as deputy assistant secretary of defense for policy plans. He would manage the NSC process for Kissinger in the initial months. Kissinger asked Halperin "to prepare a memo focusing particularly on how techniques for systems analysis could be used in the making of foreign policy decisions." Halperin produced a draft that laid out "an entire proposed NSC system," aimed at presenting the president with real foreign policy options (not consensus recommendations) and centering responsibility for shaping the NSC agenda in the national security adviser. This became the basis for a ten-page memo, co-drafted by Halperin and Lawrence Eagleburger (then Kissinger's principal aide), which the national security assistant-designate forwarded to Nixon on December 27. (At Nixon's urging, Kissinger also sought the advice of General Andrew Goodpaster, who had handled national security issues for President Eisenhower.)

The president-elect approved the proposed new system almost immediately, leaving Kissinger to fend off vociferous objections in January 1969 from State officials—and more nuanced concerns expressed by the secretary of defense-designate, Melvin Laird. Nixon was determined to "direct foreign policy from the White House," but resisted telling Rogers so directly. The secretary-designate, in turn, resisted acceding on the basis of Kissinger's word alone. Finally, Nixon reiterated his decision—in a terse memo to Kissinger, and via a phone call from chief of staff Haldeman to Kissinger conveying the further flourish "that anyone opposing it should submit his resignation." Hence were underscored two central facts about Nixon. First, he was determined to impose his will. Second, he found it just about impossible, psychologically, to do so directly to the person whose views he was rejecting. This left his aides to deliver the unwelcome message, and predisposed the recipient to blame the messenger.

The "grocer's son" and the "refugee" were politician and scholar. But as with Kennedy and Bundy before, there was a clear personal "fit" between them. In his acerbic critique, Robert Dallek finds both to be "self-serving characters with grandiose dreams of recasting world affairs." Like Kennedy and Bundy, both were smart, analytic, intellectual, knowledgeable, and ambitious. But the contrasts were greater. Unlike their predecessors, both were socially uncomfortable, insecure, perceiving themselves as "outsiders" spurned by the establishment. To quote Dallek again, "Their combative natures made them distrustful of others, whom they suspected of envy and ambition to outdo them." And they were both cold and methodical in their approach to issues. During a brief early 1960s consultancy for the Bundy NSC, Kissinger had found himself uncomfortable with the New Frontier style, "inflicting on President Kennedy learned disquisitions about which he could have done nothing even in the unlikely event that they aroused his interest." This experience led Richard Neustadt to observe, around mid-decade, that Henry would never make it in Washington. But Nixon liked to explore issues in depth, one-on-one. Finally, the two men shared a basic "realpolitik" approach to foreign policy, centered on the national interest and the balance of power.

Their separate personal insecurities would render the relationship unstable—and harder for the rest of government to accept. From early on, Kissinger, a master of snide invective, would trash the president in conversations with his subordinates as "my drunken friend" or "the meatball mind." Nixon would bait Kissinger with derogatory remarks about Jews in the presence of other staff aides, adding, "Isn't that right, Henry?" "For Kissinger," recalled Nixon's domestic policy aide John Ehrlichman, "being Jewish was a vulnerability as he saw it, and he was not fond of being vulnerable. But Nixon liked him to feel that way." Still, the two men's congruent policy visions and their overlapping interests in power over policy had brought them together. Their mutual dependence, a frustrating truth to both, kept them together. Contrary to myth, for the first four years Nixon was the dominant figure—as presidents almost always are. Only with the piling on of Watergate revelations in 1973 would Kissinger gain the upper hand.

Through the orders conveyed on January 20, 1969, Nixon and Kissinger sent a message: The president was in charge. What got Washington's attention, though, was the size and strength of the new NSC staff that would help make this control possible. On February 7, a White House press release on Nixon's "revitalized National Security Council system" included a list of twenty-eight substantive staff professionals. They followed the JFK-LBJ model of foreign policy analyst-activists, most without strong partisan ties, but recruited to serve a particular president. But the staff was larger, more structured, and—unlike Bundy's—recruited at the outset of the administration. It included men (initially no women) of formidable Washington reputations: Halperin, Eagleburger, East Asia specialist Dick Sneider (the most effective Foreign Service officer of his generation), C. Fred Bergsten (later to direct the Peterson Institute for International Economics), senior State Department policy analyst Helmut Sonnenfeldt, and a leading international relations scholar Robert Osgood, to name just a few.

The staff was remarkably eclectic in political views: Kissinger consciously did not demand allegiance to Nixon personally, rejected politically recommended people, and overruled concerns over alleged security risks or the liberal policy views of certain members. Indeed, in the words of one early staff member, Daniel Davidson, who worked with Kissinger before the election, "it was not clear there was [on the staff] a single . . . person, including Henry, who had voted for the President-elect," other than the Nixon campaign aide Richard Allen. Impressions of the Nixon-Kissinger takeover of foreign policy were reinforced by the substantial and overwhelmingly favorable press coverage it received in the opening months. But, as Davidson added, the staff's political coloration made "the whole group extremely suspect in the White House."

The formal system was White House–centered, but internally open. Senior officials responsible for an issue in their agencies could know where it was being analyzed. They could fight to get their preferred policy option included in the analysis and presented to the president. They could have their secretary (Rogers, Laird) argue its merits at the Council. And presumably, they would know—through a subsequent national security directive—what Nixon decided. At the same time, the system protected the chief executive from being confronted with a consensus precooked by his senior advisers.

For the first few months, the system worked more or less as advertised. The National Security Council met an average of once a week, twenty-seven times in the administration's first six months. Study memoranda led to interagency drafts that were vetted by the Kissinger-chaired NSC Review Group (which met twenty-six times) and (frequently after reworking) they were circulated to NSC members and debated at Council meetings. And the process produced significant policy changes. Among the more important were the decision to abandon the development and deployment of biological weapons; and the decision to return to Japan the island of Okinawa, conquered in World War II and the locus of major U.S. military bases, without insisting on the right to store U.S. nuclear weapons there. In both cases, the Defense Department was central, and in both cases, it was impossible to get the Pentagon to put forward the option that Nixon ultimately chose. But the system allowed the president to consider it anyway (as had not been the case, for example, in the more consensus-driven process of the Johnson administration). The formal system was also important in charting Nixon's initial course on what remained the central policy challenge: the war in Vietnam.

There was also, however, important early policy activity outside the system. And on this, normally responsible agencies were often kept in the dark—as, indeed, were members of Kissinger's staff with the relevant substantive portfolios. Nixon and Kissinger excluded Rogers—indeed, all State Department officials—from the president's first meeting with Soviet ambassador Anatoly Dobrynin in February. "Then," in Dobrynin's words, "the president went on to establish a confidential channel through Henry Kissinger, his national security adviser, the extensive use of which turned out to be unprecedented in my experience and perhaps in the annals of diplomacy." Nixon explained to the ambassador that while he had "every confidence in the secretary of state," he was worried about leaks about conversations inevitably known to a wider circle. Moreover, there were "questions that needed to be restricted to a very narrow circle," in some cases "to the president alone, who would receive information via the channel of Kissinger and Dobrynin."

Nixon made it clear very early that he wished certain matters to be kept within the White House. Kissinger, his natural instrument for maintaining such secrecy, was more than happy to oblige. Two early episodes further accelerated their move toward secretive foreign policymaking. The first was the April 1969 shoot-down, by North Korea, of a U.S. reconnaissance aircraft. The second was a series of press leaks, particularly one in May that revealed the administration's secret bombing of North Vietnamese targets in Cambodia.

On April 14, 1969, a North Korean jet downed an EC-121 U.S. Navy reconnaissance plane about ninety miles off the coast. The target was unarmed; the attack was unprovoked; and all thirty-one men aboard lost their lives. Nixon had criticized the Johnson administration for failing to retaliate when the same country had seized the USS *Pueblo* in January 1968, and his initial inclination was to respond with force. Kissinger shared this view. But when the matter came before the National Security Council, Rogers, Laird, and CIA director Richard Helms all expressed strong reservations. Against their concerns that the American response might be misread by North Korea and perhaps trigger a response requiring further military action (possibly even leading to a second Korean War), Kissinger and the president had no specific, operational plan for the limited military action they sought.

At the senior level, the system worked, as Seymour Hersh has noted, "to produce a frank debate at the highest levels." But Nixon was the opposite of pleased. His difficulty in overruling advisers face-to-face was compounded by the fact that he was provided no concrete, actionable military option. So, Kissinger recalled, "he raged against his advisers": he would "get rid of Rogers and Laird at the earliest opportunity." This latter fulmination, characteristic of Nixon, was presumably not meant to be taken literally. Nevertheless, "the result," Kissinger explained, "was to confirm Nixon in his isolated decision-making," even though the press reaction to administration restraint was overwhelmingly favorable.

The direct American response was limited to ordering two aircraft carriers into the Sea of Japan. Determined to show toughness somewhere, Nixon ordered a secret air strike against North Vietnamese bases in Cambodia—this followed one undertaken in March, and was succeeded in turn by a series of others in May and thereafter. Somewhat implausibly, Nixon characterized this in his memoirs as "an effective way to impress the Communist leaders of both North Korea and North Vietnam with our resolve to support our allies and resist aggression."

On May 9, *New York Times* reporter William Beecher published a detailed account of the Cambodia bombings; the same reporter had previously published an "inside" account of administration decision making in response to the downing of the EC-121. The Cambodia story didn't create much of a stir publicly or on Capitol Hill, but Kissinger was outraged. When he read that story in Hotel Key Biscayne in Florida, where he was staying (along with Haldeman and other senior White House aides) while Nixon was visiting his friend Bebe Rebozo several blocks away, he immediately realized that the news threatened his credibility with Nixon and the president's top aides. He demanded to see the president immediately. Nixon was "enraged . . . as well," but in response to Kissinger's conclusion that the leak "must have come from State or Defense," the president "suggested that Kissinger take a hard and objective look at his own staff."

Before morning was out, Kissinger had twice phoned FBI director J. Edgar Hoover asking that he "make a major effort" to discover the leakers. Hoover phoned back that afternoon with the tentative conclusion that the information "could have come and probably did from a staff member of the National Security Council." He mentioned both Eagleburger and Halperin as people who knew Beecher: Halperin he labeled a "so-called arrogant Harvard-type Kennedy [man]." Before the day was over, a tap was placed on Halperin's phone. The next day, Colonel Alexander M. Haig of Kissinger's staff delivered to the FBI a list of four individuals for wiretaps. Three (Halperin, Helmut Sonnenfeldt, and Daniel Davidson) were on the NSC staff. As time went by, other names would be added. All told, no less than thirteen officials from the NSC, State, and Defense, and five journalists were subjected to warrantless wiretaps (later declared unlawful by the Supreme Court because prior court orders had not been obtained), which continued until February 1971. Nixon concluded in retrospect: "They never helped us. Just . . . gossip and bullshitting."

Meanwhile, frustration was mounting within the Kissinger staff. If Bundy had pushed his most senior and capable aides forward, to deal directly with Kennedy, and Rostow had regularly brought the relevant NSC staffer with him when he briefed Johnson, Kissinger held his staff back. And if Bundy had regularly shared information with relevant subordinates, Kissinger just as regularly withheld it. When Halperin phoned CIA director Helms to coordinate on an NSC procedural matter, Kissinger rebuked him: he and he alone would deal with principals. The national security adviser kept Halperin out of at least one NSC meeting for the stated reason that "I can't show up with three people from the NSC [staff]—two of them Jewish." He also "began," in Hersh's words, "to savage Halperin behind his back," presumably for self-protection, in conversations with senior White House aides critical of his staff. Sonnenfeldt complained of "overlapping . . . responsibilities" and "insufficient exchange of information and knowledge" within the staff and with Kissinger. Nixon reinforced the staff's sense of being kept in their place when, in the wake of the leaks, he issued an order via Haldeman that "no one on the National Security Council staff [aside from Kissinger] is ever to hold any meeting with an individual or group of press people," on or off the record. And to top things off, senior NSC aides—unlike their Kennedy-Johnson predecessors—were denied access to the White House mess. "The NSC system is dead," a frustrated Dick Sneider, Kissinger's top aide for East Asia, declared five months into the administration. "Henry killed it long ago."

A striking exception to the general staff malaise was Army Colonel (soon to become General) Alexander Haig. From the start, he used his position as NSC military aide to become Kissinger's indispensable, across-the-board assistant. Kissinger had named no deputy, in part to deny the post to Nixon's campaign adviser Richard Allen—who had reason to expect it. Less than three weeks into the administration, Haig wrote a memo to Kissinger urging that he appoint a deputy. "I am not volunteering," wrote the not so subtle officer, but "would be honored" to serve. It was 1970 before Haig was given this formal designation; but in the meantime, he employed his assiduous service to Kissinger and his perceived political loyalty to Nixon to build up his role. The fact that other Council staff members did not respect Haig intellectually actually helped in his rise, for it meant they did not perceive him as a threat. Meanwhile, Kissinger—all too aware of broad White House concern over the eclecticism of his staff—protected himself by declaring, upon visiting the FBI and reading the wiretap logs, that "it is clear that I don't have anybody in my office that I can trust except Colonel Haig here."

Not only were NSC aides finding the staff a particularly hierarchical place, but they found that the psychological rewards of service were few. Winston Lord—who stayed the course and was ultimately one of the most successful—spoke later of staying up late at night, more than once, to write and rewrite a report. Each time he submitted it, Kissinger would ask, "Is this the best you can do?" Finally, with the ninth draft, and the same question, Lord responded, "Henry, I've beaten my brains out. . . . I can't possibly improve one more word!" "In that case, now I'll read it," Kissinger responded. Staff secretary William Watts wrote his boss a late 1969 memo highlighting problems of staff morale in the wake of "contradictory instructions" from Kissinger, "downgrading [staff] in front of their peers," and the failure to debrief subordinates on decisions made at meetings with Under Secretary of State Elliot Richardson and other senior administration officials. And two aides exceptionally close to Kissinger wrote, upon their resignations in spring 1970, of "the atmosphere of suspicion, manipulation and malice that we have seen over the past year," especially in dealings among senior administration officials.

By September 1969, no less than ten senior members of the staff had left, largely of their own volition, including Halperin, Eagleburger, Sneider, Davidson, and Allen. Three others would resign the following April because they could not support Nixon's controversial decision to broaden the Vietnam War theater of combat by sending American ground forces into Cambodia. By April 1971, only nine of the original twenty-eight were still on board. This turnover among newly recruited aides is unique in NSC history. But others were available to replace them. It became a larger, still high-quality but more compliant group, expanding to thirty-eight (including one woman) by September 1969, forty-six in August 1970, and fifty-four in April 1971.

"No more NSC meetings," Nixon decided, after he had read in the papers accounts about his administration's decision making on the return of Okinawa and the situation in Vietnam. H. R. Haldeman's diary entry for June 4, 1969, cryptically continued: "Result of leak. Can't trust to papers. Will make decisions privately with K." Haldeman's "informal, handwritten notes" of Nixon's musings went on: "Skip NSC Weds—P. has decided to skeleton them. Cut NSC to one every 2 wks—or once a month. Less papers. More brought privately to P. for his decision w/K., go right from subcomm to P—*not* to NSC. . . . Because of leaks—no NSC mtg on SALT [Strategic Arms Limitation Treaty] talks. . . . None from now on until further notice. . . . No paper on any of this."

Haldeman interpreted such outbursts as Nixon "letting off of steam." It was "not an order that was intended to be carried out." Making such a call was "a challenge I faced frequently," he observed retrospectively, as Nixon was given to venting. As Kissinger and Haig noted at the time, it was impossible—and not in Nixon's interest—to call an immediate halt to NSC meetings. But Nixon's words proved a harbinger of things to come. He was becoming more and more uncomfortable with the formal policymaking system Kissinger had built to Nixon's own specifications. And it was of course within his power to render it meaningless.

Concern over leaks ballooned, becoming far greater than their real-life policy impact could justify. But they struck directly at the president's insatiable need for control. They threatened Kissinger, too. He believed in secrecy; his power was enhanced by it. And he knew that his own credibility with Nixon demanded that he empathize with, and respond to, the president's anxieties as well as his policy priorities.

But Nixon's frustrations with the system were broader. As vice president, he had valued Eisenhower's weekly NSC meetings because they gave him a guaranteed seat at the table, a chance to speak his mind. He saw, moreover, how this open process of debate helped build broader loyalty to Ike and his administration, even as he recognized that the consensus policy papers sometimes limited Ike's options. So it was natural in 1968 for Nixon to campaign for a restoration of the Eisenhower process—with the proviso that the papers to be debated before the Council include real policy choices. The formal system he ordained on inauguration day was exceptionally well crafted for this purpose.

Once fully in charge, however, Nixon quickly found that he did not like the system. It might formally give him options, but it also confronted him, face-to-face, with strong-willed advisers arguing for choices he did not wish to make. And a key element of his convoluted psychology was his weakness in such confrontation: he found himself virtually incapable to tell individuals that he was rejecting their advice, that he had decided to do what they opposed, or (even harder) that he no longer wanted them in his administration. This excruciating discomfort became public in November 1970 when Secretary of the Interior Walter Hickel refused to accept firing via Haldeman and insisted on hearing it from Nixon directly. (Hickel had sealed his fate months earlier by writing the president a letter, which leaked, urging him to communicate more with young anti-war protestors and meet regularly with his cabinet.) On lesser matters there was a recurrent pattern. Someone would penetrate the "Berlin Wall" of senior staff aides (Haldeman, Ehrlichman, Kissinger) that Nixon had constructed to protect himself, and urge the president to take a specific action. He would agree. After the person left, he would call in Haldeman and say he had no intention of doing what he had just agreed to, and to make sure that person never gets into the Oval Office again!

National Security Council meetings posed a similar threat—that Nixon would be cornered, confronted with strong pressure to do what he did not want to do, or not to do what he wanted to do, as in the case of the aircraft shot down by North Korea. The solution was "no more NSC meetings," or, realistically, fewer and fewer as time went by. Hence, the frequency dropped from twenty-seven in the first six months of the administration to just ten in the six months thereafter. The gap widened between the system as described and the system as it operated. In February 1970, the president discussed the "National Security Council System" up front in the first of his annual reports to Congress on U.S. foreign policy. In it, he stressed how "all agencies and departments receive a fair hearing before I make my decisions," knowing that their "positions and arguments will reach the Council without dilution," and that they would be "fully informed of our policy" when he made his decision. But while this might have been true nine months earlier, it was true no longer.

Nixon was forced to hold two NSC meetings in late April 1970 before his controversial decision to attack North Vietnamese bases in Cambodia, but he managed the second in a way that avoided serious discussion with Rogers and Laird, both of whom he knew opposed the operation. Immediately thereafter, he signed a Kissinger-drafted directive ordering the invasion. Nixon's discomfort from even this limited confrontation reinforced his penchant for isolation. In the entire, policy-rich year of 1972, Nixon convened a grand total of three meetings of the Council he had pledged four years earlier to "restore." Noting this decline, an internal NSC staff memo asked at year's end: "in our writings do we want to start downplaying the role of the NSC in the NSC system?"

The main alternative to the Council was the adviser, who maintained his oft-shaky presidential relationship by assiduously catering to Nixon's needs. After a press conference, when the president called to ask how he did, Kissinger would invariably praise Nixon's substantive grasp and coolness under fire, regardless of the actual quality of the performance. When an issue needed to be resolved in a direction contrary to Nixon's inclinations, Kissinger would talk around the problem, setting forth a broad range of considerations, until the president found a way to do what he had to do. And though the national security adviser was initially skeptical of the Cambodia decision, he provided steadfast support and reassurance once the decision was made, in the face of an eruption of protest within the government and across the nation.

As the months went by, the "NSC system" underwent formal structural change—from one centered on preparation for explicit presidential decisions to one that emphasized detailed action along policy lines already decided (or to be addressed by Nixon outside the system). The most visible manifestation of this change was the creation of a set of new NSC committees. First to take form was the Washington Special Actions Group, established on May 16, 1969, in the wake of the North Korea aircraft shoot-down, to consider "policies and actions affecting crises" on a worldwide basis. It was followed in July by the Verification Panel to review "U.S. capabilities to monitor arms control agreements." In September, the Vietnam Special Studies Group was created "to more systematically assess the facts upon which Vietnam policy decisions should be based." In October was born the Defense Program Review Committee, charged to review "major defense policy and program issues." All of these were chaired by Kissinger, with State and Defense represented by their number two officials, and CIA and other agencies by their directors.

And finally, conforming to this pattern, the assistant secretary–level NSC Review Group was replaced, in September 1970, by the Senior Review Group (SRG), with membership and chairmanship comparable to the others.

In practice, these committees addressed matters from broad policy to details of implementation. They were of varying effectiveness—the special actions group became the true locus of interagency crisis coordination, whereas Secretary Laird effectively resisted defense program committee efforts to get leverage on defense budget decisions. But all five put Kissinger in the catbird's seat, and all operated just below cabinet level—convenient for Kissinger in avoiding direct conflict with Rogers or Laird.

These committees helped Kissinger to manage policy for Nixon on a range of issues, particularly those where State and Defense had unavoidable roles. But contributing most to Kissinger's power—and his indispensability to the president—was the assistant's role as secret presidential negotiator on just about every issue that his boss considered important. This role he typically played without the knowledge of U.S. negotiators officially assigned to the task (such as the chief SALT negotiator, Gerard Smith). An atypical but revealing example was Kissinger's secret effort to nail down a U.S.-Japan textile agreement and thus fulfill a Nixon campaign promise to the U.S. textile industry. Prime Minister Eisaku Sato's need to have Okinawa returned to Japanese sovereignty gave the White House leverage: the substantive outrageousness of U.S. textile demands (not understood by Kissinger) generated fierce resistance across the Pacific. The national security adviser's frustrating, sometimes comical efforts to resolve the matter with a similarly unexpert Japanese intermediary, code-named "Mr. Yoshida," are now a matter of public record. Though his efforts were sincere, his failure ended up making the problem worse and embittering, for a time, U.S.-Japanese relations. Kissinger states that "because of my ignorance of the subject, I kept the key players on our side meticulously informed"; but he did not include among them his international economic assistant, Fred Bergsten, or any other staff aide elsewhere in government with the relevant expertise.

On other international economic issues, Kissinger's basic response was neglect, together with failure to empower Bergsten to act in his stead. Overall, administration foreign economic policy was a mess in 1969–70, featuring inaction about pressures on the dollar and loss of control over trade policy, as a restrictive import quota bill passed the House of Representatives and made it to the floor of the Senate. This led, in January 1971, to the creation of a Council on International Economic Policy parallel to the NSC, and to the designation of Peter G. Peterson as assistant to the president for international economic affairs. Kissinger's continuing unconcern for this area was reflected in his absence from the crucial Camp David deliberations leading to Nixon's landmark action on August 15, 1971, severing the link of the value of the dollar to the price of gold. Leading the charge for that action was not Peterson but Nixon's new secretary of the Treasury, John Connally, and the international economic policy council had only modest policy influence until Jimmy Carter abolished it in 1977. However, a pattern was set. Under Kennedy and Johnson, foreign economic policy had been coordinated by a deputy national security adviser. But almost every president from Nixon onward would look to another institution, separate from the NSC, to handle most foreign economic issues.

What was important to Kissinger, the president, and history were the assistant's efforts on the three issues that came to define Nixon's national security policy: Vietnam; U.S.-Soviet relations; and the opening up to the People's Republic of China. Kissinger and Nixon saw the three as intertwined—pressure on Moscow could bring flexibility to Hanoi; overtures to China would bring concessions from the USSR.

Early in his presidency, Nixon elected to continue the Paris Peace Talks with North Vietnam inaugurated in Johnson's last year, and named Henry Cabot Lodge to succeed Averell Harriman as chief negotiator. In early August 1969, however, Henry Kissinger and his aide Anthony Lake "split off" from President Nixon's nearly completed round-the-world trip and flew to Paris, ostensibly to brief French leaders about it. Their real purpose was to launch a secret dialogue with representatives of Hanoi that would continue for over three years. Lodge was not informed, although, as one thoroughgoing analyst noted, the new channel "had the effect of completely downgrading all the work being done" by his delegation.

Kissinger hoped they could, by manipulating offers and threats, bring the North Vietnamese into serious negotiations. Nixon was more skeptical, but allowed Kissinger to continue the meetings. At the same time, Secretary Laird was determined to respond to congressional pressure on the war by reducing the American troop presence in South Vietnam. Nixon agreed, opting for a policy of "Vietnamization," which would steadily transfer combat responsibilities to the South Vietnamese military. This meant Kissinger had to square a circle: persuade Hanoi that mutual withdrawal of forces was in its interest even as the United States was withdrawing its forces unilaterally. Recognizing the contradiction, he and Nixon looked for actions that would keep the heat on the North Vietnamese, such as the Cambodia bombings in 1969 and the U.S. troop incursion there in 1970. But there was little movement in the talks.

The president bought political time at home with a brilliant, Nixonesque television speech on November 3, 1969, turning public resentments from the war itself to the scruffy demonstrators who were flooding Washington in increasing numbers. He appealed to the "great silent majority" of Americans, and unleashed Vice President Spiro T. Agnew to launch alliterative attacks against the "nattering nabobs of negativism" in the media. Nixon's decision to send troops into Cambodia the following April, however, reenergized the antiwar movement and its growing number of congressional supporters. Meanwhile, Kissinger continued his intermittent secret rendezvous with the North Vietnamese negotiator Le Duc Tho and his colleagues in Paris, meeting twelve times before Nixon made the negotiating record public in January 1972.

Next to Vietnam, the second most prominent issue for Nixon was U.S.-Soviet relations, where he sought to build on the thaw initiated under Kennedy and Johnson. In November 1969, the two nations launched comprehensive strategic arms control negotiations in Vienna, with Gerard Smith, director of the Arms Control and Disarmament Agency, leading the American delegation. But Nixon didn't trust Smith (as he told Smith's deputy, Paul Nitze, upon his appointment) and wanted the issue controlled from the White House, so that he—not Smith or Secretary of State Rogers—would get the credit for any achievement.

The big initial issue was whether an agreement would address both offensive and defensive weapons, or limit itself to anti-ballistic missile systems as Moscow initially proposed. Washington needed offensive weapons ceilings to constrain the rapid expansion of Soviet deployments, and Kissinger was working on a formula with Dobrynin when, in early May 1971, the official Soviet arms negotiator presented a concession to Gerard Smith through the regular channel in Vienna. "Kissinger confronted Dobrynin in a rage," notes the national security adviser's biographer, seeing this as an effort to take advantage by playing off the two channels against each other. If the Russian side persisted, Kissinger recalled telling Dobrynin, "the President's anger at what he could only construe as a deliberate maneuver to deprive him of credit would be massive." Moscow got the message, making the final concession via Dobrynin to negotiate both systems.

At noon on May 20, Nixon announced the procedural breakthrough, with Kissinger's background briefing following two hours later. Kissinger told Smith about the deal at breakfast the day before; Nixon himself informed Rogers the same morning. Smith was concerned on both procedural and substantive grounds, believing that the deal was technically flawed (omitting, for example, submarine-launched missiles). He shared William Bundy's retrospective judgment that it was a "sloppy negotiating performance." But he held public fire until the publication of his memoirs in 1980.

The secretary of state was "very upset," unloading on H. R. Haldeman at length. His focus was on process and reputation. "Both K and the P had promised him that they would not have any other further meetings with any Ambassadors, and particularly Dobrynin, without letting him know. He said he would bet a large amount that all the magazines would have a full report on the number of meetings K had with Dobrynin, etc. This would make him a laughingstock again; it destroys his effectiveness and credibility." Nixon talked further with Rogers by phone: after he hung up, the president declared that "it would be goddamn easy to run this office if you didn't have to deal with people." But he did seek to limit the damage to the secretary's reputation, telling Kissinger that, in his briefing, "Henry must not discuss at all how it happened, not one word [about] any of his sessions" with Dobrynin. Nonetheless, for Kissinger it was "a milestone in confirming White House dominance of foreign affairs. For the first two years White House control had been confined to the formulation of policy; now it extended to its execution." And it was followed in September by another agreement—also completed through the back channel by Kissinger and Ambassador Kenneth Rush—on the perennial Cold War issue of the two Germanys and the status of West Berlin.

Rogers's fury underscored the downside of employing the national security adviser in this manner. The Nixon-Kissinger mode of making foreign policy brought a degree of fractiousness to State Department–White House dealings that made Kennedy-Bundy relations with Dean Rusk look like a Sunday School picnic. In a memo to Kissinger, Lake summarized the situation late in the first year, before the full magnitude for the White House takeover was manifest:

- relations between the NSC staff and the State Department are at their lowest ebb in years;
- the State Department sees the NSC now in an adversary role in a way that it has not before;
- some comments attributed to you denigrating the State Department have been given fairly wide circulation in some Bureaus. . . .
- all of these factors have contributed to a vicious circle of reactions and counter-reactions between the staff and the State Department;

> • the major consequences [include] the serious inconsistencies we have displayed to foreigners with regard to critically important substantive issues and the impression of indiscipline and lack of coherence we have displayed to the press.

Prior to that, Haig had twice drafted (presumably at Kissinger's behest) detailed memos citing the State Department's multiple deviations from White House decisions, and maintaining that they added up to "a fundamental disloyalty to presidential policy." Rogers's failure "to adhere to broad policy lines approved by the President," Haig wrote, meant that "the most serious damage to the national interest cannot but result." In February 1970, the national security assistant had Haig draft a "bill of particulars" for an ultimatum to the president: either Nixon would order Rogers to toe the line, or Kissinger would "leave the administration." There is no evidence that he actually delivered such a message (Haig counseled against it), but Haldeman noted in his diary two days later that although Nixon expressed the view that they hadn't been "hard enough on backsliders" within the administration who didn't follow his policy, "Problem is that P is not willing to stand tight on unpleasant personnel situations and won't back us if we do." And Kissinger was unable to translate his position of power into effective working relationships with either Rogers or Defense Secretary Laird.

Nixon clearly favored Kissinger on the substance, but found his "tantrums" frustrating. Haldeman's diary is replete with entries, as those chosen from October 1969 through February 1971 show:

> Problem [with K] is his insistence on perfection and total adherence to the line in every detail. Also injects himself too much into everything, between P and Cabinet officers, and they just won't buy it, so he becomes ineffective even at getting them to do what they already were ready to do.
>
> P . . . feels K is impairing his usefulness and is obsessed beyond reason with this [Rogers] problem. . . . Tough one,

because there *is* some real merit to K's concern about Rogers' loyalty.

P . . . knows what the Rogers problem is, but he feels K is too self-concerned and inclined to overdramatize. Solution lies in better understanding both ways, but it's not likely. . . .

K called at home tonight to say Rogers had called him in a blind rage, yelling at him, about the briefing [a Kissinger press backgrounder]. Said K tricked P into hard line about Cuba. . . . said "One of us has got to go and is going to P." . . . [The next day] P then had Haig in and went over the whole thing with both of us. Made it clear he felt K had erred in briefing yesterday, Haig said K knew it. . . . [Re the] K-Rogers battle, wants me to get into it and try to work it out. . . . Asked if I felt time had come that one had to go. I said no. . . . He indicated that if one did go it would have to be K, and he's obviously still thinking of Haig as replacement.

After K went out, he [the president] got into a discussion of Rogers. . . . Wants me to put a fully documented case together and sit down with Rogers and make it clear that State has broken its pick at the White House . . . I think he's basically concluded that he's not going to be able to keep Rogers on for much longer. . . . [The next day] go ahead on the talk with Rogers, making the point that there are two different fights involved here. One is with K and Rogers, and that the P, of course, has to side with Rogers on. But the second one is much more important: that's the foreign service vs. the P. There it's unforgivable, and the P is going to have heads rolling. Since Cambodia, they've been taking on the P . . . from now on, it's us or them.

We had a long meeting . . . at Henry's request to discuss in detail his problems with the State Department. He walked into the meeting with . . . all kinds of papers . . . documenting the terrible things State has been doing. . . . He did an extremely good job, for a change, of presenting his case quite unemotionally and very rationally. . . . He would not continue this method of operation. If it couldn't be resolved, he would leave; if it could be, he'd be perfectly willing to work within a new approach as long as NSC has complete control and Rogers is, as he puts it, "brought to heel."

I had a three-hour lunch with Rogers. . . . Rogers' principal concern was to try to work out the Henry K problem, and he specifically asked for ways that he could direct communications to the P directly . . . Henry caught me later and made it clear that his dissatisfaction is again reaching a peak, so we have a lot to do.

The root problem, Nixon observed to Haldeman in June 1971, was that "the Secretary of State, Bob, does make foreign policy in other administrations," as Rogers was doing for the Middle East. "Rusk would be perfect for me [as a secretary of state] because he'd do what the hell I said." Since the president was incapable of confronting his senior advisers, he needed people who would accede to subordinate roles without his having to discipline them. When they didn't, the result was continuing conflict that spilled over into the press and rubbed all the participants raw. But one month later, an event would occur that sealed Kissinger's primacy vis-à-vis Rogers, even as it sewed the seeds of a new problem between him and the president. That was, of course, the secret opening to the People's Republic of China.

Winston Lord had become, by mid-1971, an intimate aide to Kissinger, a key player in the "staff within the staff" that the national security adviser maintained to handle the foreign policy business he cared about. In early July, as Lord recalled,

We were on this small plane, purportedly going to India, Pakistan, Vietnam, and Thailand. I had to maintain three sets of briefing books. . . . One set [was] for those who were going into China, namely [Richard] Smyser, Lord, [John] Holdridge, and Kissinger. Another set were for those knowing that people were going into China, but were part of the cover team staying back in Pakistan. . . . And then the third briefing book was for those who didn't even know there was going to be a China leg . . . we'd get them all updated and I'd put my head on a pillow, and Kissinger would then wake up and look at it and want it redone again. . . . You can't have people looking over your shoulder. You['ve] got to hand out the right book to the right person.

"O what a tangled web we weave / When first we practice to deceive!" Sir Walter Scott's aphorism, aptly applied by William Bundy to Nixon's entire foreign policy presidency, catches perfectly the convolutions required of the staff aide here. But Lord was successful in his task. The secrecy held. Kissinger and his aides slipped away from a "lengthy 'information trip' through Asia," got to Beijing from Pakistan, and back to the "Western White House" in San Clemente with astonishingly few Americans privy to the historic journey. (Nixon did not inform Secretary Rogers until July 8, after the trip was under way, suggesting falsely that the opportunity had arisen suddenly.) Late in the evening of July 15, Nixon appeared briefly on network television and made the world-shaking revelation that Kissinger had just returned from "talks with [Chinese] Premier Chou En-lai." He then read an "announcement . . . being issued simultaneously in Peking and in the United States," which declared that the president had accepted an invitation "to visit China at an appropriate date before May 1972."

With this one stroke, Nixon transformed U.S.-China relations. He devastated the pro-Taiwan "China lobby," which had blocked normal relations with the People's Republic for decades. He gained new leverage with the Soviet Union, which shifted from dragging its feet on the Moscow summit that Nixon so desired to asking whether Nixon might come to Moscow *before* he visited Beijing. (The response: the summits would take place in the order that they were announced.) Last but not least, the opening was singularly Nixon's achievement. He, not Kissinger, had envisaged the possibility for years, and his persistence and boldness had brought it to fruition. The covertness was not necessary from the Chinese point of view: Chou had offered to "receive publicly" a representative of Nixon, and the Chinese were, in Kissinger's later words, "extremely suspicious of our desire for secrecy." But in the United States, and across the world, the clandestine initiative followed by sudden revelation surely multiplied the impact.

For Nixon, however, there was one serious downside: it was Kissinger who made the secret journey, and its success elevated the assistant to supercelebrity status. This increased the risk that Kissinger, not Nixon, would get the bulk of the credit. Nixon clearly anticipated this problem. After Chou had issued the invitation to "a special envoy of the President of the U.S." in late April, "through the good offices of President Yahya Khan" of Pakistan, Nixon had discussed with Kissinger other possible messengers (including Nelson Rockefeller and Thomas E. Dewey, who had died a few months before), perhaps to avert the super-K problem, or perhaps simply to underscore the fact that Kissinger's power was overridingly dependent on Nixon's will. But in the end, the secret process left the president no choice—there was simply no one else inside or outside the administration who knew Nixon, his person and policies, well enough to be trusted with such a critical mission.

Kissinger had been, from the start, a relatively prominent national security adviser. During his first two years of service, his name had appeared in the *New York Times* five times as often as had Bundy's during the comparable period. This was true although Nixon had ordered that he make no on-the-record statements for the press. The number of mentions would double in 1971, and double again in 1972, as the China trip made Henry Kissinger a celebrity around the world. There were cover stories in *Time* and *Newsweek*. Nixon sought to arrest the tide. He had asked, impractically, that Kissinger's name not appear in the joint statement of July 15. Thereafter, he ordered the national security adviser and others in the White House not to cooperate in stories about Kissinger's role, while at the same time writing Kissinger, at length, of how he should stress to reporters certain personal Nixonian qualities—"Cool. Unflappable . . . tough bold strong leader . . . knows Asia. . . . You could also point out that most of these attributes are ones that you also saw in Chou En-Lai. . . ." Kissinger did push this line, but he did not abide by the prohibition, to Nixon's frustration.

In addition to his relentless cultivation of the press, Kissinger made himself an item on the social pages. Virtually alone among senior administration officials, he was a regular on the Washington social circuit, and an exchange with rising young *Washington Post* Style Page writer Sally Quinn caused him to be dubbed a "secret swinger." Though there was clearly more smoke here than fire, Kissinger relished the public dates with Hollywood stars, Jill St. John in particular. During long stays near Nixon at San Clemente, he would frequently escape to Hollywood for recreation. "Power is the ultimate aphrodisiac," he declared. This activity provided enormous gratification to the assistant, and relief, presumably, from the enormous tensions within the Nixon White House. The president and his aides were sometimes amused, sometimes not. But it removed one Nixon-Kissinger commonality. When they began their collaboration in 1969, each man had seen himself as socially awkward, an outsider. Kissinger did so no longer.

The larger danger, for Nixon, was that reporters and the liberal establishment would conclude what he felt (not without reason) that they wanted to conclude: that Kissinger was responsible for the administration's foreign policy "successes" and the president for its failures. While Kissinger, in his words, "did not consciously encourage the process, there is no consistent record of my resistance either." And the unprecedented publicity Kissinger was receiving increased the need for a vindictive Nixon to put him in his place when he misstepped. The South Asia crisis of late 1971 offered the perfect opportunity.

For most of the year, the same Yahya Khan who had played middleman for the China venture was engaged in brutal suppression of the rising autonomy movement in East Pakistan, which was separated by 1,000 miles from the dominant, western portion of the country, with Pakistan's rival India in between. Its leader was imprisoned; civilians in the capital city were massacred; ten million refugees flooded across the border to India. India began to call for autonomy for what would shortly become the nation of Bangladesh. The world largely agreed. Within the United States, State Department officials and the larger expert community were virtually united in condemning Yahya's brutality, and seeing the proper and likely outcome as independence for a region that had little in common with its western compatriots other than the Muslim religion. They viewed it as a regional problem, with a regional solution.

Nixon and Kissinger saw matters differently. For them, the main devil was India, which they saw as determined to dismember Pakistan, supported by an opportunistic Soviet Union. Moreover, the crisis was a test of U.S. loyalty to Yahya and his Chinese "ally," one that threatened, potentially, the nascent relationship with Beijing. Kissinger seized on isolated intelligence, believed by few others, and concluded that Indian prime minister Indira Gandhi (despised by Nixon) was determined to attack and break up *West* Pakistan. (In fact, it was the Pakistanis who, foolishly, opened hostilities on that front.) After Indian troops crossed the border into East Pakistan in late November, the outcome there seemed assured. But two weeks later, the White House received word that the Chinese government wished to deliver a message about the conflict. Kissinger "took this—as it turned out, wrongly—to be an indication that China might intervene militarily." He and Nixon envisaged the Soviet Union moving in on India's side. Nixon then made a "lonely and brave decision," as Kissinger characterized it. "Without informing either his Secretary of State or Secretary of Defense," the president made clear that if "the Soviet Union threatened China, we would not stand idly by," and he ordered a carrier task force to proceed into the Bay of Bengal. Throughout the crisis, moreover, Kissinger was simultaneously giving the press background briefings insisting that the United States was not anti-Indian, and telling his colleagues in Washington that

Nixon was determined to "tilt in favor of Pakistan" and that "I am getting hell every half hour from the President that we are not being tough enough on India."

Fortunately, Kissinger was wrong on all counts: China's message was simply that it would support a UN cease-fire resolution; Moscow was counseling restraint; and India did not exploit the matter in the west, eschewing even an attack on the Pakistani sector of the disputed province of Kashmir. But Kissinger was slow to recognize all this, and he declared in a mid-December, not-for-attribution press briefing that if the Soviet Union didn't change its approach, the president would have to reconsider the Moscow summit meeting, now booked for the following May. The *Washington Post* decided this was too important to report on background, so it published the threat and attributed it to Kissinger. Here Kissinger had gone too far—although Nixon had apparently mentioned this possibility in private conversation, he did not mean it: he had far too much invested in the prospect of being the first U.S. president to visit Moscow. In response, White House press secretary Ron Ziegler declared that Kissinger was wrong, the summit was not being reconsidered, and other presidential staff members spoke of Kissinger's exceeding his authority. Then, less than a week later, columnist Jack Anderson published the language from the meeting minutes about the "tilt," exposing at once administration hypocrisy and bitter conflict within the U.S. government.

Nixon was unhappy—and Kissinger took the heat. The search for the leaker was, in this case, successful: it was a young naval yeoman, Charles Radford, who worked on the NSC staff as a junior liaison officer with the Joint Chiefs of Staff. (Radford was pro-India, and a friend of Anderson.) The investigation further revealed that this was the tip of a very large iceberg. For more than a year, Radford had been systematically copying reams of limited-distribution NSC documents and passing them on to the Joint Chiefs of Staff, where they reached the desk of the chairman, Admiral Thomas Moorer. When he heard the news, Kissinger was outraged. The previous June, he had stoked presidential ire over the *New York Times* publication of *The*

Pentagon Papers, the secret history of the Vietnam War commissioned by Defense Secretary Robert McNamara during the Johnson administration. Now he demanded that Moorer be fired.

Nixon, however, responded quite differently. "The P was quite shocked, naturally," Haldeman recorded in his diary, "and agreed that strong action had to be taken, but very carefully, because we don't want to blow up the whole relationship with the Joint Chiefs of Staff." Three days later, he told Kissinger's deputy, General Haig, "we got to remember that basically [Moorer is] our ally in terms of what we believe in," so "we're going to cool this thing." So the yeoman was transferred and no serious action was taken. But Nixon's commitment to secrecy was validated. "I tell you whenever there's anything important you don't tell anybody," he told Haldeman. "We don't tell Rogers, Laird, anybody. We just don't tell any son-of-a-bitch at all."

The fact that Nixon discussed all this directly with Haig underscored a new Kissinger problem: the president was now using the assistant's deputy as an alternate source of information and advice, one whose substantive, political, and personal loyalty he did not doubt. And the press, egged on by the State Department, continued to highlight the "tilt," treating it as a first-level foreign policy fiasco, and placing the blame primarily on Kissinger. Nixon was expressing concerns about Kissinger's mental stability, ordering him, through Haldeman, not to respond to the attacks, and the White House was not issuing statements in the assistant's defense ("why is a presidential assistant under attack with no word of support from his boss?"). The assistant saw his situation as bleak indeed: "The policy became *my* policy. For several weeks Nixon was unavailable to me. . . . The departments were not admonished to stop leaking against me. Nixon could not resist the temptation of letting me twist slowly, slowly in the wind. . . . It was a stern lesson in the dependence of Presidential Assistants on their chief."

"And then suddenly, it was all over," Kissinger noted. By mid-January 1972, he was back in presidential favor, the indispensable aide for what would prove historic and triumphal presidential summits in Beijing and Moscow. It was Kissinger and his staff who crafted the "Shanghai communiqué," which was signed during Nixon's visit to China and prepared the way for regularized relations between Washington and Beijing. It was Kissinger who concluded the landmark SALT agreement that was subsequently attacked for disadvantageous sloppiness in detail, but assured that Nixon could sign it in Moscow and the White House would get the credit.

Nixon was also on a roll at home. Senator Edmund Muskie, regarded as his strongest potential opponent in the presidential race, faded in the early primaries, leaving the Democratic field clear for the more liberal and vulnerable George McGovern. By the end of summer, it was clear that Nixon would be reelected, perhaps by a record margin. To be sure, his insecurities had fueled an extralegal campaign against his enemies that would come to be labeled "Watergate," after White House agents were caught breaking into the office of Democratic National Committee chairman Lawrence O'Brien. But the significance of all this would not be felt until after the election.

The Moscow Summit had been preceded by a major North Vietnamese offensive and an aggressive U.S. military response, including heavy bombing and the mining of the North Vietnamese port of Haiphong. Moscow's decision to go ahead with the meeting anyway demonstrated that Nixon could be tough on the war front and still do business with Hanoi's erstwhile allies. And after election day, he would plausibly have an even freer hand. Perhaps for this reason, North Vietnamese negotiators dropped, in early fall, their consistent prior demand that the South Vietnamese government of Nguyen Van Thieu be removed from power as part of any peace settlement. Kissinger saw this as the opportunity he had spent four years waiting for, and he believed it would not last. When Congress reconvened in January 1973, virtually all U.S. combat troops would be out as a result of the "Vietnamization" program, and the Democratic majority would surely crank up the pressure to complete the withdrawal. Now was the time of maximum American leverage. Since Nixon had revealed the existence of the peace talks nine months before, Kissinger no longer had to sneak around Paris with disguises provided by U.S. military attaché General Vernon Walters. But he and his aides were no less in charge of the negotiations. And there was no doubt that Kissinger was determined to close the deal.

Nixon was driven by a different calculus. Contrary to the popular assumption that he wanted a Vietnam agreement prior to the November 7 election to further undercut McGovern's peace candidacy, he was in fact extremely wary of one. It would look political. Moreover, his aide Charles Colson told him, it would soften his "tough guy" image and undercut support from the blue-collar constituency he had cultivated ever since his "silent majority speech" in 1969. Nonetheless, presented with an agreement on the basis of an early October proposal from Hanoi, Nixon "ordered steak and wine to celebrate the event" with Kissinger and Haig. Kissinger now sought to follow a demanding, made-in-Hanoi timetable: He would travel to that city on October 22 to pin down final details; the deal would be announced on the 26th and signed on the 30th. But first he had to go to Saigon, and when Kissinger brought Nguyen Van Thieu the accord, the South Vietnamese president rejected it—on grounds of substance, and because he had not been consulted on critical details. Nixon backed off, with Haig, who had previously endorsed it, now fueling his doubts about whether it was the best attainable accord.

Then, to force matters, Hanoi Radio broadcast the substance of the draft agreement two weeks before the U.S. election, asserting that Nixon had, in essence, agreed but was now employing various "pretexts" to delay signing. In response, Kissinger held his first televised press conference. Aiming both to reassure Hanoi and to send a message to Saigon, he famously declared that "peace is at hand," that the North Vietnamese had essentially accepted the position advanced by Nixon earlier that year, and that the eleventh-hour "difficulties" were normal given the stakes involved. Nixon was "enraged" by the "peace at hand" phrase, which many Americans read as an election ploy. "I suppose now everybody's going to say that Kissinger won the election," he remarked bitterly to Colson.

Twelve days later, Nixon won the election, carrying 61 percent of the popular vote and forty-nine of fifty states. The latter was a record unmatched since 1820. But November and December were unhappy months for the reelected president and his chief national security aide. Nixon was vindictive in his hour of triumph, demanding the morning after the election that all of his aides submit their resignations (on a preprinted form) so he could have a free hand to choose who would serve in his second term. Then he receded from public view. Kissinger felt that his relationship with the president was broken, perhaps irreparably: his memoirs refer to an "emerging competitiveness that was certain to destroy sooner or later my effectiveness as a Presidential Assistant." He exacerbated matters with a wildly inappropriate interview with the Italian journalist Oriana Fallaci, in which Kissinger characterized himself as "like the cowboy . . . entering a village or city alone on his horse," a metaphor that may have reflected his feelings as he single-handedly sought to salvage the Vietnam peace accord, but grossly misrepresented his actual position as an aide dependent on presidential favor. So shaky was his relationship with Nixon by now that when Kissinger learned that *Time* was about to name the president and him, jointly, "Men of the Year," he appealed to the editor in chief, Hedley Donovan, "to take me off the cover." Donovan replied that if Kissinger didn't shut up, he would be named "Man of the Year" solo.

In any case, the peace accord was salvaged in the worst possible way. The failure of negotiations to patch things up in November was followed by the Christmas bombing of Hanoi, undertaken mainly to assuage Saigon. There were also secret Nixon promises to President Thieu, made with no discernable U.S. domestic support, that the United States would respond with force to serious North Vietnamese violations of the cease-fire. Nixon was the dominant figure in this final stage. For the peace agreement concluded in January 1973, Kissinger would become, in October, the only American awarded the Nobel Peace Prize for his work as national security adviser—receiving the honor jointly with Le Duc Tho. But the balance struck in that accord would collapse less than two years later.

(Kissinger then offered to return the money and the prize, but the Nobel Committee refused.)

———

Immediately after the election, Nixon decided to replace Secretary of State Rogers with his old Duke law professor, Kenneth Rush, and he was thinking of replacing Kissinger as well. But Rogers insisted on staying another six months, and Nixon was unwilling to remove him face-to-face. Kissinger was upset at this extension, about which he was not consulted, and he himself considered resigning. He was in fact reappointed national security adviser on December 2, four years to the day from Nixon's original public designation. Still, as 1973 began, he recognized that he "had become too public a figure for the post of national security adviser," and noted that he had "decided to resign by the end of the year."

Events were to unfold quite differently: it was a measure of Kissinger's weak grasp of the U.S. domestic scene that he did not recognize the seriousness of the gathering Watergate storm until he was alerted in mid-April by White House aide Leonard Garment. In January, Judge John Sirica presided over the trial of the burglars who had been caught breaking in to Democratic National Committee headquarters, pressing skeptical questions about the involvement of higher-ups. (Press reports had by then linked former Attorney General John Mitchell to the affair.) In February, the Senate voted 77–0 to establish an investigating committee under Sam Ervin with broad subpoena powers. In March, the leader of the burglars, James McCord, wrote Judge Sirica informing him of pressure applied to the defendants to "plead guilty and remain silent." On April 30, Nixon would accept the forced resignations of Haldeman and Ehrlichman, whom the legal process was now implicating in the scandal; and in May, Attorney General–designate Elliot Richardson, at congressional insistence, appointed former Solicitor General Archibald Cox as special Watergate prosecutor with independent authority. Early in the year, Kissinger "had found it difficult to get Nixon to focus on foreign policy." Now he knew why.

Haldeman's replacement as chief of staff was Alexander Haig, a choice Kissinger viewed with considerable trepidation, given his erstwhile deputy's attempt to undercut his peace efforts in the fall of 1972. But he need not have worried: Haig soon recognized that the president needed Kissinger now more than ever. When Kissinger's role in the 1969–71 wiretapping of his aides became public in May, Haig urged journalists to go gentle: Henry was "a national asset." And this was the year when the Gallup Poll found him to be the "most admired" American (with Billy Graham second and the president third). As the Ervin Committee Bearings dramatized the breadth of the Watergate scandal, and former White House counsel John Dean implicated the president himself, Haig began (with the national security adviser's active concurrence) to push the idea that Kissinger be appointed secretary of state. Nixon "did not really want to," he told Walter Isaacson seventeen years later, and he delayed the matter well past the June 1 date when Rogers was committed to leaving. Finally, in an astonishing exhibition of awkwardness toward the man with whom he had achieved so much, Nixon—floating on his back at his San Clemente swimming pool on the afternoon of August 21—suddenly told Kissinger, with no prior preparation: "I shall open the press conference [tomorrow] by announcing your appointment as Secretary of State."

Kissinger retained the title of national security adviser—through Nixon's forced resignation in August 1974 and the first fifteen months of the Gerald Ford presidency. But he quickly ceased to play that role. The statutory cabinet position, combined with Watergate, gave him a degree of autonomy vis-à-vis Nixon that he could hitherto only have dreamt of. A sudden Middle East war in October 1973 thrust him first into the role of prime policymaker, wielding military threats on his own with Nixon in an alcoholic stupor in the White House residence, and then into the role of negotiator, shuttling between Egypt and Israel, and achieving cease-fire and then withdrawal agreements. But he left it to Lieutenant General Brent Scowcroft, his deputy national security adviser since January, to oversee the interagency policy process. In November 1975,

President Ford would recognize that role by elevating Scowcroft to the NSC job.

In stark contrast to his predecessor, Scowcroft worked constructively and cooperatively with the still-ascendant secretary of state. His performance sufficiently impressed one member of the Ford national security team, CIA director George H. W. Bush, that Scowcroft would later be asked to serve as Bush's national security adviser when he became president.

Measured by the roles he played and the policy impact he had, Henry A. Kissinger was more influential than any other national security adviser, before or since. He began by leading Nixon's restructured policy formulation process. He soon became the president's primary negotiator, achieving landmark results on all three of the administration's top-priority issues. On one of these, the opening to China, his role was the stuff of legend. Kissinger was also the administration's principal off-the-record policy articulator and spokesman. With his pre-election "peace is at hand" press conference, he went public in this role.

All that he did was made possible, of course, by his president, Richard M. Nixon, who made Kissinger his vehicle and charted much of the course—toward Beijing, above all. Institutionally, they built upon what Kennedy had created, making the NSC staff larger and more structured. They added important process innovations: the system of national security study memoranda producing real options for presidential decision, and interagency coordinating committees chaired by the adviser himself. These would become standard practice in later administrations.

Kissinger's impact on the top-priority issues was enhanced by the secrecy that the two men maintained. In part, this was planned; in part, it was the product of deep insecurities in both of them, insecurities that fueled distrust of colleagues, which was heartily reciprocated. And the distrust extended to each other: neither man seems ever to have had full confidence in the relationship; neither had full confidence in the other's support when waters turned rough; and each resented his dependence on the other. They bad-mouthed one another, with Kissinger labeling the president "our drunken friend" and Nixon questioning his assistant's mental balance.

If the secrecy undeniably facilitated some of their achievements, it limited their reach within the U.S. government and motivated other senior players to work against rather than with them. Secretary of Defense Melvin Laird developed his own network of information sources—in part through the National Security Agency, which was under Pentagon authority—and successfully resisted NSC efforts to influence defense planning. Secretary of State Rogers never accepted the legitimacy of Kissinger's role, believing that he was manipulating the president and others. Hence the endless personal and policy conflicts that fill the documentary record. Nixon's personality made things worse: his incapacity to enforce, face-to-face, the White House–centered system that he had mandated put the burden on his aides to do so, and made them scapegoats for unwelcome procedures and decisions that the president imposed. The system lacked internal legitimacy. Thus, on issues necessarily involving the State Department—the South Asia crisis, the Middle East—Rogers and his people successfully resisted presidential authority. On issues of lesser Nixon-Kissinger interest, the departments essentially ran the show.

Some of this reflected limitations in Kissinger. Unlike Bundy, he lacked the confidence to empower his staff deputies by sharing information and authority. Quite the opposite, he used his monopoly of information as a weapon to maintain his power—against them as well as against his senior bureaucratic rivals. And most of the fifty-plus NSC aides saw little of their boss: in the insightful words of Chester Crocker, his "personal style provided much of the staff with so little access to the top man and so little feel for his interests" that they could not be effective in advancing those interests. Because there were no lines of trust reaching beyond Kissinger (and his tight support group) into the broader staff and the departments, the system at once fueled resentment, suspicion, and ignorance of what the top leaders wanted and how they might be effectively supported.

Kissinger did of course draw upon the larger government; he

had to. But a policy memo system initially designed as an internally open process of analysis and decision degenerated into one where the national security studies were used to provide relevant background information about issues and departmental views without the promised formal consideration at the National Security Council level. It is no doubt true, as Kissinger wrote later, that he "never negotiated without a major departmental contribution even when the departments did not know what I was doing." This did not prevent those departments from seeing the order to produce detailed study memos as make-work, intended to occupy them while the president and "Henry" did the real policy business. And though secrecy avoided time-consuming fights with the bureaucracy, it also led to mistakes that effective expert input would have identified. The 1972 Strategic Arms Limitation Treaty, for example, became a target of arms control skeptics due to sloppy provisions that Gerard Smith and his Vienna delegation would surely have corrected had they been given the opportunity to do so. "You don't tell anybody" exacted a substantial price.

Hence the Nixon-Kissinger experience demonstrates, at once, the policy power potential of the national security adviser position *and* the costs of a closed system that concentrates so much in that official's hands. What is unclear is how much more openly Kissinger could have operated had his style inclined him to do so. For he worked for Richard M. Nixon, "the most peculiar and haunted of presidents," who combined lonely if intelligent policy purpose with an unrivaled penchant for self-destruction. As noted most recently by Elizabeth Drew, "the paranoia, the anger, the determination to wreak revenge, the view that the opposition should be destroyed, even the excessive drinking"—all these were inextricably part of Nixon and his presidency. Ultimately, they led to Watergate and his resignation. They would also make his substantial foreign policy achievements more limited and less durable that they ought to have been.

4

"I Would Never Be Bored"

B y the time of Jimmy Carter's election in 1976, the position of national security adviser had been well established. There was still no statute providing for the job. But there was a general expectation, inside and outside government, that the president would choose to have, in the White House, a senior analyst-adviser-coordinator handling foreign policy who would be given the title of assistant to the president for national security affairs.

There was also a presumption that this person would be an academic. Now that McGeorge Bundy, Walt Rostow, and Henry Kissinger had shown the way, it was natural for other ambitious, policy-oriented scholars to seek the job. The best way to position oneself for it was to get close to a promising presidential candidate, by serving as a prominent campaign adviser in foreign policy. Columbia University professor Zbigniew Brzezinski was the first to secure the position through this route. He would not be the last.

Brzezinski would become one of the most controversial national security advisers, one whose outspokenness and strong views highlighted conflict with Secretary of State Cyrus Vance. His priority to policy over process ensured that the process would be chaotic, and that policy differences would be visible. In the words of Soviet ambassador Anatoly Dobrynin, the most informed and sophisticated foreign diplomat in Washington, "under Carter there was probably more controversy and heated debate among top officials than under any modern American president." By 1980, "Zbig"—as he was known—had supplanted Vance and become the president's primary foreign policy adviser. But he had also brought the legitimacy of the position into question. Moreover, perceived chaos in administration foreign policymaking undercut Carter's presumed advantage over international neophyte Ronald Reagan, contributing to his devastating defeat in his bid for reelection.

———

In the wake of the experience with Bundy and Kissinger, many in the policy community were already worried, in the 1970s, that the NSC adviser had become too powerful. Concerned about Kissinger's dominant role, and his inaccessibility to congressional oversight, Congress established a Commission on the Organization of the Government for the Conduct of Foreign Policy. Its report in 1975 was little noted nor long remembered—Senate majority leader Mike Mansfield described it as "thin gruel, served up in a thick bowl." But the study generated seven thick volumes of appendices, providing grist for an important Council on Foreign Relations book by the Commission's research director, Peter Szanton, and Harvard scholar Graham Allison. Drawing on these studies, and on advice from a blue-ribbon Council study group, they cautioned the next president to resist the "dangerous" tendency toward overreliance on White House aides, and urged that "the assistants closest to him" be chosen importantly for their "concern for procedure—for the balance and openness of the process of decision rather than the triumph of a particular cause." (To ensure that senior statutory officials remained close to presidential concerns, they urged that the chief executive govern via a compact "executive cabinet," including the secretaries of state, defense, and treasury, and use it to address "all major issues that combine 'foreign,' 'domestic,' and 'economic' concerns.")

But as those who write on such matters know all too well, it is the chief executive's own process priorities that dominate. And as president-elect, Jimmy Carter had a different concern. He had

indeed criticized Kissinger's role, repeatedly, but he wasn't thinking of his service as Nixon's oft-clandestine aide. Rather, he attacked
his dominance as Gerald Ford's secretary of state. "As far as foreign
policy goes," Carter declared in the second Ford-Carter presidential
debate, "Mr. Kissinger has been the president of this country." He
wanted balance among his advisers: they would be like spokes of a
wheel, with himself at the center. He was determined that "the final
decisions on basic foreign policy would be made by me in the Oval
Office, and not in the State Department."

This determination was hardly atypical for an incoming president, and like Kennedy and Nixon before him, Carter was determined to be the foreign policy leader of his administration. In terms
of relevant prior experience, however, he was not at all like his predecessors. He came to office following an unusual forty-eight-year
span of "insider" presidents, from Herbert Hoover through Gerald
Ford, chief executives whose main prior achievements had been on
the national political stage. As a man whose most important job
had been governor of the state of Georgia, Carter became the first
in a string of Oval Office outsiders—Ronald Reagan, Bill Clinton,
George W. Bush—broken in the middle by the four-year incum-
bency of Bush the elder.

As an outsider, Carter had fewer obligations to people and policies
than a candidate who had been part of the Washington process. This
was perhaps the reason for the famous, and astonishingly inaccurate,
campaign assertion of his chief political adviser, Hamilton Jordan:
"If, after the inauguration, you find a Cy Vance as Secretary of State
and Zbigniew Brzezinski as head of National Security, then I would
say we failed. And I'd quit." But as an outsider, Carter was also less
sensitive to how his advisory choices and decision processes would
play out in the broader Washington milieu, and in the world at large.
He did have exposure to the Washington establishment via membership in the Trilateral Commission, an entrepreneurial creation of
Brzezinski and Citibank executive David Rockefeller, designed to
repair and strengthen ties among North America, Europe, and Japan.
But for Carter, membership was an avocation. His main focus from

January 1975 onward was running for president—relentlessly, without the burden of an ongoing public office, since his term as governor expired at the beginning of that year.

Brzezinski attached himself to that long-shot quest, briefing Carter repeatedly, and connecting him to other policy experts, particularly those at the Brookings Institution program for Foreign Policy Studies run by veteran analyst-operator Henry Owen. But the Columbia professor remained at least first among equals. By October 1976, he was widely recognized, in the words of *New York Times* correspondent Leslie H. Gelb, as "the most influential figure in the Democratic nominee's stable of foreign policy advisers." And "it was no secret," as Brzezinski says in his memoirs, that he wanted the national security job.

The appointment was widely expected. Columbia law professor Richard Gardner, who would become Carter's ambassador to Italy, invited fellow New Yorkers Vance and Brzezinski and their wives to dine and view the returns with him and his wife on election night. When early returns indicated a strong Carter victory, Zbig reached for the champagne, but Cy cautioned—"Wait, let's be sure." As the count dragged on, the two men would repeat the sequence each time it seemed the deciding state might fall their way. Finally, at 3:30 a.m., NBC called Mississippi for Carter. ABC followed one minute later. The former Georgia governor now had his Electoral College majority, and all agreed it was time to toast the victory. This was, of course, a harbinger of the Carter administration to come: on issue after issue, Brzezinski would push for action and Vance would counsel caution.

Concern about Zbig was conveyed to Carter directly through a number of channels—Henry Kissinger and Richard Holbrooke (soon to become assistant secretary of state for East Asia) were among those who questioned his suitability for a senior position. But, though the thirty-ninth president later acknowledged as "accurate" the criticisms of Brzezinski as being "aggressive and ambitious," and inclined to "speak out too forcefully" on critical subjects, Carter clearly wanted him anyway. He deferred to the sensitivities of the foreign policy community by first naming Vance as secretary of state, reversing the Nixon sequence. Vance, a partner at the venerable New York law firm of Simpson, Thacher E Bartlett, was broadly liked and respected. He was seen as smart, collegial, practical, and strong, having risen to the position of deputy secretary of defense in the McNamara Pentagon. He had worked discreetly to secure the leadership post at State, and Carter came to like and respect him for his advice during the campaign.

But after the key cabinet appointments were set, Brzezinski received a phone call while attending a December 15 Christmas party hosted by a New York labor negotiator. "Zbig," said a familiar voice, "I want you to do me a favor . . . [pause] . . . I would like you to be my National Security Adviser." Carter added reassuringly that while he "had to go through these processes of selection . . . I knew as of some months ago that you were my choice." Needless to say, Brzezinski was both relieved and overjoyed.

———

Like Henry Kissinger, Zbigniew Brzezinski was an émigré, forced to leave his homeland by the events leading up to World War II. He was born in Poland in 1928, and emigrated to Canada with his diplomat father ten years later. A brilliant student, he earned academic degrees from McGill University in Montreal, then went to Harvard for his doctorate, receiving it in 1953, one year before his fellow student Henry Kissinger. Kissinger was older, however, and established himself as more senior through his engagement at the Council on Foreign Relations and the publication of his best-selling Council book, *Nuclear Weapons and Foreign Policy*. A late 1950s incident tells something about the contentiousness of their relationship. Brzezinski was sitting with Stanley Hoffmann, another young Harvard faculty member, outside the office of the eminent senior scholar Carl J. Friedrich, awaiting an opportunity to see him. Kissinger (a lecturer, but not yet with tenure) breezed by them into Friedrich's office, completed his business, and walked out. Brzezinski was livid—he had, after all, co-authored with Friedrich a landmark book defining the features of totalitarianism. Kissinger terribly enjoyed the put-down, quipping as he left the professor's office, "This is how junior faculty at Harvard should be treated." It could not have improved Brzezinski's mood when Kissinger was soon awarded a tenured Harvard professorship and his "junior" Polish colleague was not.

But Brzezinski persisted, moving to Columbia University, where he published another brilliant analysis, this one a book on the Soviet bloc. Now a U.S. citizen, he got himself involved at the Council on Foreign Relations, and took leave to serve on the State Department's Policy Planning Council during the Johnson administration. Returning to New York, he resumed his prolific writing and engagement in the policy community. He won election to the board of the Council on Foreign Relations by exploiting a new nomination-by-petition procedure designed to open up that "old boy" organization—one that had been recommended, interestingly, by a Council committee headed by Cyrus Vance. He created, with David Rockefeller, the Trilateral Commission. All the while he watched what Kissinger was doing in Washington. And he positioned himself to do likewise if and when opportunity beckoned. He found it with Jimmy Carter. They fashioned a unique relationship, albeit one that often brought confusion and frustration to other players in the administration's policy process.

The Kennedy-Bundy and Nixon-Kissinger relationships both worked due to similarities in personality. Carter-Brzezinski would flourish because of differences. Both men were smart: Elizabeth Drew wrote that they shared the distinction of being "always the brightest kid in the class." But their intellects were of very different sorts. Carter's was that of an engineer: linear, logical, straight-line. Give him the requisite information about a problem, and he had confidence he would figure out the solution. Brzezinski was, by contrast, a conceptualizer: his mind was fluid, imaginative, creative, ever propounding possibilities and drawing connections. He was, in Drew's insightful depiction, a "skilled entrepreneur of ideas," "bright and quick." But, she added, "hardly any" of the people she spoke to about him "used the word 'thoughtful.'" Rather, he was viewed as brash, contentious, and impulsive. Moreover, as one of his senior aides later put it, Brzezinski "thrived on conflict," and "almost seemed to go out of his way to twist the knife." But Carter wanted ideas, alternatives to those he'd get from people with institutional responsibilities. And Brzezinski had a seemingly endless supply: "sometimes wanting to pursue a path that was ill-advised," the president noted in retrospect, "but always thinking."

No doubt Carter saw himself as supplying the corrective, the necessary balance. But his lack of international experience limited his ability to do so. Moreover, Carter himself could be willful, insisting on what he saw as "right" policy, even if it was impractical. He also had a tendency to revisit issues, to remake decisions. He needed an adviser who would stabilize the system, not destabilize it. Yet, like Lyndon Johnson before him, he was determined that he, not the foreign policy establishment, would decide which intellectual would serve him in the national security post.

Nor were Carter and Brzezinski particularly in sync substantively. As illustrated by his greatest achievement in office, the Camp David peace accords between Egypt and Israel, and later by his post-presidential career, Carter was at heart a conciliator, a searcher for positive-sum compromise, with a broad commitment to human rights. Brzezinski was much more in the realpolitik mode, the most conservative among the administration's senior policy players. He believed in human rights, but gave priority to the issue's tactical utility: in putting the Soviet Union on the defensive; in widening fissures between Moscow and the Communist states of Eastern Europe. (The Helsinki accords signed by President Ford in 1975 offered one vehicle for doing this.)

These differences mattered because the humiliating loss in Vietnam had generated deep divisions within the U.S. foreign policy community. The dominant initial conclusion was that the nation had overreached, engaging in an "unwinnable" war marginal to its vital interests. To prevent recurrence, a liberal-moderate coalition in Congress enacted in 1973–75 a stream of legislation limiting presidential war powers, arms sales, and covert intelligence activities, as well as specific measures forbidding or limiting bombing in Indochina, arms sales to Turkey after its troops had occupied disputed land in Cyprus, and CIA involvement in the civil war in Angola. This was also the heyday of détente—a U.S.-Soviet commitment to arms control and stability, if not to political rapprochement. By 1976–77, however, the conservative reaction to détente had gained momentum. Ronald Reagan had drawn on it and mounted a serious challenge to Ford's nomination as the Republican Party's presidential candidate in 1976, causing Ford to back off Kissinger's proposal to complete a SALT II agreement on available terms.

At around the same time, a "Team B" exercise staffed by conservatives was challenging the more moderate CIA estimates of the Soviet military threat, and a coalition led by Paul H. Nitze and Eugene Rostow emerged to reform the Committee on the Present Danger, a group originally established in 1950 to mobilize America against what it perceived as rising Soviet power. Deep and visible division over the handling of U.S.-Soviet relations would become a hallmark of the Carter administration.

Brzezinski gained the initial advantage through the formal processes established by the new administration. Aided by the staff he quickly assembled, he had originally proposed seven formal NSC committees, patterned after the prior regime but most chaired by State or other agencies. Carter rejected this. "Zbig, I prefer a more drastic change," he wrote in late December 1976. "Since the committees are almost identical [in membership], I see no reason for a multiplicity of them. . . . Please strive for maximum simplicity." So, the seven committees were compressed into two, both at cabinet level: the Policy Review Committee, chaired by the head of the department, with primary responsibility for the issue at hand (usually State); and the Special Coordinating Committee, to be chaired by the national security assistant. This was a first: never before had the NSC adviser chaired a standing committee at cabinet level.

The system was put in place by presidential directive on inauguration day. In his journal, Brzezinski called this "a system I can use effectively." But he showed no particular sensitivity to others' concerns that he might use his unique presidential access to tilt the system to his advantage. He did declare in his memoirs his feeling that he had not "usurped excessive authority." But Secretary of State Vance was particularly unhappy with the procedure adopted for communicating the substance of committee discussions to the president, and for drafting presidential directives on matters where the principals had reached agreement. The meeting summaries and draft directives were written by Brzezinski and his staff, and in neither case were these circulated for review to those who participated in the meetings before the documents went to the president. "The national security adviser," Vance later observed, "had the power to interpret the thrust of discussion or frame the policy recommendations of departmental participants." Vance objected to the arrangement from the start, and "said so to the president," who defended the procedure as necessary to prevent leaks. "In retrospect," Vance concluded that he himself had "made a serious mistake in not going to the mat on insisting that the draft memoranda be sent to the principals before they went to the president." He found that there were "discrepancies, occasionally serious ones," between what Brzezinski wrote and what he recalled as having been said in policy meetings.

At the beginning, however, the process was relatively amicable. When his appointment was announced, Brzezinski described his position modestly. It was not a "policy-making job"; rather, he saw it as "heading the operational staff of the President, helping him to integrate policy, but above all, helping him to facilitate the process of decision-making." And he would give policy advice only when asked. An early *Washington Post* report highlighted assurances about what the "NSC chief will not do." And Brzezinski and Vance seemed to be working together amicably. Collegiality and teamwork were the watchwords. The president made Vice President Walter F. Mondale a member of his senior team, and regularly included him in advisory meetings. Mondale would join Carter's regular Friday foreign policy breakfasts with Vance and Brzezinski. This group was later expanded to include Secretary of Defense Harold Brown and top White House aide Hamilton Jordan.

Moreover, Carter's initial policy priorities were not conventional national security but energy independence ("the moral equivalent of war") and executive reorganization (giving America "a government as good as its people"). On foreign policy, the new administration declared itself moving away from Kissingerian realpolitik to greater emphasis on human rights and the Third World. Carter wanted to place less emphasis on U.S.-Soviet relations. Brzezinski set up a "global issues" office within the NSC. The administration's first formal policy study addressed the Panama Canal and whether the United States should conclude negotiations returning the Canal to Panamanian sovereignty by the year 2000.

Finally, there were changes on the NSC staff. Brzezinski and his deputy, former Mondale aide David Aaron, preempted Carter's drive to reduce the White House staff by cutting the size of theirs from the mid-fifties under Brent Scowcroft to the mid-thirties. Zbig also made the staff a much happier, less hierarchical place than it had been in the Nixon-Kissinger days. He eliminated the distinction between senior and junior people, though he kept the full range of regional and functional coverage begun by his predecessors. He generally supported his staff and some, like Latin America policy expert Robert Pastor, developed their own relationships with the president. He was open to their input and opinions. Brzezinski, observed Gary Sick, who handled Persian Gulf issues for him, "had little respect of yes men. He much preferred someone who would stoutly defend his own convictions, even if those were contrary to his own." But if he was not a Kissinger, keeping staff members firmly in their places, neither was he a Bundy, pushing them forward: memos went to Carter in Brzezinski's name, not in the name of those who drafted them, and the staff of the domestic policy assistant, Stuart Eizenstat, had "more direct dealings with the President than Brzezinski's."

New administrations are defined not just by the priorities they choose, however, but also by their handling of the issues they inherit. The most prominent of those issues was the SALT II (strategic arms limitation) negotiations carrying over from the Ford administration. Nixon and Soviet leader Leonid Brezhnev had concluded an interim offensive arms agreement in 1972, one which (reflecting existing deployment plans and perceived U.S. technological advantages elsewhere) allowed Moscow a larger number of missiles than Washington. The aim of follow-on talks was to convert this into a treaty. However, the specific provisions would have to meet the terms set by the Senate amendment to the resolution approving the interim agreement, put forward by arms control skeptic Henry Jackson, which mandated that "a future treaty . . . not limit the United States to levels of intercontinental strategic forces inferior to the limits provided for the Soviet Union." Shortly after Nixon's resignation in 1974, President Ford and Secretary of State Kissinger had gone to Vladivostok and initialed a framework accord setting limits of 2,400 strategic weapons launchers (including bombers) for each nation, with the terms to be incorporated in a formal treaty. But facing rising resistance from the Republican right, Ford had opted not to conclude that treaty prior to the 1976 elections.

Carter and his chief aides were all very much committed to arms control, but they had different views on how to proceed. Secretary Vance quickly established himself as the senior administration negotiator, as well as the principal interlocutor of Ambassador Anatoly Dobrynin. Vance worked closely with Arms Control and Disarmament Agency director Paul Warnke, who led the day-to-day talks. Their preference was to build on what was there: seek modest improvements in the Vladivostok framework, quickly conclude a treaty with Moscow on that basis, and seek significant arms reductions in the next stage. Brzezinski's druthers were to step back and review priorities and goals in overall U.S.-Soviet relations, à la Nixon-Kissinger, before moving on the arms front. But he did not press this idea very hard.

Jimmy Carter, though, had ideas of his own. He had expressed in his inaugural address his hope, one day, that mankind could achieve "the elimination of all nuclear weapons from this earth." He saw the two nations' nuclear arsenals as far larger than necessary. Following his bent to propose what was "right" and compromise later if required, he mandated a proposal involving "deep cuts" in the American and Soviet arsenals, and instructed Vance to take this to Moscow during his first negotiating trip there in March 1977. The specific formula for achieving deep reductions would require Moscow to cut substantially more forces than Washington.

The Soviets made clear, via Dobrynin, that they were unwilling to go this route, at least until after a SALT II treaty was concluded and ratified. But Carter persisted, ordering Vance to make the proposal in Moscow. The chances of success, already slim, were further undermined by Carter's outspokenness on Soviet human rights abuses. The president believed, in Raymond Garthoff's authoritative analysis, that "his continued vocal agitation on the human rights issue should have no effect [on] other aspects of bilateral relations." Moscow, though, saw this as "a major and dangerous shift" in policy, one that "created the impression in the minds of the Soviet leaders that the United States would be satisfied only with a fundamental change in their system." This would not be the last time that Carter's insensitivity to this sort of spillover would generate trouble for his advisers, and his foreign policy.

The result was a failure: the Soviets rebuffed "deep cuts" and refused even to consider a fallback proposal—which Vance had been authorized to present—that was much closer to Vladivostok. Brzezinski thought the Soviets had behaved badly toward the new president, and the American response should be to "cool it." Vance believed it wiser to leave deep cuts to the future and resume talks essentially based on Vladivostok. Carter, not wishing to risk failure to achieve some arms control, sided with Vance, devoting in the process what Brzezinski felt was "an inordinate amount of time to the SALT effort." By May 1977, the arms control dialogue resumed. But the administration's reputation had suffered—with hawks charging retreat and doves seeing naïveté. The administration was already on the defensive on arms control because Senator Jackson had mounted a vigorous February challenge to Warnke's confirmation as arms control negotiator. (Warnke received forty votes in opposition, more than enough to derail a SALT II treaty in the Senate). Now, as Vance later recalled, "the comprehensive proposal gave a weapon to anti-SALT and anti-détente hard-liners, who held up the deep-cuts proposal as the only standard against which to measure the success of the ultimate agreement." The administration would remain on the defensive on arms control issues for the rest of Carter's presidency.

Both Brzezinski and Vance favored a SALT II treaty, but as 1977 moved to conclusion significant differences emerged about how to view and manage the U.S. relationship with Moscow more generally. It involved, of course, both competition and cooperation, but what was the balance between them, and which side should the United States highlight? Brzezinski saw relations as overwhelmingly competitive, and thought Washington should challenge Moscow across a broad range of issues. Vance too recognized that competition was central, but he saw more opportunities for cooperation, and favored a relaxed approach to matters of limited global significance where the United States was unlikely to affect Soviet behavior.

The issue of broader Soviet geopolitical behavior surfaced in late 1977 in the Horn of Africa. Somalia—previously a Soviet ally—moved forces into the Ogaden region of its larger neighbor, Ethiopia, which had recently undergone a Marxist revolution. Ethiopia turned to Moscow for aid, and Soviet and Cuban forces arrived to help. The United States rejected Somali requests for arms, but in November, Brzezinski began, in Garthoff's words, "background briefing the press in such a way as to inspire a spate of articles describing and criticizing the Soviet role and growing Soviet-Cuban military presence in Ethiopia." This was done "with Carter's approval," the adviser recalled, to send a message "that their conduct was not compatible with the notion of mutual restraint." The following February, Brzezinski proposed that the United States send a naval task force to the region as an expression of concern. Vance demurred, seeing it as an ill-advised "bluffing game." He was backed by Defense Secretary Brown, who questioned whether such a force could do anything useful when it arrived on the scene. Carter agreed with the two secretaries, and rejected the proposal. As Brzezinski recalled later, he "was very much alone in the U.S. government in advocating a stronger response" to Soviet-Cuban engagement in the Horn.

Such differences of view on substance and tactics are a normal feature of high-level decision making. What made this episode stand out was that Brzezinski went out of his way to highlight his position publicly, to represent himself as seeking to "toughen" the administration's policy—even when the president was on the other side. From late 1977 into early 1978, Brzezinski became more and more visible in the media in his advocacy of these positions. State Department officials complained, and made counterstatements, some for attribution, some on background. So "foreign policy disarray" began to be a staple characterization in press reporting about the Carter administration. Public statements gave substance to this view. In the first two days of March 1978, Brzezinski, Carter, and Vance all provided different on-the-record takes on whether the SALT negotiations were linked to Soviet geopolitical behavior in Africa. The adviser said, "we are not imposing any linkage, but linkage may be imposed [by the Soviets'] unwarranted exploitation of local conflict for larger international purposes." Carter stressed that his policy was not linkage, but declared that Soviet behavior might "make it more difficult to ratify a SALT agreement." In this sense, he warned, "the two are linked because of actions by the Soviets." Vance, by contrast, made the bald statement that "there is no linkage between the SALT negotiations and the situation in Ethiopia."

To combat this impression of internal division, Secretary Vance "recommended that the president give a major speech on U.S.-Soviet relations" that would "realistically describe our policy." Carter agreed to do so: the event chosen was a June 7, 1978, address at the U.S. Naval Academy in Annapolis. But the drafting involved, necessarily, inputs from both NSC and State, and the result was a "stitched-together speech," employing both Vance's cooperative and Brzezinski's confrontational language. With the two aides' disagreement public knowledge, reporters seized on these differences in substance and tone. The *Washington Post* characterized the address as "two different speeches." "Instead of combating the growing perception of an administration rent by internal divisions," Vance later observed, "the image of an inconsistent and uncertain government was underlined."

Brzezinski also heightened divisions when he traveled to Beijing in May 1978 in order to accelerate the process of normalizing Sino-American relations. In seeking Carter's approval for the trip, the national security adviser argued, among other things, that his "reputation as the more hardnosed member of the foreign policy team would be helpful in generating understanding with the Chinese." Vance resisted, believing that "such a highly publicized trip would bring into sharp relief the question of who spoke for the administration on foreign policy." (Brzezinski would later admit that it "probably did" undermine the secretary.) Vance was also concerned about Brzezinski's tendency to play the "China card" vis-à-vis the Soviet Union, and not without reason. During his touristic visit to the Great Wall, Brzezinski was reported in the *Washington Post* as challenging his Chinese colleagues to a race: "If we get to the top first, you go and oppose the Russians in Ethiopia." This dismayed Vance, and while Zbig later denied he had said exactly that, the story "caught on." Brzezinski didn't help matters by going out of his way to marginalize the participation of State's top regional official, Assistant Secretary of State for East Asia Richard Holbrooke, a member of his negotiating delegation. The fact that the visit was diplomatically successful further exacerbated relations with State; Secretary Vance had led a less successful mission to Beijing the previous year.

What brought matters to a head internally, though, was Brzezinski's performance on NBC's *Meet the Press* shortly after his return from Beijing. He engaged in a sweeping denunciation of Soviet behavior around the world, concluding that this "pattern" was not "compatible with what was once called the code of détente." The *Washington Post* headlined the adviser's "Attack on the Soviets" the next morning. "Never before has any senior strategist in the Carter administration thrown down the gauntlet to the Soviet Union so starkly, and at such a sensitive point," wrote Murrey Marder in a front-page analysis.

Carter chastised his aide severely: "You're not just a professor; you speak for me. And I think you went too far in your statements" claiming that the Soviets "were conducting a worldwide vitriolic campaign." Vance used this occasion to go to Carter and demand a curbing of Brzezinski's role. At a Friday breakfast meeting with his senior advisers, the president agreed that his national security adviser should sharply reduce his press exposure, and Brzezinski receded substantially from public view in the months that followed. (The *New York Times Index*, published annually, contains 144 entries under Brzezinski's name for calendar year 1978, but only 26 of them are in the period between that early June breakfast meeting and the end of November.)

The impression that Vance was reestablishing himself as Carter's primary foreign policy adviser was reinforced by the secretary's central role in the president's single greatest foreign policy triumph, the Camp David peace accords between Israel and Egypt. Carter had inherited the cease-fire and military disengagement agreements that Kissinger had negotiated following the October 1973 War. But Israel's right to exist remained unrecognized by all bordering Arab states. Prospects for any further negotiating breakthrough seemed to grow dimmer when the long-ruling Israeli Labor Party was replaced by the hard-line Likud coalition under Menachem Begin. Then, in the summer of 1977, as NSC aide William Quandt recalled, "Vance essentially took charge of Middle East policy at a PRC meeting," and he retained this role until the signing of the Egyptian-Israeli peace treaty in March 1979.

Peace hopes rose when President Anwar Sadat of Egypt made his epochal visit to Jerusalem in November 1977 and addressed the Israeli Knesset. Thereafter, as Carter decided upon and moved toward hosting Sadat and Begin at a negotiating summit at Camp David, Vance convened a staff preparatory weekend in August 1978 at the Harriman estate in Middleburg, Virginia, working with his regional assistant secretary Harold Saunders, his ambassador-at-large for Mideast negotiations Alfred Atherton, and Quandt from the NSC. Progress was reinforced by the strong working relationship between Saunders—who had long handled the issue for the NSC until moving over to State—and Quandt, who essentially functioned as a member of the State Department policy team.

"Of all the Americans who dealt extensively with both Arabs and Israelis," Quandt wrote later, Vance "was the one who best retained the confidence of both sides." The secretary of state became the point man for putting things back together after the quick Camp David agreement Carter had anticipated in early September 1978 did not materialize, and the near-venomous relations between Begin and Sadat threatened to blow the negotiations out of the water. Vance, Brzezinski wrote later, was "tireless in seeking compromises and persistent in pressing the two sides to accommodate." (Brzezinski characterized his own contribution as "quite secondary.") The president's own role was crucial, of course. Carter "turned his extraordinary capacity for mastering detail to the negotiations between Egypt and Israel," Quandt later recounted in his comprehensive treatment of Middle East peace efforts. "And twice he put his political reputation on the line by engaging in summit negotiations that could easily have failed." But, Quandt added, Vance "deserves much of the credit for patiently shaping the Camp David Accords and the text of the peace treaty."

The Middle East accords offered one model of NSC-State cooperation at its most effective. Carter and Brzezinski also established an effective NSC role in the making of international economic policy, through the designation—under the Council umbrella—of Henry Owen (Brzezinski's boss at the State Department ten years earlier) as the president's "special representative" backstopping his participation in annual international economic summits among the Group of Seven advanced industrial nations. With Carter's support, Owen expanded this brokering role to encompass international trade and financial policy more generally. This was particularly useful given the shaky relationship between the president and his secretary of the Treasury, Michael Blumenthal.

Though Carter had reined in Brzezinski in June 1978, the president's confidence in Zbig remained. Carter minimized the matter in his memoirs, saying: "There were periods when we would agree that he refrain from making any public statements." And he privately assured his national security adviser that they would continue to operate as before. The stage was set, therefore, for the assistant to rise again. Top-level tensions would reemerge, with a vengeance, in late 1978 and early 1979. Conflict centered on the timing of normalization of relations with China; the terms of the SALT II accord, then nearing completion; and the rapid decline and fall of the Shah of Iran, a major U.S. ally.

Administration leaders were hoping to complete no less than three major accords before 1978 became history. One was a formal Egyptian-Israeli peace treaty based on Camp David. The others were SALT II and "normalization" of the relationship with China. Only the last of these made this goal. But the way Carter and Brzezinski handled the final stages of the deal with Beijing exacerbated relations with both State and Congress, not to mention Moscow. With Vance off negotiating in the Middle East, the president and Brzezinski decided suddenly to advance by two weeks the announcement of the date for normalizing relations with China, to December 15, five days before Vance was to leave for Geneva to try to finalize the strategic arms deal. The reason Carter gives for this abrupt change was "to expedite the public announcement so that we could explain the decision in its totality and not risk its being leaked piecemeal to the news media."

Brzezinski suggests another motive—a quick agreement, he told the Chinese, meant that a visit by the Chinese premier Deng Xiaoping "could be scheduled before any meeting between Carter and Brezhnev on SALT." To minimize any chance of delay or leaks, the key interlocutors at State—Deputy Secretary Warren Christopher and Richard Holbrooke—were "blacked . . . out of the decisionmaking" by Brzezinski, Vance reported, during a crucial six-hour period. Congress was not consulted—despite an overwhelming Senate vote calling for such consultation, and Vance's strong recommendation that this request be honored. Carter, though, was delighted with the outcome, and he gave his national security adviser full credit, telling Brzezinski he had been "the driving force behind the entire effort." Congress responded by passing the Taiwan Relations Act of 1979, providing strong support for that now-derecognized island, causing problems with Beijing that have persisted to this day.

Brzezinski's triumph was followed, eight days later, by Vance's failure to close the SALT II deal. From the first day of the December Geneva negotiations with Soviet foreign minister Andrei Gromyko, Vance sensed that Moscow was looking for ways to postpone the final agreement, raising "secondary and technical" issues, and one matter that he saw as a "red herring." This "sudden surge in Soviet inflexibility," he concluded, was "due primarily to developments related to China." In particular, the Soviets were reacting to the fact that the U.S.-China communiqué announcing the normalization included a statement of the two nations' opposition to "hegemony," a code word for Soviet influence. This was one of a number of instances in late 1978 and early 1979 when Brzezinski was able to tilt U.S.-China relations toward a tacit alignment against the Soviet Union, something Vance vehemently opposed and Carter repeatedly asserted was not his intention.

Formally, however, conclusion of the arms control talks was blocked by a technical matter. The capacity for independent verification of Soviet missile testing and deployments was crucial to SALT's substance and its credibility with Congress, and one issue was Soviet practice regarding the treatment of "telemetry," electronic signals produced during flight testing that contained valuable information about missile characteristics and performance. Vance urged that the United States should compromise, going twice to the president on this issue within six hours. Defense Secretary Brown and CIA director Stansfield Turner did not feel that Vance's compromise proposal was viable, however, and Carter, following their (and Brzezinski's) advice, rejected Vance's appeal. Moreover, since by the time of Carter's final response, the secretary of state was negotiating at the Soviet Embassy (and unreachable via normal secret channels), the national security adviser conveyed Carter's decision on an open telephone line easily susceptible to Soviet eavesdropping. Aware of this, he used general language, simply saying that "the previous instruction stands"; but the meaning was quite clear. "The whole scene," recalled Ambassador Dobrynin, "was rather embarrassing to us, as if Brzezinski was giving the secretary of state strict instructions." It was presumably embarrassing to Vance as well.

Meanwhile, the Shah of Iran was losing his grip on power. Mohammad Reza Pahlavi had sat on the Peacock Throne since 1941, with his waning strength restored and reinforced via a CIA sponsored coup in 1953. He had been an ally and anchor of U.S. Persian Gulf policy for a quarter of a century. The Shah pursued an aggressive modernization program, which brought economic gains but fueled middle-class restiveness over the lagging progress in democracy and human rights, as well as resentment among clerics who saw economic and social change as threatening traditional religious practices (not to mention their own power and role in society). Within the U.S. government, conflict over policy at the staff level had festered through 1978, with the State Department Iran desk under Harry Precht pressing anti-shah policy views (perhaps prescient in retrospect) in a persistent and contentious style that estranged Precht from Gary Sick at the NSC and to a lesser degree from his State Department superiors.

In early November 1978, an urgent cable from Ambassador William Sullivan highlighted the Shah's eroding position and forced Iran onto the agendas of senior officials, whose policy plates were already overfull. As matters deteriorated, and it began to look like the Shah might not survive, Brzezinski and Vance pressed for sharply different courses. The national security adviser argued increasingly for active American efforts to bring about a military takeover. Vance saw this as dubious in principle and unlikely to work in practice. Carter sided *de facto* with Vance on that issue, but would not approve State's recommendation to open lines of communication with the Grand Ayatollah Ruhollah Khomeini, Iran's leading religious authority, then in exile in Paris, who would shortly return to lead a successful, radical revolution. George Ball, whom Brzezinski invited to review the situation (to his later regret), recommended that the Shah convene a "council of notables" to broker the establishment of a successor regime, under which the Shah might remain as a constitutional monarch with limited powers. Both Brzezinski and Sullivan, who agreed on little else, opposed this proposal, and Carter rejected it, though Ball did argue vigorously and decisively against the president's plan to send Brzezinski on a mission to Tehran. Meanwhile, Sullivan was pursuing his own initiatives, often without the full knowledge of other senior U.S. players.

In retrospect, Vance and Brzezinski agreed on one thing: whatever chance might have existed for Washington to affect the situation was undercut by "internal divisions," as the secretary of state put it, or, in Brzezinski's similar words, "disagreement within the U.S. government." To George Ball, the source of these divisions was clear: he told Vance, "as an old friend," that he had found a "shockingly unhealthy situation in the National Security Council, with Brzezinski doing everything possible to exclude the State Department" and sending "back channel . . . telegrams of which the State Department was unaware." Brzezinski denied this charge; Vance "told him I believed otherwise," and protested to the president, after which, the secretary declares in his memoirs, "the back-channel communications ceased." But from Carter's perspective, the problem was that the ambassador to Iran and other State Department officials were resisting his policies and leaking details to the press about internal disarray. Urged on by Hamilton Jordan, he summoned a group of midlevel State officials to the White House and coldly chastised them, denouncing their leaking, and saying that if it recurred, he would "direct the Secretary of State to discharge the officials responsible, Carter recalled." "Then I got up and left the room," giving the accused no chance to respond.

For the president—in the view of NSC aide Gary Sick—this was in part a matter of "getting it off his chest." And to balance matters,

Carter also met with NSC staff aides, cautioning "Zbig's people," as he recalled, about "the contention and excessive competition that sometimes existed between the White House and the State Department" and directing "that they take the initiative at every level to form closer working relations with their equivalents at State." In his diary, the president revealed the underlying problem: "I hardly know the desk officers and others in State, but work very closely with NSC people. When we have consulted closely, like in the Mideast area . . . we've never had any problems." But the very fact that he saw them so seldom meant that his cold chastisement was particularly hurtful, and deeply resented. The "desk officers and others at State" saw themselves as victims of a distrusted policy process, with Brzezinski using his access to Carter to misrepresent and undercut their efforts to serve the president and his policies. And while Ball's specific characterization of Brzezinski's behavior on Iran appears exaggerated in retrospect, it underscores the distrust with which he was viewed by those—mainly in State—who were Ball's main source of information.

Nonetheless, Zbig's influence with the president was clearly increasing, at the expense of Cyrus Vance. So visible had he become that a member of the Senate Foreign Relations Committee, Edward Zorinsky, began calling for Senate confirmation of the national security adviser: "It's clear that we have two secretaries of state . . . and it's time that we made the other one accountable too."

If Brzezinski was rising, the Carter administration was sinking. The previous year had brought significant policy achievements: the Camp David peace agreement, normalization of U.S.-Chinese relations, and success in a protracted political struggle to win Senate ratification of the Panama Canal treaties. But the situation in Iran was a huge setback, at home as well as abroad. Brzezinski does not exaggerate when he labels it "a political calamity for President Carter." In addition to its impact on U.S. national security policy, which included the loss of two important intelligence stations for monitoring Soviet nuclear weapons tests, the Iranian revolution drove oil prices up and helped trigger the excruciating economic conditions—double-digit inflation, incipient recession—that did much to doom Carter's presidency. Meanwhile, Republicans were rising politically, and conservatives mounted attacks against administration "weakness" in foreign policy. "Disarray" became the standard characterization in the press.

Insofar as administration policymaking was to blame, much of the problem lay with President Carter himself: his willfulness, his insensitivity to how his process preferences affected others, and his tendency to make and remake detailed policy decisions without a clear guiding philosophy all fueled division among his advisers and uncertainty about what "the policy" was. The national security adviser himself, however, had become an important part of the problem. And the core reason was simple. He was so driven by the desire to shape the substance of policy—in a direction outside the prevailing consensus within the administration—that he undercut his indispensable role in managing the process.

Brent Scowcroft summarized the problem in general terms two decades later in a roundtable with several of his peers. He began with the fact that the adviser has two roles: that of policy manager–coordinator–broker for administration decisions and actions, and that of senior policy adviser to the president. And the two are inevitably in tension:

> It's always more exciting to be the adviser, but if you are not the honest broker, you don't have the confidence of the other members of the NSC. If you don't have their confidence, then the system doesn't work, because they will go around you to get to the president and then you fracture the system.
>
> . . . In order for the system to work, you first have to establish yourself in the confidence of your colleagues to convince them you are not going to pull fast ones on them. That means when you are in there with the president alone, which you are more than anyone else, that you will represent them fairly.

In other words, for the system to work, the national security adviser must give priority to establishing and managing what is—and is perceived to be—a fair and balanced policy process. He must fit his advocacy within that process, subordinating it as necessary. In fact, as Scowcroft would demonstrate in his own service for George H. W. Bush, gaining acceptance as an "honest broker" frees the national security adviser to become a strong advocate on a particular issue without upsetting the overall process. Trust is the key. Once established, it can help a president—and a national security adviser—across many rough patches. Once lost, it is difficult to restore.

For Brzezinski, the priority was clearly not the process but the substance of policy, and his capacity to influence it through his privileged White House position. Being generally the most hard-line of senior administration players, he actively and visibly sought to "toughen" policy. Time after time—on Iran, on Soviet activity in Africa, on relations with Moscow generally—he pushed, aggressively, positions at variance with those of Vance and Brown, positions that President Carter had not endorsed and was usually not ready to endorse. And his tendency was to advance these views through his personal advocacy, rather than by pursuit of more subtle tactics, such as bringing others of similar mind into the policy game. Meanwhile, administration procedures denied Vance and Brown and their staffs access to the crucial Brzezinski memos that summarized key meetings and formulated recommendations to the president—unless a secretary could himself come to the White House to review those memos in draft. It was natural for them—Vance, in particular—to believe that Zbig would use his position and access to their disadvantage.

Brzezinski was not unaware of this problem, of course. At a forum in 2001 in which national security advisers reflected on their roles, he treated the matter as too obvious for serious debate:

> I think that one would have to be awfully stupid to misrepresent the views of your colleagues to the president, because you know that if the issue is important, there will be discus-

sion. The president will go back and discuss it, in your presence or . . . absence . . . with his principal advisers, be they secretary of state or secretary of defense. And it would very quickly be evident that you distorted their views if you did. So you have to be absolutely precise. . . .

But although Brzezinski did take seriously his obligation to report others' views fairly and objectively, and no doubt did so in the preponderant majority of cases, other players were suspicious. Vance in particular found "discrepancies, occasionally serious ones," between what he said and what Brzezinski said he said on those occasions when Vance got to view, retrospectively, the adviser's memos to the president.

Broader inattention to process in the Carter-Brzezinski NSC was clinically diagnosed and summarized in mid-1979 by a former NSC staff aide, Philip Odeen, in a report for the President's Reorganization Project that Carter had established at the outset of his administration. The current staff was "by all reports exercising the personal advisory role effectively," Odeen noted, and "President Carter has put particular emphasis on this function." But "the staff's institutional role must not be neglected," Odeen quickly added, and he questioned "whether the current structure and processes are adequate" for fulfilling "institutional tasks," including "managing the decision process."

This core problem was exacerbated by Brzezinski's activities as policy spokesman. Carter sometimes encouraged him to play this role because of his bent for policy articulation and a taste for public advocacy that Vance clearly lacked. But the assistant's impulsiveness and tendency to push the policy envelope made others see his public activity not just as undercutting the leadership role of secretary of state, but as challenging him on policy. Some future assistants would in fact play the policy spokesman role to a greater degree—Sandy Berger under Bill Clinton, Condoleezza Rice under George W. Bush. But their care in sticking to positions the president had clearly endorsed made this at least somewhat more acceptable to their peers. By contrast, as Carter's adviser concedes in his memoirs, his "public appearances did fuel the image of an Administration in which the National Security Adviser overshadowed the Secretary of State," with "adverse consequences" for the president. "In retrospect," he adds, "it probably would have been wiser for me to have been the invisible man."

Brzezinski under Jimmy Carter never reached anywhere near the degree of advisory and process dominance that Kissinger achieved under Richard Nixon. Vance did the preponderant share of cabinet-level negotiating: the main exceptions, Brzezinski later recalled, were China normalization (where U.S. Ambassador to Beijing Leonard Woodcock handled the details), and lesser ventures to convey a Carter message to Anwar Sadat, help plan the agreed-upon deployment of cruise and Pershing missiles in Europe, and organize a response to the Soviet invasion of Afghanistan. And in sharp contrast to the Nixon-Kissinger practice, exclusion of Vance from knowledge of policy happenings was rare and short-lived. There were regular meetings at the presidential and principals' level; top players were consistently included; and serious policy was made there. When Carter was unhappy with a particular senior aide, he could treat that individual quite coldly—in others' presence—but he didn't cut off personal contact as Nixon had done. Indeed, Odeen's expert analysis concluded that the administration had too many top-level meetings. The number of principals-only meetings grew from an average of seven per month in 1977 to eighteen per month in January–July 1979. "As a result," Odeen concluded, "attendees don't have adequate time to prepare, and meetings often fail to reach firm conclusions or recommendations."

Notwithstanding the national security adviser's limitations as honest broker and process manager, Carter continued to look to Brzezinski and the advisory service he was providing. And he, like Brzezinski, continued to show insensitivity to the damage to policy and U.S. interests from the way the adviser's role was being played—and perceived. Of course, Zbig's influence was reinforced by the president's regular engagement in daily decision making. The assistant himself later noted that he was "the inevitable bureaucratic beneficiary of deep presidential involvement." As with other incumbents before and since, the national security adviser's leverage was importantly a function of the volume of presidential national security business.

Finally, the political tides were moving in Brzezinski's conservative direction. He was dominant in the last phase of the SALT II negotiations, and the United States won concessions on telemetry monitoring and other matters in the treaty that Carter and Brezhnev signed in Vienna in June 1979. By then Vance's ally, arms control negotiator Paul Warnke, was gone, replaced by a general; and his strong director of politico-military affairs, Leslie H. Gelb, had departed as well. It was not Vance but Defense Secretary Brown who would lead the administration's public advocacy of the treaty, together with the new chairman of the Joint Chiefs of Staff, General David Jones.

By summer, however, Carter was declaring a national "malaise" and retreating to Camp David, where he consulted various outside experts on what had gone wrong with the nation—and his presidency. He famously demanded the resignations of all the members of his cabinet (redundantly also, since they served only at his pleasure), and fired two of the more prominent: Treasury Secretary Michael Blumenthal and Secretary of Health, Education and Welfare Joseph Califano. So much did this drama dominate the summer headlines that the president got virtually no public credit for the overwhelming congressional approval of the most comprehensive international trade deal in history, the Tokyo Round accords, whose negotiations had been rescued from stasis by Carter's dynamic trade representative, Robert Strauss. Yet the shake-up brought "no tremors for Brzezinski," the *New York Times* reported. "After two years of public controversy and private bureaucratic jostling . . . the energetic and feisty Columbia University professor is said by his admirers and critics alike to have become the dominant force within the foreign policy apparatus."

The final two months of 1979 brought the events that would define Carter's last year of foreign policy. On November 4, militant Iranian students stormed the U.S. Embassy in Tehran and took sixty-six American officials hostage there and at the Iranian Foreign Ministry. The action soon gained the backing of the ruling ayatollahs, and fifty-two of the diplomats remained in captivity for 444 days, until the end of the Carter presidency. Then, on December 24, Soviet forces launched an invasion of Afghanistan and, three days later, assassinated its leader Hafizullah Amin, a Marxist who had been exhibiting anti-Moscow tendencies reminiscent of the Yugoslav leader Josip Broz Tito in the 1940s. Brzezinski had anticipated some form of increased Soviet intervention in Kabul. Carter, however, was shocked by the blatant and brutal invasion. "This action of the Soviets has made a more dramatic change in my own opinion of what the Soviets' ultimate goals are than anything they've done in the previous time I've been in office," Carter declared.

In response, the president decided to press the U.S. Olympic Committee to withdraw all American athletes from participating in the 1980 Moscow Summer Games. The suddenness of this action surprised many—not least America's allies in Europe. The president asked Senate majority leader Robert Byrd to defer Senate consideration of the SALT II treaty, since the Soviet invasion had rendered ratification infeasible. He also imposed a partial embargo on the sales of grain that the United States had been making to the Soviet Union since 1972. And support of sanctions came from across the government: Carter noted in his memoirs that "on these punitive measures, the State Department advocated stronger action than the National Security Council staff, a reversal of their usual attitudes." Vice President Mondale worried about the political impact, since Senator Edward Kennedy was mounting a challenge to Carter's renomination. Noting that Carter had ordered the creation of a rapid deployment force for Persian Gulf contingencies, Mondale asked the defense secretary whether it was ready: "I'm going to Iowa and I could use some protection." (In fact, patriotic Iowans backed the president in their first-in-the-nation caucuses, and Carter—temporarily boosted by a public that rallied round the flag in the months after the hostage capture—disposed of the Kennedy challenge more easily than most expected.)

In February 1980, Brzezinski traveled to Pakistan to mobilize support and pressure against the Soviets in Afghanistan, accompanied by Vance's deputy, Warren Christopher, and Zbig's press secretary, Jerrold Schecter. This included a trip to the Khyber Pass, which connects the two countries. As Schecter recalled, "When Brzezinski was handed an AK-47 Kalashnikov rifle to examine, he waved it in the air, a symbol of defiance against the Soviet invasion of Afghanistan. News cameras caught the moment and the next day his gesture of American opposition to the Soviet invasion appeared on the front pages of newspapers around the world."

It was the hostages in Tehran, though, who became a presidential obsession. Carter declared he would remain in Washington to work for their release, and he ordered that the lights on the ceremonial Christmas tree on the Mall be left unlit. Beginning in early November 1979, there were—according to NSC aide Gary Sick, who took notes—"daily cabinet-level meetings over the next six months and more," chaired by Brzezinski and including, in addition to the regular national security officials, the secretary of the Treasury, the U.S. attorney general, and the secretary of energy. Carter received reports from the meetings daily, and made decisions on issues they generated. He also convened frequent advisory meetings under his own chairmanship—reviewing intelligence, developing initiatives for international support, imposing and tightening economic sanctions, and encouraging any diplomatic effort that held any promise whatsoever.

The most extensive—and for a time, hopeful—such effort was carried out outside the normal framework of the NSC structure, by Hamilton Jordan and Harold Saunders, reporting directly to Vance and the president, and working through Paris-based intermediaries with ties to the Iranian president and foreign minister, each of whom favored the U.S. hostages' release. Sick's authoritative inside account labels this "a long shot that just missed," and it offered intermittent hope until the second week in April 1980.

Its ultimate failure turned Carter toward military options. Months earlier, he had rejected any general military action against the Islamic Republic, but ordered tightly held plans for a rescue mission. Outside of those operationally involved, only cabinet-level officials knew of their existence. Now this option moved to front and center on the president's agenda. On Friday, April 11, with Vance having departed the previous day "for a long weekend's rest in Florida," Carter took the astonishing step of suddenly summoning his senior advisory group for a decision on whether the rescue should go forward. There is no evidence that Zbigniew Brzezinski resisted this egregious breach of procedural propriety. Warren Christopher, representing State at the meeting, learned of the matter for the first time and could say only that while he had not been briefed and hence couldn't comment on the specifics, he thought other options should be pursued. All others present argued that the time for waiting was over, and at the end of the meeting, Carter announced his decision to proceed with a rescue mission.

When Vance returned on Monday, Christopher briefed him on what had transpired. The secretary's "reaction was volcanic—the angriest I'd ever seen him," wrote Christopher, when he learned that "a matter of such moment had been raised and decided in his absence." He raised strong objections that afternoon with the president, and on Tuesday with Carter again and the reconvened senior advisory group. Vance argued that the rescue attempt would risk the hostages' safety. It was unlikely to work; if it did, the Iranians could simply "take more hostages from among the American journalists still in Iran." U.S. officials had just won European support of broader sanctions on the tacit assumption that no American military action was contemplated. But Vance failed to change any minds. On Thursday, he told Carter that he would leave office if the mission went forward, whether or not it was successful, and the following Monday, April 21, he delivered a formal letter of resignation to the president.

On the morning of April 24, JCS chairman General Jones informed Brzezinski that eight U.S. Army helicopters were on their way, as planned, to a remote Iranian desert location, accompanied by three C-130 transport aircraft. After refueling, the plan called for a minimum of six helicopters to fly directly to the embassy compound in Tehran, extract the hostages, and return to the desert, from whence the transports would fly them to freedom. But two of the helicopters were unable to make it to the desert rendezvous point for mechanical and weather-related reasons, and a third failed on-site. This reduced the number below the minimum judged necessary for success, and the mission was aborted less than twelve hours after it began. Then the failure was tragically compounded when one of the helicopters crashed into a C-130, killing eight of the men aboard.

On April 29, Carter announced the appointment of the respected senior senator from Maine, Edmund S. Muskie, as secretary of state. The choice was widely applauded, and the new chief diplomat showed a flair for public exposition his predecessor had lacked. At the same time, Vance's departure triggered a "torrent" of public criticism of Brzezinski and his now-confirmed foreign policy preeminence. Carter, however, stuck by his national security adviser, asking him to stay on at the NSC, and rejecting—at a special Camp David meeting—proposals put forward by Muskie and Christopher to modify established NSC procedures. In the months that followed, Brzezinski's primacy as presidential adviser was solidified. Muskie had little of Vance's taste for deep immersion in foreign policy issues, and proved significantly weaker than Vance as an inside policy player. Moreover, he hurt himself with the president when, on the eve of the Democratic Party Convention where Carter would be renominated, the former senator did not immediately distance himself from demoralized Democrats suggesting that he might replace Carter at the top of the ticket. In October, however, Muskie spoke out publicly against Brzezinski's role. He "let it be known that he wants major changes in the way foreign policy is managed if he stays on in a second Carter administration," the New York Times reported. "If I were President," Muskie said, "I would appoint somebody as Secretary of State and make sure that the NSC role is that of coordinating and not anything else."

Notwithstanding the support he enjoyed from his most important constituent, the president, Brzezinski had few public defenders, and won little if any of the public acclaim that had come Henry Kissinger's way in 1972 and thereafter. In his informative memoirs, Brzezinski speculates that "a major showdown over my role . . . might have taken place if Carter had been reelected." Muskie might, he thought, have been joined in his challenge by his former Senate colleague, Vice President Walter Mondale. This proposition was never tested, but judging from Carter's memoirs, Brzezinski would likely have prevailed. For Carter liked him, and valued his service: "Next to members of my family, Zbig would be my favorite seatmate on a long-distance trip; we might argue, but I would never be bored."

"Of all the senior foreign affairs advisers in the government, he was closest—both personally and ideologically—to President Carter." These were the words of Gary Sick, senior aide to Brzezinski and chronicler of the Iranian hostage crisis, reflecting five years after the end of that crisis, and of the Carter administration. He was writing, however, not about his boss, but instead of Brzezinski's main competitor: Secretary of State Cyrus R. Vance.

Henry Kissinger had dominated the policy process under Nixon over a weak secretary of state who was unprepared for the post and who was kept at arm's length by his president. Brzezinski, by contrast, achieved ultimate primacy (though not dominance) vis-à-vis a strong, highly competent, determined secretary of state, who was close to his president substantively and personally, and who retained Carter's confidence until his waning months in office. Brzezinski's achievement was a triumph of persistence and propinquity, aided by the flow of events. It underscored the advantages of the White House position: the first to brief the president in the morning, the closest at hand when problems arose. Vance had powerful counters: Carter's basic trust, reinforced by a daily summary foreign policy report that the chief executive read consistently and carefully. But in the contest for power that is a staple of life in Washington, D.C., Vance's strengths proved no match for the advantages of the articulate policy aide serving at the president's right hand.

At the same time, Zbigniew Brzezinski's performance undercut the legitimacy of the post of national security adviser to a degree that Kissinger's, curiously, had not. An activist aide, stressing policy over process, he brought an avalanche of criticism down on him and the job that he held. McGeorge Bundy, who together with John F. Kennedy had essentially invented the position, was only one of those who concluded that the role had gotten out of hand, and he urged his successor to downgrade the job: it was "one place where less would be more," he wrote in the *New York Times*. Brzezinski himself recognized there was a real problem: "I was perceived as having usurped Vance's legitimate prerogatives." His solution, interestingly, was that the national security adviser's role should be "openly acknowledged and even institutionalized," with "consideration given" to "making the nomination of the Assistant to the President for National Security Affairs subject to senatorial confirmation," like that of the director of the Office of Management and Budget. (He has since had second thoughts on the matter of confirmation.)

Ronald Reagan's response was the opposite. Carter's successor would choose to downgrade the position, denying his first national security adviser direct access to him. This weakness, alas, also had adverse policy consequences. Brzezinski proved successful and influential as an individual policy player. But through his controversial performance as a policy manager and broker, he left the job far weaker than when he entered it. It would take six years and four unsuccessful national security advisers before balance was restored.

5

"Serious Mistakes
Were Made"

———

R onald Reagan sensed a vulnerability. President Carter's foreign policy was in disarray. The Iran hostage drama had paralyzed the administration, and differences within it had led to the unexpected resignation of the secretary of state. The Soviet invasion of Afghanistan had exposed problems with Carter's worldview. In one last speech, just weeks before the election, the Republican candidate summarized his indictment against the incumbent and laid out nine specific steps that would "put America on a sound, secure footing in the international arena." The biggest problem with the Carter administration, Reagan declared, was that it had been "unable to speak with one voice in foreign policy." As president, he would do things differently. As a first step, he would reorganize the policymaking structure. "The Secretary of State will be the President's principal spokesman and adviser. The National Security Council will once again be the coordinator of the policy process. . . . The National Security Adviser will work closely in teamwork with the Secretary of State and the other members of the Council."

The idea to make reorganization of the foreign policy machinery a priority came from Richard Allen, Reagan's chief foreign policy adviser in the campaign. Allen had occupied a similar position in Richard Nixon's successful run for the White House twelve years earlier, only to find himself on the outs when Henry Kissinger muscled his way into the inner circle. He had resented this, for sure, but he had also come to believe that in the 1970s, the national security adviser had become too powerful and too intent on isolating the State Department and humiliating the secretary of state. "From my point of view, that was not very useful or productive." So he proposed that Reagan use his final speech on foreign policy and national security to commit "then and there to return the task of the national security adviser to that of an honest broker and a staff position."

This time, Allen did get what he wanted when his candidate won. He became Reagan's NSC adviser, but with the clear understanding that his role would be secondary to that of the cabinet officers, including in particular the secretary of state. Yet, while this solved the problem of having a vocal White House competitor to the occupant at Foggy Bottom, downsizing the NSC adviser created problems of its own. Ronald Reagan was the kind of president who needed strong staff support. Clear in purpose, he was less interested in process and policy. He got such support initially from a strong White House staff—but not from his NSC adviser. During his first six years in office, Reagan had a succession of different advisers—four in all—each of whom proved unable to bring order to an unruly process, ultimately with disastrous results for Reagan, his presidency, and indeed the country.

Allen, the first of Reagan's advisers, was shut out of the process by Reagan's top White House advisers and by a voluble secretary of state. His successor, William Clark, lacked the depth of knowledge to settle the increasingly bitter policy disputes between Reagan's second secretary of state, George Shultz, and his defense secretary, Caspar Weinberger. Next came two midlevel military men, Colonel Robert ("Bud") McFarlane and Vice (later demoted to Rear) Admiral John Poindexter, who sought to advance what they thought were the president's priorities by bypassing the secretaries of state and defense. They did so most calamitously in their secret dealings with Iran and their assistance for the contra rebels in Nicaragua. This Iran-Contra scandal was the logical, though not inevitable, culmination of a sloppy, unfocused process in which four successive NSC advisers were at once too weak to bring order to the process, yet sufficiently unconstrained to perpetrate a landmark abuse of power.

Ronald Reagan is a hero to many Americans, who believe that his firmness vis-à-vis the "Evil Empire" centered in Moscow hastened the end of the Cold War. Historians will be debating this matter for decades to come. It is unlikely, however, that many of them will write positively about how he presided over his government—especially during the first six years of his tenure. In office, Reagan combined brilliance in policy articulation and uncommon clarity in setting basic goals with astonishing indifference to the specifics of governance. This indifference almost brought him down. But after the shock of scandal, he agreed to put the NSC and White House management in professional hands and was able to recoup much of what he had lost.

Ronald Reagan had a relaxed, even detached view of governing. His preference was for a collegial form of decision making, in which key advisers would discuss with him the issues and options under consideration. Reagan liked to hear different points of view, but not if these disagreements became too heated or personal. Decisions had to reflect his core beliefs: that government was the problem rather than the solution; that the struggle with communism was a fight between good and evil; that peace was attainable through building up American military strength. But he had little sense for how to translate these core beliefs into workable policies. Decisions often took the form of compromises, reflecting an effort to satisfy differing points of view. When disagreements among his advisers were too stark, Reagan's inclination was to defer making any decision.

Ronald Reagan was no policy wonk. He came to the presidency with a few core convictions and a multitude of anecdotes that helped strengthen his belief in their self-evident truth. But he was neither steeped in the details of policy nor very interested in finding out more. Leslie Gelb, a national security correspondent for the *New York Times*, once did an analysis of "the mind of the president" and found that "not one of the friends and aides interviewed . . . suggested that the President was, in any conventional sense, analytical, intellectually curious or well-informed. . . . His mind, they said, is shaped almost entirely by his own personal history, not by pondering on history books—he thinks anecdotally, not analytically." One of Reagan's biographers, the *Washington Post* correspondent Lou Cannon, agreed. "He did not know enough," Cannon said of the man he had observed for many years. "And he did not know how much he didn't know."

Reagan worked diligently, but not all that hard. Most days, he would arrive in the Oval Office after nine, and leave by five-thirty for a private dinner with his wife Nancy, often clad in pajamas in front of a television. He would dutifully go through all his reading materials at night, but aides knew not to give him too much. He tended to take Wednesday afternoons off, and on Fridays he would leave early for weekends at Camp David. His schedule also included, whenever possible, two or three hours of "personal staff time" each day, which Reagan spent writing personal correspondence and, frequently, taking a nap. He would fly off to his ranch in California as often as he could. In his eight years as president, Reagan spent almost an entire year (345 days) in California.

Reagan's relative ignorance and easygoing work habits made him highly dependent upon his staff and his cabinet. His was "the delegated presidency," in Cannon's apt phrase. He was particularly dependent on his White House staff, upon whom he relied for information, to bring issues to him for decision, and to make sure his decisions would be implemented. They would run his day, by providing him with "a daily schedule that told him what he had to do. Once he had the schedule he followed it scrupulously. He was never late for an appointment; he never allowed any discussion to run beyond its allotted time; and in the evening he never failed to deal with all the papers he took with him." Reagan was the actor in a drama largely written and directed by others. His effectiveness depended on the directors being scrupulous, fair, loyal, and competent.

In Reagan's first term, a troika consisting of Ed Meese (presidential counselor in charge of policy), James Baker (chief of staff in charge of personnel, communications, and politics), and Michael Deaver (deputy chief of staff in charge of scheduling) managed the White House with reasonable effectiveness. In combination, they knew Reagan, they knew his policy preferences, and they knew Washington. As one aide summarized their strengths: "No one can put himself in the President's shoes, when it comes to personal and many political considerations, the way Deaver can. No one can put himself in the President's mind, when it comes to difficult policy questions, the way Meese can. And no one can understand the intersection of the White House and the bureaucracy, the bridge between intention and action, better than Baker." These strengths served Reagan well, but his dependence on them exposed the weakness and danger of Reagan's presidential style. His presidency needed strong staff support, and would flounder without it. During the first term, Reagan had the staff he needed for domestic and political questions—but not during the first two years of his second term, when Iran-Contra developed. And from his inauguration until the Iran-Contra scandal became public, he lacked adequate staffing for foreign policy.

At the beginning, this was more or less intended. For Reagan had an alternative: "Cabinet government." The president would rely on his secretary of state to formulate and implement his foreign policy. Appointing the right person to this position would be key. Two people who were close to him were eager to get the nod: Caspar Weinberger, who had known Reagan since his first run for governor in California; and William Casey, Reagan's campaign manager. But Reagan followed the advice of former President Nixon and instead chose Alexander Haig, who, Nixon had told Reagan, was "the meanest, toughest s.o.b. I ever knew, but he'll be a helluva Secretary of State."

Haig had a distinguished Army career, retiring in 1979 after four years as NATO's top commander. As Kissinger's deputy on the NSC staff and, later, Nixon's chief of staff, Haig also had firsthand Washington experience—something most of Reagan's closest advisers from California lacked. As a well known hard-liner, Haig shared Reagan's antipathy toward communism and thus met the new administration's foreign policy litmus test. When the president-elect called Haig to ask him "to join my team and be my Secretary of State," he immediately reassured Haig that his national security adviser would coordinate, not formulate or implement foreign policy. "I won't have a repeat of the Kissinger-Rogers situation. I'll look to you, Al." To Haig, Reagan's words and intentions could not be clearer: the secretary of state would be in charge of foreign policy.

To make sure that this would indeed be the case, Haig used his first meeting with the president-elect, two weeks before inauguration day, to spell out in detail his conception of the job. He would be "Vicar for the community of Departments having an interest in the several dimensions of foreign policy," he told Reagan. He would be the "single manager who can integrate the views of all your Cabinet officers and prepare for you the range of policy choices." To support him in this role, he would "establish a number of interdepartmental groups," most of them chaired by State. And he promised to be "rigorously objective in reporting to you the views of all of your Cabinet Officers within the national security community." To avoid "friction between the National Security Adviser and Secretary of State," Haig added, "contacts with foreign officials must be conducted at the State Department—otherwise allies and adversaries will exploit the opportunity to drive a wedge between us on matters of policy." Finally, he told Reagan, "there must be no independent press contact with the office of your National Security Adviser. I must be your only spokesman on foreign affairs." In his memoirs, Haig recounts that Reagan agreed with each point and "repeated his desire that his National Security Adviser should be a staff man, not a maker of policy or a spokesman."

On the last point, Haig won immediate satisfaction. Dick Allen, having finally gotten the job he had wanted twelve years earlier, agreed that his role should be limited. "The policy formulation function of the national security adviser should be offloaded to the Secretary of State," Allen told reporters shortly after the election. His role, in contrast, was "a clear-cut staff function." Allen's model for the job was Gordon Gray, who had handled national security planning in Eisenhower's final years. And he sought people for his staff who shared this perspective. Yet even in this reduced role, Allen thought he would deal with Reagan the same way he had done during the campaign. But Ed Meese, who was formally in charge of coordinating and supervising the NSC, insisted that Allen report to him rather than directly to the president. The NSC adviser, Meese explained, "will be a staff person and act like a staff person. He will be much less visible. He will be a coordinator and the NSC staff will be used as a coordinating vehicle rather than to formulate foreign policy." To underscore his reduced status, Allen occupied an office in the White House basement rather than the large, corner office near the Oval Office that Kissinger and Brzezinski had used and that Meese now made his home. Again unlike his immediate predecessors, Allen chaired no interagency committees. He was politically cast at the level of a deputy secretary, rather than as the co-equal of his cabinet colleagues.

Allen tried to make the best of it: "The important thing to me is the shape of policy [looking forward] two or three years," he explained. "The day-to-day stuff really ought to be gotten out of here." But without regular access to Reagan and without engagement in day-to-day affairs, he was deprived of the leverage he needed to coordinate the different foreign policy interests within the executive branch, the main function assigned to Allen's NSC staff. Allen, Haig later recalled, was "irrelevant," and no one picks bureaucratic fights with those who cannot influence the course of policy. Haig, it was clear, intended to play the senior coordinating role himself.

Haig's proposed process was not without its logic. Henry Kissinger had served as both secretary of state and national security adviser in the late Nixon and early Ford administrations. And secretarial dominance of foreign policy suited Reagan's priorities and perspective.

Reagan came to office determined to give priority to economic policy. Indeed, the White House's edict, according to Allen, was that "no foreign policy initiative was to be undertaken until the domestic economic reform was passed," which didn't happen until September 1981. Reagan lacked both the knowledge and the inclination to be involved in the details of foreign policymaking. His propensity to delegate, and his avowed belief in cabinet government, further suggested that he would be well served by a system of foreign policy formulation built around the secretary of state.

Haig, however, was never able to make it work. From the onset of the Reagan administration, he found himself in regular conflict with the trio—Meese, Baker, Deaver—that controlled the Reagan White House: "Guerrilla warfare with a bunch of second-rate hambones," he called it. One problem was politics. Haig had considered running for president in 1980, and Meese and other Reagan advisers feared that he still harbored political ambitions. Before the appointment was made, Meese, Baker, Allen, and Reagan's close friend and political ally Senator Paul Laxalt had vetted Haig on the question directly. Did he "want to be president?" they had asked him in December. Haig found the question "curious"—Reagan had just won a landslide victory and was surely beyond challenge by any Republican. Haig "answered in the negative." But it was not clear that Reagan's aides-to-be really believed him; and Haig would in fact seek the Republican nomination in 1988.

The White House also clashed with Haig on policy priorities. During the transition, Reagan's political and economic advisers had carefully devised a plan for the first one hundred days to begin turning his electoral mandate into the reality of tax cuts, a stronger military, and smaller government. They were determined not to dissipate their political energies as they felt Carter had done, and they saw foreign policy as an unwelcome distraction from getting their priorities enacted on Capitol Hill. "It was essential to Reagan's success that we focus unremittingly on the economic agenda," David Gergen, a White House aide, recalled. Yet Haig wasn't singing from the same songbook. He frequently raised foreign policy issues—with gusto.

Early on, for example, he declared that Moscow was infiltrating guns into Central America through Cuba, and he warned that the United States might have to "go to the source" in response. Immediately, the media focus shifted from the president's economic reform agenda to the possibility of a military confrontation over Central America. An infuriated Baker called Haig to tell him in no uncertain terms that he should get off television and stop making threats that the president would not support.

This episode underscored Haig's fundamental failing—his insensitivity to how the Reagan White House operated, and his inability, and/or unwillingness, to work effectively with the president's most trusted aides. Hours after Reagan had been sworn in as the fortieth president of the United States on January 20, 1981, Haig went to the White House for a meeting with Meese, Baker, Deaver, Allen, the new secretary of defense, Caspar Weinberger, and William Casey, the incoming CIA director. There, Haig presented a twenty-page memorandum outlining his proposed organizational structure for foreign policymaking. Drafted in part by Bud McFarlane (Haig's counselor), it was a more detailed version of what Haig had presented and Reagan had endorsed at their meeting two weeks earlier. Haig now proposed to launch it on inauguration day, as Kissinger had done with the Nixon system twelve years before—and Brzezinski had done with Carter's. The memo put the State Department in clear control of the organizational structure. State would chair the interagency committees dealing with broad-range policy issues; Defense and CIA would chair interagency committees for issues clearly within their own jurisdictions. Responsibility for crisis management would shift from the White House, where it had resided for decades, to the State Department. At the apex of the entire organization would sit the secretary of state, with others clearly subordinate to his dominant role. The national security adviser and his staff were assigned staffing functions, with no policy or coordinating role.

Haig's aim was clear: to lock in a set of procedures giving him unchallenged primacy. He would "steal their underwear before they realized their pants are unbuttoned," Haig explained to an aide.

Weinberger, Casey, and Allen—all of whom had seen an earlier draft—apparently were willing to go along with Haig's proposal. Not so the White House staff. Meese subjected the draft to a thorough, line-by-line critique, while Baker expressed incredulity at the power grab, telling one reporter, "Haig wants everything beyond the water's edge." At the end of the meeting, Meese, rather than sending the proposal over to Reagan for his decision, tucked Haig's memo into his briefcase—where it would disappear forever.

This first meeting of the Reagan presidency sowed the seeds of conflict between the secretary of state and the president's White House aides—a conflict Haig could not hope to win. Meese, Baker, and Deaver all saw in Haig's attempt to take control over the foreign policy apparatus—"before [Reagan] even had a chance to change clothes," as one of them later put it—confirmation that the secretary of state was not a team player. Haig, who had been asked by Reagan to pull together the organizational memorandum, and who knew from previous experience that these documents were among the first a president signed upon coming to office, was astonished to find that he somehow needed to gain approval for his actions from White House aides rather than from the president. "I left the White House that day with the distinct feeling that Ed Meese and his colleagues perceived their rank in the Administration as being superior to that of any member of the Cabinet."

The larger problem, however, was that Haig's hierarchical conception of his own role in the administration was incompatible with the much more collegial way that the White House—including Reagan himself—viewed the secretary of state's proper relationship with other senior aides. Haig believed that he was in control of foreign policy, including domestic issues with a foreign policy component, be it automobile imports from Japan or grain sales to the Soviet Union. In his first press conference, he repeated publicly what he had told Reagan, that he would be the president's foreign policy "vicar." Within weeks of taking office he was on the cover of *Time* magazine, chin up, hands on hips, arms jutting—a pose that said "Taking Command" as much as the title on the cover. And when Reagan was shot on March 30, an out-of-breath Haig, perspiring profusely, entered the White House press briefing room to declare that with the president incapacitated and Vice President George H. W. Bush on a plane returning from Texas, "as of now, I am in control here, in the White House." A more memorable line never was spoken from that platform. Haig intended to reassure the public, America's friends, and adversaries that things were in fact under control; but for many it confirmed, as one White House aide put it, a widespread sense that "Haig thinks he's President."

Reagan liked to have his advisers sit around and argue issues—"roundtabling," Ed Meese called it. Everyone was encouraged to have their say, including cabinet members or senior staff who had no responsibility for, or direct knowledge of, the issue at hand. Reagan would listen, and often make his decision after the meetings were over. This collegial system was quite alien to Haig, who believed that as the chief foreign policy person in the administration, he should have the last—if not the only—word on matters of foreign policy. He behaved accordingly. "I used to describe Al Haig as 'a cobra among garter snakes,'" staffer Donald Gregg recounts. "At cabinet meetings, whereas everybody else would be sort of slithering happily around the table, he was up there, with his lips spread, looking for somebody to bite." And Weinberger, who sat through more meetings with Haig than most, observed that he "seemed to be constitutionally unable to present an argument without an enormous amount of passion and intensity, heavily overlaid with a deep suspicion of the competence and motives of anyone who did not share his opinions." Haig in turn was amazed that Baker and Meese sat at the table during cabinet meetings (even though Meese had full cabinet rank). "Robert Haldeman and John Ehrlichman, at the height of their pride, would never have dared such an act of lese majesty."

After Haig's initial organization memo disappeared in Meese's briefcase, he sent a revised one, co-authored with Weinberger, and granting Defense greater power, directly to the president for his signature on February 5, 1981. Three weeks later, he heard back from Meese and Baker: they were prepared to move ahead on the memorandum, but they had made some changes. Rather than a single senior interagency group chaired by the secretary of state, there would be three: one chaired by State, dealing with foreign policy; one by the Pentagon, dealing with defense policy; and one by the CIA, dealing with intelligence matters. Under this structure, Haig was institutionally and in fact co-equal with Weinberger and Casey. Gone was the notion of State being in control, or even *primus inter pares*. Moreover, the NSC was given the important task of assigning issues to the interagency groups for their consideration—thus placing in Allen's (and Meese's) hands the determination over what issues State and Haig would control. Finally, nothing was said about the function of crisis management shifting from the White House to the State Department, as Haig had wanted.

A month later, in fact, Meese and Baker convinced Reagan to make his first formal statement on foreign policy organization not on the new system that had just been agreed upon, but on how future crises would be managed by the White House, with Vice President George Bush rather than Haig in charge. Unfortunately, no one had told Haig of this decision, and when it was leaked to the *Washington Post*, Haig made his unhappiness clear before a congressional committee. Baker and Meese were furious, and responded to Haig's public challenge to the president by having the White House issue a statement "*confirming . . .* the President's decision to have the Vice President chair the Administration's 'crisis management' team." The statement went on to note that "management of crises has traditionally—and appropriately—been done within the White House." There was no mention of a role for Haig or the State Department. Having read the statement, Haig prepared to resign, and told Reagan as much. Reagan, who thought Haig "was seeing shadows in a mirror," nevertheless persuaded Haig to stay on by publicly affirming that his secretary of state was his "primary adviser on foreign affairs."

On other matters, too, Haig was losing out. Foreign policy issues with real domestic consequences—Japanese automobile imports, grain sales to the Soviet Union, and immigration and refugee matters—were decided within White House–led cabinet councils in which

State had a place at the table, but not the lead. By March, the White House was put in charge of preparing the president's trips abroad, after the State Department had mishandled preparations for Reagan's first trip to Canada. At the same time, Bush, not Haig, was asked to lead the effort to prepare for the Ottawa economic summit later that summer. Haig's access to Reagan also began to be curtailed. Although he had been promised private meetings with President Reagan three times a week, Haig was never allowed to meet with the president alone—and often failed to secure a meeting even when he thought one was necessary. Whatever the president had said about Haig being his "primary adviser," the reality proved different. Haig was increasingly isolated—from the White House and from foreign policy. That might have satisfied Reagan's protective and ambitious aides; yet it created a problem for the president and his administration. If not Haig and the State Department, who would fill the foreign policy vacuum that now existed at the center of the administration?

Ed Meese could have filled the vacuum. As the White House policy czar, he certainly had the authority to coordinate the different foreign policy interests. But Meese lacked the necessary expertise. Foreign policy wasn't his strong suit. And he wasn't much of a manager, either. All paper sent to the president on policy matters would flow through Meese's office, and it would often get stuck there. "Even his friends in the administration," Jim Baker wrote later, "referred to his briefcase as a black hole. Once something went in there, it often would never come out again." Meese once slyly suggested that "that's the way we like it," because the decision-making process should not "get a great deal of public or even internal Government attention." Others were not so sure. "Instead of having Ed Meese as a two-ton running and blocking back," Allen recalled, "he was a two-ton elephant in the middle of the door." Nothing much could get done this way. By the early autumn of 1981, Allen had some twenty different issues requiring full NSC attention that were languishing in the black hole that was Meese's inbox.

If Meese couldn't keep up, and neither Allen nor Haig was allowed to run the system, the only other way to fill the policymaking vacuum was to create a structure chaired by the president and involving all the major foreign policy players. This was tried through the establishment of the National Security Planning Group (NSPG), a high-level body that consisted of the president, vice president, the secretaries of state and defense, the CIA director, the national security adviser, and Reagan's top three White House lieutenants. Its aim was to centralize decision making at the top, and to provide the president an opportunity to meet informally with his key advisers to discuss and decide on foreign policy issues. Similar to Lyndon Johnson's Tuesday lunches, the structure could have worked, but only if it had adequate staffing support to prepare meetings and ensure that decisions would be implemented. That was the job of the NSC adviser and staff; but Meese wouldn't relinquish control and Allen was unable to grab it. As a result, issues were often discussed without proper preparation. Decisions were sometimes reached without clear consideration of the consequences. Whatever was decided went unrecorded and was not disseminated throughout the bureaucracy with clear guidance on implementation. And more often than not, disagreement among Reagan's advisers led to stalemate. While the president liked to hear different views, he hated to have to choose among them. So final decisions would often be postponed, and the arguments would then resume at the next meeting.

This failure to fill the foreign policy vacuum had significant consequences for policy. The administration was so disorganized on the question of selling sophisticated surveillance planes (AWACS) to Saudi Arabia that the president himself had to persuade no fewer than ten senators to switch from opposition to support in order to prevent what would have been a devastating congressional veto of the sale. Arms control policy was also deadlocked for many months, as Reagan failed to decide whether to adopt the uncompromising line of Weinberger's Pentagon or the more pro-engagement line pushed by State. So key players worked around the system. Richard Perle, the Pentagon's arms control hard-liner, was the first to exploit that system to get Reagan to agree to his proposal for a "zero option" on European-based missiles—consisting of an agreement by the United States not to deploy planned new missiles in Europe if the Soviet Union eliminated the hundreds of missiles it had already deployed. Having learned how the system really worked, Richard Burt, Perle's State Department nemesis, fought back with a proposal outlining a more negotiable framework for strategic weapons. He appealed to Baker's political sensibilities by arguing that State's position was preferable to that of Defense, which, if adopted by the president, would make Reagan look like "a knuckle-dragging Neanderthal."

A particularly egregious abuse of Reagan's lack of a system was the decision to set up a covert action to support the Nicaraguan contras in late 1981. The idea for the program came, strangely enough, from Bill Casey, the CIA director. Normally, the CIA's role in policymaking is informational and analytical, not decisional. Not so in the Reagan administration. As the chair of the interagency group on intelligence matters, Casey was the bureaucratic co-equal of Haig and Weinberger. At times, he would see the president alone. "I didn't mind at all because it was Casey," Allen admitted. "With another director, I may have minded." Neither did it concern Meese, who early on suggested that Casey would be "virtually a full partner" in the administration's decision-making process.

As one of the administration's anti-Communist hard-liners, Casey wanted to get the United States more involved in Central America. The administration itself was deeply divided on how to proceed, with Haig arguing for going "to the source" of instability in Cuba, and Weinberger, paralyzed by fears of another Vietnam, resisting any use of American troops. Faced with this deep division, Reagan, as usual, refused to take sides. So, in the fall of 1981, Casey sought to break the logjam with a proposal for covert support of the anti-Sandinista rebels. He made his proposal at an NSPG meeting without having discussed his specific ideas with anyone else. The ploy worked. Rather than considering the full panoply of options or even the broader context of U.S. policy toward the region, the administration simply addressed the issue of whether or not to support Casey's proposal.

A consensus in favor soon developed among the top decision makers—not because others thought the plan stood much chance of success,
but because Haig, who preferred overt steps, reluctantly acquiesced
in this as better than nothing, while Weinberger (supported by the
White House troika, who feared the political consequences of military intervention) saw covert action as a way to forestall U.S. military involvement. On December 1, 1981, Reagan accordingly signed
a finding authorizing Casey to lead a covert action in support of a
500-strong rebel force in Honduras that aimed to overthrow the San-
dinista regime in Managua. Thus was launched a process that ultimately would derail Reagan's foreign policy for the region.

The failings of Reagan foreign policymaking were not lost on Jim
Baker, the White House's most experienced Washington hand. He
saw the process as a "witches' brew of intrigue, elbows, egos, and separate agendas. From day one, the level of suspicion and mutual distrust was utterly out of control among many of the major players."
Michael Deaver shared Baker's assessment, and both men concluded
by the summer of 1981 that they had to wrest the White House foreign policy portfolio from Meese's control by replacing Allen with
someone who had an independent relationship with Reagan. Their
choice was William Clark, who had been Reagan's chief of staff in
Sacramento and later served on the California Supreme Court.

"Judge Clark," as he liked to be called, had had a rough bap-
tism when he was nominated by the president to be Haig's deputy at State. Washington insiders said he was chosen to serve as a
"White House spy" on Haig. More serious was his apparent utter
lack of foreign policy knowledge, revealed in embarrassing detail
at his Senate confirmation hearing, which caused *Newsweek* to label
him "a completely open mind," and twenty-five senators to oppose
what would normally have been a routine choice. But once in office,
Clark had performed yeoman's work, winning Haig's confidence by
keeping the channels between the White House and State Department open through the most difficult of times. Reagan was soon

persuaded that Clark would be the right man to bring order to the foreign policy process—and so was Haig, who hoped to have an ally in the White House with direct access to the president. The opportunity to remove Allen came when it was reported that he had carelessly placed a $1,000 gratuity given to Nancy Reagan just after the inauguration in a safe and left it there, triggering an investigation. He was forced to take a leave of absence. Though he was later cleared of any wrongdoing, Dick Allen never returned to the White House.

In accepting Reagan's offer of the NSC job, Judge Clark insisted that he must have direct access to the president and control the foreign policy process within the White House. Reagan agreed. Clark was to serve as the White House contact for Haig and Weinberger, in the hope that his good personal relations with both could help manage the disputes between these two key players. A White House statement subsequently announce that Clark's "expanded role" would, in consultation with NSC members, include responsibility for "the development, coordination, and implementation of national security policy." The formal downgrading of the national security adviser position had been reversed.

Once ensconced in the White House, Clark moved to consolidate his position. When Meese, who had opposed elevating the NSC adviser's role, asked Clark on his first day in office to review the national security briefing with him prior to delivering it to the president, Clark declined. "I'll be reviewing that with the President." Next, Clark established a rule that all public statements on foreign affairs by senior White House officials would have to be cleared by his NSC staff. Then, in an effort to control policy pronouncements and curb national security leaks, Clark drafted a presidential directive requiring any person working in the White House, State and Defense Departments, or the CIA to obtain advance approval before talking to the news media. The directive, signed by Reagan and publicly released within a week of Clark's arrival at the NSC, put Clark in charge of its implementation. Finally, as an additional means of exercising control, Clark insisted that all executive branch international travel at the level of assistant secretary or above be cleared by the NSC.

Clark also moved swiftly to put a more effective NSC machinery in place. President Reagan finally signed a presidential directive on the national security process in January 1982, a year after having taken office. The directive essentially codified the interagency structure that had been agreed to in late February 1981, with its peculiar tripartite structure making the secretary of state the president's principal adviser on foreign policy, the secretary of defense his principal defense policy adviser, and the director of Central Intelligence his principal adviser on intelligence matters. Parallel interagency groups were established at the deputies' level (with the national security adviser a member of each), as were regional and functional interagency groups at the assistant secretary level.

Next, Clark took steps to strengthen the NSC staff, which under Allen had been short on government experience and long on ideology. He brought Bud McFarlane, the State Department counselor, over to the White House to serve as his deputy. And he restructured his staff into a series of regional, functional, and operational officers, each headed by a senior director who, to enhance at least the appearance of influence, was also given the title of special assistant to the president for national security affairs. Finally, Clark moved to gain control of policy by issuing a slew of national security directives. Whereas no study directives had been issued during Allen's tenure, fourteen of them were signed by Reagan in 1982, asking for studies covering everything from broad national security strategy to policy toward the Horn of Africa. The number of decision directives signed by Reagan also exploded in this time—from fourteen in 1981 to fifty-eight a year later. Through these directives, Clark was able to centralize the policymaking process at the NSC and exercise better control over the administration's foreign policy.

Clark's move from State to the White House was seen initially as strengthening Secretary Haig. But now the Judge had Ronald Reagan as his one and only constituent. In a rare public speech, Reagan's national security adviser had defined his role as "the conversion of [the president's] philosophy to policy." This was not easy for an adviser with such limited substantive knowledge. And it was sure to generate tension with a secretary of state who was duty-bound to resist its application in spheres—such as U.S.-European relations—where the market for Reaganite ideology was limited.

Matters came to a head at a fractious economic summit at Versailles in June 1982. The central issue was economic relations with Moscow, and especially the projected pipeline for carrying Soviet natural gas to Western European markets. This was anathema to American conservatives, including President Reagan. But European governments across the political spectrum all supported the pipeline. Haig sought the best deal he could get: reluctant U.S. acquiescence in the pipeline in exchange for greater European restraint on economic credits granted the Soviet Union. The hard-liners back in Washington would have none of it. Clark convened an NSC meeting on a day Haig was required to be in New York and convinced Reagan to extend a previous presidential order barring involvement in the project by U.S. firms to their licensees and subsidiaries based in Europe. Haig's compromise with the Europeans was now a dead letter.

The pipeline disagreement wasn't the only one between the secretary of state and his erstwhile deputy that month. Days earlier, Haig and Clark had crossed swords over Lebanon, which was in great turmoil following the Israeli invasion earlier that June. This was a delicate time for the president, who, while a strong supporter of Israel, opposed the Israeli incursion of its northern neighbor and the large-scale bombing of Palestinians in West Beirut. But Haig insisted on being in charge and sent detailed instructions to the U.S. negotiator, Philip Habib, then in Lebanon, without first clearing them with Reagan as Clark had insisted he should. The president had had enough. Reagan didn't like to fire anyone. ("You never shoot your own horse," he had told Clark on a previous occasion. "Your neighbor does it for you.") But now he called the general into his office and handed him a brief letter accepting his resignation—though Haig had not formally offered one. In his place Reagan named George Shultz, a longtime supporter who had held several posts under Nixon, including secretary of the Treasury. Shultz's collegial style was much more suited to the Reagan presidency, and he would remain in office until its conclusion.

Clark continued to be assertive and influential in the months thereafter. As the foreign policy person who saw Reagan most frequently—and often alone—he knew best what Reagan wanted. He was able and willing to impose what he believed was the president's perspective on the rest of the administration, even if that meant going against the advice of a cabinet member or having to move ahead without informing them of what the president intended to do. By 1983, Clark had emerged as a major player in key policy areas, including the Middle East, where Israeli and Syrian interventions had further destabilized a Lebanon wrecked by civil war; Central America, where American support for the anti-Sandinista contra rebels had become politically controversial at home; and arms control, where the perspectives of the State and Defense Departments on how to proceed with U.S.-Soviet negotiations remained very far apart.

On the Middle East, Clark succeeded in appointing his own deputy, Bud McFarlane, as the president's envoy to the region. On arms control, Clark sought to break the State-Pentagon deadlock by seizing control of the interagency process—putting McFarlane in charge of a deputies-level interagency group to work on the issue and creating a new Senior Arms Control Policy Group ("sack-pig") with himself in the chair. And on Central America, Clark sided with other hard-liners in the administration—notably CIA director Bill Casey and UN Ambassador Jeane Kirkpatrick—to forge an uncompromising line toward Marxist Nicaragua, one that eschewed diplomatic negotiations and emphasized military support for the contras seeking to overthrow that regime.

But Clark had one major liability that would ultimately prove his undoing. Though he was close to the president and convinced he knew what Reagan wanted, he remained someone with little knowledge of or appreciation for the complexities of foreign policy. George Shultz paints a picture of the Judge in his memoirs as someone very much out of his depth on policy matters. "Clark simply didn't com-

prehend the subtleties or the nuances" of foreign policy, Shultz writes.
"The complexity of reality was a threat to him. To avoid looking ill
at ease and uninformed, Clark took refuge in two simple principles:
all of his decisions or recommendations would be hard-line, and he
would try to control real access to the president." Shultz could have
added a third principle: a penchant for secrecy, to include cutting out
the secretary of state.

This combination ultimately brought about Clark's downfall. Just
as he was seemingly emerging as the dominant foreign policy force
in Washington—with cover stories appearing in *Time* and the *New
York Times Magazine* in early August 1983—he made two fatal mis-
steps. One was an attempt to undermine Shultz's effort to search for
a diplomatic breakthrough in Central America by ordering a show of
military force off the coast in Nicaragua. Not only did Clark fail to
inform Shultz of the decision to conduct these unprecedented naval
exercises, but the maneuvers took place just as the House of Representatives was considering whether to cut off funding for the contras. Opponents of the president's Central America policy were able
to play to the growing concern on the Hill that CIA support for the
contras could end in direct U.S. military involvement in the region,
and they defeated the president's contra aid request. Clark's second
misstep was his determination to investigate yet another leak of security information—this time concerning a pending decision to autho-
rize the use of force by the U.S. Marines who had been deployed to
Beirut in 1982 as part of a multinational peacekeeping force—by
ordering polygraph tests of all those who had known about the decision, apparently including members of the cabinet. Shultz pointedly
refused, and Reagan sided with his secretary of state.

By summer 1983, it was clear that Clark was in over his head—
an "amateur in a professional's job," as Scotty Reston put it in the
New York Times. Baker, Deaver, and Nancy Reagan (worried that her
husband's image was being damaged by Clark's machinations) were
all convinced Clark had to go. Even the president, while he would
never fire a loyal friend, became distinctly cooler when Clark was
around, indicating that just as *Time* magazine was reporting Clark's

triumphs, his stock was falling rapidly in the one place that mattered: the Oval Office. Shultz, "increasingly convinced that Clark was miserable in his role," decided to take matters in his own hands. He complained bitterly to the president, both when senior aides were present and when they were alone, about "a disgrace" of a foreign policy process, and Clark's increasingly brazen attempts to cut him out of the action. Unless matters improved—including having regularly scheduled meetings between the president and secretary of state—Shultz said he would have to leave. Reagan could not afford the resignation of a second secretary of state in as many years, and in any case he looked to Shultz as his main foreign policy adviser. He agreed to scheduling two sessions with Shultz a week, on Wednesday and Friday afternoons. When Shultz suggested the national security adviser sit in the meetings, as a listener, Reagan pointedly responded, "let's try it with just the two of us first."

Clark soon saw the writing on the wall, and when an opening emerged with the resignation of James Watt, the secretary of the interior, Clark suggested to Reagan that he be nominated to head the department. That decision set off a scramble for Clark's replacement. Baker and Deaver were long disturbed about the rising influence of the administration's conservatives under Clark. They came up with the idea of Baker taking Clark's place, with Deaver moving up to become chief of staff. They took the proposal to Reagan, who immediately agreed. But when Clark got wind of the move, he rallied his conservative colleagues, who persuaded Reagan to abandon the idea. Their counterproposal that Jeane Kirkpatrick should move from the United Nations to the White House foundered in turn on opposition from Baker and Deaver, as well as Shultz. In the end, Reagan settled for promoting Clark's deputy, Bud McFarlane, who at least had the distinction of being "everybody's second choice."

It would prove a fateful choice. Had the president stuck to his guns and appointed Baker as his NSC adviser, it is inconceivable that the kind of shenanigans and outright illegalities that characterized the NSC during the next three years would have occurred. Baker was too aware of the political context of the presidency and the conduct of foreign policy and much too savvy to let anything like that come to pass. Reagan would later admit that his failure to appoint Baker was "a turning point" for his administration—but the recognition would come too late.

Robert ("Bud") McFarlane had the substantive knowledge that William Clark so clearly lacked, but he did not have Clark's stature or the personal connection to Reagan. To be sure, as someone who had served on the NSC staff during the Nixon administration and as Clark's deputy for over a year, McFarlane had the requisite experience for managing the policy process efficiently. And like his immediate predecessor, McFarlane remained the principal foreign policy player in the White House, even moving up to the coveted first-floor corner office in the West Wing once Meese left to become attorney general in Reagan's second term. But that was not enough for McFarlane to succeed as national security adviser; his bigger challenge was to somehow overcome the increasingly nasty feud between the secretaries of state and defense. Reagan did not deal well with conflict among his closest advisers and he generally refused to side with one for fear of disappointing the other. Instead, he looked to McFarlane to resolve the differences dividing Shultz and Weinberger. That was no easy task in the best of circumstances, but the new NSC adviser simply lacked the authority to do so. "I was not able to contribute very much to a decision-making process that relied foremostly upon the Cabinet officers, the secretaries of state and defense," he later admitted. "My own credibility with the president seemed to be rather modest, and he was looking to others for ideas and results."

The Shultz-Weinberger feud was both personal and substantive. The two men had known each other for over a decade before serving in Reagan's cabinet: Weinberger was Shultz's deputy at the Office of Management and Budget during the Nixon administration, and later, at the Bechtel Corporation, Shultz was president and Weinberger general counsel and vice president. The disparity in stature seems to have grated on Weinberger, who appeared determined to use his close and long-standing relationship with the president to make up ground on his rival. "When Weinberger learned that he would get Defense," Reagan political advisers told Hedrick Smith, "he subtly blocked Shultz from becoming secretary of State by privately suggesting that it would be inappropriate to have 'two Bechtel men' in Reagan's cabinet." Reagan likely would have appointed Haig anyway, but the story is telling nonetheless.

Their disagreements also reflected very different styles. Shultz, the academic and economist, was coldly analytical, a problem solver interested less in positioning than finding ways to move forward. In contrast, Weinberger, a lawyer by training and temperament, demonstrated a dogged determination to get his way, refusing ever to give up his position. In this he had taken to heart Churchill's wartime admonition—to "never give in, never give in, never, never, never, never; in nothing great or small, large or petty, never give in"—and even hung it on the wall in his Pentagon office. In the words of Colin Powell, the defense secretary's military assistant in the early 1980s, Weinberger's general approach was "all sails up, full speed ahead, where is the brick wall—I wish to run into it now, sir!"

At bottom, though, the disagreement between Shultz and Weinberger was substantive. They differed on how to deal with the Soviet Union, for example. Shultz sought to negotiate deep cuts in nuclear weapons, resolve outstanding bilateral disputes, improve the internal human rights situation, and gain Moscow's cooperation in addressing regional security problems. Weinberger characteristically took a harder, uncompromising line, insisting that arms control agreements be absolutely verifiable, demanding that Soviet force advantages be eliminated without limiting the U.S. capacity to respond, and refusing to engage seriously on issues other than those that posed a direct threat to American interests. These disagreements effectively stalemated arms control discussions, and U.S.-Soviet relations more generally, during Reagan's entire first term. The process was ultimately broken open in 1985 when, with the emergence of the Soviet leader Mikhail Gorbachev, Shultz convinced Reagan to take a more positive approach. Weinberger would still seek to enforce a hard line in U.S.

negotiating positions, but McFarlane, sensing that Reagan favored Shultz's more accommodating approach, succeeded in tilting policy in State's direction—helped in part by an interagency process that was effectively "State-driven," even if nominally NSC-led.

The two senior cabinet members also, importantly, diverged on the role of military force in American foreign policy. Deeply influenced by the Vietnam War—and a military still traumatized by that experience—Weinberger believed that force should only be used in the rarest of circumstances. The interest at stake had to be vital. Congress and the American public would have to support it. The purposes had to be both clear and achievable. Overwhelming force would be necessary to win. And force would have to be used only as a last resort. Few situations could meet these tests—and that was just the way Weinberger intended it. Reflecting his departmental responsibilities, Weinberger insisted on building a strong and capable military—and making sure that it would hardly ever be used. Sitting in Foggy Bottom, Shultz saw military force as an important and necessary tool for achieving America's foreign policy objectives, from buttressing diplomatic negotiations in the Middle East to deterring and responding to state-sponsored terrorist attacks. To Shultz, force and diplomacy had to go hand-in-hand. Its use might therefore well be warranted in a wide variety of circumstances; even when the interests were not vital, the objectives were less than victory, and its extent was limited.

The disagreement on the use of force took its most concrete form in U.S. policy toward Lebanon, although it also infused policy toward terrorism, Central America, and insurgencies in other parts of the world. After the Israeli invasion had routed the Palestinians from Beirut, a struggling Lebanese government battled against foreign-backed militias for power and control. The United States strongly backed the government, and Shultz, supported by McFarlane, was firmly convinced that this support required the demonstrable willingness to use military force. He consequently championed the deployment of U.S. Marines into Beirut and U.S. naval assets off the coast to buttress diplomatic efforts. Shultz also called for striking back vigorously when terrorists bombed the Marine Barracks in November 1983, killing 241 Marines. Weinberger opposed all of these steps. The Pentagon chief objected to deploying the troops to Beirut, argued against their using force, and apparently failed to execute a direct presidential order for U.S. carrier–based aircraft to participate in retaliatory strikes following the Marine Barracks bombing.

Throughout this debate, Reagan refused to take a clear position. Instead, he sought to split the difference between his two top advisers—with disastrous results. He supported Shultz in deploying the Marines, but sided with Weinberger in constraining their use. He followed Shultz's advice in beefing up the U.S. military presence in the region, but backed Weinberger in employing it sparingly, if at all. He agreed with his secretary of state to buck up a Lebanese government under fire from Syria, but accepted his secretary of defense's argument that threatening or using force against Damascus would court disaster. Only in the end, after terrorists bombed the Marine Barracks, did Reagan make a definitive call. He endorsed Weinberger's recommendation to "redeploy" the remaining Marines some miles west of Beirut—aboard U.S. ships in the Mediterranean. Shultz had still argued for a more modulated approach, combining the selective use of force with a more intense diplomacy in support of the Lebanese government, but Weinberger prevailed.

More often than not, Reagan administration foreign policy was its Lebanon policy writ large—incoherent, contradictory, if not paralyzed by disagreement and indecision. Shultz and Weinberger would bicker, often openly and bitterly in front of the president. Reagan would sit silent, unwilling to choose sides. McFarlane would formulate a compromise that was usually so broad as to be meaningless. On secondary issues, the bureaucracies would gain great latitude on moving ahead, but on the primary questions, paralysis would almost invariably set in. As McFarlane commented after he had left the White House (a decision due in no small measure to the Shultz-Weinberger feud), "You have two very, very fundamentally opposed individuals—Cap and George—both men of good will . . . each believing that they are expressing what the president wants. Now this cannot be. [It] leads basically to paralysis for as long as the decision-making model is cabinet government where the president looks to his cabinet officers to be the center of policy initiative and advice."

Before leaving, however, McFarlane tried various ways to craft a workable process. He instituted the Wednesday breakfast, at which Shultz and Weinberger met with the national security adviser and his deputy, alternatively at the Pentagon and Foggy Bottom, to go over the main foreign policy issues in a less formal environment. These meetings were well prepared, with clear agendas and framing of issues. Much of the government's foreign policy business—especially in the security and arms control policy areas—was conducted at such breakfasts. Yet, even in this less formal atmosphere, the disagreements would go on unrelentingly. "They would say hello to each other," remembered Richard Armitage, who as an assistant defense secretary attended the meetings alongside Weinberger. "And the two would begin to argue about the breakfast menu, and it continued for an hour, and then we'd leave."

So McFarlane tried again, organizing an even more informal set of meetings, the "family group" lunch, so called because it would take place in the family dining room of the White House residence. There Shultz, Weinberger, Casey, and McFarlane would meet once or twice a month without aides, notetakers, or an agenda. It was a venue for often "very candid dialogue," McFarlane said later, that "led to some resolution of disagreements here and there." But the luncheons could not overcome the basic disagreements—which Casey's presence, if nothing else, only helped to make even wider—and they were convened too infrequently to make much of a difference.

In the end, no forum could make up for the fact that the president of the United States was unwilling to make clear decisions that would favor one of his top cabinet secretaries over the other. Upon Reagan's landslide reelection in 1984, McFarlane told the president that the time had come for him to choose sides. Reagan could succeed, McFarlane said, if he built his foreign policy team around either Shultz or Weinberger, but not around both. If he kept them both on, policy would remain paralyzed unless the president "was willing to play a greater role in intervening between them." He, McFarlane, just couldn't do it on his own.

Reagan understood the problem, but he wasn't prepared to resolve it. "These are my friends," the president told his national security adviser. "I'm not going to fire either one. And I know that if Cap were secretary of state, I would get very bad policy advice. But he's my friend, and I'm not going to change that. I'm going to look to you to manage the relationship." A welcome vote of confidence, but not much of a solution to a fundamental problem. Days later, Shultz would take up McFarlane's pitch, only to be told again by Reagan, "I want you to stay, work with Bud, and let's try to find a way to minimize these confrontations." And so the confrontations continued.

All of this came with a price. Not only was the process often paralyzed, but the Reagan policymaking became so "constipated," in Hedrick Smith's apt phrase, "that high officials felt moved to short-circuit the normal interagency process." The result was a virtual free-for-all, in which Shultz, Weinberger, Casey, and, ultimately, the NSC sought to get to Reagan and sell him on their latest ideas. Getting the president's approval, and then quickly acting on it before opponents of the proposed policy could stop you, was how foreign policy was increasingly made in the mid-1980s. Given their proximity to the president, the NSC adviser and his staff were in a privileged position to exploit this increasingly secretive form of decision making. The NSC staff, moreover, had motive as well as opportunity: with State and Defense effectively stalemating policy, the best if not the only way to get anything done was by moving ahead without them. Hence Reagan's NSC moved along an increasingly secretive and operational path—culminating in the selling of arms for hostages and the illegal funding of the Nicaraguan contras.

———

Lou Cannon put his finger on the central problem: "Reagan's national security advisers wielded insufficient influence and excessive power," he concluded. "Their influence on broad policy decisions was limited because of Reagan's deference to his cabinet and his concept of cabinet government. At the same time, their authority on day-to-day operational decisions was often enormous and unchecked because Reagan provided them with minimal guidance and even less supervision." With the cabinet deadlocked, the power of initiative on selected issues shifted to the NSC adviser, who was encouraged by Reagan's frequent admonitions to "work things out" to take matters into his own hands. And successive national security advisers, from Judge Clark to Vice Admiral John Poindexter, did so with ever greater frequency and gusto.

Clark started the NSC on this operational path in 1982–83. On Central America policy, Clark got the regional assistant secretary of state reassigned and a new special envoy appointed who was more responsive to his hard-line direction. And on a number of important decisions related to the region—from the CIA's mining off the harbors in Nicaragua to conducting military maneuvers off the Nicaraguan coast—Clark moved forward without Shultz's consent, and often without his knowledge. On the Middle East, Clark authorized secret trips by NSC staffers unbeknownst to the State Department. He insisted that McFarlane, his own deputy, be appointed as the new Middle East envoy when Philip Habib stepped down. McFarlane not only retained his NSC title but was told to communicate directly with Clark through a new satellite communications link, thus bypassing the State Department entirely on a crucial aspect of U.S. diplomacy.

Last but not least was Clark's role in the secret deliberations underlying Reagan's decision, announced March 23, 1983, to launch a major missile defense program. That decision was pulled together by the NSC and White House staffs without any input from the State or Defense Departments, including the military chiefs. Despite its revolutionary nature, there were no NSC meetings on the topic. Shultz and Weinberger only saw the text of the president's speech announcing the Strategic Defense Initiative, or "Star Wars," forty-eight hours before Reagan was due to address the nation. It was a powerful reminder of the power of the presidency—and of the national security adviser who serves at the president's whims and wishes.

After he succeeded Clark as national security adviser in October 1983, Bud McFarlane continued down the same operational path. This, most conspicuously, involved U.S. policy toward Iran. Already as deputy NSC adviser, McFarlane had demonstrated a great interest in thinking through Iran's future, once its aging Islamic revolutionary leader, Ayatollah Khomeini, departed the scene. Quite properly for a senior NSC official, McFarlane had placed the issue on the Council's agenda. He continued to have an interest in the subject when he moved up to head the NSC in 1983, hoping perhaps that if he could fashion a strategic opening to Iran, he might be hailed in ways that Kissinger was for the U.S. opening to China a decade earlier.

McFarlane's initial forays consisted of pushing the interagency process to come up with a new policy for Iran. Early studies by the State Department did little more than reaffirm the status quo. A CIA study in 1985, which McFarlane's staff worked on with the agency, concluded, among other things, that the Soviet Union stood to gain from instability in a post-Khomeini Iran, but that the United States might be able to gain influence with some Iranian moderates if Washington allowed weapons to be sold to that country. McFarlane used the study to draft a presidential directive seeking an opening to Iran, including by using arms sales to encourage potential moderates in Tehran. An "eyes-only" draft was sent to Shultz, Weinberger, and Casey. The CIA director endorsed the move, but Shultz and Weinberger were dismissive. The idea was "almost too absurd to comment on," Weinberger wrote on his copy of the memo. "It's like asking [Libyan strongman Muammar] Quadaffi to Washington for a cozy chat." Shultz agreed with Weinberger that it would be both wrong and counterproductive to weaken the arms embargo against Iran, and they insisted that there were neither moderates in Iran willing to engage the United States nor many opportunities for the Soviet Union to gain advantage there.

Up to this point, McFarlane was basically doing his job as national security adviser (although the adviser's hands were improperly all over the CIA's intelligence estimate). He had tasked the departments for new ideas, and pushed consideration of alternative policies. The consensus from the operating departments was clear: existing policy was preferable to any of the alternatives. Having pushed not once but twice for a different answer, McFarlane should have left it at that. But he didn't. He pushed on, convinced that an opening to Iran was both possible and desirable. He went to the president and argued that a new initiative was needed because Tehran had effective control over terrorists in Lebanon who were holding a number of Americans hostage. McFarlane knew that the human drama would get Reagan hooked. And so it did. In the hope of obtaining their release, Reagan would come to support every wild idea his staff came up with, even after he was told that certain actions, such as selling arms to Iran, violated not just his own publicly stated policies but U.S. law as well.

Having secured the president's blessing, McFarlane moved ahead. He worked with Israeli officials, and Iranian middlemen of uncertain repute, to sell arms to Iran in exchange for the release of the American hostages. Even after he had left his post in November 1985 and John Poindexter took over day-to-day responsibility for the policy, McFarlane remained centrally involved, linked by computer to the NSC. Ultimately, he and Poindexter, urged on by Casey, but vehemently opposed by Shultz and Weinberger, convinced Reagan to sell U.S. arms directly to Tehran. That shipment resulted in no release of hostages. But apparently accepting the old maxim that "if at first you don't succeed, try, try again," McFarlane and his NSC co-conspirators were determined to push on—including a journey by McFarlane secretly to Tehran, with a Bible and key-shaped cake in hand, for three-plus days of unproductive talks. Returning to Washington, McFarlane told the president it was time to quit. Reagan refused, and McFarlane's direct involvement came to an end at that point.

Not so for Poindexter, and his key NSC aide on this issue, Marine Lieutenant Colonel Oliver North. Backed by Casey, they continued the effort to sell arms for hostages. And even while those efforts failed to produce any results, there were other apparent benefits—notably a financial profit from the sales that North, with Poindexter's knowledge, used to purchase weapons to arm the Nicaraguan contras. By the fall of 1986, however, even that effort failed when the Iranians found out that North was inflating prices for the weapons they were buying by nearly 400 percent. And although some hostages were released in response to the arms sales, additional Americans were kidnapped to even the score.

———

The whole sordid affair was first publicly exposed in November 1986. Soon, a major political storm engulfed Washington. Congress set up a select Senate-House committee to investigate the matter, and convened months of nationally televised hearings. An independent counsel was appointed to investigate any criminal wrongdoing. And the president appointed his own "Special Review Board" (the Tower Commission) to investigate the role of the NSC staff in the affair and recommend improvements in its future procedures and operations. Reagan survived the inquiries; but the investigative efforts clearly demonstrated that his administration had made profound mistakes and broken laws in its pursuit of an opening to Iran and support of the contras.

The Tower Commission provided a scathing critique of the process and where it had led. Its membership was bipartisan, senior, and serious: John Tower, former Republican chairman of the Senate Armed Services Committee; Edmund Muskie, former senator and secretary of state; and Brent Scowcroft, national security adviser to President Ford (and adviser-to-be to Reagan's successor). Its counsel (and the report's principal drafter) was Stephen Hadley, who would serve as NSC deputy and then adviser in the administration of George W. Bush. The commission completed its work in three months. It concluded that the Iran-Contra affair was the result of a flawed decision-making process:

> Established procedures for making national security decisions were ignored. Reviews of the initiative by all the NSC principals were too infrequent. The initiatives were not adequately vetted below the cabinet level. Intelligence resources were

underutilized. Applicable legal constraints were not adequately addressed. The whole matter was handled too informally, without adequate written records of what had been considered, discussed, and decided.

This pattern persisted in the implementation of the Iran initiative. The NSC staff assumed direct operational control. The initiative fell within the traditional jurisdictions of the Departments of State, Defense, and CIA. Yet these agencies were largely ignored. Great reliance was placed on a network of private operators and intermediaries. . . .

In all of this process, Congress was never notified.

The critique was unassailable, and universally accepted. But what caused the process to be flawed? Though it offered devastating criticisms of individual policy players from the president downward, the commission failed to provide a broad, systemic answer to that question. The answer, however, is pretty clear. In a policy process deadlocked by the insatiable quarreling of its chief foreign policy and defense personalities, an inattentive president was unwilling, and a series of weak national security advisers was unable, to use the regular process to make policy and achieve results. This created both motive and opportunity for national security advisers, supported by entrepreneurial aides and the CIA director, to take matters into their own hands.

The presence of strong-willed secretaries of state and defense in the same cabinet is nothing new. Their disagreements can often contribute positively to the formulation of a better policy. But the differences between Shultz and Weinberger went both deeper and were far more personal than is the norm. Their world outlooks diverged in fundamental ways, as did their styles of governing. And the personal animosity that characterized their relationship certainly did not help matters. Too often, very real policy disagreements gave way to the "pettiest of petty quarrels," ensuring that differences would be aired again and again, never really to be resolved. Reagan may have despaired of the situation—many of his key advisers surely did—but not enough to do anything about it. The result was a paralyzed policy process, through which it was often impossible to push new initiatives.

At the apex sat Ronald Reagan, the inattentive president, who believed that governing was the same as making a few broad decisions. Both the formulation and the implementation of these decisions were delegated to others—to his cabinet secretaries and, most of all, his trusted White House aides. In presenting his commission's conclusions, John Tower maintained that it was these people who had "failed the President. They failed to advise him. They failed to insist on periodic review. They failed to expose him to expert judgments and briefings." But of course the real failure was not theirs but Reagan's: the president had failed to ask for advice from his senior advisers; he had failed to insist on a policy review when the promised results did not materialize; and he had failed to get the expertise necessary to make decisions of fundamental import on how to proceed. It is true, as Lou Cannon has observed, that Reagan's aides did not hesitate to manipulate him: "The sad, shared secret of the Reagan White House was that no one in the presidential entourage had confidence in the judgment or capacities of the president." But it is equally true that Reagan allowed himself to be manipulated.

The success or failure, propriety or impropriety, of the Reagan administration's foreign policy process was therefore ultimately dependent upon the managerial skills, intellectual strengths, and political stature of its national security advisers. Yet never in the history of this position of awesome responsibility had there been a succession of men who so lacked one or more of these essential qualities. Richard Allen certainly possessed the intellectual heft, but lacked the skills and stature to be a player, let alone an effective one. As the president's close friend and confidant, William Clark had stature, but his intellectual capacity for the job was lacking. Bud McFarlane may have had the skills for the job and possibly the strength, but he did not have the stature to work effectively with cabinet giants like Casey, Shultz, and Weinberger. And John Poindexter—well, he had neither the skills nor the substantive strength nor certainly the stature to be national security adviser.

Rear Admiral John Poindexter was the first and only national security adviser to rise up from the trenches. He had originally been hired by Dick Allen as his military assistant. For more than two years, he busied himself with improving communications within the NSC system—setting up its first e-mail system and overseeing the creation of the crisis management center. These were his pride and joy. McFarlane made Poindexter his principal deputy in 1983 and put him in charge of managing the Council staff and the internal paper flow. Then, when McFarlane abruptly resigned in late 1985, Reagan looked to Poindexter to take his place. It was a surprising— and troubling—choice. Undoubtedly smart, having graduated first in his class at the U.S. Naval Academy, Poindexter proved to be totally unsuited for the job. His was a peculiarly narrow, unreflective form of intelligence. His preference went to clear and crisp command systems. He worked behind closed doors, accessible to neither his staff nor anyone on the outside. He ignored both the press—"they were not my friends"—and the Congress, for which he said he bore no responsibility.

Most disturbing, Poindexter was obsessed with secrecy. "Need-to-know was second nature with him," said one administration official. "Covert man," another called him. His closest assistants did not know everything that went on, as he received "eyes-only" papers in sealed envelopes, talked one-on-one with key staffers behind perpetually closed doors, and met daily or more frequently alone with both the White House chief of staff, Donald Regan, and the president himself. He held everything to himself, sharing nothing that came out of these channels with anyone. And that included not just members of the cabinet (who, unlike him, were accountable to the Congress) but ultimately also the president himself, to whom he deliberately did not divulge the diversion of funds from the Iranian arms sales to the contras. "I made a very deliberate decision," Poindexter would later tell Congress, "not to ask the President so that I could insulate him from the decision and provide some future deniability for the President if it ever leaked out."

Anyone who arrogates to himself the decision-making authority that is rightly the president's should not be in a position of power where he can do just that. Ultimately, though, Reagan had no one but himself to blame, for he had put Poindexter in that very position. In selecting his national security advisers, Reagan would choose the path of least resistance. Allen was his foreign policy aide during the campaign and moved into the same position when Reagan entered the White House. Clark had been the choice of Baker and Deaver, and Reagan accepted it unquestionably. Baker then proposed himself, and Reagan concurred, only to drop the idea as soon as it ran into resistance from Clark, Meese, Weinberger, and Casey. So he opted for Clark's deputy, McFarlane, and then for *his* deputy when McFarlane left. After Iran-Contra would come Reagan's first solid choice, Frank Carlucci—though his designation, the president told him, was solely because he was "the only person that Cap and George can agree on." And when Carlucci left to succeed Weinberger at the Defense Department in 1987, Reagan followed his established pattern and turned to Colin Powell, Carlucci's deputy. Sometimes deputies turn out to be good at the top job—Scowcroft was in 1975, and so was Powell—but that is not always the case. As the Reagan administration was to demonstrate over and over again, the job of national security adviser is just too important to be left to chance.

The Iran-Contra revelations devastated the Reagan presidency. The chief executive's public approval rating plunged from 67 percent in October 1986 to 46 percent in November, the largest one-month drop in the presidential job approval rating ever recorded. Writing at year's end, conservative realist (and former defense and energy secretary) James Schlesinger depicted the damage. "The nation is in an uproar. The Administration is in disarray," he observed. "It has lost control over the national agenda. Public confidence in the President has been seriously eroded. The question remains whether the Administration can partially recover or whether it will be permanently crippled." The scandal was particularly devastating for this president because, Schlesinger continued, "Ronald Reagan was elected to be strong—to stand up to the nation's enemies." Now it had been learned that this strong president had negotiated with terrorists and sold arms to the very ayatollahs who had taken Americans hostage. "Perhaps it was best put," Schlesinger concluded, "by a Chicago lawyer and Reagan appointee: 'It's like suddenly learning that John Wayne had secretly been selling liquor and firearms to the Indians.'"

The hearings of the joint Senate-House investigating committee would carry into the summer of 1987, highlighted by the charismatic performance of Oliver North and the difficult, but deeply honest, testimony of Secretary of State George Shultz. Even as the facts were coming out, however, the Reagan administration was reshaping itself—at first chaotically, but thereafter with increasing coherence and purpose.

Before November 1986 was out, Poindexter and North had been fired and Carlucci had been named Reagan's fifth national security adviser. In December, CIA director Bill Casey—who was still pressing for negotiating with Iran—was taken to the hospital and diagnosed with a brain tumor. (He resigned a month later, and died in May 1987.) In January 1987, David Abshire—a veteran Washington hand—took up residence in the Old Executive Office Building with the title of special counselor to the president, with cabinet rank and the mission of "saving the Reagan Presidency" by assuring a full and truthful administration response to all investigators. At the end of February 1987, Donald Regan—White House chief of staff since the start of the second term—wrote out a letter of resignation, forced above all by First Lady Nancy Reagan, who was determined that her husband rebound from the depths to which he had fallen. Regan had known of and supported the Iranian arms sales, though he was ignorant of North's diversion of funds to the contras. His replacement was a widely respected Republican, former Senate majority leader Howard Baker. Then, in the spring of 1987, the directorship of the CIA was assumed by the venerable William Webster, who had spent the previous nine years restoring the reputation of the FBI.

By the time the Tower Commission issued its report on February 26, 1987, the Reagan White House cleaning was already well advanced. "The NSC process did not fail, it simply was largely ignored," the commissioners concluded. The remedy lay not in creating a new structure, much less in new legislation, but in using the structure that was already in place. Responsibility for putting such an orderly process into practice fell to Frank Carlucci, a widely respected former Foreign Service officer who had served as ambassador to Portugal under Ford, deputy CIA director under Carter, and as deputy defense secretary earlier in Reagan's term. He had known the secretaries of defense and state well, having worked with Weinberger and Shultz at the Office of Management and Budget in the early 1970s. As his deputy, Carlucci, in turn, selected Army Lieutenant General Colin Powell, a White House fellow in Carlucci's budget bureau office, who had served as both Carlucci's and Weinberger's military assistant at the Pentagon.

Carlucci had a big job to do when he came to the White House on January 2, 1987. His most immediate task was to streamline and reorganize the NSC staff. Poindexter's penchant for secrecy had resulted in a flat organization, in which the adviser dealt with everyone directly in order to ensure that information was not widely shared among members of the staff. Carlucci and Powell changed all that, instituting a pyramidal structure, with themselves up top and a coterie of senior directors below them, each of whom would be responsible for their own staffs. As part of this system, the staff's work was delineated into eleven separate directorates, each responsible for a different region or functional area. Gone first was the NSC's political–military affairs directorate, North's old office. "I didn't bother to look into what went on there before," Carlucci said of his decision. "Everything that the NSC does is political-military, so why have a separate office that is called political-military affairs?"

Carlucci insisted on a strong role for the national security adviser, though he promised to tell the secretary of state, but not necessarily his department, "everything I do." By mid-May, this put him, Shultz recalls, in "a steady—though initially unexpected—struggle" with the secretary of state "over the proper role of the NSC staff." Shultz hadn't been all that happy with the Tower Commission Report, which to his mind "offered the NSC staff an opportunity to *increase* its authority—exactly the opposite of the remedy needed." He was particularly perturbed about its "recommendation that the NSC staff should chair interagency groups including cabinet-level meetings." To Shultz, this was unacceptable. It would "put the NSC adviser, who is not accountable to the Congress, in a senior position over cabinet officers who *are* accountable." The battle was joined that spring and summer over a presidential directive providing that Carlucci would play just such a role.

Taking the Tower Commission as its guide, Carlucci drafted two presidential directives that aimed to reorganize how the NSC would go about its business. A key recommendation was that the NSC adviser should chair the senior-level interagency meetings, including meetings attended by the secretaries of state and defense, the CIA director, and the JCS chairman. Shultz "confronted Carlucci directly" on the draft directive. He had no problem with informal principal-level committees "being coordinated by the national security adviser"—in fact, he had initiated the earlier "family group," where he, Weinberger, Casey, and McFarlane lunched informally in the family dining room of the White House to discuss pending issues. This process had continued when McFarlane was replaced by Poindexter. But to Shultz, the NSC staff chief was below the cabinet in the chain of command, and the formal structure should reflect this. "Forgive my annoyance," he recalled Carlucci replying, "but I did not return to government in order to be an executive secretary."

Carlucci won the formal battle. In June 1987, President Reagan signed a new presidential directive that formally put the NSC adviser in the chair of meetings among the principals. Shultz, however, resolved to "work with the president and ignore" the directive—and he largely did so. But Carlucci finessed the problem by using the deputies-level group: "If you don't want me to chair meetings, I'll get Colin Powell to chair them instead. That worked out fine," he recalled in retrospect. As his deputy, Powell, put it, "Weinberger had confidence in his seconds. Shultz had confidence in his seconds. Carlucci had confidence in his seconds. And so we generally could fight out most of this stuff and then bring it up" to the cabinet/NSC level.

Once this matter was finessed, the relationship between Shultz and Carlucci improved. And when Weinberger decided in October to resign as secretary of defense, Shultz was happy to back Carlucci as his successor—recommending that he be succeeded as national security adviser by Colin Powell, who had "proved to be extraordinarily knowledgeable and gifted intellectually." Shultz invited Carlucci to participate in the negotiations for the pending treaty on Intermediate Nuclear Forces with Soviet foreign minister Eduard Shevardnadze. "The final agreement was negotiated," Carlucci recalled, "with just George, Shevardnadze and me sitting in George's office." It was celebrated in Reagan's triumphant December summit meeting with Mikhail Gorbachev, and ratified overwhelmingly by the U.S. Senate in May 1988.

With Carlucci now at Defense and Powell as national security adviser, the three of them formed, in Shultz's words, "by far the best team, and in fact, the first genuine team, assembled in the entire Reagan presidency." Shultz had finally achieved clear foreign policy primacy with the president. Powell proved an effective and congenial adviser. Stressing the informal, he hosted—at Shultz's suggestion—a meeting with the two secretaries "every morning when we were all in town. Alone. Every single morning." In the general's vivid recollection,

> George would come in and tell me what evil he had perpetrated at the State Department. Frank would scream at George, George would scream at Frank. We would leave at 7:30. . . . And so we started off the day with the three principals kind of knowing what each was thinking and what we were going to do. . . . So it was not just the Policy Review Group and not just the paper process but the three guys talking to each other every single morning.

Both the formal structure promulgated in the presidential directive and the informal cooperation would provide a model for subsequent administrations. After six years of policy chaos culminating in the virtual demise of a presidency, the Reagan administration had finally gotten it right. Substantively, with Gorbachev's help, the last years of the administration saw the beginning of the end in the decades-long Cold War confrontation. Procedurally, professionalism had been brought to national security operations. It proved a happy ending for Reagan's "role of a lifetime."

6

"Brent Doesn't Want Anything"

W hen Brent Scowcroft arrived at the residence of the vice president one Sunday in late November 1988, he found Jim Baker there as well. Vice President George H. W. Bush had named Baker as his secretary of state the day after his landslide electoral victory. When Scowcroft got the call to visit with the president-elect that Sunday, he thought he might be offered the second national security job in the new administration, and he hoped it would be secretary of defense. Instead, Bush asked Scowcroft to be his national security adviser, a job the retired Air Force lieutenant general had held under President Ford a dozen years earlier. Though somewhat disappointed, Scowcroft accepted on the spot, excited about the prospect of working with a man he had known and admired ever since Bush had served as Ford's CIA director.

Baker's presence in the small study behind the living room of the Naval Observatory home was significant. He was Bush's best friend, and the man most responsible for his rise to the presidency. Bush clearly intended him to be the "chief action officer and source of foreign policy advice" in his administration, as well as its leading spokesman on these matters. His national security adviser would be an honest broker and policy coordinator, not a policymaker. "He will convey to me exactly the feelings of the Cabinet members," Bush said, when announcing Scowcroft's appointment a few days later. "He will bring those together," and then also "convey to me, unvarnished, his own view on policy matters of tremendous importance." Bush's model for the job was the way Scowcroft had done it under Ford, when the national security assistant focused on coordinating the different agencies, and Secretary of State Henry Kissinger had been the undisputed leader of the president's foreign policy team.

Like Bush, Scowcroft was keenly aware of the pitfalls facing an adviser who sought to compete directly with the secretary of state in making and implementing foreign policy. As a member of the Tower Commission, which had investigated the Iran-Contra affair that had almost destroyed Ronald Reagan's presidency, Scowcroft knew better than anyone how such tugs-of-war ill-served the president—and the nation. He had drafted the final report's section on what the role of the national security adviser should be, including the clear admonition that the adviser should focus on coordination while the secretary of state (and other cabinet members) focus on implementation and operations. The national security adviser "should not try to compete with the Secretary of State or the Secretary of Defense as the articulator of public policy," the report had concluded; rather, he "should generally operate offstage." Less than two years after the report's release, Scowcroft had the opportunity to put these prescriptions into practice.

And yet, by the end of Bush's presidency, Scowcroft would be undisputedly the closest adviser to the president on foreign policy and national security affairs. There were signs early on of Scowcroft's influence, but certainly by the time of the Gulf War crisis in the second half of 1990, it was clear that the national security adviser had become the president's indispensable policy companion, and the two of them together drove the international agenda of the administration—for good and for ill. Remarkably, Scowcroft's growing influence did not so much diminish as augment that of Baker, and he was able to avoid the usual conflicts over policy and power that had beset relations between secretaries of state and national security advisers in other administrations. Even so, in 1992, Baker would be called back to the White House to try to salvage Bush's faltering reelection campaign, and Scowcroft effectively administered Washington's relations with the outside world. When it came to writing his memoirs of his years in the Oval Office, Bush turned to Scowcroft as his co-author. There could be no clearer signal that Bush had come to see this man as his most important and trusted foreign policy adviser.

Brent Scowcroft was in many ways the ideal national security adviser—indeed, he offers a model for how the job should be done. Born in Ogden, Utah, in 1925, Scowcroft grew up under the formative influences of the Mormon Church and his father, a successful greengrocer. He entered West Point in the midst of World War II, and soon made an impression as a quiet, studious, serious, yet very determined young man. At five eight and weighing just 130 pounds, Scowcroft wasn't exactly prime material for the football team; but he wanted to make a contribution and became the team's manager, showing the kind of determination and skill that would become evident in the White House years later.

The young lieutenant graduated from West Point in 1947 and joined the new Air Force, earning his fighter pilot wings a year later. His flying career was cut short, however, when his P-51 Mustang crashed—"I prefer to call it a forced landing," Scowcroft insists— in a training exercise over New Hampshire. He broke his back and spent two years in a military hospital. Instead of flying combat missions, Scowcroft turned to academia, earning degrees in Russian history from Columbia University and teaching at West Point and the Air Force Academy. In the late 1950s, he served a stint as a military attaché at the U.S. Embassy in Yugoslavia, learning Serbo-Croatian and meeting Larry Eagleburger, a young Foreign Service officer who would later become Baker's deputy and ultimately his successor as Bush's secretary of state.

Scowcroft's Washington experience didn't start until he had reached his mid-forties, but once he arrived in the nation's capital in 1970, his rise to power and prominence was meteoric. His first Washington job was on the Joint Staff, the military's policy planning wing, where he quickly learned the ins and outs of the interagency process. A year later, in November 1971, he was appointed military aide to President Nixon, where he could observe the presidency and White House from a unique vantage point. Fourteen months after that, Kissinger hired him as his deputy on the NSC staff, replacing Al Haig, who had become Nixon's new chief of staff after Watergate forced the resignation of the dominant H. R. Haldeman. Kissinger, who had admired the way Scowcroft once stood up to Haldeman, later recalled that he turned to the lieutenant general because he "needed a strong person as my deputy, who would be willing to stand up to me if necessary—not every day—but to stand up for what he thought was right." Scowcroft doesn't quite remember it the same way. "I heard he wanted me because I was a Mormon," he recalled. "Mormons were supposed to be loyal and faithful." But whatever the reason, he did his job so well that thirty months later—only five years after he arrived in Washington—President Ford elevated Scowcroft to the top NSC job.

Scowcroft's first stint as national security adviser proved challenging, but it demonstrated why he was made for the job. Even after Ford stripped Kissinger of his post as national security adviser in late 1975, Kissinger remained as secretary of state and very much the dominant player in the administration. Scowcroft was willing to take a backseat, and focused instead on serving and staffing the president: keeping him informed, making sure that perspectives in addition to Kissinger's reached his desk, and yet doing so in a way that never undermined Kissinger's preeminence. He had the temperament of a team player—wanting to get along with his colleagues, insisting on dealing openly and aboveboard with everyone, working hard to build consensus where possible, and standing ready to offer his advice and counsel without ever insisting that it be taken. And, rare for Washington, Scowcroft was the kind of person willing and able to park his ego to ensure the process moved smoothly. It was, all in all, an impressive staffing job for Ford, and one that the director of the CIA at the time would remember when he was looking for his own national security adviser a dozen years later.

———

George H. W. Bush arguably came to the White House as well prepared for the job as anyone before (or since). He certainly had the longest résumé. The son of a senator, Bush had been elected to the House, run the Republican Party, served as ambassador to the United Nations and America's second diplomatic representative to the People's Republic of China, and directed the Central Intelligence Agency. During his eight years as Reagan's vice president, he had traveled to seventy-two countries, in the process getting to know many of the world's leaders on a first-name basis. As president, he would make these personal relationships a central element in his diplomacy, frequently calling his counterparts around the world to see what was going on or to gain some new insight or information.

Bush made clear from the start that he would be a "hands-on" president. "I wanted the key foreign policy players to know that I was going to involve myself in many of the details of defense, international trade, and foreign affairs policies," he recalled. Foreign policy was Bush's passion, the driving interest of his presidency. If he often appeared to view his domestic and economic policy responsibilities as a chore, his foreign and national security responsibilities were what kept him charged and going. At times he would hear about a meeting of key principals taking place in Scowcroft's office and scurry over to join the discussion. Without question, George Bush was going to be a foreign policy president; what he needed in his national security adviser was someone who could help him succeed.

Brent Scowcroft was that person. His temperament and experience were a perfect fit with Bush's preferences and management style. Their formative experiences had been the same; both men were members of the Greatest Generation, having been called to military service by the attack on Pearl Harbor and World War II, flown fighter planes, and survived plane crashes. They shared a passion for foreign affairs, and had learned the same lessons from history: that aggression must never be appeased, that America must lead, and that Washington's credibility must always be preserved. They witnessed the ups and downs of the Nixon administration, learning firsthand the dangers of the duplicity and dysfunctions growing out of deep-seated disagreements among top aides. They were both fascinated with China, which Scowcroft visited with Nixon on the president's first trip in 1972, and where Bush served as Washington's representative; they would become the co-desk officers of U.S.-China policy when they returned to the White House years later. And their strengths complemented each other's well, with Bush more oriented toward solving problems one at a time and Scowcroft more focused on providing overall strategic direction.

As important as these shared experiences was the fact that Bush and Scowcroft saw the practice of policymaking in much the same way. "Prudence" was their favorite word; "vision" something for others to worry about. These were deeply pragmatic, cautious men, who abhorred ideological rigidities. They would pursue a "Rockefeller Republican" foreign policy, Scowcroft suggested: "tough, hard-headed, sort of power politics oriented—but with a relatively low ideological content." It would be a "mainstream" foreign policy, he said at another point. "Unimaginative, perhaps. But mainstream." Bush and Scowcroft were realists when it came to America's power and purpose, motivated more by notions of stability and order than by the need for change or justice. They were small "c" conservatives, determined, as one top Scowcroft aide put it, "to preserve what is working, not embracing departure for departure's sake. We prefer what is, as opposed to the alternative. We don't want to reinvent the world. This is not an administration hell-bent on change." Change, they believed, equaled risk, and risks were things to be avoided. "I don't want to make any early mistakes like Kennedy and the Bay of Pigs," Bush exclaimed early on. "I don't want to do anything dumb."

This world outlook made Bush and Scowcroft reactive rather than proactive, and extremely cautious when confronting unexpected developments. Often, their first instinct was to do nothing, to hold firmly to the status quo. Thus, when in October 1989 Panamanian officers launched a coup against Manuel Noriega, the strongman whose ouster Bush had publicly supported, the president opted not to assist the plotters for fear that the coup might fail. And when the Chinese leadership massacred hundreds of young people peacefully protesting Communist rule on Tiananmen Square, Bush's first instinct was to contact Deng Xiaoping, China's de facto leader, to see how the relationship with Beijing could be preserved. Once contact was established, he sent his personal emissary, Brent Scowcroft, not only to make clear his concern about what had transpired but to underscore the need to maintain the strong relationship between Washington and Beijing, Bush and Deng.

Caution and suspicion were also Bush and Scowcroft's first inclination when it came to change in the Soviet Union. Both men had been deeply concerned about Ronald Reagan's uncritical embrace of Mikhail Gorbachev and the changes his *perestroika* policies purported to entail. They had regarded Reagan's efforts in 1986 to eliminate ballistic missiles and nuclear weapons at the Reykjavik Summit and elsewhere as "unrealistic" (Bush), even "insane" (Scowcroft), and viewed the search for an impenetrable "missile shield" as wild fantasy. They distrusted Gorbachev and his motives, and both came to office firmly convinced that the Cold War wasn't over. Bush had said as much during the campaign, and Scowcroft made this clear when he appeared on ABC's *This Week with David Brinkley* the Sunday after Bush's inauguration. Gorbachev, the new national security adviser warned, seemed "interested in making trouble within the Western alliance. And I think he believes that the best way to do it is a peace offensive, rather than to bluster, the way some of his predecessors have." Indeed, Scowcroft thought that Gorbachev was "potentially more dangerous than his predecessors [because] he was attempting to kill us with kindness."

Even when Bush and Scowcroft accepted the irreversibility of change (after the collapse of the Berlin Wall in November 1989 both men concluded that Gorbachev was indeed for real), that change became the new status quo, to be preserved in the face of calls for more change, as Russian President Boris Yeltsin offered in 1990–91 in response to the crisis besetting the Soviet Union. In the words of Dana Carvey, who brilliantly spoofed Bush week after week on NBC's *Saturday Night Live*, "Wouldn't be prudent!"

Bush was determined to avoid the "personality battles and turf disputes" that so often beset relations among top foreign policy officials. He had witnessed their destructive impact on U.S. foreign policy firsthand during the 1970s and 1980s, and he wanted none of it within his own administration. He looked to people he had known for a long time, friends who would work with him and with each other—who together would constitute a well-knit team. He liked making decisions within small groups and in informal settings, where everyone could relax, let their hair down a bit, put their cowboy boots on the table, crack (naughty) jokes, banter about the issues of the day—and where he could be sure that what transpired there wouldn't end up on the front page of the next day's *Washington Post*. Such informality required people to be comfortable with one another, to be respectful and loyal. Above all, it required friendship, a trait Bush valued more than anything else. "I would hate to be President without friendship," he told the *New York Times* in an interview. Friendship, to Bush, was more important than issues or ideas, and he used it as "a catalyst for decision-making or bull-sessions. [If] you were making decisions in isolation, from reading briefing papers and selecting options a, b, or c, it just wouldn't be the same."

It was no surprise, therefore, that Bush offered "Jimmy" Baker—the person he called his "younger" brother and placed "in the inner circle in the sense of friends"—the all-important job of secretary of state. The two men had been best friends for more than thirty years, ever since the young Bush family decamped from Connecticut to Midland, Texas, in 1959. Baker had run every one of Bush's political campaigns: the ones he lost (for the Senate in 1970 and the Republican presidential nomination in 1980) as well as the ones he won (for the House in 1966, the vice-presidential nomination in 1980, and finally the presidency in 1988). The two friends had long dominated the doubles tennis circuit in Houston, and now they were determined to dominate the Washington political scene.

Within days of his nomination as secretary of state, rumors were flying around the capital that Baker might not only involve himself in foreign affairs but also domestic and economic policy—areas he had run as Reagan's chief of staff and Treasury secretary in the preceding eight years. Word had it that he would be some kind of "deputy president"—not quite the president's equal, but still much more than a mere aide or member of the cabinet. In these initial days, Baker's star was shining so brightly that even before Bush had uttered the oath of office, people were beginning to speculate about a possible Baker run for the presidency in 1996.

Such were the ambitions of James Addison Baker III, one of the most accomplished political and bureaucratic operators in Washington of the last quarter of the twentieth century. He had shown his mettle in running campaigns for three different presidential candidates in 1976, 1980, and 1988, leading two to landslide victories and one (Ford) to an almost-come-from-behind win. He had served in the most senior positions under Ronald Reagan, and remained unsullied by the scandals and difficulties that had beset that administration—a masterful ability to manage the press may help explain how and why.

Now, he was eager to tackle the tough job of managing America's diplomatic relations. He brought to it a lawyer's feel for negotiations rather than the statesman's sense of geopolitics. He wasn't interested in policy so much as in solving problems—of which there were only two kinds: hard ones and easy ones. He'd leave the easy ones for the bureaucracy to resolve and take on the four or five hard ones himself. He'd tackle these problems much like a turkey shoot, of which he was an acknowledged master. "The trick is in getting them where you want them, on your own terms. Then you control the situation, not them. You have the options. Pull the trigger or don't. It doesn't matter once you've got them where you want them. The important thing is knowing that it's in your hands, that you can do whatever you determine is in your interest to do." Baker was stalking turkeys; but he could just as well have been talking about the way he stalked his diplomatic and political opponents.

Yet, as an accomplished hunter, Baker knew not only what prey he should go after but also which ones he should let go. "There were a whole range of issues that Baker didn't want to know about," said Richard Burt, a chief arms control aide to Baker when he was at State. "And some of those issues blew up." China after Tiananmen was one such issue, which Baker, according to Richard Solomon, his assistant secretary for East Asia, dropped "like a hot potato." Another was the former Yugoslavia, where on the eve of its violent disinte-gration, Baker famously declared that "we have no dog in this fight." But there were big problems he did take on—managing relations with the Soviet Union, securing German unification within NATO, and building a diplomatic and military coalition to confront Saddam Hussein—and he did so brilliantly.

Brent Scowcroft not only wanted to be secretary of defense; he would also, Bush knew, "be wonderful in the job." But Bush needed him in the White House, not just to manage the policy process, but to provide strategic direction and advise him on defense and arms control questions—neither of which played to Bush's or Baker's strengths. Bush also wanted a strong national security adviser, as he had learned about the pitfalls of advisers being weak or secretaries of state being too strong. For Defense, Bush had settled on Senator John Tower, the former chairman of the Senate Armed Services Commit-tee and a fellow Texan. Tower was an acquaintance, not a friend, and he had a reputation for liking his liquor and his women, preferences that ultimately doomed his nomination in the Senate. The defeat gave Bush a do-over, and this time he chose a person he had known well and who would be a good addition to the team he was building: Dick Cheney, a congressman from Wyoming who had risen to num-ber two in the Republican House leadership.

Cheney had been appointed President Ford's chief of staff on the same day in 1975 that Brent Scowcroft was elevated to the top NSC job and George Bush was recalled from Beijing to run the CIA. He had worked closely with Scowcroft during their time at the White House, worked well with Bush when he was at Langley, and had also come to know Baker when the future secretary of state joined the Ford reelection campaign. Of the three, Cheney was closest to Jim Baker, with whom he had developed a real friendship—sharing a love for hunting and fishing in the wilds of Wyoming. They'd go camping together, sometimes sleeping in the same tent. "Dick washes dishes. I dry," recounts Baker.

As the youngest and perhaps least experienced member of the Bush team, Cheney was determined to get along with everyone. He would have his hands full running the Pentagon, the government's largest and most unwieldy bureaucracy, and little time or inclination to get involved in policy matters that were beyond his purview. Within eighteen months of arriving at Defense, he had two wars on his hands (Panama and the Gulf), even while facing the reality of having to adapt—and downsize—the armed forces to the new, post–Cold War world. Though he may have been more conservative on some issues—for example, on the Soviet Union, which, he insisted well into 1991, remained a potential adversary—he would plead his case and then go along with the decision that was made. Dick Cheney, as defense secretary, was very much a team player.

The final key member of the team was General Colin Powell, the chairman of the Joint Chiefs of Staff. Powell had been Reagan's national security adviser, and someone Bush and everyone else much admired. Indeed, the day after his election, Bush had bumped into Powell near their West Wing offices and asked the general whether he might consider staying on—as national security adviser for a while, or otherwise as Baker's deputy or to head the CIA. Powell, then a three-star, wasn't ready to hang up his uniform, and instead took a command assignment that got him his fourth star. Nine months later, though, he was back in Washington—a place where he had spent much of the 1980s, first as Defense Secretary Caspar Weinberger's military assistant and then on the NSC staff as the deputy and the adviser. Now he would serve as the nation's chief military officer. Wise in the ways of Washington, Powell had great presence and communications skills.

He was loyal to the chain of command, and ready to salute when commanded. But he had his own ideas and perspectives—on how policy should be made and what policy should be—views he shared not only with his colleagues but with journalists like Bob Woodward to make sure posterity would know where he stood.

There were other important players, including the vice president, Dan Quayle; Bush's chief of staff, John Sununu; and Scowcroft's deputy, Bob Gates, but they weren't the people Bush generally looked to for counsel and advice when it came to making policy. These three officials were part of Bush's regular decision-making circle—known colloquially as the "Big Eight"—which Scowcroft set up after it was clear that formal NSC meetings, with lots of staff sitting along the walls, produced discussions that were often stilted and pro forma, and regularly leaked to the press. But Bush, Baker, Scowcroft, Cheney, and Powell were the inner circle, where the real discussions often took place and the real decisions were made. At times, Bush even relied on a smaller group—an "inner inner circle"—consisting of Bush, Scowcroft, and Baker (or Cheney, when it came to military matters during the Gulf War). Though one reason for relying on such small groups was that Bush was more comfortable with them, another was his penchant for secrecy. He loathed nothing more than reading in the newspaper what he had discussed the day before. And the best way to make sure this did not happen was to leave people in the dark, including, at times, his most senior advisers. For example, Cheney wasn't told about Bush's decision to meet with Gorbachev in Malta in 1989; Quayle and Sununu were absent from the meeting where Bush decided to invade Panama; and Powell was kept in the dark on many key discussions that Bush, Cheney, and Scowcroft had during the run up to the Gulf War.

The peculiarities of this president, his people, and his preferred process for making decisions, presented major challenges for a national security adviser. Scowcroft would have to deal with a president who wanted to be the player-manager of his foreign policy team, eager not only to coach his players but to play many of their positions himself. Bush would phone West German chancellor Helmut Kohl and try to seal the deal. He would handle the details of issues like China as if he were the desk officer at State rather than the president of the United States. And he would check on the information in daily intelligence reports by calling other leaders around the world to get their take—as he did in the summer of 1990 when Saddam Hussein was massing forces on the Kuwaiti border, only to be reassured by his Arab counterparts that Saddam would not invade.

Managing such an activist president would prove a major challenge for any national security adviser. But this wasn't Scowcroft's only challenge. He also had to figure out a way to deal with a secretary of state who was not only the president's very best friend but his generation's most effective bureaucratic player. There was no way this secretary of state could be cut off from the president; but given that the two of them would talk on the phone sometimes as often as a dozen times a day, it was not inconceivable that Scowcroft himself could be left in the dark.

Finally, Scowcroft had to find a way to mitigate the potential downsides of a closed, informal decision-making process, which offered the possibility that decisions would be made on the basis of insufficient information or inadequate considerations of the options available, or that subordinates would not know enough about the decisions to implement them effectively. Especially when things go wrong, as at some point they invariably do, closed decision-making circles tend to aggravate rather than mitigate faulty analyses and mistakes.

All of which raised the question: How could a national security adviser operate effectively in that kind of decision-making environment? Brent Scowcroft had a winning formula, which consisted of three key ingredients: gain the trust and confidence of the key players; establish a cooperative policy process at all levels; and cement an unbreakable relationship with the president.

It is true, as the *New York Times* put it when Bush announced his appointment, that Brent Scowcroft was someone who "inspires trust." But for Scowcroft, trust was something that you earn more than inspire, and gaining it was essential to being an effective national security adviser. "I think it is important that the national security adviser should have the confidence of all agency heads involved in the process," he observed in April 1980, shortly after the years of open warfare between Cy Vance and Zbig Brzezinski had led to Vance's resignation. "If you don't have their confidence, then the system doesn't work, because they will go around you to get to the president and then you fracture the system," he explained two decades later. The adviser can gain such confidence by running a transparent process, representing the views of others fairly, allowing open access to the president, and setting clear limits on his own role.

Scowcroft worked hard to ensure that his key counterparts were fully aware of what he was doing. He met with Baker and Cheney every Wednesday over breakfast at the White House to iron out any differences that had not been resolved during the frequent phone calls and larger meetings. They would also use the occasions to plan for the week ahead. In a crucial innovation, he established a "Principals Committee," which he would chair and which the regular members of the NSC, minus the president and vice president, would attend. These formal and informal meetings allowed Scowcroft to get a good sense of where the other key players stood on a particular issue, and he always made sure he fairly represented such views to the president. "The first responsibility is to present what you know of the community views," Scowcroft said of the adviser's role. Only then can you offer your own advice. Gaining the confidence of the others requires that they trust you will present their views to the president, and that any advice you yourself give will be shared with them as well.

As important as gaining the confidence of others was to allow them ready access to the president. Scowcroft would work hard, through the Principals Committee and other venues, to develop a consensus among the key advisers on policy issues—and he mostly succeeded, helping to preserve that most valuable of all presidential commodities: time. But there were occasions when the president would have to get involved, or when one of the principals wanted to hear from or make his case to the president directly. And Scowcroft was eager to have them do so. "Everybody knew they had free access to the president," Robert Gates recounted. "And if they had a real concern about an issue, not only would no one stand in their way, they were encouraged to bring that difference forward."

A good example of this practice occurred in the run-up to the Gulf War. In private meetings with other principals, Colin Powell had argued the case for continuing sanctions on Iraq as the preferred way of forcing Saddam to retreat from Kuwait. Having talked about this to Cheney, Baker, and Scowcroft, he was then encouraged to make his case directly to the president in the Oval Office (to no avail, as it turned out). More generally, communications between the principals and the president were open and frequent. Bush and Baker spoke often on the phone. The secretaries of state and defense held regular meetings with Bush in the Oval Office, which Scowcroft would usually join. And larger meetings—of the inner circle, the Big Eight, and the NSC (at least in the first two years of the administration)—occurred virtually every day, and offered plenty of opportunities for any of the principals to speak with Bush directly. Scowcroft might see the president more than anyone else, but everyone could count on having their say whenever they wanted.

Finally, Scowcroft clearly understood that there had to be limits on his own role. "The secretary of state should be the chief spokesman for the president's foreign policy. And the president makes foreign policy," Scowcroft said the day after Bush's inauguration. The national security adviser, while "not exactly invisible," should play mostly offstage. That didn't mean that the adviser should not be operationally involved in foreign policy—meeting ambassadors, speaking publicly about policy, or even going on occasional diplomatic missions—but he should do so only in close consultation with and the full knowledge of the secretary of state. This was important, especially early on, since, as Scowcroft suggested, Baker, who "was not deeply versed in foreign policy," was at the outset "very ill at ease." So, from the start, Scowcroft told Baker when he would meet with ambassadors, go on television, or make a public statement.

On those few occasions when he went abroad, such as the secret trips to China after Tiananmen, Scowcroft would take Baker's deputy, Larry Eagleburger, along to make sure the secretary would be fully informed. "I bent over backwards not to appear to be repeating, frankly, what Henry Kissinger did," he later recounted. Within a year, though, Baker had gained his sea legs and theirs had become a relationship of mutual trust, so that Scowcroft no longer felt the need to inform Baker of his public appearances or private diplomatic contacts in advance. "With few exceptions," Baker recalled, "the NSC left the conduct of diplomacy to State—and I was always told about and concurred with those exceptions in advance."

The second ingredient of Scowcroft's winning formula was his creation of a cooperative policy process at all levels. In interviews, memoirs, and other reflections, there was uniform agreement that the process of foreign policymaking in this administration was an exceedingly cooperative one. This was a "team," where people "trusted" each other and everyone had their "egos under control." There was a deep sense of "camaraderie," and all were "loyal" to the president and his wishes. Of course, there were disagreements, often big ones on important issues. There were times, as Bush recalls, when Scowcroft and Baker "did get moderately crosswise," each worrying that he might be cut out by the other. But these differences were always worked out amicably, and they were never played out in the press, which Bush made clear he detested more than anything else. Importantly, people knew when to push their position hard, and when to fold. For example, when Cheney strongly opposed a proposal by Baker and Scowcroft to seek a ban on multiwarhead land-based missiles in arms control negotiations with Moscow, they decided not to push the issue further, even though the president had in principle sided with them. The secretary of state and national security adviser "were not about to proceed with the de-MIRVing proposal over the objections of the secretary of defense."

What made the system work was, above all, the fact that the spirit of cooperation that emanated among the principals was extended to lower levels as well. The importance of a structured, cooperative process below the principals became evident early on in Bush's administration, when the high-level decision-making process clearly broke down over Panama. During the presidential campaign, Bush had repeatedly called for the ouster of Manuel Noriega, the Panamanian strongman who had profited handsomely from the drug trade. But when coup plotters approached Washington in October 1989 for assistance, the administration was unprepared and opted to do nothing.

The coup failed, and Bush was excoriated in the media for being too cautious and heading what George Will concluded was an "unserious presidency." Within the administration there was "considerable soul-searching," Baker recalls. "An opportunity to remove Noriega had been squandered. Our reaction had been wholly defensive." The decision-making process also left much to be desired. Powell, who had joined the administration as JCS chairman only days earlier, marveled about the "free-swinging" debate in the Oval Office that substituted for a structured process in the administration. "Critical deliberations were taking place with no preparation or follow-up planned," he complained. Baker concurred: "It's an understatement to say that administration decision making was less than crisp."

Just as other crises such as the Bay of Pigs in 1961, the downing of a reconnaissance aircraft by North Korea in 1969, the Soviet rejection of the ambitious Strategic Arms Control proposal in 1977, and Iran-Contra in 1986 had produced needed changes in the way previous administrations made decisions, so the failed Panama coup led to a welcome revamping of the process in the Bush administration. Most important, Scowcroft decided to assign responsibility for crisis management to the "Deputies Committee." The DC, as this committee was known, was chaired by Bob Gates, Scowcroft's deputy, and included the top aides to the principals of all the key departments and agencies: State, Defense, CIA, JCS, and whichever others needed to be present. It had operated from the start of the administration mainly as a forum for policy development, sifting through different options and narrowing choices for the president and his principals to consider. Now it would also be responsible for meeting regularly at times of crisis, summarizing information, developing options, and following up on any decisions that the president had made.

The DC would prove to be extraordinarily effective in times of crises, notably during the Gulf crisis of 1990–91, when the deputies would meet at least twice a day and often more frequently to keep track of the fifty to seventy-five detailed items that had to be handled each and every day. As Robert Kimmitt, State's representative on the DC, recalls:

> At 11 a.m., the deputies committee would get on the video conference and talk. That would go until about 12:00 p.m. You can get about seventy-five percent of your work done there. And then we'd get together in a small group, in the situation room, just seven or eight of us. Gates would then attend the meeting of the Big Eight. Importantly, very importantly, we would also meet on the way back down, and have another small group meeting, back to a video conference with deputies, and then we would meet inside the department, because, frankly, policy implementation is much tougher than policy formulation. Making sure what people say should be done gets done is crucial to the policy process.

A good process, though, is only as effective as the people who run it. And what made this DC so effective was the quality and standing of the people who participated. It was agreed from the outset that everyone attending the DC would have to have the total confidence of, and ready access to, their principals. It had to be "somebody who could come back from a Deputies Committee, place a call to the secretary or walk down the hall, and get in to see him immediately and get his reactions, or could speak for him in the meetings authoritatively," Gates explained. All of the key agency deputies—Kimmitt from State, Paul Wolfowitz from Defense, General David Jeremiah of the Joint Staff, and Richard Kerr from CIA—were so empowered by their principals.

And so was Gates, the chair of the committee. He was the first deputy national security adviser also to be an assistant to the president (the most senior White House designation), which gave him real and visible access to the president himself. (For example, he traveled in the cabin on Air Force One rather than "back in the cattlecar" with the other deputy assistants.) He was also the first deputy to sit in on the morning intelligence and policy briefings with the president and national security adviser. And he was the only person who was not a principal to be included (as notetaker) in meetings of the Big Eight. All of which gave Gates tremendous power with his colleagues. "When I would go into a Deputies meeting," Gates recounts, "I knew exactly where the president was, I knew where his concerns were, I knew what the issues were." And people in the meeting would know, too. If there ever was uncertainty about what the president really wanted, as happened on a few occasions, Gates "would simply say, 'Well, I'm just going to go up and ask the president.' And I would leave the meeting for five minutes, come back down, and say, 'Here's what he thinks.' You only have to do that once or twice." As a result, the deputies were frequently able to resolve issues among themselves, which explains why there were so few Principals Committee meetings during Bush's term, since any issues the deputies could not resolve would invariably require the president's direct intervention.

Not all issues could be dealt with by the deputies, of course, and some had to be handled by a different set of people. This was the case in dealing with Europe's transformation in the wake of the fall of the Berlin Wall, as well as for formulating arms control policy. In the case of Europe, which was on the top of the State Department's agenda throughout the first two years of the administration, Baker wanted not only Bob Kimmitt, his under secretary for political affairs, involved in the process, but also some other key advisers on his staff, notably Robert Zoellick (counselor), Reginald Bartholomew (under secretary for international security), and Dennis Ross (head of policy planning). Part of his insistence on their being included stemmed from the fact that there were deep suspicions at State about the NSC's intentions with respect to issues like German unification and the need to reach out to Gorbachev. And vice versa. "There was hostility in the White House and a lot of suspicion," recalls Philip Zelikow, who served on the NSC staff and co-authored (with future national security adviser Condoleezza Rice) the definitive history of America's role in Germany's unification. "Brent was suspicious. He was suspicious of Baker personally. And at the level below Brent, that suspicion was acute and spilled over in consultations with people in Bonn, and so on." The suspicion concerned many key issues at a time of dramatic change, including how much to concede in negotiations with Moscow and the extent to which the unification discussions should be mainly a German affair.

To accommodate Baker, Scowcroft and Gates decided to create a European Security Strategy Group, which was basically the Deputies Committee, but with four State representatives rather than just one. This helped smooth the differences. The cooperative spirit of the deputies meetings was now transposed to this issue area, and soon State and NSC were able to agree on new strategies for addressing the challenges before them.

One major reason for the amicable resolution was that not only the principals but their key subordinates were close friends and had worked together for many years. A second was that none of their differences ever leaked to the press. This was crucial, as Dennis Ross recalls:

> When people saw that things didn't leak that would put them in a disadvantageous light, then it built a level of confidence so that you really could totally unburden yourself with others and you didn't have to worry that somehow it would be used against you. There's nothing like building that kind of trust that allows you to air everything. And we really were quite good. You could have really intense debates, and we did have some really intense debates, but they were among friends in the end because there was that level of trust.

Moreover, with trust established and all the key people in the room, it was possible to consider bold new moves at a time of radical change. "The Steering Group was no less than a way to bypass the U.S. bureaucracy," recalls Gates. "There was little time and a need for bold departures." Reshaping NATO, unifying Germany, ending the occupation of Eastern Europe, transforming the Soviet Union—all of these were policies made possible by a cooperative interagency process.

The other issue that required a different mechanism was arms control. Of all the questions addressed by the administration, those dealing with nuclear weapons, conventional forces, and their control proved to be the most contentious, not least because they involved the equities of multiple agencies. There was, of course, the Pentagon, which developed, procured, and deployed the weapon systems, fielded the forces in question, and housed competing service interests. There was also the State Department, which not only led the negotiations with the Soviet Union and others involved in arms control talks but increasingly viewed arms control agreements as a crucial indicator of the transformation of Moscow's internal politics and external behavior. And there was Brent Scowcroft, who had built much of his Washington career on being an expert on strategic weapons and arms control, and who came to his new position with very definitive views on what should—and should not—be negotiated. Indeed, his perspective on these issues proved to be crucial, since Bush, who did not have such strong views, had appointed Scowcroft in part because "Brent more than made up for my failings in arms control and defense matters."

On arms control issues, then, the national security adviser was as much a player and advocate as he was an honest broker. Moreover, because the issues were highly contentious and often very technical, the normal interagency process was not up to the task of formulating policy. Since the deputies weren't particularly well versed in the intricacies of policy (nor were most of them terribly interested in these issues) and the principals were preoccupied with other matters, a special interagency team—known as the "Un-Group"—was created instead. Chaired by Arnold Kanter, the NSC's senior director for arms control and defense policy, and the person formally in charge of the arms control policy coordinating committee, this Un-Group included representatives from all the key agencies who could both speak on the issues for their agency heads and were willing to work on them while leaving their bureaucratic hats at the door. It was an eclectic group, which included a principal (Ron Lehman of the Arms Control and Disarmament Agency), a deputy (Reginald Bartholomew of State), and key assistant secretary–level people (Stephen Hadley of the Office of the Secretary of Defense, Lieutenant General Howard Graves of the JCS, and Douglas MacEachin of the CIA).

Much of the real arms control business within the administration was conducted by this small group of people. They worked hard to achieve a consensus on issues such as whether to place limits on warheads, how to count tanks and troops, and what kind of measures could verify the absence of a chemical weapons production capability in an industrial plant. The Un-Group members possessed the requisite expertise, and they mostly addressed the issues from a problem-solving rather than a bureaucratic perspective. In many cases they were able to develop common positions, and when that proved impossible, they would present clear options for the principals to consider. (The DC never got involved in any of these issues.) Baker, Cheney, and Powell would come to Scowcroft's office, and the four of them would try to bridge their disagreements. Mostly, they succeeded. In rare instances, an issue was left for Bush to settle. In even rarer cases, the issue had to be taken up by the principals with Bush directly. Overall, though, the Un-Group proved to be an effective process for resolving many of the most contentious issues within the administration. Though it differed from that originally envisaged, the Un-Group "was a regular, structured, predictable process," Kanter insisted. "It was analytical. It had all of the attributes of what you would want an interagency process to be."

What made the Un-Group work—indeed, what made so much of the interagency process run so smoothly in the Bush administration—was the people who participated in it. In each of the key agencies, there were four or five people who worked most of the important foreign and national security policy issues; meaning that some twenty to twenty-five people in all effectively ran policy in these areas. Most of these people had worked together for years, and many preferred pragmatic problem solving over ideological posturing. Their ethos was one of cooperation rather than confrontation. "You didn't get the feeling that this was an administration where food fights would be tolerated for long," recalls Richard Haass, Scowcroft's senior Middle East person. "The work-to-bullshit ratio was better in this administration than any other . . . and less of your calories went into the bureaucratic game." And this culture of cooperation radiated downward in the bureaucracy. "If there were a problem between CIA and the military, Dick Kerr and Dave Jeremiah could deal with it directly. And their subordinates knew that their bosses were trying to solve a problem," recalls Gates. "You had a dialogue among the members of the Deputies Committee that extended to bilateral issues between agencies that really changed the culture or the atmosphere of the way the government was run." For Scowcroft, Gates, and the rest of the NSC staff, that reality made their work both simpler and more effective.

———

At first blush, Brent Scowcroft did not look the part as one of the most powerful personas in the Bush administration. Balding, gray-haired, just five feet eight in his stocking feet, he had what one journalist called the "gaunt demeanor of a church elder." The retired lieutenant general possessed nothing like the confident pose of natural-born leaders such as James Baker or Colin Powell. He was more comfortable in the shadows, invisible and off to the side. In appearance, he looked more like a presidential aide than a presidential adviser; more servant than sidekick.

Yet looks can be deceiving. For Scowcroft's real effectiveness—the third ingredient in his winning formula—was that he was closer to the president than anyone else during the four years of the Bush presidency, closer even than Baker. He was constantly at Bush's side—in the Oval Office, at Camp David, sailing on the waters off Kennebunkport. On an average day, he could spend as many as four hours with the president. That's how Bush wanted it. Operating in the shadows, Scowcroft was the president's close and constant confidant. More, he was, Bush confided, "the closest friend in all things"—as close to family as one could get without being blood-related.

It wasn't just about friendship, though that was important, especially to a Yankee aristocrat like Bush. It was also, and especially, about the exercise of power. Whereas many in Washington sought power through publicity, Scowcroft achieved power through proximity. He built a relationship with the president based on loyalty and trust. His self-effacement helped, as did the fact, as Bush noted, that "Brent doesn't want anything." At times, one NSC staffer recalls, "Bush and Scowcroft were like two dimensions of the same person. He was almost like a kind of doppelganger for Bush." That reality gave Scowcroft tremendous power, both within the administration as a person everyone knew spoke directly for the president and to the world outside. Scowcroft used that power skillfully and judiciously, always making sure that he would not encroach on the responsibilities of other key presidential advisers, like Baker or Cheney, who in turn respected his close relationship with the president.

Aside from proximity, Bush's activism in foreign affairs helped to empower his national security adviser. The near-instantaneous access to all the latest information enabled Bush to act quickly in response to crises or evolving situations without having to involve other departments. Information would come into the Situation Room; the NSC staff could help analyze and evaluate it; and Bush could get on the phone with leaders around the world to address the issue at hand. During August 1990, the first month of the Gulf crisis, Bush would make no less than sixty-two phone calls to foreign leaders—and not only to such close and important allies and partners as British Prime Minister Margaret Thatcher and Saudi King Fahd, but also to more obscure leaders such as Carlos Andres Perez, president of Venezuela. Such activism naturally enhanced the centrality of the White House in America's foreign relations—and with it the power of the person in charge of managing foreign policy for the president. To underscore that reality in procedural terms, Bush agreed from the outset of his administration to have Scowcroft and Gates chair the most important interagency committees (of principals and deputies), something that had never been done until that point. This guaranteed that all important business would be channeled through the NSC to the White House, which was exactly how Bush and Scowcroft wanted it.

Brent Scowcroft's emergence as the preeminent foreign policy adviser to the president evolved over the first eighteen months of the administration. During the first year, when relations with Moscow and Europe's post–Cold War evolution stood central, Scowcroft's influence was more noticeable in some areas (arms control) than in others (diplomacy with Germany and the Soviet Union). The conventional wisdom at the time was that foreign policy was largely the domain of the president and his secretary of state—"The Fabulous Bush and Baker Boys" was how the *New York Times* portrayed it—though that underestimated the already vital role of the national security adviser. By the time of the Gulf crisis of 1990–91, however, there was no doubt anymore that Scowcroft had a uniquely influential, and in many ways unrivaled, relationship with the president.

When the Bush administration took office in January 1989, there was a great deal stirring in Europe and the Soviet Union. In the preceding years, Mikhail Gorbachev had embarked on far-reaching, historically unprecedented, economic and political reforms—*perestroika* and *glasnost*—at home and large-scale change abroad. The latter included agreement with the United States in 1987 to eliminate an entire class of nuclear missiles and Gorbachev's announcement at the United Nations in December 1988 that the Soviet Union's massive conventional forces would be unilaterally reduced by 500,000 men and 10,000 tanks in two years. A significant portion of these cuts (including 5,000 tanks) would come from Soviet forces stationed in Eastern Europe.

The new, dynamic Soviet leader was clearly on the offensive. But whereas the Reagan administration and most of America's allies in Europe were enchanted by the changes—Britain's Iron Lady, Margaret Thatcher, had said of him that "this is a man I can do business with"—the new Bush administration was deeply skeptical. "There are those who want to declare the Cold War ended," Dick Cheney said upon taking office at Defense, "but I believe caution is in order." The Pentagon chief's sentiment was shared by Bush and Scowcroft. So, rather than continuing Reagan's embrace of the Soviet leader, they ordered a months-long review of U.S. policy toward Europe, the Soviet Union, and arms control.

Time, though, would not stand still while the administration conducted its strategic review. Ever the political operator, Baker increasingly worried that Gorbachev represented a major challenge in the battle for public opinion, not only in Europe but in the United States, and he urged Bush to take the initiative away from the Soviet leader. As public criticism of the administration's passivity mounted (including from former President Reagan), Bush told Scowcroft that the administration needed a more forward-leaning message. "We've got to make clear that we know important stuff is happening and we're not just sitting here on our duffs." Scowcroft responded by going on NBC's *Meet the Press* to acknowledge the changes that were going on and claim them as evidence "that the West has won." He also began to look for ways to challenge the Soviet leader on the one issue that really counted: the future of Eastern Europe.

Ultimately, real change in Moscow would require the end of Soviet dominion over the countries of Eastern Europe, and Scowcroft believed that this would only come about if Soviet troops were removed from those countries. Already during the transition, he had suggested to Bush that he might consider proposing the withdrawal of U.S. and Soviet forces from Central Europe; now, with public pressure for an American response to Gorbachev's peace overtures growing, the national security adviser pressed again for a bold initiative along these lines. Although the Pentagon was initially opposed to any consideration of manpower reductions, Bush and Baker liked the boldness of trying to best the Soviet leader at his own game. Weeks of intense discussions in the small core group followed, with Cheney, Baker, Scowcroft, and others all making their case before the president. In the end, Bush endorsed Scowcroft's idea of using troop cuts to effect change in Europe, and he used his first NATO summit meeting, in May 1989, to introduce a proposal that would impose an equal ceiling on U.S. and Soviet troops in Europe. Because Soviet troop levels in Europe were so much higher to begin with, Bush's proposal, though cutting American deployments by 25 percent, required far larger reductions in the number of Soviet troops deployed in Eastern Europe. The allies reacted enthusiastically to Bush's ideas, and Moscow indicated it was ready to negotiate on the issue. Scowcroft's initiative was starting to bear fruit.

In the months that followed these dramatic developments, change enveloped the Soviet Union and Europe. In the autumn of 1989, the East witnessed unprecedented political upheaval—first in Poland, then in Hungary and Czechoslovakia, and finally in East Germany, Bulgaria, and Romania. On November 9, the Berlin Wall, symbol of Europe's division and Soviet repression, came tumbling down. While Scowcroft still privately worried that Gorbachev might not last, Baker saw these historic developments as an opportunity to lock in lasting change. In the months that followed, the secretary of state was the one pressing to move forward, winning Bush's backing for a speedy negotiation of Germany's unification within NATO, a remarkable achievement, and making major strides in negotiating agreements on conventional, chemical, and nuclear arms. Scowcroft played the insider role, making sure that everyone's equities were protected and pushing his own positions, in particularly on nuclear weapons issues. It was an effective effort, which saw the Bush administration help broker peaceful—and lasting—change throughout Europe.

By late 1990 and early 1991, with the steady consolidation of positive political change in Eastern Europe, a new worry came to dominate the administration's deliberations: the stability of the Soviet Union itself. Gorbachev was increasingly challenged from within, not only by hard-liners on the right but also by reformers from the left. Having at first regarded the Soviet leader with considerable unease, Bush and Scowcroft grew increasingly concerned that the man they now viewed as the main proponent of positive change might be ousted. As a result, they were wary of backing any policies that might weaken Gorbachev's hold on power—be it greater autonomy (let alone independence) for individual Soviet republics or calls for more far-reaching political and economic reforms by Boris Yeltsin, who had been elected president of the Russian Republic. "Our policy has to be based on our national interest, and we have an interest in the stability of the Soviet Union," Scowcroft explained at an NSC meeting in 1991. "The instability of the USSR would be a threat to us. To peck away at the legitimacy of the regime in power would not be to promote stability."

Bush shared Scowcroft's perspective, though less for the realist reasons his national security adviser embraced than for the fact that he came to see Gorbachev as the personal embodiment of everything positive that had occurred. To Bush, Gorbachev was *perestroika,* and he was not about to turn his back on him—even though many of the Soviet Union's own citizens were doing just that. "It's tempting to say, 'Wouldn't it be great if the Soviet empire broke up?'" Bush told Scowcroft privately. "But that's not really practical or smart." So Bush supported the unity of the USSR, even when it concerned the Baltic Republics, whose forcible incorporation into the Soviet Union in 1945 the United States had never recognized. And he traveled to Ukraine in August 1991 to deliver a speech in support of Gorbachev—soon dubbed the "Chicken Kiev" speech—in which he denounced the stirrings for independence as "a suicidal nationalism." In the end, though, loyalty and friendship, even from the president of the United States, could not save Gorbachev. Following a failed coup in late summer 1991, it had become clear to all that power in the Soviet Union had slipped ineluctably from the center to the republics. On Christmas Day 1991, Gorbachev recognized the dissolution of the Union of Socialist Soviet Republics, and resigned as its last president. The Cold War had ended. A new world lay ahead.

The reality of this new world had already become evident a year earlier. On the evening of August 1, 1990, news reached Washington that hundreds of thousands of Iraqi troops had crossed into Kuwait with the express purpose of making the small Arab oil state Iraq's nineteenth province. From the very first moment of the crisis, Brent Scowcroft took charge of the effort to fashion an American response. He literally took control of the process overnight, chairing a series of deputies meetings (Gates was on vacation), drafting presidential orders freezing Iraqi and Kuwaiti assets, and preparing for an NSC meeting the president would chair early the following morning. Having gained the confidence of other key players in the administration, built an effective and cooperative interagency process, and established his close proximity to the president, Scowcroft now sought to make his own views of the stakes, goals, and strategies the president's.

Others within the administration also saw the importance of responding strongly and without equivocation to Iraq's invasion. But Scowcroft, Bob Gates recalled, "was perhaps a step ahead. He played a central role in bringing together the consensus that formed rather quickly and in the crystallization of the U.S. response." Baker, who was in Siberia when news of the invasion first hit, initially viewed the crisis primarily through the prism of U.S. relations with the Soviet Union. He worked assiduously during the days, weeks, and months that followed to keep Moscow as an ally in the confrontation with Baghdad. Cheney, meanwhile, focused on the military demands of the response, including the deployments of hundreds of thousands of troops, tanks, planes, and ships to the region. It was left to the national security adviser to pull these disparate efforts together into a single, successful strategy to counter Saddam Hussein's Iraq.

Scowcroft's crucial role was apparent from the start. The first NSC meeting on the crisis, which convened in the Cabinet Room at 8:00 a.m. on August 2, got off to a bad start. In a photo-op prior to the meeting, the president made clear that "we're not discussing intervention." He wanted to hear from his advisers about possible military options, but reiterated that "I'm not contemplating such action." That wasn't quite the way Scowcroft would have wanted to signal America's intentions. Bush's "choice of words was not felicitous," he later recalled, and the statement would have to be corrected. Worse, the actual meeting that followed once the press had departed proved meandering, chaotic, and lacking in passion. Much of the discussion focused on how to cope with the consequences for the oil market and the U.S. economy of Iraq's seizure of the Kuwaiti oil fields. It was as if the invasion had become a fait accompli to which the United States would have to accommodate itself. "I was frankly appalled at the undertone of the discussion," Scowcroft noted later. Much of the discussion "tended to skip over the enormous stake the United States had in the situation, or the ramifications of the aggression on the emerging post–Cold War world." Afterward, Scowcroft mentioned his concerns to Bush. He proposed that at the next NSC meeting the following day, he should start off with a statement about the stakes involved and the need to reject the occupation of Kuwait as intolerable to American interests. Bush readily agreed, even proposing that he make such a statement himself, which Scowcroft suggested would stifle the discussions.

Scowcroft expanded on his concerns in a memo to the president in preparation for the August 3 NSC meeting. Non-military measures, he suggested, might fall short of achieving the goal of having Iraqi forces withdrawn completely and Kuwait's full sovereignty restored. The choice then would become living with the status quo or challenging Iraq directly. "I am aware as you are how costly and risky such a conflict would prove to be," Scowcroft wrote. "But so too would be accepting this new status quo. We would be setting a terrible precedent—one that would only accelerate violent centrifugal tendencies—in this emerging 'post Cold War' era. . . . We don't need to decide where to draw any lines just yet, but we need to take steps—moving forces, pressing allies and reluctant Arabs, etc.—that would at least give us a real choice if current efforts fall short."

Bush got the message. Opening the NSC meeting, the president noted that "the status quo is intolerable," and then turned the floor over to Scowcroft, who contended that the previous day's meeting might have suggested "that we may have to acquiesce to an accommodation of the situation. My personal judgment," the national security adviser went on, "is that the stakes in this for the United States are such that to accommodate Iraq should not be a policy option. There is too much at stake." And it never was an option from that point on. The next day, Bush gathered his main advisers at Camp David to hear a briefing on military options from General Powell; General Norman Schwarzkopf, the head of Central Command, with direct military responsibility for the region; and Lieutenant General Charles Horner, CENTCOM's air commander. Upon returning from Camp David the next day, Bush expressed publicly what he had concluded privately a few days earlier: "This will not stand. This will not stand, this aggression against Kuwait."

In the first weeks after the invasion, the focus of American efforts was twofold: to get as many U.S. and other troops into Saudi Arabia as possible to deter any further Iraqi incursion south; and to build a grand international coalition to squeeze Iraq economically. Baker's brilliant diplomacy, combined with Bush's indefatigable phone calls to leaders around the world, succeeded in forging a mighty coalition in support of a UN-authorized effort to reverse the Iraqi invasion and restore Kuwait's sovereignty. Many hoped that economic sanctions and the threat of military force might suffice to bring Saddam Hussein to his senses, but neither Scowcroft nor Bush ever really believed that would be enough. "I never had any faith in sanctions and I don't think the President did either," Scowcroft recalled. "I think he made up his mind early on that if Saddam did not withdraw of his own accord that we would force him out." Indeed, just three weeks after the invasion, in a discussion with Scowcroft on his speedboat *Fidelity*, while fishing for bluefish in the Atlantic, Bush made clear he was getting impatient. He wanted to know "when we could strike." He thought the Pentagon was overestimating Iraqi strength and resolve, and believed U.S. airpower might be enough to take out the Iraqi armor and planes. "I just didn't see the Iraqis as being so tough."

Once a sufficient number of U.S. forces had been deployed to Saudi Arabia to defend the kingdom from a possible Iraqi attack, the president and his top advisers turned to the question of whether to continue the troop buildup to the point where the United States would be able to force the Iraqis out of Kuwait. Whereas Powell and Baker leaned toward waiting to see if sanctions and diplomacy might work, Scowcroft and Bush believed military force was necessary. The decision to move from a defensive to an offensive posture was made with little debate or analysis of the possible consequences. The deputies were never involved in evaluating alternative options, and the actual decision to double the number of U.S. troops in the Gulf region was made by Bush, with only his inner circle—Baker, Cheney, Powell, and Scowcroft—in the room. Given Scowcroft and Bush's view of the matter from the start, there was little doubt that it would ultimately have to come to this. But the sudden and secretive decision provoked a strong political response, with Senator Sam Nunn, chair of the Senate Committee on Armed Services, holding hearings at which retired generals expressed concern about the apparent rush to war.

Although Bush and Scowcroft agreed that force would be required to reverse Iraq's aggression, they differed on the reasons why. Scowcroft, the historian and a close student of the classical realist Hans Morgenthau, saw the crisis in traditional realist terms. Iraq's invasion had upset the regional balance of power, and it was now up to the United States to restore that balance by forcing Iraq out of Kuwait and making sure that its military capacity to do harm in the future was severely (though not completely) degraded. At the same time, after the status quo ante had been restored in Kuwait, the need to maintain a stable regional balance of power required a united Iraq that was strong enough to balance Iran. Though Bush understood and shared such realist thinking, his outlook on the crisis was driven by a far more personal assessment of the danger Saddam Hussein represented. "Saddam is irrational," Bush had told his advisers on August 5. "We are dealing with a madman who has shown he will kill." By October, the president was comparing the Iraqi dictator to Adolf Hitler. He had been reading Martin Gilbert's massive study *The Second World War*, a "great, big, thick history," and he continually spoke out about the "parallel between what Hitler did to Poland and what Saddam has done to Kuwait."

Scowcroft was deeply concerned about such "flights of rhetoric."

It suggested that the real goal of any military action would not just be to ensure Iraq's ouster from Kuwait and the restoration of Kuwaiti sovereignty, but the end of Saddam's regime. As the president flew around the country campaigning for Republican candidates in the 1990 midterm elections, Gates or Scowcroft began to travel along to remind Bush that the Hitler rhetoric wasn't helpful. This seemed to have its intended effect; whereas Bush had mentioned the Nazi dictator nine times publicly in the second half of October 1990, he stopped doing so afterward. Even so, there was no denying the president's strong feelings. When Richard Haass, Scowcroft's top Middle East hand, drafted a memo to the president in late January 1991 on how the war might end, he concluded that regime change in Baghdad should not be a condition for ending the war. Not only would such a change be difficult to bring about, but it would make the critical aim of shaping a stable regional balance of power after the war more difficult to achieve.

Bush didn't buy it. He wanted a clean victory. And he wanted Saddam go. Haass drafted two more versions of the memo, each sticking to Scowcroft's realist view of what it would take to end the war. A heated Oval Office debate on the third memo showed that the president continued to believe that at the end of the day, Saddam had to go. "Mr. President, I know what you want, I just don't see how it's going to happen," Haass argued, noting that to guarantee Saddam's ouster would go beyond the administration's domestic and international writ, break up the international coalition Bush had so painstakingly assembled, and require an indefinite occupation of Iraq.

Bush's hope for Saddam's removal did not become official policy. Indeed, the National Security Directive authorizing the use of military force was silent on the matter. The purposes of the authorization, the directive stated, were the more realist ones that Scowcroft had championed: effect the withdrawal of Iraqi forces; restore Kuwait's government; and promote the security and stability of the region. To that end, U.S. military forces were ordered to destroy Iraq's weapons of mass destruction and command and control capabilities, and to eliminate the elite Republican Guard as an "effective fighting force."

And while the aim would be to "weaken Iraqi popular support for the current government," the directive explicitly ordered any military action to stop short of replacing "the current leadership of Iraq" unless Iraq used chemical, biological, or nuclear weapons, supported terrorist acts, or destroyed Kuwait's oil fields.

As Scowcroft and Bush debated how the war might end, they forgot to focus on the one issue that might arguably be even more important: what would happen after the fighting had stopped. In a serious oversight in strategic planning, there was little if any discussion of the aftermath of the war within the U.S. government or among its top leaders. It was assumed that America's overwhelming military might would suffice to meet the explicit goals of the war: restoring the status quo ante in Iraq and sufficiently degrading Iraq's military capacity to ensure a stable regional balance of power ex ante. Key officials had also begun to think about how the United States and the rest of the international community might ensure that Iraq was permanently out of the chemical, biological, nuclear, and missile business. But they had given little thought to the effects of the war on the political shape of Iraq itself—or of the region as a whole.

The national security directive authorizing the war did not address the matter. Even the terms of a cease fire, and what Iraqi military forces would and would not be allowed to do, were ignored in the planning phase and, worse, at the time of the actual cease fire negotiations. The U.S. commander of the war effort, General Schwarzkopf, was sent out to negotiate a formal end of hostilities without any political aides present to help him sort out some of the political fallout of particular cease-fire provisions. According to Chas Freeman, the U.S. ambassador to Saudi Arabia who worked closely with Schwarzkopf, there was "a total failure of integration between military and political strategy"—exactly the kind of integration that a national security adviser and his staff are supposed to do.

The guiding assumption of all the policymakers was that Saddam Hussein was unlikely to survive a major defeat at the hands of America or the world. "It was our hope that the magnitude of the defeat would lead the Iraqi generals to throw Saddam out," Gates later admitted. "Here's where we fell down." Rather than the generals rising up against Saddam Hussein, it was Iraq's Shi'ites in the south and its Kurds in the north, both of whom had suffered grievously under Saddam's rule, who seized the opportunity of Iraq's massive defeat in Kuwait to rebel against the regime. Their actions may have been spurred by a statement the president made on February 15, 1991, shortly before the ground war started: "There is another way for the bloodshed to stop," Bush had declared. "And that is, for the Iraqi military and the Iraqi people to take matters into their own hands—to force Saddam Hussein, the dictator, to step aside and to comply with the United Nations resolutions and then rejoin the family of peace-loving nations." The intent of this statement was to have the generals rise up; it never occurred to Bush or Scowcroft that the Iraqi people would do so themselves (despite the direct appeal "to take matters into their own hands"). It proved to be a deeply flawed assumption— with fateful consequences for U.S. policy in the region.

The uprising was brutally crushed by Saddam's forces—including Republican Guard forces that had escaped destruction, as well as attack helicopters that had not been grounded by the cease-fire terms. Though Bush had been adamant in wishing Saddam's ouster, he was now equally adamant not to see Americans "bogged down in a civil war." The net effect was not only that the rebellion supported by large majorities of the Iraqi people failed, but that by crushing it, Saddam Hussein was able to rebuild much of the power his military defeat had undermined just weeks earlier. As a result, U.S. policy toward Iraq and the region had to be refocused—and it was, precisely in the direction that Scowcroft had worked so hard to resist.

By April 1991, it was clear that the future stability of Iraq and the region required the removal of Saddam Hussein. "The U.S./international community continues to support Iraq's territorial integrity," the State Department cabled key ambassadors previewing the change in strategy, "but now wants a new Iraqi leadership. Because of the invasion and occupation of Kuwait and the brutal repression of his people, Saddam is discredited and cannot be redeemed." The second major change was the necessity to maintain a significant U.S. military presence in the region—both to deter Iraq from invading any of its neighbors and to provide a modicum of protection for Iraqi populations, and especially for the Kurds up north. Most significant, the open-ended presence of American military forces in Saudi Arabia, which both the Bush administration and the Saudi royal family had sought to avoid, had now become a reality, with consequences that would be felt only many years later.

Brent Scowcroft proved to be an extraordinarily effective national security adviser, especially during the turbulent times that engulfed America and the world in the first two years of the Bush administration. His winning formula for effectiveness—gain the confidence of colleagues, run a transparent and collegial process, and secure power through proximity to the president—is one that every other person who holds the office would do well to make their own. The most important lesson Scowcroft taught during his second stint as national security adviser was that power in Washington need not be a relative concept: you can gain and exercise power and influence without having to deprive other players of theirs. In this respect, the Scowcroft process resembled the one that McGeorge Bundy had put in place for John F. Kennedy almost thirty years before.

But while Scowcroft's tenure as George H. W. Bush's closest adviser was effective, the four years he served in this position were not an unalloyed success. The decision-making process suffered from two main weaknesses during the Bush presidency. The first was a closed, and exceedingly small, circle of decision makers, which tended to stifle new thinking. Part of the problem was Bush's desire to make decisions surrounded by friends, many of whom saw the world and its challenges in the same way. "Bush wants twins around him," observed the presidential scholar James David Barber, "and that can be dangerous." Another part of the same problem was the natural consequence of making decisions in small groups. "By the midpoint of the administration," Robert Hutchings, an NSC staff aide, recalled, "a closed and self-contained decision-making circle [had become] increasingly impervious to new and unconventional ideas at the very time that unconventional thinking was most needed." And part of the problem lay with Scowcroft, who, as time went by, increasingly became an advocate for a particular position rather than the guardian of an open and analytical process. Although in the run-up to the Panama invasion in December 1989, Scowcroft would probe the military commanders on their plans through a series of difficult but important questions, when it came to the Gulf War, that critical probing role was played more by Colin Powell (by then the president's chief military adviser) than by Bush's national security adviser.

The second weakness lay in the fact that Bush and Scowcroft's experiences and perspectives made them better at dealing with the breakdown of the old world than with building a new one. Their much vaunted "New World Order," which stressed the importance of upholding international rules for maintaining global order, was decidedly old-school—focusing on states, and relations among them. It said nothing about what the United States should do when empires break up, ethnic conflicts engulf nations, or states suffer internal collapse—precisely the kinds of problems that came to dominate the second half of their administration. As a result, they proved largely incapable of dealing with these problems. When Scowcroft briefed Bush on the conflict in the Balkans, for instance, the president seemed confused by the complexity of the region, "asking again and again which side was which, who were the Bosnians, who were the Bosnian Serbs, who were the Bosnian Muslims," as David Halberstam writes. "The more Scowcroft talked the more the shadow of perplexity seemed to come over Bush's face."

The disintegration of Yugoslavia, the breakup of the Soviet Union, the collapse of Somalia—these and other conflicts engulfing the world in the early 1990s were in many ways beyond the conceptual worldview of the president and his national security adviser. In most cases, they decided to do too little about the dangers that accompanied these violent upheavals, leaving them to the next president and national security team to deal with.

7

"You Have to Drive the Process"

———

I t's the economy, stupid!" With that campaign slogan, a small-state governor, inexperienced in foreign affairs, beat an incumbent president running on that very experience in 1992. Bill Clinton was the first person born after World War II to run for and win the presidency. He understood, in a way George Bush did not, that in the wake of the Cold War, economic issues and domestic concerns rather than national security were uppermost in people's minds. Bush's successful management of the Cold War's demise and his Gulf War victory in 1991 amounted to little when it came to his reelection. By November 1992, he was able to muster just 37 percent of the national vote—the lowest percentage for an incumbent president in eighty years.

There was a lesson here for the victorious candidate: never forget that the American people wanted their president to put their economic and domestic concerns first. Clinton promised to "focus like a laser beam on this economy" in his first postelection interview. "Foreign policy will come into play in part as it affects the economy." Though he returned congratulatory phone calls from domestic supporters immediately, he asked Warren Christopher, who headed the transition, to return some of the calls from foreign leaders. In contrast to his predecessors, Clinton chose his economic team first, and then organized a large symposium with business, labor, and other leaders to consider how to get the economy on track. The first assistant to the president he named was Robert Rubin, chairman of Goldman Sachs, as assistant for economic policy, not national security. Rubin was to run a new White House entity, the National Economic Council, whose creation sent a strong signal of changed priorities. Clinton shared the widely held view that the national security apparatus under Bush and previous presidents had given only subordinate emphasis to economic aspects of foreign policy. This he wanted to change. Setting up a White House–based Council, led by a senior economic adviser who had his full confidence, would ensure that economic concerns would receive at least equal consideration in foreign policy.

The transition period set the tone for the first year of Bill Clinton's presidency. In a meeting with his entire cabinet in Camp David shortly after his inauguration, Clinton laid out his priorities for the first one hundred days: economic recovery, health care, welfare reform, political reform, national service. Foreign policy was notably absent. "That's why he is president and George Bush isn't," explained a top Clinton aide, when asked about the omission. "He's interested in foreign policy, but right now that's not where he is focused," said another. Instead, Clinton delegated much of the foreign policy business to his advisers—leaving one frustrated top national security aide to suggest wryly that Tony Lake, Clinton's NSC adviser, was in effect the president for foreign policy.

The problem for Clinton, however, was that while he hoped his advisers would take care of brewing foreign crises in Somalia, Bosnia, and Haiti, none of these conflicts was easily taken care off. Thus, even as he was making progress on his economic and domestic agenda during his first year in office, these crises required high-level attention. The president failed to give them that attention early on—with significant consequences both for the course of the conflicts abroad and for his political standing at home. Then, recognizing the problem, Clinton and Lake as his national security adviser moved during their second year to revamp the way they approached foreign policy. They built a tighter, more decisive process. Front-burner issues, including Haiti and Bosnia, were addressed with clear resolve, while priority questions such as NATO enlargement, the Middle East, China, Russia, trade, and international financial stability were being handled more directly from the top. Aided by a new team in his second term, Clinton increasingly focused on a growing set of issues arising out of globalization—the environment, weapons proliferation, and terrorism high amongst them. By this time, a president more comfortable and confident of his abilities had come to understand that success at home required full engagement abroad.

With the initial focus on economic issues, Clinton's national security team was assembled almost as an afterthought. A top concern for the new president was collegiality. He wanted to avoid the struggles over policy and power that had characterized the last Democratic administration, when the secretary of state and national security adviser were constantly at each other's throats. His model was the Bush national security team, which had worked cooperatively and collegially in dealing with the big challenges around the world. "There was a real determination on the part of key architects of the transition," recalls James Steinberg, who was a member of that effort, "both in terms of personnel selection and in terms of certain styles that they wanted to convey, that the Scowcroft-Baker model was quite successful. They didn't agree with the policy, but they thought that this was the way people ought to do business."

The choice of national security adviser was a difficult one for Clinton. He was close to Samuel (Sandy) Berger, an international lawyer who served as the State Department's deputy director of policy planning during the Carter administration. They had met during the 1972 McGovern campaign, and over the years Berger had introduced Clinton to the Washington foreign policy establishment. During the 1992 campaign, however, Berger had brought in the more experienced Anthony Lake because he believed the Arkansas governor needed the counsel of someone with a more substantial inside track record. Lake, a former Foreign Service officer turned academic, had been Berger's boss at State and had served at the NSC under Kissinger. Once elected, Clinton had to choose between Berger's friendship and Lake's experience. In the end, Berger decided for him, telling the president-elect that he should make Lake his national security adviser while he, Berger, would serve as Lake's deputy.

Lake was reluctant to take the job, telling some friends during the campaign that he would not go back into government even while knowing that he could never really say no to a president if he were asked—as he knew Clinton might. His ambivalence was personal rather than professional; his previous experience working in the White House, as an executive assistant to Henry Kissinger, as well as the long hours he had toiled as head of policy planning in the Carter administration, had taken their toll on his family.

Lake knew that another stint on the inside, this time in the most demanding of all national security jobs, would come at a high personal cost. Initially, he thought he would do the job for a year, "simply because I'm more experienced than anybody else," and then return to his farm in western Massachusetts to raise his herd of cattle, tap maple trees for syrup, and teach at Mount Holyoke on the side. But he stayed on through the entire first term, driven in part by the need to resolve the festering problem of Bosnia, somewhat to the frustration of Berger, who had gotten him the job and had thought that he might take over a year or two earlier.

Despite his ambivalence, Lake had been preparing for the NSC job all of his life. After earning his bachelor's degree at Harvard and doing graduate work at Trinity College, Cambridge, he joined the Foreign Service in 1962, following the clarion call of John F. Kennedy for a new generation to "ask what you can do for your country." His first posting was to Vietnam. He was convinced America could do anything, including bringing democracy to this far-flung corner of the world. On the plane over to Saigon he read Graham Greene's *The Quiet American*, whose main character was as young and idealistic as Lake, but whose endeavors to instill the values of liberty and democracy abroad proved unsuccessful. "I remember thinking to myself,

'What does Graham Greene know?'" Lake recalls. "Because that's exactly what I believed." Such idealism was still possible in these early years of America's involvement in Vietnam, and Lake worked hard to spread American ideals. He rose rapidly, becoming a staff assistant to Henry Cabot Lodge, the U.S. ambassador in Saigon.

The young Foreign Service officer returned to Washington in 1965, serving first on the Vietnam desk at State and then as staff assistant to Nicholas Katzenbach, the under secretary of state. He had been hired by U. Alexis Johnson, Katzenbach's deputy, despite some skepticism about Lake's personnel report. "No foreign service officer that young is that good," Johnson had said. But throughout this time at the State Department, doubts about America's Vietnam policy had begun to grow in Lake's mind, and in 1967 he decided to take academic leave rather than try to defend a policy he found increasingly indefensible. While at Princeton, from which he eventually earned his doctorate, he received a call from Henry Kissinger, Nixon's national security adviser, requesting that Lake be his special assistant. Kissinger told Lake that the president was committed to ending America's involvement in the war, so Lake joined the team, accompanying the national security adviser to the secret Paris talks with the North Vietnamese in 1969. But he was soon disillusioned again, and he resigned a year later in protest over Nixon's decision to invade Cambodia.

Lake subsequently signed on with the 1972 presidential campaign of Maine Senator Ed Muskie as his foreign policy coordinator. When the Democrats came to power in 1977, he became a close aide to Secretaries of State Cyrus Vance and Muskie, serving as their policy planning chief during the Carter administration. A decade later, Lake and Sandy Berger became, in Lake's words, a "wholly owned subsidiary" of the Clinton presidential campaign, and the two of them were provided "a lot of running room" on developing its foreign policy aspects. After the election, Lake only had a "pro forma" conversation with Clinton about the job; he was basically expected to continue the pattern of the campaign—keeping Clinton informed but otherwise taking care of the problems that were out there.

In contrast to Lake, Warren Christopher really did want to be secretary of state. He had served as deputy attorney general in the Johnson administration, and he was Vance's number two under Carter. There, he had worked his heart out to secure the release of the American hostages held in Tehran. When Vance resigned over the ill-fated hostage rescue mission in April 1980, Christopher had hoped and expected to take his place, and he was deeply disappointed when Carter appointed Muskie instead.

Christopher's courtly demeanor masked an intensely ambitious man. When Clinton asked him to chair the transition (along with Vernon Jordan), Christopher had told the president-elect that he "assumed in undertaking this role that I would not have a major responsibility in the future." Indeed, Clinton considered others for the job of secretary of state—Senators Sam Nunn and Bill Bradley, and even Colin Powell, then still the chairman of the Joint Chiefs of Staff. So it was somewhat of a surprise to those who did not know Christopher that Clinton asked the sixty-eight-year-old lawyer to assume the position. Though he hadn't actively campaigned for the job, he had indicated in subtle ways that he very much wanted it; and so, at Vernon Jordan's strong urging, Clinton ultimately decided to offer it to him. "People ask me all the time, how did you ever decide to make Warren Christopher your first secretary of state," Clinton once recalled. "And I say, you know, I don't know—it just sort of came to me in the transition process—which Warren Christopher *ran!*"

A seasoned hand, Christopher seemed a safe choice. He understood that Clinton wanted to focus on domestic issues, and the president trusted his secretary of state to make sure foreign policy would not get in his way. The lawyerly and precise Christopher would approach the job with great care, steadiness, and without any of the showiness that others might bring to the task. What wasn't so obvious was whether Christopher had any clear vision of how the United States should behave in this very new, post–Cold War world. A firm hand when the direction was clear, he might not be able to chart a steady course in uncharted waters. "Dean Rusk without the charisma," was how some of his critics greeted the choice. The "perfect Number Two," others concluded.

Les Aspin, the powerful chairman of the House Armed Services Committee, was selected to head the Pentagon more for what he knew than for what he could do. Aspin was one of Robert McNamara's original whiz kids, a brilliant defense intellectual, who had challenged the outgoing administration on the strategic direction of its overall defense policy (though not, importantly, on the Gulf War, as had his Senate counterpart, Sam Nunn). He came to the Pentagon armed with big ideas on how to downsize the military and remake the policy arm of the secretary's office into a major national security player. Instead of the usual two assistant secretary–led policy bureaus, Aspin proposed to create six new offices—for counterproliferation and nuclear security, democracy and peacekeeping, strategy and resources, plans and policy, economics, and environmental security—and he nominated prominent public policy professionals to head each of them. The idea, apparently, was for Defense to do much of State's job as well.

Missing from this initial organizational activity was a clear sense of how the incoming defense secretary would relate to the department's main constituency, the uniformed military. Indeed Colin Powell, who remained as chairman of the Joint Chiefs, had warned Clinton in their first meeting that Aspin, while brilliant, might not be quite up to the job. "Smart's not everything in running the Pentagon," Powell noted when the president-elect asked what he thought about Aspin. "Les might not bring quite the management style you're looking for." Rumpled and professorial, Aspin had never run anything larger than a House committee staff—and certainly nothing like the behemoth bureaucracy that is the Pentagon. His interests lay in policy not process, in discussions not decisions. The military and many civilians within the Pentagon were used to a culture of command; Aspin failed to provide it, with big consequences. "He lost the building," one senior administration official observed, "and once you lose them, it's very, very hard to win them back."

Aside from collegiality, the guiding philosophy for picking Clinton's national security team—and the cabinet as a whole—was to ensure broad diversity among its members, so that it would "look like

America." The public announcement of the team therefore included not only Clinton's choices for the top three posts (all white men) but also the nomination of Madeleine Albright as U.S. Ambassador to the United Nations and Clifton Wharton, an African-American agricultural economist who had served as a university president in Michigan and New York, as deputy secretary of state. Clinton was determined to have a conservative at Defense or the CIA, and he nominated R. James Woolsey, a Democrat who had served as an arms control negotiator in the Bush administration, to head the intelligence agency.

Most of the new players knew each other well: Lake had worked with Christopher at State under Carter; Aspin had been a close friend of many; Albright and Berger had traveled in the same Georgetown circles for two decades; even Woolsey had dabbled in the same kinds of national security get-togethers that many of the others had. But this group of players did not constitute a team, in the sense of the one Bush had assembled four years earlier. Most critically, unlike Bush's team, Clinton's lacked a captain. The president would be involved in national security issues whenever necessary. He was interested in many of them, much more than he generally let on, and he would make all the important decisions. But he would not be spending a lot of time on foreign policy. He did not attend many of the meetings, nor did he engage in the kinds of informal, freewheeling discussions that Bush had liked and that Clinton himself loved on domestic and economic policy.

David Gergen, who joined the Clinton White House a few months into the administration to improve communications, observed that while most presidents spend about 60 percent of their time on foreign affairs and Bush might have spent as much as 75 percent of his time, Clinton barely spent 25 percent during his first year. "My premise," Clinton explained "was that the American people were hungry for a president who showed that he knew something had to be done here to address our problems at home that had been long neglected." At one point, the president even sounded a note of apology when he said that he "had to take a good deal of time off to deal with the foreign policy responsibilities of the President."

Without its captain, the incoming national security team was left to its own devices. The guiding philosophy was to avoid the power struggles of the Carter years and to keep foreign policy off Clinton's desk. Both factors influenced the decision to maintain the same basic organizational structure that had operated under the previous administration. Aside from the statutory National Security Council, which met only infrequently, there was a three-level structure: a Principals Committee for cabinet secretaries, chaired by Lake; a Deputies Committee for deputy and under secretaries, chaired by Berger; and Interagency Working Groups ("I-wigs") for assistant secretaries, chaired either by a senior director at the NSC (in the case of most functional issues) or by departmental assistant secretaries. The only real change was the decision to expand the membership of these committees. For example, in addition to its statutory members and advisers, the NSC now included the Treasury secretary, Lloyd Bentsen; the chief of staff to the president, Thomas (Mack) McLarty; the U.S. representative to the United Nations, Madeleine Albright; and the assistant to the president for economic policy, Robert Rubin. The last two also served on the Principals Committee. In another departure from past practice, Vice President Al Gore's national security adviser, Leon Fuerth, was a member of the Deputies Committee (and generally attended meetings of the principals as well).

The decision to retain the previous organizational structure reflected not only appreciation for the Bush-Scowcroft system, but also a belief that by mimicking that structure they could enhance collegiality and smooth operations. "This administration wanted to put foreign policy on autopilot," recalled one former NSC staffer, "and the Clinton people consciously chose the Bush model to do that." Even more unusual, Lake made a conscious effort during the transition to meet with many of Scowcroft's people because he wanted to be as non-partisan as possible. Lake kept on ten staffers from the Scowcroft NSC (out of forty-five overall). He also sought to hire a large number of career people, both to stress continuity and to reduce the pull of partisanship. The decision to opt for organizational continuity—even though the two administrations were run by different political parties—was an important one. It institutionalized the basic operation of the National Security Council and its staff. Indeed, the next Bush administration would follow the Clinton example and keep the basic structure, leaving the organization (as opposed to its actual operation) essentially unchanged for the past twenty years.

This continuity solidified the central role of the national security adviser and his staff in the making of America's foreign policy. Interestingly, there was little debate about the decision. Neither Christopher nor Aspin objected to the notion of Lake chairing the main policymaking committee, even though the prerogative of the national security adviser had been a major bone of contention during the Carter administration—and many others. One reason why they accepted Lake's proposed role was that he was junior to them and they believed he would be more the coordinator than the advocate, as was indeed his intent. Another was that Christopher may not have appreciated the importance of the document—Presidential Decision Directive 2 on the organization of the NSC—that Lake had drafted and the president signed. "Tony understood the politics of the NSC," Berger suggested. "I am not sure whether Chris understood [the impact of the document on] how the government was going to be organized in the Clinton administration."

At the outset of the administration, though, Lake did not seek preeminence over foreign policy. He conceived of his job in textbook terms; indeed, he (along with Leslie Gelb and one of the present authors) had written the book on the topic. In *Our Own Worst Enemy,* a critical look at U.S. foreign policymaking published eight years before Clinton's election, Lake and his colleagues had argued that the NSC adviser should be "strictly an inside operator. [He] should not speak publicly, engage in diplomacy, nor undermine the Secretary with Congress or the news media."

Lake took his own prescription to heart. One of his role models for the job was Andrew Goodpaster, the quiet, efficient, and effective aide

to President Dwight D. Eisenhower. Another was Brent Scowcroft—
during his first stint, under President Ford. Stronger, perhaps, were
the negative role models, Henry Kissinger and Zbigniew Brzezinski.
Lake wasn't going to go out and speak publicly, conceal things from
the secretary of state, push his own views much, or be operational in
any way. He had a self-described "passion for anonymity," so much
so that when the *New York Times* published an article about Eric Liu,
a junior White House speechwriter, the accompanying photograph
of Clinton, Liu, and Lake referred to the national security adviser as
"an unidentified man"—much to Lake's amusement. Some referred
to him as "the submarine," and when he did surface publicly to give
his first speech as national security adviser some nine months into the
first term, others dubbed his debut "Garbo speaks."

As self-defined policy coordinator, Lake worked hard to forge a
consensus among the president's top advisers. That was what Clinton
wanted. Although the president would always want to know what
the options were, "he liked to have that consensus," Lake explained.
"There is a comfort you get in hearing that all your advisers agree."
It also reduced the amount of time he had to devote to these issues.
Of course, the search for consensus could at times prove arduous,
especially on tough issues that might involve the use of force or on
those in which a particular agency would have a great stake. In the
early months of the administration, issues could be debated endlessly
in what Powell called a "Renaissance Weekend style of policy making." On some of these issues, though, Lake believed it important to
discuss first principles. When it came to Bosnia, for example, Lake
wanted to go back to basics, in order to find a good answer and avoid
simply applying the rhetoric of the campaign. The simple solutions
bandied about by Clinton as a candidate all of a sudden didn't look
so simple when you actually were responsible for bringing them
about. On other occasions, the problem was the strong objection of
an agency and Lake's reluctance to overrule it. This was particularly
the case when it was the Pentagon objecting. "A very big part of the
national security adviser's role," Berger argued, "is to avoid putting
the president in a situation where he had to do something that over-

ruled the Pentagon." And so, in the absence of consensus, there often was no decision—just endless discussion and debate.

The administration's indecisiveness in foreign policy reflected the absence of a team captain. With Clinton focused on other issues, there was no one who had either the president's confidence or the capacity to lead in his stead. Though Warren Christopher had played a key role in heading the vice-presidential selection process and the transition, Clinton had hardly known him before. And Christopher wasn't about to take the lead without the president telling him to. At State, Christopher remained the lawyer he had always been, trying to anticipate his client's needs and desires, but not charting any clear direction for the president to follow. This might have worked for a president with great confidence and interest in foreign affairs, but it didn't in the case of a president who was uncertain about what to do and how much to engage. "What Clinton needed," John Harris has argued in his study of the forty-second president, "was someone who could quiet Clinton's doubts through the force of certitude." Bentsen's strength as Treasury secretary was his ability to do just that. Christopher either couldn't or wouldn't. Instead, he sought to "read and respond to his boss's wishes and second-guessing in ways that amplified uncertainties rather than put them to rest."

Lake was no more able to lead. Not only had he defined his role as coordinator, but Clinton knew Lake little better than he knew his secretary of state. They had met only eighteen months before the elections, and during the campaign Lake had remained at his Massachusetts farm, dispensing advice from afar and leaving much of the direct contact with Clinton and his staff to Sandy Berger and Nancy Soderberg (a former Ted Kennedy staffer, who had been based in Little Rock, and traveled with the candidate throughout the campaign). Nor, once in office, did Lake seek to establish the kind of close, friendly, and huggable relationship Clinton valued so much. Lake believed that he could not do his job as well if he succumbed to being the president's "friend," he later recalled. "It could be hard to draw the line between a friend and being a courtier." It would take some time for the two very different men—"the gregarious, schmoozing Arkansan and the reserved, business-like New Englander"—to understand and accommodate each other's style.

Nor, of course, could Berger take the lead. He clearly had the president's confidence. But he was a deputy, not a principal, which made it impossible to be the captain. Moreover, by his own rueful admission, Lake felt threatened by Sandy Berger's closeness to the president in the first year or so—leading Berger to complain that while he would dribble the ball up the court, Lake would always make sure that he was the one to put it in the basket. One other person could have been the team's captain: Al Gore, the vice president. Clinton and Gore had agreed that the vice president would have a very large and substantial role in the administration, and his key national security staffer Leon Fuerth was closely integrated into the NSC process. The vice president did take the lead on a number of issues: reorganizing the government was one; broadening and deepening the relationship with Russia was another. But although his role was to be larger and more powerful than that of any vice president before, Gore was always careful to lead alongside, not in place of, the president.

There was, of course, competition within the national security team, though never as backbiting or ugly as it had been during the 1970s and 1980s. Both Lake and Christopher were deeply devoted to an open and transparent process, in which neither would try to undercut or cut out the other. But they were not indifferent to their policy impact, real and perceived. Christopher was, as Elizabeth Drew notes in her magisterial study of the administration's first year in office, "constantly concerned about his place in the administration's firmament—more concerned than a man of his experience, who had the trust and respect of the President, should have been." As for Lake, "Tony is the most competitive person I know," said a close friend. "He is even competitive at being obscure." A few weeks into the administration, a quiet struggle broke out between Christopher and Lake over who would accompany Clinton in his first one-on-one meeting with Russian president Boris Yeltsin. Both couldn't do so, but neither wanted the other to have the prominence that accompanying the president naturally implied. In the end, Lake suggested to the president that he take along instead his close friend Strobe Talbott, a fluent Russian speaker Clinton had put in charge of his Russia policy—setting a pattern that would endure through the rest of the administration.

The team also lacked a common worldview. All of its members favored broad international engagement, working with allies and within multilateral institutions, and promoting America's core values of democracy, human rights, and open economies. But they differed over the means, especially when it came to the question of using military force. Aspin, perhaps reflecting the sentiment of the uniformed military, was skeptical about its utility or appropriateness, particularly in conflicts where there was no clear national interest at stake. Gore and Albright believed that force was necessary to end such conflicts, and they consistently pushed to deploy it. Christopher's views were less settled; he tended to move back and forth between more or less engagement, often reflecting where he thought the president might end up. Lake was sympathetic to the views of Gore and Albright, but Vietnam weighed heavily on him. He warned that even good intentions "can lead to a war of murderous naïveté." When Albright challenged Colin Powell early in the administration—"What's the point of having this superb military that you're always talking about if we can't use it?"—Lake supported the JCS chairman's insistence that before deciding whether and how to use military force, it was necessary to have clear political goals. "You know, Madeleine," Lake explained, "the kinds of questions Colin is asking about goals are exactly the ones the military never asked during Vietnam."

When Tony Lake entered his spacious corner office in the West Wing on January 20, 1993, he found a full inbox but empty cabinets. Every single sheet of paper—and, nowadays, every electronic file—that is generated by the president and the people who work for him in the Executive Office of the President is moved out of the White House and archived the day the president leaves office. When the new occupants arrive at their offices the next day, they will find their file cabinets empty and hard-disk drives erased. They have to start completely anew.

The world, of course, does not work this way. Conflicts do not end and new crises do not erupt according to the American political calendar. And so it was in 1993. The incoming administration faced a rash of issues left unresolved by its predecessor. There was Somalia, where President Bush had decided the previous Thanksgiving (weeks after Bush's electoral defeat) to send 20,000 American troops to maintain security so food supplies could reach starving millions. Somewhat naively (and contrary to the military's own projections), Brent Scowcroft had told the incoming national security team not to worry. Combat "could be completed in two weeks," he had said reassuringly. "We'll have the troops out by January 20," with only a small U.S. naval presence remaining offshore to support a UN peacekeeping force on land. But when Clinton took the oath of office, the American troops were still there. Conflict was raging. And there was no plan for how to put a state that had failed and descended into anarchy back together once the fighting had ended.

There were Bosnia and Haiti, two other conflicts that had exploded on Bush's watch. In Bosnia, many tens of thousands of people had been killed in the murderous interethnic fighting that followed the dissolution of Yugoslavia. In the summer of 1992, the world had been witness to pictures of concentration camps in which emaciated men stood behind barbed-wire fences in images reminiscent of the Holocaust. A newly confident Europe had hoped to be able to resolve this conflict itself, and the Bush administration had decided that it had "no dog in this fight." During the campaign, Clinton had repeatedly urged stronger action, such as lifting the arms embargo that prevented the majority Muslim population in Bosnia from defending itself and launching air strikes to support the government against Serb and Croat attacks. Now, the responsibility for action lay with the new administration, including the difficult task of trying to turn campaign promises into viable policy.

The same challenge existed with regard to Haiti, where an elected president, Jean-Bertrand Aristide, had been ousted by the military in 1991, and thousands of Haitians had taken to the seas to seek safety and a better life in America. With Clinton's election, many more Haitians threatened to take to rickety boats in the hope that the incoming president would allow them to stay, as he had promised during the campaign. Even before he took the oath of office, Clinton had to make clear that the door to new refugees would remain closed. But this reversal left open what the United States should do to resolve the Haitian crisis.

And there were other pressing issues. In Iraq, the unsettled end of the Gulf War still required American vigilance, including the enforcement of the prohibition on flying aircraft over the northern and southern parts of Iraq (so called no-fly zones) as well as direct support to the United Nation's effort to ensure the removal of all Iraq's weapons of mass destruction and ballistic missiles. In Russia, Boris Yeltsin's hold on power was becoming increasingly precarious, as revanchist forces in and outside the Duma tried to challenge the first freely elected president in Russian history. During the campaign, Clinton had chastised the Bush administration for doing too little to support Yeltsin's efforts to transform the Russian state-run economy, and he had promised to do much better once in office. In China, finally, the human rights situation had not improved much since the 1989 massacre at Tiananmen Square, and many in Congress were determined to use the leverage of the U.S. market to force a change in policy. One such lever was the annual determination whether to extend normal trade access to Chinese products (so-called most favored nation, or MFN, status). Clinton had accused Bush of "kowtowing to tyrants" during the campaign, and now he had to decide whether to condition granting China MFN on human rights criteria.

All of this amounted to one very full inbox. Though the issues differed significantly, they either posed immediate political challenges for Clinton at home or raised the difficult question of whether to employ force abroad. In some cases, such as Bosnia, they raised both challenges at once. Clinton had made it quite clear that he did not want to spend a lot of political capital on foreign policy issues. He was determined to put the American people first—which meant getting control of a ballooning budget deficit, addressing health care and welfare reform, and dealing with other domestic needs. As a result, the administration tended to decide foreign policy issues by choosing the most politically expedient course: start bringing troops home from Somalia, bar Haitian refugees from entering the United States, rule out deployment of ground forces to end the fighting in Bosnia, find a way to tie China's most favored nation status to its human rights performance.

The one exception was Russia, where Clinton insisted on fully embracing the embattled Yeltsin and supporting the Russian president's economic reform efforts financially with a big, $2.5 billion aid package. Importantly, it was the president who from the outset pushed for this decision, rejecting the counsel from his political advisers that he should limit his requests for aid from Congress and preserve his political capital for the big domestic issues. Clinton would have none of it. On this crucial issue, the president chaired all the meetings, drove the process, and pushed his aides: "You guys go out and be bold," he told his top aides. "Tell me what you think substantively needs to be done. Don't worry about how Congress will react to the price tag. I'll worry about Congress. That's my job." Not only did he get a bold proposal to Congress early in his administration, but he got Congress to pass it with overwhelming majorities in both houses.

On the use of force, though, the president and his advisers were far more cautious. Clinton's relations with the military were strained from day one. During the campaign, questions had been raised about his draft status during the Vietnam War. Immediately after coming into office he had a tense confrontation with the entire top brass over the ability of gays to serve openly in the military (which he had favored as a candidate, but many in the military strongly opposed). The president was clearly uncomfortable in his role as commander in chief, having to learn how to salute properly and finding it difficult to gain the respect from many in uniform that his constitutional role demanded. With such tense relations, it wasn't all that surprising that the president and his top advisers (just one of whom, Berger, had any military experience) were extremely reluctant to take on the Pentagon on matters relating to the use of force. Nor was there a flag officer in a senior NSC position who could help bridge such differences.

Complicating matters even more was the widespread belief in the Clinton White House that the highly popular JCS chairman Colin Powell might make a run for the White House after his retirement in 1993. Powell had close connections to major powers in the Republican Party, and as the first African-American ever to have served as national security adviser and the first to chair the Joint Chiefs, he would pose a major challenge if he decided to run. Clinton courted Powell assiduously, asking for his advice on senior appointments, calling him regularly on the phone, and inviting him over for informal meetings at the White House. (At the last of these, on the morning he stepped down, Powell suggested to Clinton that Les Aspin was not working out at the Pentagon. That became clear to everyone a few days later over the response to Somalia, and the secretary of defense was soon gone.) Powell appreciated the attention; he "spent more quality time alone with the president during his eight months with Clinton than he had during his years with Reagan and Bush." And he became appreciative of Clinton's qualities in return. "I always felt more comfortable when the President was present at [policy] discussions," Powell recalled. "Bill Clinton had the background to put history, politics, and policy into perspective."

Given these challenges, it was little wonder that Lake found it difficult to make a big dent in—let alone empty—his in-tray. A number of issues were dealt with, more or less successfully. An early summit with Boris Yeltsin (held in Canada because the White House thought Russia was too far from home for Clinton to travel) forged a strong U.S.-Russian relationship that was to last through both of

Clinton's terms. Saddam Hussein's Iraq remained firmly contained, especially once Clinton made it clear that he was willing to use force in defense of U.S. and regional interests. (In June 1993, the president ordered a cruise missile attack on Hussein's intelligence headquarters following the discovery of an Iraqi plot to assassinate former President George Bush.) The tricky issue of China was pushed forward a year when, in May 1993, Clinton signed an executive order linking subsequent annual decisions on whether to extend China most favored nation status to specific (albeit modest) human rights improvements. And Clinton delivered on his promise to stress international economic issues: "rebalancing" the U.S-Japan relationship through "an elevated attention" to economic matters; improving and winning ratification of the agreement to create a North American Free Trade Area; and concluding the Uruguay Round of global trade negotiations.

These relative successes were overshadowed, however, by the administration's performance on more immediate crises in Bosnia, Haiti, and Somalia. Bosnia took up a tremendous amount of the principals' time. But the administration proved neither willing to deploy the type of military capabilities necessary to bring the conflict to an end nor able to convince its European allies to endorse other forceful actions to end the fighting. Christopher declared Bosnia "a problem from hell," and the rest of the administration decided to muddle through. The principals paid much less attention to Haiti and Somalia in the early months of the administration. In July, Washington helped the United Nations negotiate the Governors Island agreement between the military junta in Haiti and the ousted leadership to restore the elected president to power, but it gave little thought to how its terms were to be enforced. As for Somalia, a steady deterioration in the political and military situation on the ground produced ad hoc tactical adjustments, including the dispatch of U.S. Army Rangers in August, rather than a serious strategic reevaluation.

This neglect came to a head in October 1993. In Somalia, on the third of the month, a daytime helicopter raid by Army Rangers and Delta Forces against the headquarters of Mogadishu's most notorious warlord, Mohammed Farah Aideed, went disastrously wrong when some of the Black Hawk helicopters were shot down and eighteen Rangers were killed. Much of the urban carnage played out on cable television, including shocking pictures of American bodies being dragged around the streets. The disaster was followed a few days later by another humiliation—this one off the coast of Haiti. On October 11, the USS *Harlan County*, with some two hundred lightly armed American and Canadian soldiers, arrived at Port-au-Prince to help train and professionalize the Haitian police and military in anticipation of the transfer of power from the junta to Aristide, which was slated for October 30. They were greeted by a mob of local thugs, all jeering: "Somalia! Somalia!" After the ship sat offshore a few days, the *Harlan County* received orders to turn around and sail back to the United States rather than risk a confrontation by offloading the troops.

"Black October" proved a searing experience for the Clinton administration. It demonstrated that this White House, and this national security team, were not working properly. Not a single senior official had traveled to Somalia before the October 3 disaster in Mogadishu to see the situation firsthand—even though thousands of American troops were deployed in a shooting environment. Worse, Clinton did not actually discuss Somalia with his national security team until after Americans had died there. Nor did his top advisers focus on the issue. In the preceding nine and a half months, Lake did not convene one Principals Committee meeting on Somalia. (There had been eighteen such meetings on Bosnia during this period.) The deputies did discuss Somalia, about once a month on average, and in September they had proposed that the United Nation shift from hunting Aideed to seeking political reconciliation. But the military effort on the ground never reflected the change in emphasis.

If anything, the *Harlan County* incident was even more embarrassing. The mighty U.S. Navy turned back by a jeering mob of hundreds. "A total fuckup," Lake admitted. "It was our fault: We had sent the ship out with zero military support." A bigger problem was the unexamined notion that a military junta would give up power without a fight—and yet that is what the administration had assumed when it backed the Governors Island agreement and focused on how it might assist Haiti after Aristide had returned. To his credit, Aspin understood that the Haitian military was unlikely to leave of its own accord and he opposed sending lightly armed trainers who were bound to be caught in the middle. He predicted that the mission would end in embarrassment. But then he failed to press his case. Rather than insisting that the decision to send the trainers be reexamined in a meeting with the president, Aspin called Lake shortly before the *Harlan County* sailed to make sure Clinton was behind the decision. The national security adviser assured him that the president was. That was good enough for Aspin.

Clinton was furious. This was his Bay of Pigs. His advisers had let him down. Lake, Aspin, Christopher, not one of them had warned him of the disasters in Somalia and Haiti—or been able to figure a way out of the mess in Bosnia. A clear consensus was being formed in Washington. This was a weak president, surrounded by a weak team, pursuing a weak foreign policy. Things had to change. And they did, remarkably rapidly, as both Clinton and Lake reassessed and then adjusted the way they went about their business.

The first adjustment concerned people. Though Clinton blamed his entire team for the October disasters, he was most concerned about Les Aspin, whose tentative leadership of the Pentagon and failure to be a forceful player within the administration had clearly become a problem. The final straw was Aspin's disastrous performance before a large number of congressmen and senators in which he solicited their ideas on how to proceed in Somalia after the Black Hawk debacle rather than offer firm reassurance that the administration knew what it was doing. By December, Aspin was gone, to be replaced in early February 1994 by his deputy, William Perry. This quiet, steady defense intellectual would turn out to be exactly what the Pentagon and the administration needed. Respected and liked by everyone in the building, Perry offered the president clear guidance on issues of defense and the use of force, and proved to be an exemplary player on the first term's team. Assisting Perry in this effort was Army General John Shalikashvili, who replaced Powell as JCS chairman in October 1993. "Shali," born in Poland, was both the first immigrant and the first Army private to rise through the ranks to become chairman. In contrast to Powell, he saw his job as helping the president and his team to accomplish their stated policies with the aid of military force, rather than to warn them about why using force was an ill-considered idea.

Even though Lake offered to resign in the wake of the Somalia debacle, Clinton never seriously considered replacing his national security adviser. The same was true, at least initially, for Christopher as well. But when in 1994 an exhausted Christopher told Clinton that he wanted to leave, the president saw an opportunity to try to recruit the one man he had wanted to be his secretary of state all along: Colin Powell. Even before the election in 1992, Clinton had asked his friend Vernon Jordan to sound Powell out about a possible job. Powell had declined. A few weeks into the administration, Clinton wondered whether he shouldn't have pressed harder. "I think he would have taken it," the president confided to George Stephanopoulos. Now, nearly two years later, Clinton was determined to press again. "Call Colin," he said to Jordan, after telling him the news that Christopher wanted out. Powell told Jordan he wasn't interested, and he said the same thing to the president when they met in person the next day. Part of the reason was his desire to make some money and spend more time with his family. But part also was Powell's "reservation about the amorphous way the administration handled foreign policy." Meanwhile, Christopher had reconsidered; he now wanted to stay through the end of the term.

Clinton realized that ultimately the problem wasn't so much his advisers as it was himself. The president had to be more engaged in the process. Inattention to problems at home had clear political costs, but so did inattention to problems abroad. Clinton had always focused on the big international issues like Russia, the Middle East, and international economics (indeed, much more than people realized). But he could no longer ignore what he had considered the "second-order" issues like Bosnia, Haiti, and Somalia. He had to be involved earlier, ask the tough questions, and know the consequences of the different courses of action. "After Black Hawk Down," Clinton recalls, "whenever I approved the deployment of forces, I knew much more about what the risks were." He agreed to more regular "Foreign Policy Team" meetings, which convened instead of the NSC, and included get-togethers with his top national security aides to discuss issues more freely, rather than meeting solely when there was a need to make decisions.

In addition to giving more attention to questions of national security, the president and his White House began to operate very differently. During its first year, the Clinton White House (though not the NSC) was an undisciplined, disorganized operation. All and sundry could come to meetings, walk into the Oval Office, or speak up during the sessions. The president would be involved in many meetings in which discussions meandered for hours and ended without a clear decision. And when decisions were made, they could all too easily be reversed. Clinton understood the problem. He told Stephanopoulos early on that he felt he was "losing control of his presidency," and he feared "that his schedule and his government [were] not organized to achieve what he wants to achieve."

Clinton needed structure. He needed someone who could erase his doubts and strengthen his convictions. Someone to discipline this most undisciplined of men. Unfortunately, that someone wasn't his first chief of staff. Mack McLarty was Clinton's closest and dearest friend and an accomplished businessman. But he had neither the Washington experience nor the temperament to run a disciplined White House. The two friends came to understand they had a problem. So Clinton turned to Leon Panetta, a former congressman who was serving as his director of the Office of Management and Budget, and made him chief of staff. The president gave his new chief of staff broad license to put the White House in order. Panetta did so with great efficiency. Access to the Oval Office became tightly controlled. The number of meetings was drastically cut, and they now ran on time and only for the scheduled duration. Decisions were made, and they stuck. In short, the change in chief of staff was more than a change in personnel—it was a fundamental change in the way Clinton's White House went about its business.

Anthony Lake needed to change as well. He now realized that in this administration at least, the national security adviser could not do his job the way Andy Goodpaster had in the 1950s or Brent Scowcroft in the mid-1970s. Part of the problem was the nature of the times. Post–Cold War foreign policy was increasingly complex and, by its nature, increasingly mixed with domestic policy— and thus increasingly politicized. That, combined with a media that filled the airwaves 24/7, meant that effective communications were critical for an effective foreign policy. A president cannot do this alone, nor can he rely solely on his chief foreign policy spokesman, who must always be the secretary of state. Other top officials, including especially the NSC adviser, who is in the best position to know what the president wants, must be involved in the communication process. "I had admired the way some of my predecessors had worked effectively behind the scenes," Lake admitted. "This discreet posture was my picture of the way to do my job, and I now believe it was a mistake." Lake would do more public speaking and even appear on the Sunday talk shows, but he still would not do a lot. Others, including Gore and Albright, would help to fill the void.

Lake understood, however, that it was not just the failure to communicate policy that was the problem. It was also how policy was being made. No one was driving the process toward decisions and action. Clinton was, as Elizabeth Drew puts it, "an absentee landlord on foreign policy." Christopher was reluctant to press his views at the White House if he felt that the president had already made up his mind. Aspin had been more comfortable discussing all angles of an issue than pressing a case, even when he had a case to make. And Lake believed his honest broker role precluded him from being a strong policy advocate. No one really pushed the process; no one brought discussions to closure. The result, in many instances, was inaction—or, as in the case of the critical crises, weak and ineffective action.

The Clinton team, Lake concluded, had "over-learned the lessons of the Carter administration." In an effort to avoid debilitating conflict, the team had adopted a consensus process that proved to be no less debilitating. That had to change. "I remember Colin Powell coming to me and saying that I needed to give my own views more," Lake recalls. "I knew he was right. . . . You have to drive the process." Once he decided to do so, Lake proved to be quite adept at driving the process toward decisions and actions. Though his outward demeanor suggested someone who liked scholarly contemplation much more than bureaucratic infighting, the reality was quite different. "There are very few times that Tony ultimately is reversed or changed or modified," noted Leon Panetta, who watched from up close as Clinton's chief of staff.

But while he fought hard, Lake was still determined not to repeat the mistakes Kissinger and Brzezinski had made in the 1970s. He would remain open with his colleagues and seek agreement whenever possible. But "I would be less hesitant in voicing my own views when they differed from those of my colleagues, even if it prevented consensus or put me more at odds with them." Lake realized that this would increase tensions within the team, not least with Christopher, with whom he had a series of substantive differences. In part to diffuse the tension and to bridge differences, Lake convened more meetings with the other key advisers, adding, for example, a weekly breakfast with Christopher, Perry, Shalikashvili, Albright, and Woolsey (replaced in 1995 as CIA director by John Deutch) to the regular weekly lunches with Christopher and Perry that had been a staple of the process from the start. He also always made sure to convey the views of other principals to the president fully and fairly, and he would never stand in their way if they sought to air those views with Clinton directly. And though he would prove more active not only in pushing policy but also in executing it by meeting more frequently with foreign visitors and even engaging in direct diplomacy himself, he never tried to cut Christopher or the State Department out from anything he was doing. Lake's newfound activism was much more about good policy, and the process required to get there, than about bureaucratic prerogative.

There was one other important change in administration foreign policymaking. This was the idea, pushed by Christopher, of appointing key people to manage particularly important issue areas directly for the president and secretary of state. The model was Strobe Talbott, whose initial title of ambassador-at-large and special adviser to the secretary of state on the newly independent states of the former Soviet Union obscured the fact that he was Clinton's "go-to" man on Russia, running the interagency process that made policy and then being responsible for its implementation. Talbott enjoyed unusual leeway within the administration, not least because of his close friendship with the president but also because of his acknowledged expertise. During Lake's four years at the head of the NSC, there would only be one principals meeting on Russia—in 1996, prior to the Russian presidential election, which many feared Yeltsin might lose. In all other cases, important decisions were made in informal meetings with the president.

No other individual would gain as much control over one policy area as Talbott did over Russia policy—and none would escape the oversight and guidance of the Principals Committee the way Talbott did—but the model of presidential issue managers stuck. Dennis Ross became Middle East envoy, with particular responsibility for negotiating peace agreements between Israel, the Palestinians, and their neighbors. Robert Gallucci took responsibility for negotiating a deal to end North Korea's nuclear weapons program. Richard Holbrooke was given the task of negotiating an end to the Bosnian conflict; Robert Gelbard and James Dobbins succeeded him as Balkan envoys in Clinton's second term. Richard Clarke, finally, was put in charge of counterterrorism policy during the second term. In all of these cases, the idea was to identify a single individual within the bureaucracy (usually at State) to take control of a particularly important issue by chairing the interagency meetings and usually becoming the point person for implementing agreed policy.

———

That process matters became evident soon after Clinton decided to become more involved and Lake decided to change the way he conceived of his job. Starting in 1994, the administration began to apply the same decisiveness it had on domestic policy and a few foreign policy issues (notably Russia, the Middle East, and international economics) to a number of other issues that had languished or proven impossible to resolve before. In most cases, the mark of successful policy was a more active and directed involvement by the White House, notably by Tony Lake and the NSC staff. This would clearly prove to be the case for policy toward Europe, Haiti, Bosnia, and China. It was not true, however, for all issues. Clinton decided in October 1993 to withdraw all U.S. troops from Somalia by April 1994, and leave that country for the United Nations to handle. Failure to engage at all marked the U.S. policy toward Rwanda, where over 800,000 people were killed in a brutal genocide in mid-1994. The issue received very little attention in Washington's corridors of power—or beyond. "It didn't arise for us because it was almost literally inconceivable that American troops would go to Rwanda," Lake later confessed. "Our sin, I believe, was not the error of commission, or taking a look at this issue and then saying no. It was an error of omission—of never considering that issue." But, Lake adds, "it was nonetheless a terrible sin."

Aside from Russia, Europe was not, initially, high on the administration's agenda. "Western Europe is no longer the dominant area of the world," Warren Christopher explained, and he urged Washington to get over its Eurocentric view of diplomacy. Clinton didn't even travel to the Old World during the entire first year of his presidency. So, it was somewhat surprising to see the president become a forceful advocate of expanding America's security commitments in Europe. Yet, pressed by leaders from the newly liberated countries of Central and Eastern Europe, Clinton early on championed the enlargement of NATO's membership. Lake was instrumental in turning this presidential desire into actual policy, even though none of the other principals originally supported the idea. Working with a few key allies at State, the NSC adviser convinced the president to make clear in his first visit to Europe that "the question is no longer whether NATO will take on new members but when and how." Subsequently, Lake and other advocates would point to Clinton's speech as the definitive policy statement on the matter (although the Pentagon, caught in the transition between Secretaries Aspin and Perry, did not realize that the issue had been decided). By mid-1994, Richard Holbrooke, the new assistant secretary of state for Europe, moved swiftly and effectively to turn the policy aspiration into reality. In 1997, NATO invited Poland, Hungary, and the Czech Republic into the Atlantic Alliance as the first members of the former Warsaw Pact.

The pattern would repeat itself with respect to Haiti. "Never again," Sandy Berger had muttered after the *Harlan County* fiasco. "Never again," Lake agreed. There was no way the junta would leave without at least the threat of force—if not an actual intervention. The NSC adviser talked to Clinton in April 1994 and suggested that he devise a strategy for threatening or using force. Clinton was noncommittal. He was wary of ordering a military intervention, but he did not discourage Lake from pursuing this line of thought. Working with Berger and Talbott, both of whom shared Lake's view that the status quo in Haiti was unacceptable and force would have to be part of any solution, Lake pushed the military option forward—even though Clinton and Christopher remained doubtful and the Pentagon was strongly opposed.

By August 1994, the use of force seemed all but unavoidable, and JCS chairman John Shalikashvili presented the president with an operational plan for an invasion. Clinton now indicated that he was supportive, but he wanted more. "I know we can intervene in these little countries with great ease and the first seventy-two hours go really well," Clinton told his principal advisers. "But I'm concerned about what happens after that," noting that Somalia hadn't gone so well in that respect. "I don't want to do Haiti unless I'm confident there's a plan" for the day after. An integrated, political-military plan was swiftly developed, setting forth clear objectives, a workable strategy, and definitive benchmarks for the post-invasion phase of the operation. Much of this plan was subsequently put into effect when, in September 1994, with the 82nd Airborne on its way to Haiti, the junta was persuaded to leave the country and Haiti's elected president was restored to power.

Bosnia would prove a tougher nut to crack. For two and a half years, the administration had struggled to find a way to end the conflict without having to deploy U.S. forces in combat. It had not worked, and the brutal war had continued to take tens of thousands of lives. Convinced that Bosnia represented "a cancer on the presidency," echoing John Dean's characterization of Watergate, Lake began to push for a fundamental reassessment in late spring 1995. In what John Harris called "his finest hour in government," Lake worked with his NSC staff to develop an "Endgame Strategy," sold it to Clinton, and then convinced the rest of the government to fall in behind it. The Endgame Strategy set a goal of where the administration wanted Bosnia to be six months out, and then worked back to develop a policy for getting from the current situation to that point. It envisaged a unitary state, divided between roughly equal Serbian and Muslim-Croat entities. It combined carrots and sticks for all parties, including the deployment of large numbers of U.S. and NATO troops to enforce an agreement, and lifting the arms embargo and launching sustained air strikes if a settlement could not be reached.

In August 1995, Lake traveled to Europe and convinced the allies that Clinton was determined to end the conflict—with or without them. European leaders bought the strategy, and Lake then handed the baton of negotiating an actual peace agreement among the Bosnian parties to Richard Holbrooke. Holbrooke did so brilliantly, spending the next three months blustering, cajoling, and pleading with the Serbs, Croats, and Muslims to conclude a peace, which they did in November 1995, ending Europe's most brutal conflict since the end of World War II.

In addition to Haiti and Bosnia, Clinton had made Bush's China policy a major issue during the 1992 campaign. His own decision in 1993 to link China's future most favored nation status to definitive (albeit modest) human rights improvements reflected strong congressional sentiment, and had been driven largely by the State Department. The economic agencies had little input into the decision and, as Bo Cutter, the deputy at the National Economic Council, recalls, they were "surprised, shocked, angered by how it came out, and thought it was going to be a fairly fast disaster." Before long, these agencies went public with their anxieties, undercutting what became a disastrous trip to China by Warren Christopher the following spring. When the secretary failed to win human rights concessions from Beijing, Clinton concluded that a course correction was in order. The NSC, under Berger's lead, was put in charge of China policy in 1994.

The NSC and NEC staffs began to meet regularly, and before midyear the president decided to end the human rights–trade linkage once and for all. A strategic policy reassessment came later, when Lake and Berger, following a series of meetings with China experts from outside the government, concluded that China would have to be part of the solution rather than considered part of the problem. "It was in China's interest as well as the world's," Lake explained, "that China not only play by the rules but also help devise those rules—whether on nonproliferation, arms control regimes or trade." To implement this shift in orientation, Lake opened a direct strategic dialogue with his Chinese counterpart, once again taking on the very operational role that his original conception of the job had firmly excluded.

By the end of Clinton's first term, Lake's inbox had been emptied of many of the issues that had filled it at the outset. U.S. troops had left Somalia. Aristide was back in Haiti. The war in Bosnia had ended. NATO was adapting and enlarging. Iraq was effectively contained. America's relations with Russia and China were progressing on an even keel. Clinton had grown, adapting his style and organization to the demands of his office and the times. He had become more decisive, and by 1995, Lake recalls, "all meetings with him were far more crisp and presidential." That was one reason why the foreign policy record of the second half of his first term was so much better than in the first year. Tony Lake was the other reason. On one issue after another, Lake had taken command—forging consensus where possible, driving the process toward decision where necessary. There were times when he might have driven the process a bit too aggressively. Clinton, on occasion, would tell him that maybe he was pushing his colleagues too hard. But Clinton wanted decisions, and he knew and appreciated the fact that his NSC adviser could deliver. The results spoke for themselves: rather than a failed foreign policy president, the successes added up to a strong record on which to run for reelection in 1996.

Notwithstanding these successes, it was clear that a second Clinton term would bring a new team to run foreign policy. Both Warren Christopher and William Perry had long indicated that they wanted to return to California after the election, and Lake had never even intended to be at the NSC for all of the first term. The job had been exhilarating but exhausting, and it was time to move on. When Clinton announced the new team a month after his reelection, there were no real surprises. Madeleine Albright was appointed secretary of state, the first female to hold the top cabinet job. For Defense, Clinton, who had wanted to appoint a Republican to the cabinet, decided to nominate Senator Bill Cohen, a moderate Republican from Maine. Sandy Berger moved up to become NSC adviser, though Clinton had briefly toyed with the idea of making Berger his chief of staff and appointing Strobe Talbott to the NSC job instead. Lake would go to the CIA—but his nomination ran into partisan trouble in the Senate, and after he withdrew in March 1997, Clinton appointed the deputy CIA director, George Tenet, to the top job.

Whereas Lake and Clinton had never been a natural fit—the one committed to a clear divide between policy and politics, the other seeing a political angle to every aspect of policy—there was no such problem between Clinton and Berger. The two men had known each other for a quarter century, starting when both had worked for Gary Hart on the McGovern presidential campaign. They had remained close ever since. Berger introduced the young Arkansas pol to the Washington political scene, and Clinton always looked to the Washington insider for policy and political advice. There was a general expectation, therefore, that Berger would be Clinton's principal foreign policy adviser when the governor decided to make a run for the White House. But for Berger's insistence that Lake get the job, Berger would have been Clinton's national security adviser from the beginning. With Clinton's reelection, he finally took the job Clinton had offered him four years earlier.

It was not just their close personal relationship that made Sandy Berger the obvious choice for Clinton. Berger himself brought a lot to the job. He had been Lake's deputy for four years, though that understated his true importance and seniority. On some key issues—economic questions, China, peace implementation in Bosnia, to name a few—Berger already played the principal coordinating role in the first term. He had also been the main liaison between the NSC and the political side of the White House, even participating in the weekly political strategy sessions that were convened in the president's residence during the run-up to the 1996 election. Now that he was fully in charge at the NSC, his value to Clinton would become even more evident. A detail man, who constantly wrote long to-do lists in his precise, neat handwriting, Berger would guide the president carefully through the pitfalls ahead. Because of his political instincts, he was able to understand where Clinton was or would likely end up on any given issue. Seeking neither power nor glory for himself, Berger complemented Clinton perfectly. "He understood my strengths and weaknesses," the president later remarked, "and how to make the most of the former and minimize the latter."

In selecting the other players for his second term team, Clinton was not only looking for collegiality but also for cabinet members who could sell a bipartisan foreign policy to a skeptical public, as well as to the Republicans who now controlled Congress. As UN ambassador, Albright had already shown a knack for explaining complex policies in an effective and convincing way. She was the master of the crisp one-liners, the penetrating sound bites. Of Haiti's junta she had said, "they can leave voluntarily and soon or involuntarily and soon." When Cuban fighters shot down two small planes operated by exiles in 1996, the Cuban pilots had been overheard triumphantly boasting about how they had demonstrated their manhood. "Frankly," Albright exclaimed at the United Nations, "this is not *cojones*, this is cowardice." As secretary of state, Albright would forge a striking, and effective, relationship with the chairman of the Senate Foreign Relations Committee, the ornery, arch-conservative Republican senator from North Carolina, Jesse Helms. It helped boost spending for her department, and eased passage of some contentious treaties through the Senate. After Christopher, Clinton realized, there was value in having an effective communicator as secretary of state. At the same time, the president could be exasperated at Albright's tendency to insist on the morally right course without providing clear guidance on how to get there. "Clinton," one biographer noted, "vastly preferred solutions over sermons from his own aides."

Bill Cohen's contribution to the new team was his record of service on Capitol Hill, including on the Armed Services Committee, and his membership of the majority party. Clinton had hoped that appointing a Republican to run the Pentagon might ease his relationship with two constituencies at once: the uniformed military and the Republican Congress. It did so only partly. Cohen had a hard time thinking of himself as part of the new team. His contributions to administration deliberations often reflected the concerns of Congress and the opposition of the military more than the concerns of the administration or the president. In meetings, Cohen would refer to Congress as "us" and the administration as "you"—a sentiment that extended also to his partisan references. At one point, Berger took Cohen aside, telling the secretary of defense, "I will regard this administration as a success when you refer to the administration as *we*, and not *you*." Cohen also shared the military's skepticism toward the use of force, especially in the Balkans. "I voted against your Balkan policy," he once told Clinton, who needed no reminding. Early on in his tenure, Cohen fought a fierce (and losing) battle with Albright about the U.S. troop presence in Bosnia; and in the run-up to the Kosovo campaign, he kept emphasizing his deep doubts about using force or sending in the troops.

Berger stood at the core of the ABC team—the Albright-Berger-Cohen triumvirate. He was, Albright acknowledged, "the glue of the system." And his policy impact was such that two close observers of the Washington power scene would label him "the most influential national security adviser since Henry A. Kissinger." In contrast to Kissinger, though, Berger achieved that influence by managing his coordinating and advisory roles with great skill and determination, and never at the expense of the power of any other major player. Key to his effectiveness was his affable personality; those who knew Sandy Berger liked him. "He was the Sara Lee of our class," commented Mark Green, a classmate at Harvard Law. Though Berger had a famous temper—and not a few staff members would emerge dazed from his office after another one of his outbursts—he was protective of his staff in interagency battles and loyal to the core.

Berger ran a fair, open, and open-minded policy process. He used the Principals Committee more effectively than Lake had done, not just as an opportunity for hearing out different points of view but as a real decision-making forum, whether to make policy recommendations to the president or to set a broad framework that would then guide implementation. "Very few important decisions went to the president that hadn't been reviewed by the Principals Committee," Berger later recalled, thereby ensuring that all key advisers would have a say in the process. And whenever the president was about to go against the advice of one of his principal advisers, particularly if it involved a major issue or one with which that adviser was clearly identified, Berger would encourage Clinton to pick up the phone. "Talk to the person you are going against and hear it directly from them," he would urge the president. Clinton would do so in most instances, and sometimes it would affect his ultimate decision.

In addition to formal meetings, Berger every week convened two informal get-togethers: the "ABC" lunch on Mondays and a breakfast meeting Wednesdays that included all of the principals plus Tenet (CIA), General Hugh Shelton (JCS), Bill Richardson and Dick Holbrooke (UN ambassadors,) and Leon Fuerth, Gore's national security adviser. At the ABC luncheons, the three top advisers would work through a list of some ten to twenty topics, trying to clear away what Berger called "second-tier issues." But it was also an opportunity for each of them to express concerns about certain policies, or to work out kinks in the decision-making system. The larger breakfasts offered an opportunity for the principals to speak more openly, without the presence of aides, as was the norm in formal committee meetings. "People get a little gun-shy in terms of expressing their views candidly," Berger said of these larger meetings.

None of this is to suggest that there was no conflict or tension among Clinton's top advisers in the second term. There were plenty of policy differences, especially between Albright and Cohen on issues like the Balkans. They would argue their cases vehemently and stand their ground as long as possible, but once a decision was made—whether it was to keep troops in Bosnia longer or to threaten air strikes against Belgrade—they would all fall in line. At times, though, the tension went beyond policy, becoming personal instead. Albright worried about Berger gaining too much influence at her expense. "Problems arose when Sandy and I tried to occupy each other's space," she later remarked. "Proximity to the President sometimes tempted Sandy and his staff to assume an operational role." For his part, Berger believed that Albright was at times more interested in managing her public image than worrying about the substance of policy—a concern Clinton apparently shared. But rather than letting tensions linger, Berger and Albright agreed to work them out, which they did through frequent calls over a dedicated phone line, sometimes as often as a dozen times a day. To help smooth matters, Berger early on in his tenure had drafted "four rules for not killing each other": Rule 1: No friendly fire. Rule 2: Walk ourselves back. Rule 3: Presumption of innocence. Rule 4: No policy by press conferences.

Berger's more collegial style reflected a number of important differences from the first term: the circumstances he confronted when getting the job; the nature of the presidency in Clinton's second term; and how he conceived of his role as NSC adviser. In sharp contrast to 1993, Berger's inbox contained no immediate crises or ongoing conflicts involving American troops overseas. There were many challenges, to be sure, but also many more opportunities for shaping a better, more stable world. At the outset of his tenure, Berger worked with his staff to establish a clear set of priorities for the second term: build a peaceful, undivided, and democratic Europe; create a strong, stable Asia-Pacific community; deal with transnational threats such as terrorism and drugs; and expand global trade. These were big strategic aspirations, made more realistic by a largely quiescent global environment.

Another big difference in 1997 was the fact that Berger would be working with a president who had become supremely confident in his own abilities. In 1993, Clinton had been the first Democrat elected to the presidency since 1976 and only the second since 1964. He did not know the ways of Washington all that well, and confronted challenges at home and abroad that were fundamentally different from what he had had to deal with as governor of Arkansas. He was surrounded by people who were as green and inexperienced in their jobs as he was in his. Four years later, things were very different. Clinton was the first Democrat since Roosevelt to have won a second full term. He had learned what Washington was about the hard way—first losing control of Congress, then winning a major battle over government spending with the Republicans on Capitol Hill. And he had also confronted and successfully managed a series of major foreign policy crises: in North Korea, Haiti, Bosnia, the Taiwan Straits, and Russia. Therefore, as he entered his second term,

Bill Clinton was ready to be a foreign policy president; and Sandy Berger was the ideal national security adviser to help him succeed.

The final difference related to how Berger defined his job. Unlike Anthony Lake in the latter years of his tenure, Berger believed that the NSC should not be operational. "The secretary of state should be the chief diplomat, the chief negotiator," Berger insisted. "My job was a policy job, a coordinating job, not a conducting foreign policy job." In his four years as NSC adviser, Berger made few solo trips abroad; he went to China in 1998 to try to convince Beijing not to hold the opening ceremony for Clinton's visit at Tiananmen Square; to Europe during the Kosovo crisis in 1999 to talk with his key counterparts; and to Moscow in 2000 to try to determine whether a deal on missile defense was possible prior to Clinton's last summit visit. Though there were times when he would have liked to engage in such diplomacy in the Middle East or elsewhere, he knew that doing so would create tensions with Albright and State, and he did much less of it than Lake (though some officials at State felt that he compensated by trying to micromanage Albright and her diplomatic activities instead). He would also meet less often with foreign leaders visiting Washington (when he did, he remarked, it was "more for their optics than for anything else") and spend less time on the phone talking to foreign leaders or counterparts. There were exceptions, of course, including Ehud Barack when he was prime minister of Israel (who wanted to talk to Clinton directly and often got Berger instead) and Prince Bandar bin Sultan, the Saudi ambassador, when there was a particularly sensitive matter to discuss. But Berger's standard operating procedure was to try to leave such relationships to other parts of the government.

In contrast to his limited diplomatic and operational role, Berger attached far greater importance to playing a public role, both in the media and with Congress. That, too, stood in sharp contrast to his predecessor. "Part of my job," Berger observed, "is to explain to the American people what our objectives are." As a result, he appeared on many more Sunday talk and other TV shows than Lake (close to fifty over four years, compared to just five appearances for Lake). He made many more speeches, both in defense of particular policies and, especially in later years, in order to provide a clearer conceptual basis for Clinton's foreign policy. And he greatly expanded the number of people dealing with communications, speechwriting, and press issues on the NSC staff—from two part-time directors at the outset of the administration in 1993 to eleven officials by the end. Part of the reason for such increased public involvement was the need for the administration to play on a greatly expanded media field. A shorter news cycle and a larger number of media outlets meant that the secretary of state could not be the only one out there explaining policy on the Sunday shows; you had to have top officials on three or four of them to get the point of a specific policy across. Another reason was the increased politicization of foreign policy, especially at a time of divided government. "Since so many of the things we did were inherently unpopular and often criticized," Berger's deputy, James Steinberg, observed, "part of the reason we had the good communications strategy was because you knew the policy wasn't going to be popular initially."

An essential part of an effective communications strategy was to reach out to the other end of Pennsylvania Avenue. Berger made this a central aspect of his job. He would make calls to key senators and representatives, often as many as six or eight a day. He would go up and meet with chairs of key committees, or talk to one of the caucuses, and make the administration's case. Often, the purpose was to prevent bad things from happening—getting rid of language in a particular resolution or a provision in a bill that could hurt relations with a key ally or friend. But this strategy was also crucial to advancing the administration's agenda. For example, Berger's close consultation with Senate majority leader Trent Lott in 1997 helped secure the ratification of the Chemical Weapons Convention. The NSC adviser's efforts were also crucial in securing administration victories on such key issues as MFN for China and the enlargement of NATO. To be sure, in each of these cases, the efforts of Albright, Cohen, and other cabinet officials were crucial as well; but Berger understood better than most of his predecessors that success would often require the NSC adviser's active and direct engagement with Capitol Hill. Then again, such engagement could never guarantee success, as became clear when the administration (along with Senate Democrats) demanded an up-or-down Senate vote on ratification of the Comprehensive Test Ban Treaty in October 1999, only to discover that Republicans had quietly lined up more than enough votes to defeat the measure. The outcome was perhaps the most notable repudiation of any administration on an international treaty since the Senate rejected the League of Nations eighty years earlier.

In the case of Kosovo, the problem was oversensitivity to political resistance. When violence first embroiled this small former Yugoslav province in early 1998, the White House, already caught up in the Monica Lewinsky scandal, resisted calls from Albright and others to threaten air strikes against Serbia for fear that Congress would actively oppose them. The question was never posed directly to Clinton; Berger's opposition was sufficient to silence the calls. Over the ensuing months, Albright would press for action again and again, but Berger continued to resist because he was convinced it would incur repudiation by a hostile Republican Congress. When air strikes became unavoidable in early 1999, Berger and Clinton explicitly ruled out the use of ground forces in combat operations. "We would not have won the war without this sentence," Berger later insisted, referring to Clinton's explicit disavowal of ground troops. Asked why the administration would undercut Western leverage in this way, Berger responded that the American people, Congress, and the NATO allies would all have opposed going to war if they believed it had to involve ground forces. Such political deference, however, likely came at significant cost. A credible threat of troops on the ground might have obviated the need for a long air campaign, or at least ended the war sooner. Indeed, it was only when the ground option was finally put on the table in late spring—when winning the war became more important than risking the wrath of Congress—that Serbia finally yielded.

Berger's tenure at the NSC also represented an important continuity with Lake's, at least when it came to adapting the Council and its
staff to the reality of a world in which global forces and transnational
challenges had become dominant factors in America's engagement
abroad. From the start of his administration, Lake recalls, Clinton
"understood something before the rest of us did, and that was what
later became called globalization." Clinton recognized early on that
globalization was not just an economic phenomenon, permanently
erasing the distinction between the domestic and international economics, but something much broader. The same forces that made the
flow of labor, capital, and goods across borders possible also enabled
the flow of ideas and information, germs and viruses, weapons and
terrorists, pollution and greenhouse gases, and a whole lot more.

The challenge for the NSC—and the White House more generally—was to adapt to that new reality. One key innovation, noted
earlier, was the creation of the National Economic Council (NEC),
which helped to integrate foreign and domestic economic policy.
From the outset, Lake and Rubin agreed that those on their staff
responsible for international economic issues like trade and finance
would be dual-hatted, reporting to both the NSC and NEC advisers. This arrangement worked well in the first term when the two
councils had deputies (Sandy Berger and Bo Cutter) who not only
knew each other well but appreciated the link between security and
economic issues. It worked less well in the second term because of
changes at the NEC, which after Bob Rubin left to head Treasury
became a flatter, less hierarchical organization. "It was always a little
bit difficult to mesh gears," Berger acknowledged. More of the issues
moved to the NEC, into the very capable hands of Lael Brainard,
who was the deputy responsible for international economic issues.
"But I don't think the NSC-NEC process worked that well," Berger
concluded. That became evident during the Asian financial crisis,
which started with a run on the Thai baht in July 1997. Treasury
and the economic team decided, without much involvement of State,

Defense, or the NSC, not to contribute U.S. funds to an international bailout package, arguing that the restrictions imposed by U.S. law made such a contribution counterproductive. However, "many in Thailand—a U.S. treaty ally—and others in Asia," recalled Steinberg, "questioned what that decision said about America's commitment to its friends in the region."

The growing importance of globalization was reflected in other organizational changes as well. Lake created three new directorates with responsibility for transnational issues: non-proliferation and export controls; environmental affairs; and global issues and multilateral affairs, which dealt with a grab bag of issues like drugs, migration, international crime, terrorism, and peacekeeping. The idea was not only to enable the U.S. government to coordinate a growing number of agencies that dealt with these issues, but also to give greater prominence to these challenges in bilateral and multilateral relations. As Lake told Dan Poneman, the first person to head the new non-proliferation office, "we need to weave nonproliferation into the bilateral relationships around the world." In succeeding years, other directorates were created—for democracy and human rights, transnational threats, international health affairs, and even, briefly, for Gulf War illnesses. Since traditional national security issues—including regional stability, defense and arms control, and intelligence—remained very much within the NSC's purview, these organizational changes fueled a dramatic increase in the Council's size, from a policy staff of about 57 in 1993 to 105 people in 2000.

Nowhere was this organizational change more dramatic and more noticeable than on the issue of terrorism, which came early to the Clinton administration. On January 25, 1993, a young Pakistani walked alongside cars lining up at a traffic light to turn into the CIA headquarters in McLean, Virginia, and shot at their drivers, leaving three people dead. A month later, a van packed with explosives was driven into the parking garage under the World Trade Center in New York, and later exploded. Though the towers stayed upright, six people were killed and over a thousand wounded. Like the Pakistani gunman, some of those responsible for the New York bombing were able to leave the United States undetected. One of them was Ramsi Yousef, the nephew of Khalid Sheikh Mohammed, who would be the mastermind behind the 9/11 attacks in 2001. The hunt for Yousef led eventually to Manila, where authorities discovered a plan to simultaneously blow up eleven 747 jets bound for the United States across the Pacific. The information reached Washington on a Saturday morning, early in January 1995. Lake wanted to ground all U.S. planes crossing the Pacific. "Get me the secretary of transportation," Lake shouted into the phone, so he could order the Federal Aviation Administration to ground the flights. But no one could locate the secretary. The department was closed, and there was no answer at the secretary's central number. Eventually, the planes were grounded by presidential order.

The episode dramatically illustrated the organizational challenges posed by the global threat of terrorism. An effective government response to this quintessentially transnational threat required the cooperation and coordination not only of traditional national security agencies like State, CIA, and Defense, but also of such traditional domestic departments as Transportation, Justice, Health and Human Services, and even the Department of Agriculture. Lake gave the responsibility for pulling these different government agencies together to Richard Clarke, a holdover from the Bush administration, who headed up the directorate for global issues and multilateral affairs. Among his many responsibilities, Clarke chaired the CSG (which stood for the obscure "Coordinating Sub-Group" and was originally concerned with crisis management, but later was rechristened the "Counterterrorism and Security Group"). A bureaucratic master of the first order, Clarke turned the CSG into a counterterrorism bulwark, bringing together all of the key agencies in a concerted effort to prevent and, if necessary, respond to a terrorist attack, whether at home or abroad.

Clarke's efforts broke new ground. For nearly fifty years, the NSC had concerned itself mainly with matters overseas (even though its function, as spelled out in the original National Security Act, was, Clarke reminded critics, "to advise the President with respect to the integration of domestic, foreign, and military policies relating to national security"). Now, one of its key directorates and most forceful senior directors was deeply engaged in domestic affairs. For example, Clarke's outfit was put in charge of coordinating security for the 1996 Atlanta Summer Olympics. An effective security operation would have to involve elements of the Departments of Transportation, Health and Human Services, Justice, Energy, State, Defense, Treasury, and the CIA, not to mention state and local authorities. Only the NSC had the kind of experience to bring these people to the table, and plan and coordinate their activities to meet an agreed objective. "My job," Clarke would often say, "is to introduce the United States government to itself."

There was no doubt Clarke was effective at his job. He probably understood how Washington worked better than any other official at his senior level. He knew where to get funding for new initiatives, who had the authority to deploy critical assets, and how lines of authority could be directed to meet his needs. Even if he ruffled quite a few feathers in the process, Clarke would get things done, which is a valuable asset for any president or national security adviser to have. Clinton, Lake, and Berger recognized this quality from the outset, and they gave Clarke tremendous leeway in doing his job. In June 1998, Clarke was named "National Coordinator for Counterterrorism," gaining a seat on the Principals Committee and endowing his beefed-up CSG with both budgetary authority and policymaking responsibility. Two months later, U.S. embassies in Kenya and Tanzania were blown up, killing several hundred people. That was the day that America, and the world, was introduced to Osama bin Laden, the man behind the attacks.

Dealing with the threat that Osama bin Laden represented proved tricky. It wasn't that Clinton, Berger, and the rest of the administration didn't understand its nature. They did. But the political context within which they operated limited what they felt they could do. Even the limited military strikes against terrorist training camps in Afghanistan launched in response to the embassy bombings elicited vitriolic condemnation from political opponents on Capitol Hill and elsewhere, many of whom contended that the real purpose of the strikes was to distract attention from the sex scandal in which the president was by now deeply embroiled. This, to them, was a real-life *Wag the Dog*—the box-office hit that had political advisers fabricating a crisis with Albania to distract attention from political troubles at home. Faced with such criticism, Clinton and his top advisers felt constrained from ordering more forceful action, whether a systematic bombing campaign of terrorist training camps or an even more risky incursion of Special Forces or CIA operatives into Afghanistan to try to capture or kill bin Laden. Knowing what we know now, it is clear that more should have been done at the time to try to neutralize the terrorist threat that bin Laden and his Al Qaeda network represented. Indeed, it was this realization—and the political fallout it might imply—that may have led Berger after 9/11 to purloin highly classified documents from the National Archives. The documents suggested that more might have been done to deal with the threat during Clinton's last years in office. It was an act for which he later would plead guilty, pay a hefty fine, and lose his security clearances.

Even so, there is little doubt that Clinton, Berger, and the rest of the administration took the threats seriously. They realized terrorism was a reality that could even hit Americans at home. This became clear a year later when information reached Washington about a series of possible terrorist strikes that could take place around the turn of the millennium. The administration's top officials were kept busy for weeks trying to prevent an attack. There were daily meetings of Berger's "small group" (consisting of Albright, Cohen, Tenet, the attorney general, the FBI director, the JCS chairman, as well as Fuerth and Clarke), and many more by Clarke's CSG. They scoured every piece of information for clues and directed activity around the country. Through hard work and happenstance, a plot to blow up Los Angeles Airport was broken up, leading to further arrests in Brooklyn, Boston, and elsewhere. "We now have a foreign threat to come to the United States and attack in the United States," Clarke told us a few weeks later.

———

With the election of 2000 decided, Clinton met with his successor, George W. Bush, in the Oval Office for two hours of one-on-one discussions about foreign policy and national security. "I think you will find that by far your biggest threat is Bin Laden and the al Qaeda," the outgoing president told Bush. It was a message all of Bush's senior advisers would hear from their Clinton counterparts. Berger showed up for a briefing on the terrorist threat that Clarke was giving to Condoleezza Rice, his designated successor. "I'm here because I want to underscore how important this issue is," Berger told Rice. Later that day, when the two of them met in his own office, Berger again warned his successor, "You're going to spend more time during your four years on terrorism generally and al-Qaeda specially than on any other issue."

Berger may not have been satisfied with the organizational solution he had devised to address the threat of terrorism, he told us in an interview, but he was in no doubt about the nature of the threat. "Terrorism," he said, five months before 9/11, "is the most serious threat to American security."

8

"I'm a Gut Player"

The governor needed a tutor. George W. Bush was thinking of running for president in 2000, but he didn't have "the foggiest idea" about international politics. Throughout the summer of 1998, Bush met with foreign policy luminaries from his father's generation, including former Secretary of State George Shultz and former Secretaries of Defense Dick Cheney and Don Rumsfeld. He also met with stars of his own generation, like Paul Wolfowitz, who had been Cheney's chief policy aide in the Pentagon, and Richard Haass, who had run Middle East and Iraq policy on his father's NSC staff. And he met three times that summer with Condoleezza Rice, a political scientist who had become Stanford University's youngest provost after having served as the chief Soviet expert on the Scowcroft NSC. The last of these meetings took place during an August weekend at the Bush family estate in Kennebunkport, Maine, where over long workout sessions and fishing trips off the Atlantic coast, the Texas governor was instructed by the Stanford professor about the situation in Russia and China, and trouble spots around the world. Bush felt comfortable around Rice. He was impressed by her directness and by her ability to frame questions and answers in ways he clearly understood. She was an excellent tutor.

After winning reelection as governor of Texas in November, Bush asked Rice to be in charge of foreign policy advice in his run for the

White House. Rice agreed, and together with Wolfowitz she pulled together a small team of experts, friends, and former colleagues. It included Richard Armitage, Stephen Hadley, Richard Perle, and Dov Zakheim, all of whom had served in the Reagan or Bush Pentagon, Robert Blackwill (Rice's first boss at the NSC), and Robert Zoellick, a top aide to Secretary of State James Baker, with whom Rice had worked on German unification issues in 1989–90. They called themselves "the Vulcans," after the Roman god of fire, a huge statue of which stood in Birmingham, Alabama, Rice's hometown. When the Vulcans met with Bush, other foreign policy heavyweights, such as Shultz and Cheney, would sometimes join the discussions. Yet other Republican stalwarts, including Colin Powell, Brent Scowcroft, and Henry Kissinger, openly expressed their support for Bush's candidacy. Rumsfeld chaired a more clandestine campaign group focused on the single issue of missile defense.

The decision to bring a large number of foreign policy stars into the campaign reflected a desire to reassure the public about the Texas governor's lack of experience. "I may not be able to tell you exactly the nuance of the East Timorian situation," Bush assured *New York Times* columnist Maureen Dowd in an interview early in the campaign, "but I'll ask Condi Rice or I'll ask Paul Wolfowitz or I'll ask Dick Cheney. I'll ask the people who've had experience." The Vulcans, in turn, were impressed with Bush's qualities, if not his knowledge about foreign affairs. "His basic instincts about foreign policy and what needed to be done were there," Rice said during the campaign. "Our job was to help him fill in the details."

Once he was elected president, Bush again sought to reassure the public about his national security credentials by appointing true giants to key slots in his administration. It was the reason he had decided to make Dick Cheney his vice president. And it was why he appointed Powell and Rumsfeld to run State and Defense. They were a stellar cast, with decades of hands-on Washington experience in the national security field that many saw as useful compensation for the president's own inexperience. Bush looked to Rice, his national security adviser, to help him manage the policymaking process. Her ability to do so would depend greatly on whether Bush's other advisers could agree on the basic direction of policy, and on whether they would work cooperatively within the process she was to manage. Unfortunately, they would end up doing neither. There were deep personal and ideological differences among Cheney, Powell, and Rumsfeld, and these proved difficult to overcome. So, rather than trying to bring the process (and the top players) into line, Rice focused on staffing Bush and trying to translate his instincts into policy. She defined her job as Bush's enabler and enforcer. This earned her the president's enduring trust, loyalty, and support—and ultimately a promotion to secretary of state. But it wasn't at all clear that seeing this job primarily as staffing the president rather than managing the policymaking process was what this president needed—even though, by all evidence, it was what he wanted.

George W. Bush came to the White House knowing that foreign policy was not his strong suit. "This is a big world," he'd said. "I've got a lot to learn." But he believed that an experienced team of advisers would help him deal with that big world beyond the United States. "If I have any genius or smarts," the president told Bob Woodward later, "it's the ability to recognize talent, ask them to serve and work with them as a team."

Dick Cheney, his vice president, was such a talent. Bush had originally asked Cheney to help him find a suitable vice-presidential candidate, insisting that he was looking for someone with the Washington experience that he lacked and whose political ambitions would not conflict with his own agenda or priorities. "You know," Bush told Cheney after they'd reviewed a list of possible candidates, "you're the solution to my problem." Cheney agreed; what Bush needed most was a vice president, not a running mate—and he fit the bill better than anyone else. Cheney would be an active player in the administration, as he made clear to Dan Quayle when the former vice president told him that his job would consist of funerals and fundraising. "I have a different understanding with the president," Cheney replied. Bush agreed to give Cheney access to "every table and every meeting." To that end, Cheney hired a large staff, ensured that he had access to all information, and placed key allies in important positions throughout the rest of the administration.

Heading Cheney's staff was his close ally and confidant I. Lewis ("Scooter") Libby, who was not only his chief of staff but also his national security adviser, as well as an assistant to the president in his own right (placing Libby on a par with Rice in the White House hierarchy). For national security issues, Cheney and Libby assembled their own staff of fourteen senior people, including two deputy national security advisers, many of whom had the stature necessary to serve in senior slots on the NSC staff itself. This mini-NSC staff was not only far larger than any that Cheney's predecessors had hired. (Gore, for example, had only four midrank military officers assisting his national security adviser.) It was larger than President Kennedy's entire NSC staff. In addition, Cheney made sure he had access to every piece of information circulating within the Council staff. Two days into the administration, Stephen Hadley, Rice's deputy, advised the senior staff that copies of every memo to Bush, Rice, or himself would also be routed to the vice president's office. It soon turned out that the same was true for many e-mails, which were automatically forwarded to Cheney's office without the knowledge of their authors. Finally, to extend his influence beyond the White House, Cheney, who headed the transition from the outgoing to the incoming administration, was able to place key allies throughout the administration—including Don Rumsfeld at Defense, Paul O'Neill at Treasury, Mitch Daniels and Sean O'Keefe at the Office of Management and Budget, Stephen Hadley at the NSC, and John Bolton at State. In short, armed with a presidential mandate, and the staff and information he needed, Cheney was in an excellent position to ensure his voice would be heard at every table and in every meeting he, his staff, or his allies attended.

Though Cheney's voice was powerful, it was not the only one. Nor was it always decisive. The first appointment Bush announced after his election was that of Colin Powell as secretary of state. Powell was an irresistible appointment for Bush. The general had been a critical asset throughout the campaign, symbolizing in person what Bush meant by his claim to be a "compassionate conservative." Powell's stellar record—White House fellow, military assistant to Caspar Weinberger, Reagan's last (and best) national security adviser, youngest chairman of the Joint Chiefs of Staff, overall commander of the Gulf War, best-selling author—also helped to reassure people about the likely direction of Bush's foreign policy. And since Powell was the most popular and trusted public figure in America, many hoped that his appointment would soothe the deep divisions that had marked the contested aftermath of the election.

The announcement of his nomination, though, may have been the high point of Powell's influence in the new Bush administration. The press conference that followed set a tone that would come back to haunt the secretary of state. Bush gushed about Powell—"an American hero, an American example and a great American story"—and briefly detailed his own approach to world affairs. "I will set our priorities and we will stand by them," the president-elect insisted. "If we do not set our own agenda, it will be set by others, potential adversaries or the crises of the moment." Powell came next. After briefly thanking the president for nominating him to the highest cabinet office, the incoming secretary of state launched into a lengthy disquisition about the state of the world and how he viewed America's role in it. He started off by directly contradicting what Bush had said moments before: "Mr. President-elect, during your administration you will be faced with many challenges, and crises that we don't know anything about right now will come along." He then went on to give his views not only on the foreign policy challenges and opportunities facing the country but also on missile defense, overseas troop deployments, and other military issues not normally the purview of a secretary of state. In the question-and-answer session that followed, Powell took the questions and gave the answers—not the president he was to work for.

Powell's towering performance was not lost on the media. "Powell seemed to dominate the President-elect who had just nominated him, both physically and in the confidence he projected," reported the *Washington Post*. "At times General Powell sounded as if he were speaking not just as the next secretary of state," the *New York Times* noted, "but as the next secretary of defense, too." And the columnist Thomas Friedman hoped that "Colin Powell is always right in his advice to Mr. Bush—because he so towered over the president-elect, who let him answer every question on foreign policy, that it was impossible to imagine Mr. Bush ever challenging or overruling Mr. Powell on any issue." Nor was the performance lost on Bush, Cheney, and others in the incoming president's coterie. Bush appeared to be irritated by Powell's lengthy presentation. Cheney, always wary about what he saw as Powell's grandstanding, was outraged. Already distrustful of the retired general's popularity (and still worried that he might later decide to run for office), Bush and Cheney were determined to put Powell in his place. Richard Armitage, Powell's close friend and deputy-to-be, knew what was coming. "We're screwed," he said, when Powell called him immediately after the press conference was over. The stark contrast between Powell's eloquence and Bush's lack of depth on the issues would come back to haunt him.

Cheney and Bush were determined to counter Powell's outsized personality by appointing a strong secretary of defense. The front-runner for the job was the former Indiana senator Dan Coats, but in their interview with him, Bush and Cheney became convinced that he did not have what it would take to stand up to Powell. (At one point Coats asked Bush whether he would have the president's support if Powell tried to intervene in defense policy issues. Bush wanted someone who could take Powell on without having to rely on the White House.) Their attention soon shifted to Don Rumsfeld, originally slated by Cheney to take over the CIA. The former college wrestler had a strong résumé: Navy fighter pilot, Illinois congressman, White House chief of staff, NATO ambassador, and the youngest defense secretary ever when Ford appointed him to that position in 1975. He also had strong bureaucratic credentials. Nixon had called him a "ruthless little bastard." Kissinger, who had frequently sparred with Rumsfeld during the Nixon and Ford administrations, described him as "a special Washington phenomenon: a skilled full-time politician-bureaucrat [who] was skillful at deflecting every controversial issue into some bureaucratic bog or other."

Still, Bush's decision to choose Rumsfeld was somewhat surprising. Rumsfeld had long been a rival and critic of Bush's father. It was Rumsfeld who had engineered the older Bush's appointment to head the CIA in 1975, ending any immediate prospect for Bush to run for national office. "I see this as the total end of any political future," Bush had cabled Kissinger of his move to the CIA. As it turned out, Rumsfeld's gambit failed. Bush, not Rumsfeld, ended up on the Republican ticket in 1980, and he ran successfully for the White House eight years later. (Rumsfeld had considered running himself in 1988, believing that Bush could not win.) Because of this history, Rumsfeld had been frozen out of any job in the first Bush administration, and a still-bitter former president had urged his son not to appoint him as director of the Central Intelligence Agency. When the younger Bush sought the counsel of James Baker about Rumsfeld's appointment to the Pentagon, his father's best friend said, "all I'm going to say to you is, you know what he did to your daddy." His father's feelings notwithstanding, Bush needed Rumsfeld as a counter to Powell and soon announced his appointment. Neither Bush nor Cheney consulted Powell about the selection.

———

Though Bush entered office with a wide gap in world knowledge, he felt he had a pretty good sense of how to be president. He'd been around the White House when his father was in office, even performing occasional staffing chores, including firing John Sununu, his father's chief of staff. And he had learned the pitfalls of the presidency from his father's triumphs and failures. He would approach the job very differently. As the first White House occupant with an MBA, Bush saw himself as the country's chief executive officer. He would set the nation's agenda, its priorities, and its broad course of action. He had no interest in the complex details of policy—"I don't do nuance," he once confided. For that, he would rely on his strong team of cabinet secretaries. "One of the things that's really important for the American people to understand is, I'll be getting some of the best counsel possible," Bush explained. "General Powell's a strong figure and Dick Cheney's no shrinking violet, but neither is Don Rumsfeld, nor Condi Rice." His job was to listen to their advice and then make the call. His emphasis was on leadership and making decisions, not on administration or execution. Bush approached the challenge of running the country with a remarkable degree of self-confidence. He said he wasn't going to be influenced by polls or focus groups. He would rely on his own instincts, instead. "I'm a gut player," he explained. "I'm not a textbook player."

Bush looked to his national security adviser to help manage the process by which he would make the decisions that the cabinet secretaries were then expected to implement. "My job," Rice explained, "is to organize the decision-making for the president, not to impose my own views." Rice stepped into this role with one great disadvantage and one great advantage. The disadvantage was that she was not really a peer of the other major national security advisers in the administration. "I'm by far the baby in this group," she conceded. That was true not only in terms of age (she was in her forties while the others were in their sixties) but also in terms of experience. Before occupying the corner office in the West Wing, Rice had had a total of three years of government experience—one year with the Joint Chiefs of Staff and two years on the Scowcroft NSC. In contrast, Bush's other advisers had decades of experience at the highest level of government. Each of them had occupied multiple seats at the NSC table—two in the case of Rumsfeld (defense secretary and White House chief of staff), and three in the case of Powell (secretary of state, JCS chairman, and NSC adviser) and Cheney (vice president, defense secretary, and chief of staff).

All of them knew they had years more experience than Rice—and they let her know it. Powell saw himself as Rice's mentor. He regarded her "like a daughter," but he found it difficult to think of her as a senior strategist. Rumsfeld didn't think that much of Rice. He was, Andrew Card, Bush's chief of staff, observed, a "little bit old school" and "a little bit sexist" in his dealings with her. Rumsfeld also had great disdain for the process that Rice was supposed to run. "I report to the president of the United States," he pointedly told Rice. He ordered that all communications from the Pentagon to the White House, including the NSC, be approved by him personally. Cheney, finally, sought to usurp Rice's position by proposing that he, not Rice, chair meetings of the Principals Committee. Even attending such meetings was highly unusual for a vice president, but chairing them would completely emasculate the NSC adviser's internal power and position. Rice strongly objected, insisting to Bush that chairing principals meetings "is what national security advisers do." The president agreed. "Condi will run these meetings," Bush told the participants at his first Council meeting on January 30, 2001. "I'll be seeing all of you regularly, but I want you to debate out here and then Condi will report to me. She's my national security adviser." Even so, when the presidential directive outlining the organization of the National Security Council system was published two weeks later, it pointedly noted that the vice president would preside over NSC meetings when the president was absent.

Rice's challenge to manage these three, strong-willed titans was therefore considerable. But she had one great advantage in approaching this task: she was closer to the president than any of them, including Cheney. She spent an extraordinary amount of time with Bush—sometimes six or seven hours a day. And not just at the White House. Having lost her father just days after her nomination was announced (her mother had passed away fifteen years earlier), Rice, an only child, became an integral part of the Bush family. She would spend most weekends with the president and Laura Bush in Camp David, where she had her own cabin, and often vacation at the ranch in Crawford, Texas, where she sometimes stayed in the guest bedroom of the main house.

Though they came from very different backgrounds—one surrounded by great privilege and wealth, the other by the violence of the segregated South; one a rabble-rouser, the other a studious academic; one white, the other black—Bush and Rice proved remarkably compatible. They shared a love for physical exercise. During the campaign, she had been photographed pumping iron for a cover story in *George* magazine—"Bush's Kissinger: She Can Kick Your Butt Too." Bush loved the story. They were avid sport fans. He had run the professional baseball team, the Texas Rangers, before becoming governor; she, a lifelong Cleveland Browns fan, had long dreamt of one day becoming commissioner of the National Football League. Both were deeply religious. Bush was born-again, Rice a devout Presbyterian. And they shared one other notable characteristic: a complete absence of self-doubt. When a reporter once asked Bush to list his biggest mistake, the president, memorably, was at a complete loss of words. "I wish you would have given me this written question ahead of time, so I could plan for it," he lamented. As for Rice, "I doubt she's ever lost a night's sleep as national security adviser or secretary," one of her best friends told a biographer. Both of them were people comfortable making decisions—and uninterested in looking back.

No national security adviser had been closer to a president than Condi Rice was to Bush. The president often said she was "like my sister," empowering her in a way he empowered no one else. He relied on her for advice and guidance. She was the one person who "can explain foreign policy matters in a way that I can understand," he had said during the campaign. He called her "a close confidante and a good soul." That closeness and confidence gave Rice tremendous access and potential for power. Everyone knew she had the president's ear, and that when she spoke, she was reflecting his thinking. It was this reality that gave her the opportunity to exert major influence over the president and policy. But it was no guarantee. For her ability to translate access and confidence into power and influence depended critically on how she used them to affect the president's thinking and the way he made decisions.

The NSC staff existed to help her do just that. Rice came to Washington with little more than her two years of experience as a staffer for Scowcroft to guide her. Her model, naturally, was "an NSC that functioned a lot like Brent's NSC," as Rice recalled. "Low-key, very much more of a coordinating function, much less operational, smaller." This was in contrast to the Berger NSC, which she believed had become too large, too operational, and too public. Rice also thought the NSC staff under Clinton had become too powerful, that in particular it needed to get out of the business of implementation. "I'm the National Security Adviser; what I do is coordinate policy. I don't operate, I don't implement, I coordinate." Unlike some of her predecessors, she was not interested in weakening any of the cabinet secretaries. Rice and Hadley constantly reminded their staff of "the need to devolve down," to return power and responsibility to the agencies. "We don't implement," was a constant Hadley refrain.

In order to return the NSC to the Scowcroft model, Rice sought to reduce the Council's form, function, and focus in deliberate ways. She cut the staff by nearly a third, mainly by consolidating and eliminating some of the policy and supporting directorates. The four separate directorates that had dealt with different parts of Europe under Clinton were brought back into one; the health and environmental directorates were eliminated entirely; and staffing for press, communications, and legislative affairs was cut drastically in the conviction that these matters could best be handled by the White House offices responsible for them. Rice also explicitly limited the responsibilities of the Council staff to three overriding functions: staffing the president; pushing his policy priorities; and coordinating the rest of the government. Although she maintained that the coordinating function was important, she placed particular emphasis on the first two. "I'm not saying you can let any of them slide," she insisted. "But staffing the president and pushing his high-priority items, he has nobody else to do that but the NSC." Finally, Rice insisted on narrowing the NSC's policy focus, which she sought to return to the traditional concerns of managing relations with the great powers, bolstering alliances, and strengthening the U.S. military—starting with building a national missile defense system.

Whether the Scowcroft model could work well in this administration was the real—and unexamined—question. What made that model so effective in the first Bush administration were two factors that were noticeably absent in the second. One was a basic consensus on the goals and ways of U.S. engagement in the world not only among the top advisers but at lower levels of the administration as well. As would become clear, no such consensus existed within the new administration. The second factor was an activist president, who was deeply familiar with and interested in the world: this had greatly eased the task of Scowcroft and his staff. Bush the elder's ongoing engagement reinforced the role of his assistant in managing the process, and increased the need for cabinet members to connect to Scowcroft in order to stay in sync with the president. Since Bush the younger was far less familiar with and engaged in foreign affairs, Rice's task of helping him make considered decisions was more demanding. It required more than relying on presidential instinct, however good that may have been, and more even than presenting the president with clear differences among his advisers. It also required that the national security adviser and her staff take the initiative: present all of the logical alternatives, probe their underlying assumptions, and perform or commission the critical analysis necessary for reaching decisions. Yet this essential requirement—to assist the president in making sound decisions—was missing from Rice's list of NSC responsibilities.

Another important reason why the Scowcroft model was not easily transferable from one Bush administration to the next was the profound change in the international environment during the intervening years. Rice wasn't prepared for this new world. "I'm really a Europeanist," she had admitted during the campaign. "I've been pressed to understand parts of the world that have not been part of my scope." Even so, the issue agenda that Bush, Cheney, Rice, and others brought into the administration in 2001—great powers, alliances, missile defense, even Iraq—was the same one many of them had focused on when they were last in office in the early 1990s. It was as if they had pushed the pause button on January 20, 1993, and then the play button eight years later. But the world had changed. Instead of the familiar issues, a new set of concerns demanded attention in

2001: the rise of China and India; climate change; the scourge of AIDS and other infectious diseases; the proliferation of weapons and dangerous technologies; and, critically, the threat of transnational terrorism.

None of these issues was truly on the radar of the incoming administration. This became clear when Rice had her first substantive discussion with Richard Clarke, the national coordinator for counterterrorism under Clinton. Clarke also headed the NSC office on transnational threats, which, with fourteen people, was then by far the largest of the Council directories. "The NSC looks just as it did when I worked here a few years ago, except for your operation," Rice told Clarke. "It does domestic things and it is not just doing policy, it seems to be worrying about operational issues." She wasn't sure she wanted to keep the office on transnational threats, though Clarke tried to convince her that his office was new because the world and its many dangers and challenges had evolved considerably. Rice wasn't convinced. She decided to keep Clarke and his people for the time being, but she told him to figure out a way to shed some of the more operational activities and domestic concerns.

Neither the mind-set nor the organization of the new administration was prepared for a world of global, catastrophic terrorism. The president and his senior advisers did not see the September 11 attacks coming. But others within the administration did—and they repeatedly tried to sound the alarm. Four days after George W. Bush was inaugurated as the forty-third president of the United States, Richard Clarke sent Condoleezza Rice a memorandum "*urgently*" seeking a meeting of the principals to review strategy on the Al Qaeda network. Appended to the memo was a December 2000 paper by Clarke proposing a detailed plan for eliminating the network. Rice ignored the request. She wasn't interested in recycling old Clinton administration policies and strategies. Instead, the new NSC adviser wanted a plan that placed the terrorist threat within the regional context of Afghanistan and Pakistan. That, importantly, was also the view of

Powell and his deputy, Richard Armitage, who wanted a strategy for dealing with Pakistan, which required that the administration knew what to do about Al Qaeda. Rice also strongly believed in an ordered policy process, in which issues would first be discussed within NSC interagency meetings, then by the deputies, and finally by the principals and in the Council. Indeed, when she decided to keep Clarke on, she told him that his interagency group—the Counterterrorism and Security Group—would, like all other such groups, report to the deputies rather than to the principals, as had been the case in the previous administration.

The net effect of these decisions was to delay the development of an effective strategy. While other issues such as Iraq and missile defense were fast-tracked and quickly discussed by the principals, Al Qaeda and terrorism were moving along slowly. It would take more than three months to convene the first full Deputies Committee meeting on the issue. The principals' first discussion of a new strategy came on September 4, 2001. Clarke later noted that the first time he actually briefed the president in person on terrorism and Al Qaeda was on the evening of September 11. That may explain why the White House speechwriters hadn't actually heard of the term "Al Qaeda" until that very day.

The insistence that the issue be addressed within a South Asian regional context also seemed to miss the point. "Al Qida [sic] is not some narrow little terrorist issue that needs to be included in a broader regional strategy," Clarke had stressed in his January 25, 2001, memo to Rice. "Rather, several of our regional policies need to consider centrally the transnational challenge to the U.S. and our interests posed by the *Al Qida* network." And in actual fact, the discussions in the Deputies Committee showed that some key officials were not focused on or even convinced of the threat. For example, Rumsfeld's deputy, Paul Wolfowitz, complained about the focus on Osama bin Laden and the threat he might pose. "There are others that do as well, at least as much. Iraqi terrorism for example," he insisted. As a result, the policy review proceeded slowly—too slowly. "We weren't going fast enough," Armitage later complained to the 9/11

Commission. Hadley disagreed. "For the government, we moved it along as fast as we could move it along."

Clarke, though, wasn't the only one to warn of the pending danger. In March 2001, George Tenet, whom Bush had kept on as the CIA director, went to Hadley to present him with a list of new "covert action authorities" the CIA would need in order to launch a more aggressive strategy against Al Qaeda, including an explicit authorization to kill Osama bin Laden. Tenet was told that he should hold off on the request until a new policy had been put in place. (President Bush would finally approve the authorities on September 17, as part of the new war against terrorism.) During the summer of 2001, the CIA repeatedly warned that a terrorist attack against U.S. interests was imminent.

One particularly urgent warning occurred on July 10. Tenet's counterterrorism team had put together a strategic assessment based on the accumulated set of indicators of a likely attack. The assessment, Tenet said, "literally made my hair stand on end." The CIA director picked up the white secure phone with a direct connection to Rice and told her he had to see her immediately. Fifteen minutes later, Tenet and his team were sitting in Rice's West Wing office. Hadley and Clarke were there as well. A CIA operative identified as Rich B. opened the briefing: "There will be a significant terrorist attack in the coming weeks or months," he stated. It would be "spectacular," and designed to inflict mass casualties. "Attack preparations have been made," the operative declared. "Multiple and simultaneous attacks are possible, and they will occur with little warning."

The message was unmistakable: An attack was coming. "This country needs to go on a war footing *now*," Cofer Black, the CIA counterterrorism chief, told Rice. How? she asked. By signing the covert action authorities the agency had asked for since March, came the reply. Three days later, the deputies met to discuss the authorities as well as a presidential directive drafted by Clarke, which was largely based on his original strategy paper of December 2000. It would take another seven weeks for the principals to meet and approve the directive and authorities, which, on September 10, 2001, were awaiting President Bush's signature.

Bob Woodward was the first person to reveal the dramatic meeting in Rice's office that July afternoon, which the 9/11 Commission had failed to report. Once Tenet had confirmed the meeting, and offered more detail, Woodward accused the CIA director of failing in his duty by not presenting his warnings directly to the president. Tenet, who met with the president daily, insists that he warned Bush about a possible attack throughout the summer of 2001. But in seeking a change in policy, the CIA director believed it was important to go through regular channels, which was why he called Rice. "I remember directors that went directly to the President, around a policy process, to get a covert action going," Tenet recalled. "That doesn't work. You don't jump the principals and say, 'Give me covert action.'" Particularly in the disciplined Bush White House, in which the president was the CEO who didn't want to be bothered by details, Tenet's insistence that "you bring the action to the national-security adviser and people who set the table for the President to decide on policies they're going to implement" seems correct from the perspective of good governance.

Woodward's ire is misplaced. Rather than asking why Tenet did not go directly to the president, the veteran journalist might better have asked why Rice didn't do so. Indeed, why, when confronted with a threat briefing that made people's hair stand on end, did the national security adviser not pick up the phone to the Oval Office and say, "Mr. President, George is here, and I think you need to hear what he has to say"? Rice later suggested that the Tenet meeting wasn't all that important—even though it was the only time in Tenet's seven years as CIA director that he called over to the White House to say he needed to see the national security adviser immediately. The meeting came "in the context of very high threat warnings almost every day," Rice remembered. "We would talk about them in the Oval," suggesting that even if Tenet had gone to Bush rather than Rice, the outcome would have been no different.

Tenet did not give up. Less than four weeks after the July 10

White House meeting, the CIA prepared a paper—a top-secret presidential daily brief—detailing all it knew about the possibility that Al Qaeda might attack in the United States. Prepared in answer to Bush's queries about a possible terrorist threat at home, it carried the ominous title "Bin Laden Determined to Strike in U.S." The paper discussed a variety of threats to underscore bin Laden's determination, including hijackings, casing of buildings in New York, and approximately seventy ongoing FBI investigations in the United States that were bin Laden–related. "All right," Bush told the CIA briefer who had read the paper to the president at his Crawford ranch. "You've covered your ass, now." After 9/11, Bush, Cheney, Rice, and others would dismiss the August 6 presidential daily brief as little more than "historical." The paper, Bush later testified to the 9/11 Commission, told him little more than that Al Qaeda was dangerous, which he had known since the day he became president. He was heartened, he told the commissioners, that the FBI was investigating reports thoroughly, but he did not think it necessary to inquire about their progress with his national security adviser, the attorney general, or the FBI director.

Rice shared Bush's perspective—on the presidential daily brief and the threat more generally. "This was not a threat report to the president or a threat report to me," Rice testified before the 9/11 Commission. "If there was any reason to believe that I needed to do something," she continued, "I would have been expected to be asked to do it. We were not asked to do it." Rice also told the 9/11 Commission that her job did not include coordinating domestic agencies—or between foreign and domestic agencies. "I didn't manage the domestic agencies; no national security adviser does." Instead, she looked to Clarke and his Counterterrorism and Security Group as the bridge to those agencies (even though when she came to the White House she had ordered Clarke to shed such responsibility to other entities). In the end, Rice blamed "structural" problems in the U.S. government—a word she used forty-two times in her three-hour testimony before the 9/11 Commission. There was the structural problem of the CIA and the FBI not sharing information; the structural problem of foreign and domestic agencies not talking to each other; and the structural problem of law enforcement requirements clashing with intelligence needs.

It is, of course, the national security adviser's job to break down these structural barriers and ensure effective coordination across agencies. Indeed, Rice had come to Washington pledging "to work the seams, stitching the connections together tightly." Yet, in this crucial instance, when stitching the seams was more important than ever, she pleaded that it was not her job to coordinate domestic agencies or, worse, that no one asked her to do anything. Neither, though, had she asked what she could do. As the warnings multiplied, she could have convened the key principals repeatedly and asked each of them what they were doing to chase down the threat information that was coming in. How were the FBI investigations proceeding? What evidence was there of known terrorists or Al Qaeda affiliates seeking visas to enter the United States? Were airplanes secure against possible hijackings? Did we find the men who were casing buildings in New York?

These and other questions would have forced the principals in turn to go back to their agencies and begin asking more questions. And maybe, just maybe, information would have emerged that would have led investigators to one or more of the hijackers before they boarded their planes and committed their murderous acts. Though there was no actionable intelligence—no information on the time or place or type of attack—Rice did little to shake the system in a way that might have produced just that.

The 9/11 attacks may not have been avoidable—even the best efforts can fail—but the process leading up to the attacks was seriously flawed. As the 9/11 Commission pointed out, there was a lot of continuity in terms of personnel and organization from the Clinton to Bush administrations. George Tenet and the counterterrorism center remained at the CIA. Dick Clarke and the Counterterrorism and Security Group remained at the White House. Dale Watson remained as assistant director for counterterrorism at the FBI. And all of them "did their utmost to sound a loud alarm," the commission noted. "The system was blinking red."

The change was at the top—and within the National Security Council itself. And there, Tenet later noted, "there was a loss of urgency." The new president and his senior advisers just didn't take the threats all that seriously. "I didn't feel that sense of urgency," Bush admitted to Woodward. "My blood was not nearly as boiling." Cheney was not particularly alarmed by any of the intelligence coming in, even though he saw everything there was to see. "My impression at the time," the vice president recalled, "was not that an attack was imminent. There was noise in the system. But that's the nature of the business." Rumsfeld was focused on creating a twenty-first-century military and showed no interest in military operations against Al Qaeda. Powell did show some interest; he had asked to meet with Clarke's group during the transition and wanted to figure out how to deal with Al Qaeda in order to have a coherent strategy for Pakistan. But he had many other concerns to keep him busy in the first eight months of the new administration. In short, the system may have been blinking red, but most people at the top kept their eyes averted.

The attacks on September 11 changed George W. Bush. Up to that point, the Washington consensus seemed to be that, as one of his speechwriters put it, "Bush was not on his way to a very successful presidency." The attacks gave Bush a new lease on life—and offered him unprecedented opportunity to demonstrate his strengths as a leader. In the days and weeks that followed one of the greatest tragedies to befall Americans in their history, the president grew in stature and popularity. "I am here for a reason," Bush confided to his political aide, Karl Rove. "I will seize the opportunity to achieve big goals." History would ultimately judge whether he had acted rightly or wrongly, Bush told the Japanese prime minister later. "But it won't judge well somebody who doesn't act, somebody who just bides time here."

Always brimming with self-confidence, after the attacks Bush was "dead certain" (in Robert Draper's apt phrase) about what he now needed to do: whatever it would take to prevent another attack and defeat terrorism. "Our responsibility to history is clear," the president told mourners at the National Cathedral in Washington on September 14, 2001. "To answer these attacks and rid the world of evil." The determination was fed by a flood of information about possible new threats, this time possibly involving anthrax or some other weapon of mass destruction. To warn of pending dangers, the CIA and other intelligence agencies were now sending raw, unexamined information to the White House, which often raised the most frightening possibilities. At a meeting months after the attacks, a senior White House official greeted the German minister of the interior by saying: "Welcome to Washington. You have come to a war capital"—by which the official meant that those with access to information felt besieged by the terrorist threat. In an interview with a *New York Times* reporter, Rice acknowledged that the constant flood of threat information "had a powerful effect on Bush's state of mind and her own. She felt she was constantly on edge, in a state of paranoia, but rational paranoia, as even old threats— and Iraq would soon be one—took on new meaning."

Such a state of paranoia helps explain Bush's insistence that almost any action was justified to prevent another, quite possibly even worse attack on the United States. In the president's mind, as well as in the minds of his most senior advisers, this justified taking preemptive military action against terrorist and other threats even before they fully materialized. It justified putting suspected terrorists behind bars without judicial review or the prospect of a fair hearing or day in court, even subjecting them to abuses that almost everyone would describe as torture. It justified warrantless surveillance of e-mail and telephone conversations not only of foreigners but also of American citizens. To Bush and his advisers, the threat justified virtually any action to keep Americans safe and secure. This became known as "the one percent solution," a doctrine coined by Dick Cheney. "If there's a one percent chance that Pakistani scientists are helping al Qaeda build or develop a nuclear weapon, we have to treat it as a certainty in our response," the vice president declared in a statement that was expandable to all terrorist threats. "It's not about our analysis, or finding a preponderance of evidence," he explained. "It's about our response."

The first application of the new doctrine was the war against the Taliban in Afghanistan. On the evening of the terrorist attacks, Bush had addressed the nation from the Oval Office, and made clear that the country was now at war. "We will make no distinction between the terrorists who committed these acts and those who harbor them," he declared. The president made this far-reaching commitment without consulting Cheney, Rumsfeld, or Powell (though he did bounce the language off Rice, who encouraged him to use it). The student, it seemed, no longer needed a tutor.

The goal of the war in Afghanistan would be to capture or kill Osama bin Laden, to destroy the terrorist infrastructure that had arisen there, and to remove the Taliban from power. The decision-making process leading up to the war was focused on these goals, but never really on what would follow. Days before the actual fighting was to start, Bush, at an NSC meeting in the White House Situation Room, had asked: "Who will run the country?" An obvious question, given that the stated goal of the military operation was to remove the government from power. But Rice hadn't thought of addressing the issue until then. "Her most awful moments," Woodward writes of Bush's NSC adviser, "were when the president thought of something that the principals, particularly she, should have anticipated."

Part of the reason no one could answer Bush's question was that the administration had come to office with great disdain for nation building. During the 2000 campaign, Bush had frequently denigrated U.S. involvement in such efforts. Rice had scoffed at the thought of the "82nd Airborne escorting kids to kindergarten." Superpowers fight wars; they do not do windows. The attitude continued after 9/11 and into the Afghan war. Even after the first bombs had fallen, Rumsfeld distanced himself from any U.S. responsibility for helping to forge a more stable government once the Taliban was gone. "I don't think [that] leaves us with a responsibility to try to figure out what kind of government that country ought to have," the Pentagon chief said on October 9. "I don't know people who are smart enough from other countries to tell other countries the kind of arrangements they ought to have to govern themselves. One would hope and pray that they'd end up with governments that would provide the best possible for the people of those countries." Bush offered little more than hope and prayer two days later, when he passed the responsibility on to others. "It would be a useful function for the United Nations to take over the so-called 'nation-building'—I would call it the stabilization of a future government—after our military mission is complete."

Though Osama bin Laden escaped Afghanistan to live another day, the Taliban were quickly routed by the combination of American airpower and local insurgents—and by innovative strategies that multiplied the effectiveness of both. The war, Bush believed, showed that regime change was relatively easy and risk-free. "For hundreds of years of war," he later argued, "military power was used to end a regime by breaking a nation. Today, we have the greater power to free a nation by breaking a dangerous and aggressive regime." Prior to Afghanistan—and before 9/11—Bush had explicitly rejected repeated requests by General Tommy Franks, the regional commander for the Middle East, to do more robust planning for an Iraqi contingency. But after the attacks and the seeming ease with which the Taliban was removed from power, Bush was ready.

On November 21, 2001, Bush ordered Rumsfeld to begin quietly planning for an invasion of Iraq to remove Saddam Hussein. The president informed Rice about his decision. And he told Cheney. But not Powell. The four-star general who had been in charge of the U.S. military during the last American confrontation with Saddam's Iraq was left out of the loop. Indeed, a few days after Bush's order, Powell was quoted in the *New York Times Magazine* as saying, "Iraq isn't going anywhere. It is in a fairly weakened state." As for removing Saddam, "I never saw a plan that was going to take him out. It was just some ideas coming from various quarters about, let's go bomb."

Clearly, when it came to Iraq, the president and his secretary of state were not on the same page.

Bush was the driving force on Iraq, and responsibility for the decision to go to war is ultimately his alone. As history will no doubt record, it was a deeply flawed decision—based on an exaggerated view of the threat and a complete lack of knowledge of the local and regional consequences of launching an invasion into the Arab and Muslim heartland. But it was also the product of a profoundly dysfunctional policy process—a process that was dominated by the wishful thinking of strong-willed officials that failed to evaluate information systematically or assess alternative courses of action carefully, and that allowed control over policy formulation and execution to slip beyond the purview of the National Security Council. As it was a war of choice rather than necessity, there was time—plenty of time—to conduct a thorough review and in-depth examination of the situation, the requirements, and the consequences. The responsibility for doing so fell to Condoleezza Rice, the manager of the process.

Rice's task, of course, wasn't easy. One of the key players, the secretary of state, was an outlier within the administration. In terms of the ideological playing field, Powell saw Cheney sitting at around the ten-yard line, Rumsfeld and Rice between the ten- and twenty-yard lines, and himself at around the forty. They were in the red zone, while he was still at midfield. Powell didn't say where he thought Bush was playing on the ideological field, but he did make clear that he didn't think all that much of the president. The president, Powell said, "is guided more by a powerful inertial navigation system than by intellect. He knows what he wants to do, and what he wants to hear is how to get it done."

That perspective became evident during the one long and substantive meeting Powell had with Bush about Iraq, which occurred over dinner at the White House residence on August 5, 2002. Rice was also present at that meeting, which she arranged at the secretary's request. Powell made a strong case against a precipitous decision to go to war, warning in particular about the consequences of toppling the Iraqi regime. "You are going to be the proud owner of

25 million people," he warned. "You will own all their hopes, aspirations and problems. You'll own it all." Powell didn't say: Don't do it. Instead, he suggested that Bush take the issue to the United Nations and build a strong international coalition for action. "If you take it to the UN," he insisted, "you've got to recognize that they might be able to solve it. In which case there's no war."

Bush appreciated Powell's counsel, but he only heard the parts he wanted to hear. He would go to the United Nations, but only as a means to gain support for war against Iraq, not as an alternative to war. He appreciated Powell's warning about the consequences—"it's going to suck the oxygen out of everything," the secretary of state had said—but he had made up his mind. Asked later about his reaction to Powell's statements, Bush dismissed them as "talking tactics." His job, the president insisted, was "to secure America" and to be strategic about it. The president would listen to his secretary of state. But, he emphasized, "I didn't need his permission."

With Powell largely isolated and ignored, Rice's second problem in running the policy process was Don Rumsfeld. The seventy-year-old defense secretary didn't think a great deal of the much younger, and much less experienced, national security adviser. He would read when she spoke in meetings or make dismissive comments that left others in the room uncomfortable. Worse, he ran roughshod over the process. He would come to meetings unprepared to make a decision or even to argue his department's position. Often he would deliver a new paper to meetings and insist on an immediate decision, without allowing any of the other principals time to review the arguments. He gave his subordinates no flexibility in trying to find compromises in interagency meetings—his word was law, and neither his deputy nor anyone else could deviate from it at any point. And when he did not like the direction an issue was going, he just wouldn't show up. In early 2004, Rice tried to call a meeting to implement the president's order to commence trials of detainees at Guantanamo. Rumsfeld finally agreed to a meeting, but then didn't turn up. This happened not once, not twice, but three times. Steve Herbits, one of Rumsfeld's best friends, who the defense secretary sometimes brought in to evaluate how things were going, called Rumsfeld's style of operations the "Haldeman model—arrogant." The secretary of defense was often "abusive," Herbits wrote in a memo. "He diminished important people in front of others."

But it was arrogance with a purpose: to completely control the policy process. And Rumsfeld succeeded brilliantly. He effectively eliminated the military as an independent voice in policy deliberations. General Richard Myers, the JCS chairman, achieved what he called a "mind meld" with Rumsfeld, so that they would always speak in the same voice during meetings at the White House. The general in charge of Central Command was no different. Asked by Bush during a meeting what he thought, General Franks replied: "Sir, I think exactly what my secretary thinks, what he's ever thought, what he will think, or whatever he thought he might think." Rumsfeld derived this power and control from a rigid insistence on the chain of command, which under Goldwater-Nichols, the landmark legislation of the mid-1980s, ran from the field through the combatant commanders to the defense secretary, and on directly to the president.

The Pentagon chief made the point emphatically after the September 11 attacks, when the president decided to create a new NSC position for counterterrorism and appointed Wayne Downing, a retired four-star general, to the post. In a scathing memo to Rice, Rumsfeld objected to the decision, codified in a presidential directive, to making Downing the "principal" adviser to Bush on counterterrorism. "There is only one principal military adviser," Rumsfeld wrote, referring to the JCS chairman. Downing's mandate, he went on, "could be read as infringing on the chain of command from the President and the Secretary of Defense to Combatant Commanders." It was "dangerous, exceedingly dangerous," to think that anyone else could have any role in "fulfilling war-fighting responsibilities, including mission planning and execution." Downing's wings were clipped; he resigned the post in deep frustration months later. But so were Rice's. "You're not in the chain of command," Rumsfeld effectively told her. Neither Rice nor the NSC staff could play any part in military planning or decision making.

In playing his bureaucratic one-upmanship, Rumsfeld had important allies in the White House. He was, as the journalist Andrew
Cockburn observed, "one of history's great courtiers," and Bush
didn't mind in the least. The president appreciated that his defense
secretary didn't play out his battles in the media (unlike, say, Powell) and that he never uttered a word of disloyalty toward him. "Bush
rather enjoyed Rumsfeld's cussedness and the manner in which he
cheerfully tormented the press," and they shared a belief that policy
was best advanced by "Big Ideas" and bold action. Rumsfeld's other
key ally, of course, was the vice president, who served as Rumsfeld's
deputy first in the Budget Office under Nixon and then when Rumsfeld was Ford's Chief of Staff. Though his longtime mentee might
now outrank him in the political hierarchy, Rumsfeld's relationship
with Cheney had not really changed. "When I look at Don Rumsfeld, I see a fine Secretary of Defense," Cheney once remarked. "When
Rumsfeld looks at me, he sees a former assistant to Don Rumsfeld."

Cheney and Rumsfeld made for a powerful pair—especially when
their views were shared by the president. Together, they could dominate the policy process in a way that was very difficult for the NSC
adviser to counter. It didn't help that Cheney was no more interested
in playing the formal process game than his onetime mentor. His participation in principals meetings had "a chilling effect on the free flow
of views," Tenet recalled, as none of the principals wanted to end up
on the wrong side of an argument. More worrisome was the fact that
Cheney acted on important policy issues without involving Rice or
other key players. He had set the precedent as early as March 2001,
when he secured Bush's assent to declaring that the administration did
not favor mandating restrictions on greenhouse gas emissions. Cheney
consulted neither Rice nor Powell (nor Christine Todd Whitman, the
Environmental Protection Agency administrator, for that matter), even
though the foreign policy implications of the decision were immense.

A few months later, Cheney was at it again—this time over the
volatile issue of how to deal with people suspected of past or future
involvement in terrorist activities. On November 13, 2001, Bush
issued an executive order authorizing the military to detain any-

one the president determined had "engaged in, aided or abetted, or considered to commit" terrorism. It would be the commander in chief's call; no court would have a say. The first Powell and Rice heard of it was when CNN broadcast news of the president's order. "That shouldn't have happened," Rice later confided. But it did— and would do so again and again. On crucial detainee decisions, such as whether to apply the Geneva Conventions or what types of inter-rogation methods to use, State and the NSC were kept in the dark. Yet few decisions did more damage to America's global standing and moral authority than those that authorized locking up people with-out trial, setting up secret prisons around the globe, and allowing extraordinarily abusive methods of interrogation.

Rice, at times, would object. She once dressed down Alberto Gon-zales, the White House counsel, "in full Nurse Ratched mode," as Powell recalled, referring to the head nurse in *One Flew Over the Cuckoo's Nest.* She also complained directly to Cheney when the vice president, in August 2002, delivered an ill-conceived speech on Iraq, weapons of mass destruction, and UN inspections. But the damage had been done. Cheney's actions—and Bush's inactions—had the effect of cut-ting Rice out of the very process she was supposed to manage.

Under these circumstances, pulling the process back into line would have presented a formidable challenge. The NSC adviser never really tried. Early on, she came to believe that when the president and vice president agreed, as they often did, it wasn't her role to object. Nor did she think it was her role to construct a process that would put these policies to the test. As a result, those who thought the poli-cies ill-advised often felt they were not given a chance to make their case. To them, the process was skewed and effectively closed.

This sense, not surprising, was strongest at the State Department, where Colin Powell and Rich Armitage felt increasingly isolated from the rest of the administration. That perception was widely shared outside the administration as well. Henry Kissinger once quipped that Powell's department was viewed abroad "as a small country that occasionally does business with the United States." But the impact of such isolation on policymaking was no less real for that. State Department officials would enter interagency meetings with what they saw as the deck stacked three-to-one against them—with Defense, the vice president's office, and the NSC all likely aligned against State's position. When they raised questions, Rice and Hadley would make them feel as if "they were not on the team." Often, once the formal meetings were concluded, another separate meeting would take place upstairs, with the president in the Oval Office. Cheney and Rumsfeld would be there, as would Rice and often the JCS chairman and White House chief of staff. But Powell wouldn't be invited. Nor would Tenet. The result was a closed—and flawed—policy process. "There was not enough quality control," complained Richard Haass, Powell's chief policy planning aide. "Too many assumptions got accepted or built in."

Two-plus years into the administration an increasingly frustrated Richard Armitage, an original member of the Vulcans, went to the White House to complain to Rice that she was running a "dysfunctional" process. "You don't resolve things," he told her. Defense was running roughshod over the interagency process. Rumsfeld and his aides were conducting their own foreign policy. Deputies and Principals Committee meetings were useless. "We'd get on the gerbil wheel every morning getting ready for these DCs and PCs," Armitage said later. "Then we'd get off the gerbil wheel and wait for an answer. No answer would ever come from the NSC, so we'd get back on the gerbil wheel the next morning." And when decisions were made, there was no follow-through by the agencies and no price to be paid for failing to do so. The problem, Armitage told Rice, was an absence of execution and a complete lack of accountability—especially on the trio of issues that mattered most: Iraq, Iran, and North Korea. Powell agreed, though he made the point more gently to Rice. "We are not knitted up," he told her. "And we don't go about these things well." Rice would have none of it. "People generally think something is dysfunctional when they didn't get their way," she later explained. The situation for State was more difficult in the case of Iraq, she conceded, "because you had a structure where Defense had the lead, but increasingly, State had equities." But there was little she could do about this structural problem, Rice insisted. It "wasn't going to be solved by an interagency process."

Rice was surely right that part of the problem was that State's key players stood outside the main consensus—that they were running on a different part of the playing field. But that wasn't the only problem. Another one was that she didn't see it as her role to manage a contentious interagency process: to probe decisions, weigh alternatives, assess consequences, and prepare for the unforeseen. As Rice saw it, her primary role was to push the president's agenda. Bush had strong views, and he had no interest in having others question him, putting his views to some kind of test, or figuring out whether a different course of action might work better. He knew he was right, and was only interested in getting things done. Rice wasn't about to question these views—to try to talk the president out of, or into, any particular policy. "I don't talk the president into almost anything, all right," she snapped at one reporter. "You can't do that with the president." Her job, instead, was to translate Bush's instincts and intuitions into policy, to make sure his wishes became his government's commands. Nor did she disagree with these views. "I've been tremendously influenced by the president," Rice explained. She had come to Washington as a self-described realist, but after 9/11 she was persuaded by Bush's frequent talk about universal values—"and about the links between those and security"—that their promotion should now drive American foreign policy. "People don't understand," Rice told a close friend. "It's not me exercising influence over him. I'm internalizing his world."

"One of the great mysteries to me," George Tenet wrote some years after he had resigned as head of the CIA, "is exactly when the war in Iraq became inevitable." In the sixteen months after Bush first ordered Rumsfeld to begin serious military planning for an invasion, there never was a single meeting, Powell recalled, "when we all made our recommendation and [Bush] made a decision." As far as the secretary of state was concerned, the president had decided "in his own mind, by himself," that war was necessary. He had told Powell as much early in January 2003, during a brief meeting in the Oval Office. "I really think I have to take this guy out," Bush had said. But in many ways, Bush had reached that conclusion long before. Throughout the previous year, there was a steady move toward confrontation with Iraq. By spring 2002, Bush and Rice were talking about Iraq in, as Rice put it, a "different way." Starting in the summer, the push for war became inexorable, and war itself increasingly inevitable. It never really was a matter of whether or why; just of when and how.

The decision to go to war, particularly when it involves a matter of choice rather than necessity, is the most momentous decision a president can make. Yet there is no evidence, in any of the dozens of books, hundreds of articles, thousands of newspaper stories, or many millions of words that have been written about it, that the Bush administration's decision to go to war against Iraq was a carefully considered one. In the many interagency meetings, principals, deputies, and other senior government officials devoted a lot of attention to the question of how to go to war. But few if any of them looked at the consequences in order to consider whether war was the best way to address the problem at hand—or, indeed, what that problem was exactly. "In none of the meetings," Tenet recalled, was there ever "a discussion of the central questions. Was it wise to go to war? Was it the right thing to do? The agenda focused solely on what actions need to be taken if a decision to attack were later made."

By the summer of 2002, the die had been cast. After visiting Washington in July, Britain's top spy, Sir Richard Dearlove, reported that there had been "a perceptible shift in attitude. Military action was now seen as inevitable. Bush wanted to remove Saddam, through military action, justified by the conjunction of terrorism and WMD." Richard Haass heard the same thing from Rice directly in early July. In one of their regular meetings, Haass raised the issue of whether the administration was really sure that it wanted to put Iraq front and center, given the war on terrorism and other issues. "Don't waste your breath," Rice responded. "That decision's been made." Haass was stunned. When he returned to the State Department, he told

Powell that the decision on Iraq had already been made. The secretary of state said Haass was wrong, but after making some calls he had to conclude that his aide had been right. Powell called Rice and asked for a meeting with the president. The result was the August 5 dinner in the White House residence where Powell warned Bush that he would "own" Iraq. But even that meeting ended up being not so much about whether to invade Iraq, as how. Powell's main pitch, then and thereafter, was to convince Bush to go to the United Nations. Bush did precisely that—but as a means to going to war, not, as Powell had hoped, as an alternative to war itself.

During this period, Rice did nothing to challenge Bush's thinking. As she saw it, her job was to carry out the president's wishes and address his concerns. Throughout these many months leading up to war, Rice's biographer Elisabeth Bumiller observed, "Rice did not so much prod the process as get drawn along in its wake." The job of actually prodding the process, of raising real questions and challenging assumptions, fell to another national security adviser. Brent Scowcroft, more than anyone else, had been responsible for launching Rice's Washington career when he hired her as a young member of his NSC staff in the first Bush administration. Now he was distressed to see his onetime protégée help the son of his best friend lead the nation into a war he thought unnecessary and unwise. He felt duty-bound, both as a former national security adviser and as the former president's friend, to raise all of the questions and concerns that an effective policy process would have to consider before deciding on war. This he did in an op-ed published in the *Wall Street Journal* on August 15, 2002. Its title—"Don't Attack Saddam"—left no doubt what Scowcroft thought the answer to these questions ought to be.

Rather than taking Scowcroft's arguments seriously and wondering why this most soft-spoken of Washington insiders felt it necessary to so publicly raise a red flag, Rice reacted with fury. "How could you do this to us?" she screamed at her former boss over the phone. To her, the problem was Scowcroft's seeming betrayal; to Scowcroft, the problem was that the national security adviser had no interest in hearing what another national security adviser—one who had actually been there the last time the United States confronted Saddam Hussein—thought about the most important decision a president could make. The loud confrontation between Scowcroft and Rice was emblematic of how the younger NSC adviser went about her job. Her role was to defend the president against his critics, and to advance his agenda, no matter what. It wasn't to ask questions, to probe assumptions, or to challenge conclusions—and those who did would get Rice's famous cold treatment. "Anytime someone wasn't ready to do immediately exactly what the president wants," Armitage recalled of Rice's thinking, "it was almost disloyal."

By the summer of 2002, Rice had taken on one other role: to make the case publicly that Saddam Hussein's Iraq constituted a threat that could be dealt with only through the use of force. The national security adviser became a ubiquitous presence on the Sunday talk shows, appearing on no less than twenty-six shows in the twelve months before the war began, or about once every other week. Inside the White House, Rice was seen as by far the best and most credible spokesperson for the president's policy. "The initial response is always to put Condi out first," one White House aide told the *New York Times*. "She always has the exact tone and response the president wants. She's someone everyone feels entirely safe with." Yet such a public role came at the price of failing to do what any national security adviser must—which is to examine the evidence with a skeptical, analytical eye in order to make sure that the information being relied upon to make decisions is as accurate and indisputable as possible.

All of the top administration officials, including Rice, approached the Iraq issue in full confidence that Saddam Hussein had stockpiles of chemical and biological weapons and an active nuclear weapons program. Cheney had said as much publicly in late August 2002, and when Rice called him to express concern about the speech, it wasn't because of the vice president's claim that "Saddam Hussein will acquire nuclear weapons fairly soon" or that there was "no doubt that Saddam Hussein now has weapons of mass destruction." Her concern, rather, was Cheney's insistence that going back to the United Nations (as Bush had decided to do) would "provide false comfort." Rice didn't doubt the evidence on Iraq's weapons programs, no matter what the intelligence documents might be saying. "As a student of this business," Rice said at the time, "I know that intelligence estimates almost always underestimate capabilities. They rarely overestimate capabilities."

There was no need, therefore, to ask the intelligence community to write a formal National Intelligence Estimate (NIE) on Iraq's programs or on the consequences of a military confrontation with Saddam Hussein. Bush, Cheney, Rumsfeld, Rice, Hadley, and other top officials thought they already knew everything there was to know. And when an NIE on Iraqi weapons of mass destruction was hastily written in September at the request of senators who did not share the administration's certainty, Rice didn't feel it necessary to actually read the document or its key dissenting footnotes. "We have experts who work for the national security adviser who would know this information," a senior White House aide later told reporters. Nor did the erstwhile professor "read footnotes in a 90 page document," the official went on. "The national security adviser has people who do that."

Among the tasks a national security adviser must perform is to make sure that information reaching the president is accurate and complete, and that any gaps in knowledge are identified and reflected upon. Some of the information on Iraqi capabilities that was reaching the president directly, including in the daily presidential briefs, turned out to have been "much more assertive," according to Tenet, than what appeared in the NIE and other documents. Even so, when a key intelligence agency states that it does not agree with a principal finding—as the State Department's intelligence arm did when it came to whether Iraq was reconstituting its nuclear weapons program—the national security adviser not only needs to know that, but must so inform the president.

Instead, Rice ignored any evidence that seemed to contradict the administration's basic story line that Saddam Hussein had weapons of mass destruction, that he had close ties with Al Qaeda and other terrorists, and that Iraq therefore constituted an intolerable danger. When the CIA sent Rice and Hadley not one but two memos saying it did not believe the claims that Iraq was seeking to acquire uranium from Niger in West Africa, its objections were ignored and the president was allowed to make just such a claim in his 2003 State of the Union address. When the CIA failed to make a clear and convincing case concerning the Iraqi weapons threat in a rehearsal before the president of what could be said publicly about it, Rice did not ask whether there was a problem with the underlying intelligence. And when Colin Powell expressed repeated skepticism about the intelligence data he would outline in a speech before the UN Security Council, Rice and Hadley kept on pushing him to make a stronger and more convincing presentation. "Can't you make it any better?" she demanded. Powell, who had no intention of going far out on a limb, insisted he could go only so far as the data would let him. Even that, it turned out, was way too far.

Having pushed for war and made the case publicly that war was necessary, the next important step was to prepare for war. Throughout 2002 and into 2003, there were innumerable meetings—with the president, of the principals and deputies, and of the Executive Steering Group, an NSC-chaired group of midlevel officials that was assigned the task of coordinating preparations for the war. The main concern of nearly all these meetings, however, was the invasion itself—how many troops it would take, what strategy to follow, when to launch an attack—and not on what would come afterward. Part of the reason was that no one in the administration, least of all the secretary of defense, put much stock in postwar reconstruction or nation-building efforts. Before the war, Rumsfeld had complained about a "culture of dependency" that had allegedly been created by the long commitment of large numbers of NATO peacekeeping troops in the Balkans. Iraq, like Afghanistan, would be different. "The concept was that we would defeat the army, but the institutions [in Iraq] would hold, everything from ministries to police forces," Rice later recalled. "You would be able to bring new leadership but we were going to keep the body in place." In other words, the United States would invade, find and destroy any weapons of mass destruction, install new leaders, and then it would leave. Six months after the invasion, military planners assumed, only about 30,000 Americans would be left in Iraq.

Having been in charge of planning the invasion, Rumsfeld decided that his department should also be responsible for planning what came after. In Afghanistan, responsibility for various parts of the postwar effort had been shared across the government. State was responsible for helping set up a government, Treasury for rebuilding the financial system, the Pentagon for security, USAID for reconstruction and development. There had been no unity of purpose, nor unity of command on the ground. Rumsfeld did not want to repeat this situation in Iraq, so he proposed that the Defense Department be put in charge of both planning for and running post-invasion Iraq. Though in past conflicts reconstruction efforts had largely been run by the State Department, Powell did not object. A military man, he understood the value of unity of command. Someone had to be in charge, and Powell believed the Pentagon had the assets—the money and the people—to make it work. Nor did Rice see a problem with assigning Rumsfeld's Pentagon full responsibility to plan for (as opposed to run) the postwar effort. With Powell and Rumsfeld for once in accord, Rice accepted the argument that this decision was necessitated by the need for a unified command. "It was not at all controversial," she later recalled of the decision. "I mean, how else were you going to do it?"

It was a good question, to which, however, there was more than one answer. In the previous administration, for example, the responsibility for planning any post-conflict operations had been vested in the NSC. After repeated ad hoc efforts in Somalia, Haiti, and Bosnia, the Clinton administration had developed a set of guidelines for such operations that was codified in a presidential directive in May 1997. But Bush had rescinded this and other Clinton NSC directives, and his administration had yet to develop alternative guidelines when it faced the issue of what to do in Iraq. Rather than replicating the Clinton model, and have the NSC staff coordinate interagency planning for postwar Iraq, Rice agreed that the Pentagon was best positioned to undertake this responsibility. And so, on January 20, 2003, Bush signed National Security Presidential Directive (NSPD) 24, creating a postwar planning office within the Defense Department that would undertake "detailed planning across the spectrum of issues that the United States Government would face with respect to the postwar administration of Iraq."

The directive was notable in at least three ways. First, the range of responsibilities assigned to the new planning office was staggering—running from providing humanitarian relief, rebuilding the economy, and reestablishing civil services like electricity and health care to dismantling weapons of mass destruction, defeating terrorism, and reshaping the military and internal security forces. Second, though military planning for an invasion had been going on for well over a year, a coordinated effort to plan for this wide-ranging set of postwar tasks was inaugurated less than two months before the war was to commence. Finally, to carry out these responsibilities both before the war and in the field following the invasion, a large team of new people, to be drawn from ten different U.S. government agencies, had to be assembled entirely from scratch.

The effort was bound to fail. No one agency, not even one as powerful and resource-rich as the Pentagon, can effectively coordinate other agencies. Interests and priorities invariably compete, and no department or agency will submit to the direction or control of another. The only effective way to run an interagency process is to run it out of the National Security Council. That is what the Council and staff are there for. Yet Rice decided that in this particular instance—when the need for effective coordination among a great number of agencies was so clear and immediate—it was okay for the NSC to cede this role to the Pentagon. And not just any Pentagon, but Don Rumsfeld's Pentagon. In the preceding months, the defense secretary had refused to share information on war planning with Rice or her staff, who had to use their own contacts in the military to glean whatever information they could. Amazingly, Rumsfeld had at times refused to return Rice's phone calls when she had questions about military matters, and still refused even after the president had said something about it to his defense secretary. Once the war started, Rice and her staff had to rely on British reporting, sent over from the embassy in Washington, to learn what was going on! And, still, the NSC adviser did not object when the Pentagon—run by Rumsfeld—was put in charge of the interagency process for postwar Iraq.

Rumsfeld, of course, had no interest in running an interagency process—he was only interested in maintaining control. He completely ignored a thick study on "The Future of Iraq" that the State Department had conducted with the help of Iraqi exiles and experts over the previous year. He also rejected Powell's offer following the signing of NSPD 24 to detail seven ambassadorial-level officials, including three Arabists, to the new planning office. "I think we should have Defense Department people," Rumsfeld told Jay Garner, a retired three-star general who was the head of the new office. And he later consented to what was likely the most fateful decision of the immediate postwar period—the May 2003 order to disband the entire Iraqi army, Defense Ministry, and intelligence agencies—without consulting anyone. Not the JCS chairman. Not the secretary of state. Not the NSC adviser. Not even the president. ("Well, the policy was to keep the army intact," Bush later insisted. "Didn't happen.") Again, Rice, who learned of the directive only after it had been publicly announced, didn't see much of a problem. "The whole structure had been set up so that some of those decisions could be made in the field or through the Pentagon chain," she explained later.

It would take seven months of mounting confusion in Washington and escalating violence in Iraq for Rice to finally seize control of the interagency process on Iraq. In August 2003, she talked to Bush about her rising frustration with the course of events in Baghdad and her increasingly bad relations with Rumsfeld. The president agreed that she needed to take control. She did so in early October, when she sent a memo to her counterparts announcing the formation of the Iraq Stabilization Group, a principals-level committee that Rice would chair. The new committee would also have four separate working groups—on counterterrorism, political affairs, economic development, and communications—each chaired by one of Rice's deputies. Rumsfeld wasn't pleased. He, rightly, saw it as a direct attack on his authority and—worse—his ability to control what was happening on the ground in Iraq and within the bureaucracy in Washington. "Condi has taken over political matters," the Pentagon chief complained. "I think it's a mistake. The last time the NSC got into operational issues, we had Iran-Contra. But she seems to have jumped into this with both feet." The analogy was spurious. Iran-Contra had been a secret effort designed to circumvent a legal prohibition of support for the contras. Rice, in contrast, was asserting her rightful role of managing the policy process—it was "really kind of the traditional role for the NSC adviser," as she told the *New York Times*.

Terrorism and Iraq were certainly the most consequential policy areas the president and his national security adviser confronted during Bush's first term, but they weren't the only ones. There was a newly confident Russia, whose president, Vladimir Putin, was seeking to restore his country to its erstwhile perch as a great power. There was China, rapidly expanding economically, whose leaders sought to extend their influence throughout Asia and into Africa and the Americas. There was India, also expanding rapidly, which was beginning to feel its way in the larger world and contemplating a strategic partnership with Washington. There was the continued search for peace in the Middle East, a process that had run into trouble by the time Bush came to office. There was the prospect of a rogue regime in Tehran, Pyongyang, or elsewhere acquiring a nuclear bomb. And there were other large concerns—from battling AIDS and other infectious diseases to ending civil war and genocide in Sudan to helping build more stable, capable, and prosperous states around the world.

Rice helped Bush tackle all of these issues, some of them successfully. But two of them—the Middle East peace process and North Korea's nuclear ambitions—would come to dominate much of Bush's second term, mainly because of the way both were handled during the first.

Bush arrived in Washington in 2001 just as a last-ditch effort by President Clinton to forge an Israeli-Palestinian peace had foundered. At a meeting in Camp David the previous summer, Israel had made major concessions on a possible peace deal only to find the Palestinian leader, Yasser Arafat, unwilling to make similar concessions. This was followed by a Palestinian uprising—the second intifada—in early fall 2000, and then the resounding election of the Israeli hard-liner, Ariel Sharon, as prime minister a few weeks after Bush's inauguration. Bush had met Sharon when he toured Israel as governor, and he liked him. The same could not be said of Yasser Arafat. "You can't make a peace deal with that guy," Bush had exclaimed. "He screwed President Clinton." The 9/11 attacks further cemented Bush's views. He saw Arafat as an unrepentant terrorist—and a loser. "I'm not going to spend political capital on losers, only winners," Bush told Jordan's King Abdullah. "If people don't fight terrorism, I am not going to deal with them." As for Sharon, whose country had endured a large number of deadly suicide bombers in the previous year, Bush increasingly saw the Israeli prime minister as a kindred soul—they were two leaders standing up, unbowed, to the terrorist threat.

The State Department and Powell urged the president to seize the opportunity of the 9/11 attacks to reinvigorate the mideast peace process. But Bush, while declaring that he favored the creation of a Palestinian state alongside Israel, wasn't interested in the kind of traditional, even-handed diplomacy that had failed to produce results in the past. Peace could come only if the Palestinians opted for democracy, elected leaders "not compromised by terror," and ended support for terrorism. At the same time, Bush offered an unqualified embrace of Israel and Sharon—including its right to defend itself against terror. Unstated but nevertheless clear was Bush's decision to halt Washington's criticism of Israeli actions designed to fight terror: of its military reoccupation of the West Bank, its decision to build a fence separating Israelis from Palestinians, even its targeted assassinations of terrorist leaders. And Bush made one other change. He put

Condi Rice in charge of the Israel-Palestinian portfolio, effectively sidelining Powell and his department.

Rice established a back channel to Dov Weissglas, Sharon's chief of staff and close friend, which she used to good practical effect to goad Israel. In September 2002, for example, she told Weissglas that Israeli tanks besieging Arafat's compound in Ramallah should be withdrawn. It was a distraction from the much more important effort to get Arab countries to line up behind Washington on the Iraq issue. "The United States will never restrain you against any action which is needed to protect your people and stop terror," Rice assured Weissglas. But the seige didn't meet that test. "This is not the case. Arafat is not a ticking bomb. To me, he is not important." The tanks were withdrawn the next day. A year later, after Israel's arch enemy Saddam Hussein had been toppled by the U.S. military, Rice suggested Israel needed to do something bold to move the peace process forward. Sharon and Weissglas came up with the idea of disengaging Israel from Gaza, starting with a few settlements. Rice welcomed the move, but suggested it would not be much of a breakthrough. "If you want a different reality, it has to be Gaza in its entirety." That was a big step for Israel to take. Sharon would need something in return—which he got in the form of a letter from Bush, carefully worked out between their two aides, suggesting that Washington would support Israel's right to retain large settlements and refuse the demand by Palestinians to return to Israeli land in a negotiated peace settlement.

Rice's back channel produced results, but not without costs. For much of the first term, the formal peace process lay moribund. Washington's backing of the Israeli negotiating position on territory and the right of return made a deal with the Palestinians even less likely. When Rice sought to restart the process in 2005, she found it hard going. Arafat had been replaced by a more moderate leader, Mahmoud Abbas, uncompromised by terror, but the Bush administration was unable to deliver any Israeli concessions or positive moves to help advance the peace process. Palestinian parliamentary elections in 2005, strongly backed by Bush and Rice, produced a victory for Hamas, a terrorist movement with an uncompromising stance toward Israel. The assumptions behind the Bush policy—that elections and democracy would produce leaders willing to negotiate peace and able to confront terrorism—proved unfounded. Peace in the Middle East was no closer at the end of the administration than it had been at the beginning.

Whereas on the Middle East Rice took a firm position and a leading role in her White House years, that was not the case with the second issue that would come to dominate her time as secretary of state. When the Bush administration came to office in 2001, Bush's advisers were deeply divided on how to handle the issue of North Korea's nuclear weapons program, a program that had remained frozen for six years under the "agreed framework" negotiated by the Clinton administration in 1994. A hard-line faction, centered on Cheney and Rumsfeld, believed that the only effective way to end the nuclear and missile threat posed by North Korea was through a change in the odious regime that had ruled the country since the end of World War II. A more moderate faction, led by Powell, believed that continuing negotiations with Pyongyang was the preferable, and more realistic, course. Rice didn't fall clearly in either camp, and she was never able to bridge the differences while in the White House.

During Bush's first term, there were, in fact, two quite parallel policy processes on North Korea. One was led by the assistant secretary of state for East Asia, James Kelly, and focused on how to engage Pyongyang in a new set of negotiations (first bilaterally, then multilaterally). A second was led by Robert Joseph, the NSC's senior director in charge of non-proliferation policy. This group, which included Douglas Feith and J. D. Crouch from the Pentagon, John Bolton from State, and Eric Edelman from the vice president's office, existed primarily to make sure no serious negotiations with North Korea would actually take place. Even when Kelly was allowed to engage in direct negotiations, his guidance left him no room for maneuver, so that discussions usually boiled down to a recitation of each side's talking points. And when progress appeared possible, as it did in 2002 when the first serious sets of negotiations were to commence, new issues were raised to call the talks into question. Pyongyang responded to these mixed signals by abandoning the freeze on its plutonium program, throwing out international inspectors, reprocessing nuclear materials to manufacture enough plutonium to build six to eight nuclear weapons, and finally testing a nuclear device in 2006. The North Korean nuclear threat was serious but constrained at the outset of the administration; now it was much worse.

In her four years at the White House, Rice was never able to bring the two different strands of policy together or make clear that the administration would stand behind one rather than the other approach. As a result, all sides—both hawks and moderates—complained about the administration's policy incoherence; and all of them blamed the national security adviser. "The failure of Condi Rice" is how one official termed the policy. Implicitly, Rice accepted the critique, and when she moved to Foggy Bottom, she would take complete control of the policy—pushing the very engagement line the State Department had championed, but that she had proved unwilling to promote during the first term.

Looking back, Condoleezza Rice realized that she had not been the best national security adviser. Asked by Elisabeth Bumiller to assess her performance in those four years, Rice answered quietly: "I don't know. I think I did okay." She knew that many people inside and outside the administration didn't have a positive assessment of her tenure. In particular, the rap on Rice was that she failed to put a halt to the endless bickering between the moderates at State and the hardliners at Defense and in the vice president's office, particularly on such issues as North Korea, Iran, and Iraq. Later, Rice realized that people held her responsible. "If that's the assessment, you know, I'll accept people's assessment," she ventured. It was a difficult job, she insisted. "Everything is by remote control," Rice explained. "You do not own any of the assets," discounting the potential power that propinquity to the president can provide the NSC adviser. "I frankly prefer being coordinated than coordinating."

Rice, no doubt, was a better secretary of state than national security adviser. A line job was more suited to her temperament and strengths. It helped that she retained the president's trust and confidence when she moved from the White House to Foggy Bottom at the start of Bush's second term. From her new perch, Rice made the State Department the dominant foreign policy player in a way that really hadn't been the case since Henry Kissinger occupied the office in the mid-1970s (which, perhaps not coincidentally, was the only other time a national security adviser became secretary of state). As the senior member of the cabinet, Rice had less compunction about challenging Rumsfeld than when she was at the White House. And through her direct relationship with the president, she proved increasingly able to bypass—or defeat—the vice president. That explains why Rice was able to push the administration in a more multilateral direction when it came to issues like North Korea, Iran, and the Israeli-Palestinian conflict. These were all policies Powell had unsuccessfully pressed in the first term, but no one in the White House, including Rice, had supported him. "Ultimately," Kissinger observed after Rice had taken over from Powell, "a secretary of state can succeed only if he or she is close to the president and is treated by him as the center of the policy process."

Rice's closeness to Bush was beyond dispute—Kissinger called it the closest such relationship of any in modern times. Nor was her dominance of the policy process in the second term in question. Taking over as national security adviser was Stephen Hadley, her loyal deputy for four years. Hadley, who had first worked at the NSC under Kissinger and Scowcroft during the mid-1970s and had been counsel to the Tower Commission in the mid-1980s, was that rare Washington creature involved in policy matters for many years who never made any real enemies. A workaholic of the first order, he was lawyerly in his approach to the issues and deferential to higher authorities. He strongly believed in Brent Scowcroft's adage that a national security adviser should be seen infrequently and heard even less. Rice would continue to be the administration's real spokesperson on foreign affairs, strengthening the sense that she remained very much in control of both policymaking and implementation.

Early on in the second term, Hadley would drive over to Foggy Bottom to attend Rice's staff meetings, and word in Washington spread that the secretary of state now had three deputies: Robert Zoellick (deputy secretary), Philip Zelikow (counselor), and Stephen Hadley. Rice and Hadley also agreed to coordinate senior staff appointments, thus reinforcing the sense of a tight link between the two entities. And Rice was able to chart a new direction on important issues that had long been stuck within the bureaucracy without having to run them through the interagency process. For example, the deal with North Korea to dismantle its nuclear weapons program was reached by Rice's negotiator, Christopher Hill, in secret bilateral talks in early 2007. Rice arrived at the talks in Berlin, approved the deal, and then called Bush directly to urge his okay, thereby bypassing all the hard-liners who might oppose it.

Hadley, meanwhile, focused his energy and attention on improving policy implementation and execution. Failure to execute had been the biggest problem in the first term. "I give us a B minus for policy development," Hadley said about those years, "and a D minus for policy execution." Upon moving into the big West Wing corner office from his cubicle-sized room next door, the new NSC adviser began to demand that his staff do a better job of monitoring how agencies implemented agreed policy. "We need to be systematic and rigorous in improving implementation and execution within the government," he told David Ignatius of the *Washington Post*. The NSC would develop "action plans," "due dates," and "metrics to measure performance." A new office was set up precisely for that purpose. Officials there reviewed processes to speed up the internal paperwork and began to set up a system to monitor the implementation of past decisions. A metric called the "stoplight process" (red, yellow, green) was set up to track whether actions agreed upon in Afghanistan and Iraq were being implemented or whether policy needed to be adjusted or changed.

That concern with policy execution was not a whim on Hadley's part became clear in April 2007. After trying for two years to oversee policy execution on the two biggest issues confronting the admin-

istration—the wars in Iraq and Afghanistan—Hadley decided that
having "plans and due dates and stoplight charts" wasn't enough. You
also needed someone to manage the process, an "Iraq and Afghanistan Implementation and Execution Manager," who could ensure that
policy in these areas was in fact implemented. This "War Czar," as
the job was quickly dubbed, would be an assistant to the president—
ranked on a par with the NSC adviser—and would report directly to
President Bush, not Hadley. He would chair the principals meetings
on Iraq and Afghanistan, and make sure that agencies in Washington responded immediately to any requests coming from the field.
"This is what Steve Hadley would do if Steve Hadley had the time,"
explained Defense Secretary Robert Gates, who had replaced Rumsfeld in late 2006. Tracking demands and making sure Washington
was following through on them had become a near full-time job for
the NSC adviser. Hadley needed someone else to take on the task. In
fact, the new job came with a staff of fifteen policy people, all charged
with overseeing policy implementation in Iraq and Afghanistan.

The decision to put someone else in charge of the day-to-day
implementation and development of policy on Iraq and Afghanistan
assumed that the problem confronting the United States in these
places was a lack of execution rather than the policy itself. But before
deciding he needed a top-level official to oversee implementation,
Hadley had spent many months engineering a major policy review
on Iraq, which resulted in both a change in policy and a change in
personnel to help implement it. The effort was a good example of
how a national security adviser can operate effectively, even in a situation where strong personalities are at loggerheads—as continued to
be the case for Iraq policy in the first half of Bush's second term.

The situation in Iraq never went well in the months and years
after the invasion, but it deteriorated significantly in the first half of
2006. Sectarian violence was on the rise. Iraqi and American casualties were mounting precipitously. Chaos engulfed Baghdad and
most of the surrounding provinces. The war appeared to be lost. The
constant stream of reporting convinced even Bush that staying the
course was no longer an option. "I was worried," Bush later confided.

"I'm worried any time it looks like we're going to fail in Iraq." Hadley and his principal aides knew Bush would never agree to giving up and withdrawing in the face of adversity. He wasn't a throw-my-hands-up-in-the-air kind of a guy. They knew the president wanted to win. "He knew my anxiety," Bush later said of Hadley. "He knew my intensity on the issue. He read me like a book." Hadley's key aides—his deputy, J. D. Crouch; his principal Iraq assistant, Meghan O'Sullivan; and his strategic planner, Peter Feaver—believed that only by increasing the number of American troops in Iraq was there a chance to establish security and order in the country. And only when there was security was there a possibility to win.

This NSC view of what needed to be done was not widely shared within the government, let alone outside it, where calls to withdraw from Iraq were gaining political momentum. The uniformed military believed the problem in Iraq was political; only if the parties were able to reconcile their differences was there a possibility to establish security. Absent political reconciliation, more troops would not bring more security. Rumsfeld essentially agreed. He wanted to train Iraqi security forces so that American troops could leave. The last thing he wanted was to send more U.S. troops to the region. Rice's State Department didn't think training Iraqi forces would do the job, but neither did it favor sending more troops. Instead, State suggested pulling U.S. troops back into their bases and along the border and letting the sectarian violence burn itself out. Meanwhile, a bipartisan commission known as the Iraq Study Group, led by former Secretary of State James Baker and former chairman of the House Foreign Affairs Committee Lee Hamilton, set up to try to forge a new consensus on Iraq, proposed a "way forward" that would force the Iraqi army to "take over primary responsibility for combat operations."

Faced with eroding support outside and deadlock within the administration, Hadley made two moves that broadened the range of choices in a way the president would find congenial. First, knowing that Bush was receptive to a strategy that offered a greater chance of success, he began to expose him to different views from sympathetic outsiders. He organized a weekend session at Camp David in mid-June 2006, and invited supporters of the war like Fred Kagan, Robert Kaplan, Michael Vickers, and Eliot Cohen to brief the president. Their message: the war was being lost and a change in course was necessary. More troops were needed. They needed to work aggressively to protect the population and defeat the insurgency. The president needed to take back control of the strategy from the generals.

It was a message, Hadley knew, that would speak directly to the president. Bush wasn't ready yet to embrace the need for more troops, but he was convinced that a new direction was necessary. By August, the president was tipping his hand—at least internally. "If the bicycle teeters, we have to put our hand back on," Bush told his principal advisers, using one of Rumsfeld's favorite metaphors, though the Pentagon chief had long argued that the Iraqis needed to learn to peddle by themselves, even it meant their falling over a few times. "We have to make damn sure they don't fail," Bush went on. "We have to have enough military personnel."

Having implanted the idea of more troops and the need to change strategy, Hadley next instituted a formal, interagency review of Iraq policy. The review examined alternative strategies: continuing the current course (favored by the Pentagon); "surging" the number of troops and shifting tactics on the ground (favored by the NSC); and the burnout strategy (favored by State). The review was serious, even though Hadley knew where the president was likely to come out. It forced Bush to consider the pluses and minuses of alternatives, and it gave everyone a chance to make their best case. What may have clinched it for Bush was his decision finally to replace Donald Rumsfeld, who he had come to view as an obstacle to change. As his successor, Bush interviewed Robert Gates, who, the president recalled, told him "he favored a surge of additional troops in Iraq." Though Cheney didn't agree with the decision to fire Rumsfeld, he too, Bush said, "was a more-troops man."

Only the military still stood in the way. The JCS chairman, the regional commander, and the Iraq force commander all believed that additional troops were unlikely to make much of a difference. Sending more troops would also put too much strain on the U.S. ground forces, which were already stretched thin by the burdens of fighting two wars simultaneously. Their preference was to stay in Iraq with a substantial force for the long haul. To overcome this opposition, new commanders were rotated into all of the key slots. General David Petraeus, an advocate of the surge, who had been in charge of writing the Army's new counterinsurgency doctrine, was sent to Iraq as the new force commander. The outgoing regional commander was replaced by a Navy admiral. And the JCS chairman was told his term would not be extended for two more years, as had long been custom. He, too, was replaced by an admiral.

More troops, a new strategy, different commanders—it all added up to a new Iraq policy. The "surge" would prove effective in helping to reduce the level of violence in Iraq, even if its long-term success depended on Iraqi political progress that had yet to emerge. A year later, Iraq had receded from the headlines. Americans still viewed Bush's Iraq policy as a major blunder, one that more than anything else would define the president's tenure in office. But the NSC policy review had served an important purpose: it had given the president, and perhaps even the country, hope that the worst possible outcome in Iraq could be avoided. Few thought this likely in 2006, when Hadley decided to launch the review. But Hadley believed that he could best serve the president by at least trying. It may have been his most important contribution to the administration in the eight years he served.

———

Few Americans would recognize Stephen Hadley's name, much less identify the office he held in George W. Bush's second term. Unlike his prominent predecessor, he labored anonymously, in the shadows. And he lacked Rice's close relationship to the president. Yet he accomplished something on Iraq policy that Condoleezza Rice was never able to bring about: a reality-driven review of policy choices, culminating in a serious and consequential presidential decision. Iraq was a war of choice. Hence there was plenty of time to assess whether it was the right choice before it was carried out. Unlike many issues that confront a president and his national security adviser, the administration controlled the timetable for war with Iraq. Rice did not use that time wisely.

Four years later, Hadley also had time to explore Iraq alternatives—months rather than a year, but time enough to develop alternatives and manage an effective presidential decision process. And while he lacked Rice's relationship with Bush, he did not face the all-powerful cast of senior presidential aides. Rumsfeld was discredited and on his way out. Cheney was a less dominant force than he had been. And the hubris of all senior players had surely been diminished by the reality of policy catastrophe in the one theater that, more than any other, defined their foreign policy.

Still, Hadley exploited his advantages and overcame his limitations. Six years of hard work had paid off. Bush had full confidence in his national security adviser to get the job done. "Hadley drove a lot of this," Bush told Bob Woodward. "Why? Because I trust he and his team a lot." This trust proved well-placed. Hadley ran a serious policy review that resulted in a consequestial and constructive policy change that served his president and his nation well. Faced with a far more consequential choice, Rice failed even to launch such an intense policy review. Perhaps it would have made no difference, given Bush's determination. But given the costs ultimately paid by her nation—and her president—she should surely have tried.

9

"Trust Is the Coin
of the Realm"

N owhere in the U.S. code is there a provision establishing the position of the assistant to the president for national security affairs. The job is the creation of presidents and its occupants are responsible to them alone. The position gained prominence after John F. Kennedy's election nearly half a century ago, and since then has become central to presidential conduct of foreign policy. Fifteen people have held the job during this time. Some proved successful; others less so. But the post of national security adviser is now an institutional fact. By all odds, it will remain so.

It all started with McGeorge Bundy, back in 1961. Previous presidents had aides who managed the National Security Council, established under Truman in 1947 and given greater prominence by Eisenhower in the 1950s. Ike, in fact, created the position of "Special Assistant for National Security Affairs," as it was then called. But he did so for policy planning, not day-to-day action. Kennedy was skeptical of long-term planning and wanted to handle foreign policy directly, hands-on. So he and Bundy converted the job into one of managing the president's current policy business, and connecting the broader national security bureaucracy to presidential purposes.

Bundy came from outside government, as did most of his successors. Within a few months, he emerged as Kennedy's most senior aide on national security affairs. He moved his office to the West Wing. He recruited a small staff—soon dubbed Bundy's "Little State Department"—that provided independent advice and analysis to the president and watched over the broader government. And for the first time, the president, the adviser, and their staff gained direct access to information, including cable traffic and intelligence assessments, which enabled them to reach independent judgments on what needed to be done. Together, these innovations created within the White House an independent staff and analytical capability to help the president manage and execute the nation's business abroad. No previous president had had such a capability, yet it was one that no subsequent president would do without.

Kennedy and Bundy were very compatible individuals, and they worked well together during the 1,000 days Kennedy was president. Kennedy desired lots of information. He thrived on debate and disagreement as a method to help him sort out the best ways to proceed. A speed reader, he devoured books and documents, and sought out information from all and sundry—even calling a junior desk officer at State to get the answer to a question. Bundy, the unusually bright Harvard dean, was very much in his element within this intellectual environment. He was happy to feed Kennedy more and more information, drawn from a wide range of government and outside sources. After the Bay of Pigs fiasco, Bundy knew that he had to do a much better job of advising and warning the president. He needed to look at problems from all angles, even switching positions if necessary, in order to assure the diversity of views and perspectives Kennedy so clearly needed and wanted. He did so especially during the Cuban missile crisis, which turned out to be Kennedy's finest hour. And as those deliberations exemplified, Bundy ran an internally open process, with the president exposed to information and advocacy from a broad range of people inside and outside the government. He came to be trusted as an honest broker and communicator by the principal cabinet secretaries and their subordinates.

But what works with one president does not necessarily suit another. Bundy's uncomfortable relations with Kennedy's sudden successor underscore that there is no single formula for being an effective national security adviser. It depends very much on what the president wants and needs. Lyndon Johnson was a domestic policy man, an extraordinary wheeler and dealer focused on pushing through new legislation. He was responsible for many of the great initiatives—on civil rights, social justice, health care, poverty—that helped make America what it is today. But he wasn't much of a foreign policy man. He was uncertain about the direction America needed to take in the world, especially when it came to the Vietnam War. He feared being seen as weak or responsible for a prominent geostrategic loss, but he was unclear about how America could win. Perhaps because of this basic insecurity, he relied on his most senior advisers—particularly the secretaries of state and defense—to help him chart his course. Unlike Kennedy, Johnson did not seek out the more junior staffers who might have real expertise. Nor did he want or need a mass of background information to make his choices. Instead, he trusted Rusk and McNamara—and later his senior military commanders—to advise him well.

Bundy was uncertain about how to operate within this environment. He didn't have the same personal relationship with LBJ that he had had with JFK, nor, frankly, did he regard Johnson in the same light. He realized that he had to change in order to do his job well. Johnson didn't want or need mountains of information, nor did he like to debate options or analyze the alternatives. He was a man of action, uncomfortable with dissent, which he feared could leak out and undercut him. Bundy responded by becoming less of a channel for alternative views and more of an advocate—particularly on Vietnam, the issue that dominated the times. Johnson may not have needed another advocate for escalation in Vietnam, but that's what he got. Bundy, moreover, came to differ sharply with Johnson on the manner of his wartime leadership. He believed the chief executive should tell the nation the full magnitude of the commitment, while the president sought to downplay the war in order not to undercut his domestic programs. The breach grew, and Johnson was happy to see Bundy go in early 1966.

Walt Rostow was far more compatible with Johnson; the two of them got on very well. But Rostow, the unquestioning booster of the Vietnam War, wasn't nearly so effective with the rest of the administration. He wasn't trusted to reflect the views of other officials in his conversations with the president, and Johnson never really put him in charge of managing the overall policymaking process. And that highlights a fundamental dilemma: Bundy was a superb process manager, but ultimately failed with Johnson because of their shaky and deteriorating personal relationship. Rostow, on the other hand, had a good relationship with the president, but failed as a process manager. The trick, as Kennedy had demonstrated, was to find someone who could both manage the process in the way the president needed and relate to the president in ways he wanted.

Richard Nixon and Henry Kissinger built on what Kennedy and Bundy had begun. Both were foreign policy aficionados, eager to put their stamp on the world. They had a similar, realist view of how the world operated—one in which power and its balance between states was of primary importance. They used the institutions established by Kennedy to establish a strong, White House–centered system of foreign policymaking. And at the beginning, they seemed to have the balance right, creating a policy process that engaged officials across the government yet protected the president's power to choose. Under Kissinger's direction, interagency groups drafted study memoranda on a wide range of issues, lengthy documents that tried to consider all possible angles of the matter in question and present the president with all realistic options. The issues would then be discussed at the National Security Council, with all the senior advisers weighing in. Nixon would examine the analysis, listen to the arguments, and then make his decisions.

Yet Nixon found the system not to his liking. He was determined to impose his will, but had a deep aversion to overruling his advisers face-to-face. And he hated the intermittent press leaks that came from an internally open process. So, within six months, the well-

calibrated analytical system crafted by Kissinger to Nixon's specifications was abandoned. Increasingly, the president and his adviser
decided what they wanted to do and set about doing it, with little
regard for the perspectives or prerogatives of other key players, including Nixon's own secretary of state. Kissinger became the implementer
of Nixon's most important policies—on Vietnam, the Soviet Union
and arms control, and China. They would make policy in secret, and
then execute it in secret. Kissinger negotiated with Hanoi, keeping
the talks secret for well over two years. Kissinger employed a secret
back channel with the Soviet ambassador to the United States, Anatoly Dobrynin, and negotiated there many of the key arms control
issues. Kissinger went on the first trip by a U.S. official to China since
1949—secretly, of course—and opened the way to establishing relations with the Communist government. All of this was done with
Nixon's authority, and in some cases it led to extraordinary results.

Kissinger and Nixon demonstrated the great potential for power
that inheres in the position of national security adviser. But their tenure also demonstrated the great potential for the abuse of that power.
Secrecy feeds upon itself, and under Nixon and Kissinger, it became
a dangerous obsession. It was made worse, in this case, by each man's
insecurities and the resulting fragility of their trust in one another.
To protect himself from blame for leaks, Kissinger authorized the
wiretapping of even his own staff. And the inability of both to share
power cut out from policy deliberations people who had the knowledge and expertise that often is necessary to make the right decisions
(as became clear, for example, in technical discussions on arms control or conflict in South Asia). This undermined the cohesion of the
government as a whole, as the distrust secrecy engendered among
other top officials led them, in turn, to work around Kissinger or
even the president.

After Kissinger, no national security adviser would ever again
dominate all major negotiations. Nor would any of his successors
systematically keep other key government players in the dark about
what he and his president were doing in the area of those officials'
responsibility. There would be occasional abuses: particularly egre-

gious was the secret diversion of funds to the Nicaraguan contras by John Poindexter under Reagan. But most national security advisers came to realize that information is a key to power, that sharing it is a key to building trust, and that trust among the top officials is key to effective policymaking. This was well understood by Brent Scowcroft, Kissinger's immediate successor under Gerald Ford. Another clear lesson learned from the Kissinger experience is that the national security adviser should not be the primary negotiator on a complex set of issues. The adviser can help open doors or try to clinch the deal. But to be the negotiator is to replace the secretary of state. On that road lies certain conflict, growing distrust, and an increasing likelihood of flawed outcomes.

Zbigniew Brzezinski realized the pitfalls of Kissinger's approach when Jimmy Carter tapped him to be his national security adviser. But he also realized the glory awaiting those who succeeded on the policy field. So, while he worked to craft an open policy process, one in which information would flow freely and the positions of top players were accurately conveyed to the president, his real interest was in moving policy in a certain direction. Unfortunately, Brzezinski's views on critical issues—notably on how to deal with a Soviet Union that appeared to be becoming more powerful and menacing—clashed with those of other top people in the administration, especially Cyrus Vance, Carter's secretary of state, and often with the president himself. The ongoing battles that followed led those who opposed Brzezinski on policy to perceive him, more and more, as an unfair manager of the policy process—someone who was trying to tilt it in his preferred direction. Trust broke down and, with it, an effective process.

Carter aggravated the situation. On the one hand, as Brzezinski rightly insists, Carter wanted foreign policy to be run out of the White House—a desire that naturally gave his top aide tremendous power and influence. On the other hand, Carter's policy instincts were, at least initially, closer to those of Vance and the other doves in the administration than to his hawkish national security adviser. So Brzezinski was empowered from a process perspective even when in debates with others in the administration the president was more comfortable with the other side. The only way Brzezinski could have reconciled these conflicting pressures was by focusing on managing the process and downplaying his own views—or else by convincing the president that his views were indeed the right ones. Brzezinski never did the former, because his driving interest was policy. After the Soviet invasion of Afghanistan, Carter did come around to supporting his adviser's view of the threat that America's Cold War adversary represented.

By then, however, it was too late. Vance would soon resign (over a policy difference relating to the American hostages in Tehran). America's standing in the world and the president's at home had been tarnished by the uncertain leadership Carter had shown in the wake of the Islamic revolution in Iran. And Brzezinski was widely seen as someone who had distorted the process by his policy advocacy and failed to protect the president from his own mistakes. Coming after the Kissinger experience, moreover, Brzezinski's tenure in the job delegitimized it in the eyes of many. There were calls to make the position of national security adviser confirmable by—and thus accountable to—the Senate (a call Brzezinski initially supported). And some even proposed abolishing the position altogether, arguing that its very existence generated policy conflict within an administration.

Ronald Reagan came to Washington sharing the view that the national security adviser had become too powerful a player in the previous decade and that the power of the secretary of state and other cabinet officials had to be restored. But he overreacted to the Kissinger and Brzezinski experiences and thereby helped create new problems of his own. Richard Allen, his first NSC adviser, was essentially relegated to the bureaucratic standing of the NSC executive secretaries in the Truman and Eisenhower administrations. His office was moved back down to the West Wing basement, away from the action on the first floor where the Oval Office is located. And his direct access to the president was blocked, making him a bit player in the national security process.

Allen's successors were able to restore some of the perks and procedures that put them closer to the power of the presidency. But each of the next three of Reagan's advisers—William Clark, Robert McFarlane, and John Poindexter—proved inadequate to the task. Clark, though personally close to Reagan and able to win various policy battles, lacked the knowledge and experience necessary to lead an effective process. McFarlane, affable and hardworking, lacked the stature to go up against his gigantic cabinet counterparts, especially Secretary of State George Shultz and Secretary of Defense Caspar Weinberger. And Poindexter was living proof of the Peter Principle—eventually, everyone gets promoted to the level of their incompetence. The nation, unfortunately, cannot afford inexperience or incompetence in its national security advisers. The consequences can, quite literally, be catastrophic—like the Iran-Contra scandal that nearly destroyed the Reagan presidency.

Reagan, however, didn't help his national security advisers to succeed. Uninterested in the details of policy, the president all too often proved unwilling to decide between the positions staked out by his headstrong secretaries of state and defense. He tried to split the difference among them when he could, but Shultz and Weinberger frequently disagreed on fundamentals, not tactics. So decisions were often postponed, to be debated another day. Nor did Reagan ever agree to get rid of one or other of his advisers in order to overcome the differences that way. "They are my friends," he would explain. He could not fire his friends. "You work it out," he would tell his hapless NSC advisers who, without the president's backing, really were in no position to do so. The only way they could work it out and get things done was to subvert the process, which hardly served the president's or the nation's interests.

The shock of Iran-Contra induced a much needed shake-up at the core of the Reagan administration. Strong advisers were brought in to help the president run his White House—men like former Senate majority leader Howard Baker as chief of staff, and former NATO ambassador David Abshire, who assured an honest administration response to the Iran-Contra investigations. Frank Carlucci, a former deputy secretary of defense, became Reagan's fifth national security adviser. He revamped the foreign policy process and helped restore trust across the government.

Reagan's successes in the last two years in office owe much to these personnel changes; but they would not have been possible without two other major developments. One was the emergence of Mikhail Gorbachev as the new president of the Soviet Union, who offered Reagan the opportunity to jointly find a way out of the Cold War confrontation. The other, partly a result of this first development, was the decision by Caspar Weinberger to leave his post at the Pentagon, thus ending the debilitating feud with Shultz that had paralyzed the administration for all too long. In the final year of Reagan's term, with Carlucci at Defense and Colin Powell at the NSC, cooperation replaced confrontation, both in Washington's relations with Moscow and within the Reagan administration.

The successful end of Ronald Reagan's presidency provided a perfect situation for his successor, George H. W. Bush. The NSC had been relegitimized through the changes that had been instituted in the wake of Iran-Contra and following the recommendations of the Tower Commission. Those responsible for the excesses had been punished, through forced resignation and, in some cases, prosecution. The world itself stood at the brink of major, positive change. Even before Bush had ascended to the presidency, Gorbachev had announced the unilateral withdrawal of hundreds of thousands of Soviet troops and thousands of tanks from Eastern Europe, long the focal point of the Cold War confrontation. More change was in the offing.

Bush was in many ways the perfect president for this situation. He was intensely interested in foreign policy, precisely what was needed at a time of big change. More than any president before or since, he understood both the importance of a well-run policy process and the role of the national security adviser in managing it. And he appointed the perfect adviser to help him succeed. Though Bush's best friend, James Baker, would be in charge of the new diplomacy as secretary of state, the president would rely on Brent Scowcroft to keep his policy team moving in the same direction. Scowcroft had a winning formula. He built a relationship of great trust with the other key players in the administration. He then ran an open, fair, but determined interagency process—both at the level of the principals and below, especially among the deputies. And he became the president's most trusted adviser by providing a sounding board and pushing his own ideas when he thought those best served the president's—and the nation's—interests.

The processes and practices Bush and Scowcroft instituted proved their worth during their tumultuous first years in office. The fall of the Berlin Wall, the liberation of Eastern Europe, the collapse of the Soviet Union—all of it happened on their watch. With Baker, they managed the change brilliantly. The Cold War ended without a shot being fired. Then came the challenge of Saddam Hussein, who in August 1990 invaded Kuwait. Again, Bush and Scowcroft met the test, pulling together a large international coalition to force Iraq out of its neighbor's lands and restore the status quo ante. Not everything went well—the aftermath of the Gulf War, the breakup of Yugoslavia, and the disintegration of Somalia all posed great challenges at high human cost, which Scowcroft and Bush tended to downplay. But these were failures to adapt old worldviews to new realities, not failures of process, though no less consequential for that. The process Scowcroft put in place, the way he balanced his responsibilities as presidential adviser and honest broker, the manner in which he structured interagency deliberations by emphasizing trust and transparency—these made Scowcroft the national security adviser that each of his successors sought to emulate.

For Brent Scowcroft, the 1980s provided an object lesson in how not to manage the national security process. For Tony Lake, it was the 1970s. He did not want to be the domineering Kissinger (whom he had served as an executive aide), nor repeat the feuding of Vance and Brzezinski (which he had witnessed from the seventh floor of the State Department). He wanted to be like Scowcroft—under Ford— a quiet, unassuming, behind-the-scenes honest broker who managed the policy process efficiently and without conflict. Lake also sought to keep his distance from Bill Clinton. He didn't want to be the president's best friend; rather, he wanted to keep the national security process insulated from politics. That, too, was a lesson Lake had learned from the 1970s. There were clear risks in being too close to the president. Clinton eased this final concern; after all, Lake wasn't the president's first choice for the job.

Lake's model of what an NSC adviser should be might have worked with another president—and another secretary of state—a Ford and a Kissinger, or a Bush and a Baker. But this administration was different. Unlike Ford and Bush, Clinton was a Washington novice, much more passionate about domestic policy than foreign affairs—a preference that politics at home strongly reinforced. This president, therefore, needed someone not only to manage the policy process but to push it forward. A Kissinger or a Baker could have done that; but for all his strengths, Warren Christopher was no Kissinger or Baker. He was perfectly content to have foreign policy take a backseat at the White House, not to push difficult choices on the president, and to defer actions when these might have diverted attention and political capital from domestic concerns to foreign ones.

After the debacles of the first year—over Bosnia, Somalia, and Haiti—Lake realized that the way he had approached his job from the outset did not serve the administration. So he changed. He would not only manage the process, but push it along—by trying to resolve old problems and better anticipate new ones. If that meant pushing actions (like threatening the use of force in Bosnia, Haiti, or Northeast Asia), then he would push them. If that meant he might differ significantly with others within the administration, notably the secretary of state, then differ he would. Someone had to drive policy, and make the case for action. The president, too, came to understand that he needed to be more actively engaged in foreign policy (as he had on some important issues, like Russia, from the start).

The new approach paid off. The democratically elected leader of Haiti was restored to power. The Bosnian war, Europe's most bloody since 1945, was ended. A new relationship was forged with China. Relations with Moscow were solidified. By the end of Clinton's first term, many of the issues that had piled up in the foreign policy inbox at the outset had been successfully transferred to the outbox.

A more confident Bill Clinton could try to use his second term to mold a better, more stable and peaceful world. Sandy Berger was the perfect partner for that effort. Close to the president in both personal and political terms, Berger would help Clinton steer foreign policy during the next four years. Though the execution of policy would remain the purview of the cabinet officers, the initiative would come from an energized White House. Clinton and his second national security adviser were kindred souls—tactically astute and politically brilliant, although lacking a clear strategic vision of the world and America's role in it. They were problem solvers. Good ones. And they tried to solve some big problems, such as the Israeli-Palestinian conflict. But they were also keenly aware of the political limitations at home that a hostile Republican Congress would try to impose. These political considerations played a large role—sometimes too large a role—in their deliberations, particularly when it came to whether and how to use force. In a democracy such as ours, striking the right balance between political considerations and policy desiderata is never easy—especially when they point in opposite directions.

George W. Bush came to the presidency very much determined to do things differently from his predecessor, though in one important respect he was very similar. Like Clinton's, his presidency would be focused on problems at home rather than those abroad. The terrorist attacks on September 11, 2001, came as a huge surprise to the new president and his young national security adviser, and reordered his priorities and his presidency. Condoleezza Rice was to be a key part in this reordering, though her ability to do so would depend not only on her very close relationship to the president but on the titanic advisers Bush had surrounded himself with. Dick Cheney, Don Rumsfeld, and even Colin Powell didn't make things easy for Rice. Cheney tried to take away her major responsibilities (such as chairing the Principals Committee) or went around her (on detainee matters). Rumsfeld refused to share information (on war planning). None of them was inclined to defer to her on matters of policy or process.

Rice's power lay in the president, who trusted her and liked her more than he did any of his other advisers. To maintain that power in the face of the giants surrounding her, Rice decided that she needed to channel Bush—to focus on his instincts and translate them into policy. After 9/11, Bush was increasingly certain about what he wanted to do, and how. And Rice's job was to get it done. In the process, the NSC adviser decided not to put Bush's instincts and desires to the analytical test—not to probe his assumptions, look for alternative courses of action, or even to examine the likely consequences. She asked: What does the president want? How can it be done? She did not ask: What if the president is wrong? How else can we achieve his objectives? Who among those who disagree should he hear out?

This was a serious failing. It is fair to wonder, though, whether the kinds of questions she should have posed were ones Bush was at all interested in having answered or even in asked. There is reason to believe that, particularly after 9/11, Bush would not have reacted positively to such an analytical effort and that he would have objected to Rice trying to engage him in it. Early in his administration, people meeting with the president felt that, especially on foreign policy matters, Bush was very much in receiving mode. He did not know all that much, and realized he needed to know more. But later, those meeting with him saw someone much more in broadcasting mode—telling them what he thought and what he was going to do, and far less interested in hearing what they thought or believed he should do. Bush had no self-doubt; he was "the decider." Given this sense of dead certainty, it's doubtful he would have been interested in reexamining his assumptions, taking another look at alternatives, and working out what to do if the policy he was advocating did not succeed. And so Rice never suggested that he do any of these things. Ultimately, the successes and failures of this presidency, Rice realized, would be the successes and failures of the president. Once again, what the national security adviser could do was constrained by the predilections of the president she served.

Of course, on those (rare) occasions when George Bush did realize that his policy was failing, having an adviser in the White House willing and able to push consideration of alternatives would help. Stephen Hadley was such an adviser, and he did push such an analytical effort when Bush recognized in 2006 that his Iraq policy was not working. Hadley urged a reexamination of the assumptions underlying the Iraq strategy. He had the president meet with analysts who favored different strategies. And he pushed a policy review that would give the president clear choices. By the end of that year, these efforts produced a new Iraq policy—the "surge"—which provided the president and his administration with a new basis to hope that the disaster in Iraq might turn out better than many people, including most Americans, had come to believe.

Hadley, of course, worked in a very different environment from Rice. Most important, on the issue of Iraq, the president himself had come to believe that his policy was not working and he therefore was open to considering alternative courses of action. But Hadley also operated within a different team. Unlike her predecessor at State, Rice was a close and trusted confidante of the president, someone Bush felt comfortable to hand the reins of policy to. The failure of the original Iraq strategy had undermined Donald Rumsfeld's power; his replacement, Bob Gates, proved to be much more of a team player. And although the vice president remained extremely influential within the administration and with the president, he no longer had many allies within the rest of the government. All of which enabled Hadley to play the more traditional role in a way that Rice could not. Which goes to show: national security advisers can only be as effective and successful as presidents enable them to be.

Who was the best national security adviser? This question comes up whenever we discuss our book. It's a fair question, if not an easy one. The immediate problem in answering it is summed up in another question: best at what? If the measure is the accumulation of power over policy, the prize certainly goes to Henry Kissinger, who—with Nixon's encouragement—conducted the major negotiations himself and effectively kept Secretary of State William Rogers and other senior officials out of the loop. If the criterion is the achievement of policy change, Kissinger looks like the winner again, though on his administration's signature accomplishment, the opening to China, it was Nixon himself who came up with the idea and took the substantive lead. Or if success is best measured the way presidents tend to measure it, by responsiveness to them, no one did better than Condoleezza Rice, who was as close to her boss as anyone who ever held the position. She was rewarded by being named secretary of state for the second Bush term—and unlike Nixon's grudging elevation of Henry Kissinger thirty-two years earlier, this was an appointment the president very much wanted to make.

If "best" means being able to make the process work, then there are a number of contenders. McGeorge Bundy, who let Kennedy down badly by failing to force a serious review of the CIA's Bay of Pigs plan, became a highly effective policy manager for Kennedy. He played a key role in the Cuban missile crisis by keeping options open until all the consequences had been effectively weighed. More generally, he ran a transparent process. Though his intellect and surface arrogance could be intimidating, he systematically strengthened lines of communication to the president and empowered individuals, on his staff and across the government, who were effective in advancing the president's agenda. Decades later, his colleague Robert S. McNamara pronounced him "by far the ablest national security adviser I have observed over the last forty years." Had he been as effective with Johnson as with Kennedy, and had not Vietnam blotted his copybook, Bundy's service might well have gone down as the model for all his successors.

Others played key process roles. Both Frank Carlucci and Colin Powell restored a sense of competence and purpose in the policy process during Reagan's last two years in office. Though Shultz resisted, they forged a model for an effective, NSC-led consideration of policy options and choices. And with Shultz, they helped steer Reagan into a strong and effective relationship with the Soviet president, Mikhail Gorbachev, that did much to help end the Cold War confrontation.

As the first truly post–Cold War national security advisers, Tony

Lake and Sandy Berger understood the importance of widening the scope of NSC activity beyond the traditional political military concerns. They helped integrate international economic considerations into foreign policy, gave global issues like non-proliferation, humanitarian concerns, and the environment a permanent place at the table, and began the process of coordinating domestic and foreign activities to counter terrorism. Stephen Hadley started off in a distinctly subordinate position, but he would prove quietly effective, not least in helping the president see that his Iraq policy was failing and in creating a process that allowed for a different, possibly more successful course.

But the man who stands out in his role as assistant to the president for national security affairs is Brent Scowcroft, the only person to hold the job twice. Scowcroft had a unique perspective. He had learned the job while working under Kissinger, the most dominant adviser in history, and from that experience developed strong convictions about how—and how not—to play the role. Having sat in the seat, he then had a bird's-eye view as first Brzezinski and then six more men took the chair he would himself return to twelve years later. He learned the importance of operating in the shadows. The national security adviser, he would often say, "should be seen occasionally, heard even less." Scowcroft understood the need for the adviser to be strong, but also the vital importance of being trusted and transparent in how he deals with his colleagues and the president. He became convinced of the need for an effective interagency process, chaired by the NSC, and the critically important role the deputies would have to play within that process. The deputies would be the crisis managers. And they would have to vet the policy choices so that the president and his principal advisers could make the right kinds of decisions.

Not only did Scowcroft play the role effectively. He also enhanced it through his central contribution to the Tower Commission Report of 1987. As the only commission member with White House experience, he shaped recommendations that quite literally saved the national security process—not to mention the Reagan administration.

In some respects, Scowcroft was lucky. The presidents he served had relatively easy personalities, and both were willing to address, directly, questions about the substance of policy. He might have worked less well with a Johnson or a Nixon, or with George W. Bush. None of those presidents made the job of their security adviser easy, whereas Ford and Bush senior did. This gives credence to the tongue-in-cheek conclusion of one colleague, James Lindsay, who read this book in manuscript form: that national security advisers should "choose their presidents wisely."

Be that as it may, it helped greatly that Scowcroft possessed a personality that was peculiarly well suited to the position. He was a man of quiet strength, and a quintessential team player, a straight shooter who was comfortable sharing information—and power. He naturally elicited trust from others, and gave it in return, when it was earned. Yet, while diffident, he did not shy away from pushing his own views strongly when he thought it necessary.

Scowcroft was certainly not perfect. He left unexamined a critical assumption about the aftermath of the Gulf War of 1991—that after his anticipated defeat, Saddam Hussein would be overthrown by his generals. He and his staff were too careful to promise Bush that Saddam *would* indeed lose power, even though the president sought such assurance. But they were unprepared for the consequences when Saddam Hussein retained power, and indeed strengthened his hold on it as a result of successfully crushing the Shi'ite and Kurdish uprisings within Iraq. Scowcroft also failed to force consideration of the costs and consequences of a bloody Yugoslav civil war in the midst of a Europe that was longing not only to be free but whole and at peace. And he was unable to counter the general ineffectiveness of Bush's final year, when foreign policy concerns were subordinated to domestic considerations even as major problems festered in the former Soviet Union, the Balkans, and the Horn of Africa. It is no accident that the remarkable Bush-Scowcroft joint memoir says nothing about the events of 1992.

Nonetheless, Scowcroft still stands out among the fourteen men and one woman who have held the job since Kennedy and Bundy "invented" it in 1961. Each of the four advisers who came to the White House after him—two Democrats, two Republicans—looked to his tenure in 1989–93 as the model to emulate. They all wanted to be Scowcroft. They kept the essential form of the NSC process he first fully instituted: a Principals Committee chaired by the NSC adviser; a Deputies Committee chaired by the deputy national security adviser; regional and functional NSC offices headed by senior directors, many of whom chaired interagency groups on their particular areas of expertise as well. They each sought to balance the role of adviser to the president and honest broker of the process, drawing on Scowcroft's excellent example. Some proved more successful than others, but all recognized that if they could be like Scowcroft, they likely would succeed. That may, in the end, be the most convincing answer to the question of who was the best national security adviser.

Looking forward, however, the questions are different: not who was best, but what qualities presidents should look for when choosing this close adviser and what practices should future national security assistants emulate. The answer starts from the fact that the NSC adviser has enormous potential influence. One reason is his or her proximity to power. During the course of an administration, the adviser will spend more time with the president than anyone else responsible for the nation's business overseas. She sits a few paces away from the Oval Office, briefs the president first thing in the morning, and is often the last person to see him before he retires in the evening. The other reason is freedom from competing obligations. In contrast to all the other key players, the adviser is beholden to no one except the president. Cabinet officers have departmental interests that often compete with those of the president; and as officials subject to confirmation, they also have a responsibility to Congress. Vice presidents nearly always have political interests that can compete with the president's, including a desire to one day sit where the president currently sits.

As the only person free to focus solely on what is best for the president, the national security adviser is very likely to emerge as the president's most important foreign affairs adviser. Bundy, Kissinger, Brzezinski, Lake, and Berger all ended up in this position. So did

Scowcroft, even though the president's best friend served as his secretary of state. This reality is reinforced by the increasingly complex and interconnected world in which we now live. Making effective policy to cope with this interconnected world requires integrating its varied dimensions—defense and diplomacy, finance and trade, the environment and homeland security, science and social policy—into a coherent whole. Increasingly, it is at the White House and, within it, at the National Security Council, that such integration occurs. Which is why, aside from the president himself, the national security adviser is potentially the most important person in government today.

It is an awesome responsibility, one that requires the adviser to play his or her role with great care. History is replete with cases where American foreign policy suffered because the adviser overplayed or misplayed the role—think of the distorted processes under Kissinger, or Brzezinski, or Clark. But policymaking also suffers if the adviser proves too weak, as was true through most of the Reagan presidency, and critically in George W. Bush's first term. One dilemma is that the incumbent must respond to the particular predilections of the president; but he or she must also do more. Another is that the adviser must be ready to use the power inherent in the office, but to do so in a disciplined manner, so that it serves rather than subverts the policy process.

The person who sits in the large corner office of the West Wing must strike a number of difficult balances. One is to realize that while the president is boss, he is not always right. Maybe after the September 11 attacks it made sense to consider the risks posed by Saddam Hussein and his apparent determination to obtain weapons of mass destruction to be unacceptably grave. But that was the kind of judgment call that should not have been accepted uncritically by anyone—least of all the national security adviser. Such a conclusion demanded probing analysis, detailed discussion of the assumptions and alternative conclusions, as well as possible consequences, in order to determine whether the judgment was right. And it was Rice's job to insist on such an analysis when Bush began to signal that overthrowing Saddam was his preferred course.

Scowcroft and his staff did exactly this sort of analysis when considering how to reverse Iraq's invasion of Kuwait in 1990. In this case, the adviser himself had a strong policy view, but the staff nonetheless examined all the possible outcomes of a confrontation with Iraq in the run-up to the war—including what the United States would have to do if Saddam pulled most or all of his troops out of Kuwait before the first bombs had been dropped. And they told the president that there was no way, short of occupying Baghdad, that war could guarantee the ouster of Saddam from power. It might be likely, they said, but it was not certain. Bush didn't like the answer—and he twice rejected the analysis that led to it. But in the end he accepted the fact because Scowcroft insisted it was so. It was a clear instance of a president realizing that his adviser was telling him something he did not like to hear, but accepting it nevertheless. No president is omniscient; all of them need advisers who protect them from themselves. Deference to the office is vital; and so is challenging the judgment of its occupant, particularly when the stakes are so high.

Another major balance that has to be struck by the national security adviser is to be assertive but wary of intruding on the roles of others. There is a natural temptation for NSC advisers to think they can be as good a secretary of state or defense or CIA director as the actual people who occupy those positions. At times, Kissinger, Brzezinski, Poindexter, and Lake all gave in to this temptation. Sometimes, it worked out well—Kissinger's opening to China and Lake's marshalling of European support to end the Bosnian war come to mind. But often it did not, with Iran-Contra only the most obvious case in point. Other people, generally, are better positioned to do their own jobs.

But there are some tasks that the NSC adviser and staff are uniquely placed to undertake, and it is their responsibility to make sure that they do so. These include:

- Staffing the president's daily foreign policy activity: his communications with foreign leaders and the preparation and conduct of his trips overseas;

- Managing the process of making decisions on major foreign and national security issues;
- Driving the policymaking process to make real choices, in a timely manner;
- Overseeing the full implementation of the decisions the president has made.

All of these tasks are important—and none can be left to others.

The president needs to be kept informed on the key international issues of the day. He needs to be staffed prior to communicating about these issues with leaders at home and overseas. The State Department and other departments can offer input, but it is the NSC adviser's job to make sure he gets it right. That commitments made can be fulfilled. That questions raised can be answered. That statements uttered can be relied upon as accurate. The importance of good staffing was underscored by President Bush's 2003 State of the Union address, which contained some unfounded statements about Iraq's weapons of mass destruction capabilities, notably Saddam's alleged attempt to buy uranium yellowcake in Africa. Condoleezza Rice had been warned by the CIA that they were inaccurate. But she failed to get them deleted, and the president's credibility on this issue was, accordingly, undermined.

Staffing the president, while crucial, is only a part of the NSC adviser's job. More important in the end is making sure that the president makes the right decisions, that he does so in a timely manner, and that they are implemented effectively. It is the adviser's overriding responsibility to manage the policymaking process in such a way as to give the president the best chance of getting it right. The adviser will need to make sure that all those with strong stakes in the issues are involved in the process of deciding them; that all realistic options (including those not favored by any agency) have been considered and fully analyzed; that the underlying assumptions have been fully tested and the possible consequences of every action are clearly understood by everyone before the president is asked to make a decision. The importance of an effective policy process cannot be underestimated. Its absence, as the run-up to the Iraq War demonstrated, can have truly disastrous consequences.

There is a model of how to manage this decision process effectively, and it dates back to the beginning of the Nixon administration. The new president was steeped in foreign affairs like few others; it was the abiding interest of his presidency. As a result, he didn't want to be confronted by consensus recommendations emanating from the bureaucracy; he wanted clear options that were backed up by a good analysis of the underlying assumptions, possible actions, and likely consequences. Kissinger accordingly instituted comprehensive reviews of all the major policy issues—ranging from Vietnam to strategic weapons policy to arms control to China. He put together a deliberative process that presented the president with a clear set of alternative policies, each based on a careful review and analysis. The process eschewed consensus recommendations, and produced options that were not limited to the preferences of the different agencies, but included other choices that might plausibly work.

Initially, the president and his NSC adviser were committed to the process, and it produced good, considered decisions on issues such as the abolition of biological weapons and the return of Okinawa to Japan. In less than a year, though, its credibility was undercut when Nixon and Kissinger began making decisions in secret while cutting the secretaries of state and defense and their departments out from their deliberations. Nevertheless, future presidents and national security advisers would do well to adopt the kind of careful, options-driven, non-consensual process that they instituted—and briefly practiced—four decades ago.

Putting in place an effective policy process is a crucial responsibility of any NSC adviser. No process, however effective, can guarantee good policy decisions; but an ineffectual process makes bad policy that much more likely. Also important is knowing when to force a decision—and when not. Often, a crisis will mandate the need for an immediate decision. But not every issue needs to be decided right away, even if some within or outside the administration are clamoring for a quick resolution. The national security adviser can help the process by pushing for decisions when they are needed, or not doing so when the time is not ripe. During the Johnson administration, Bundy slow-walked a decision on approving the development of the so-called multilateral force—a sea-based nuclear flotilla under the joint control of the United States and some of its non-nuclear allies in Europe. Despite clamor from a range of Europe-oriented advocates inside and outside the administration, Bundy knew that neither the president nor any of his top advisers nor the European allies were really committed to the idea. So he solicited a skeptical review and slowed the process down, until the ultimate rejection by Johnson would incur few costs. Conversely, Lake's determination in the summer of 1995 finally to push for a decision on Bosnia, coming after he convinced Clinton that the issue had become "a cancer on the presidency," demonstrates the potential value of forcing the action even when the president and key advisers are hesitant to make a choice.

Making good decisions is key, but they amount to nothing unless there is consistent follow-through. Particularly with controversial decisions, implementation may prove less prompt than is desired. In such cases, there is a temptation on the part of the president or his NSC adviser to carry out the policies directly. Nixon and Kissinger were deeply distrustful of the State Department, which led them to open up their own channels to Moscow, Beijing, and Hanoi—not always with happy results. Faced with opposition from the secretaries of state and defense to selling arms to Iran, McFarlane and Poindexter essentially kept them in the dark as they proceeded to do just that.

Instead of taking policy execution into his or her own hands, the NSC adviser serves the process much better if he or she can institute a clear system for monitoring the implementation of presidential decisions. This was one of Hadley's contributions. Dissatisfied with the pace at which policy was executed in the first Bush term, Hadley created a special office and appointed a coterie of people to focus on implementation. For big issues like Afghanistan and Iraq, they instituted a "stoplight process," in which they defined clear lines of action and the agencies responsible for them. The NSC staff then examined the extent to which these actions were being implemented, and assigned them a "green," "yellow," or "red" light for policies that were on track, needed reexamination, or were failing. In this way, the NSC adviser could focus on just how well policy was being executed, and where and when it needed to be adjusted.

If job one of the national security adviser is to manage the policy-making process, how he or she goes about this task will prove crucial to their success. The adviser has to balance this managerial responsibility against the role of advising the president. This is perhaps the most critical—and most difficult—balance of all. If other senior officials believe the national security assistant is skewing the process so his or her own preferences will prevail, then they will work around the assistant whenever they can. But if the president isn't getting serious recommendations from his closest policy aide, his confidence in that aide will suffer, with a negative impact on the adviser's overall effectiveness.

The key ingredient to getting the balance right is *trust*. The president must trust the adviser to present him with his or her best and unvarnished advice. The other senior players in the national security field must trust the adviser to convey their views fairly and openly to the president when they are not there—as will often be the case on fast-moving issues. They must also be confident that they know what the adviser is telling the president about his or her own views and advice. And they must be sure that they will be involved in any issue or decision that falls within their purview. Bundy put it well: "A good national security assistant works for Cabinet officers as well as for the President. One of his main functions is to help senior officials outside the White House understand and be understood by the President."

In helping Reagan to survive Iran-Contra, David Abshire insisted (quoting Bryce Harlow) that "trust is the coin of the realm." Not every adviser has taken this maxim to heart. Iran-Contra, of course, resulted from secrecy at the core of the NSC, when even the president was kept in the dark about the diversion of funds. But there are less egregious instances where advisers forgot the importance of trust. Brzezinski, for example, carried his oft-tendentious policy advocacy to the point that other policy players did not believe he was playing square with them. Kissinger regularly deceived other senior officials by conducting back-channel negotiations in their areas of responsibility, without their knowledge. On strategic arms talks, this resulted in their holding to positions that he himself had already secretly abandoned. The final U.S.-Soviet agreement on offensive arms completed in 1972 contained serious flaws that administration arms control experts could have corrected had they not been shut out.

Trust is also essential for building a true foreign policy "team." In addition to working to connect its members, the adviser can help make it so by limiting her or his own operational, public, and political roles. As Robert Frost wrote, "Good fences make good neighbors." There is nothing wrong with being an activist NSC adviser, but there can only be one secretary of state. The White House should not be a routine stop for foreign ministers or ambassadors; it is the job of the secretary of state and their senior subordinates to meet with these officials on a regular basis. Moreover, by avoiding such routine interaction, an administration can signal the importance of an issue or concern when it changes tack and invites a foreign official to visit the NSC adviser or even the president at the White House.

The same consideration should inform decisions to travel abroad. It was appropriate for Sandy Berger to travel quietly to Moscow in May 2000, just weeks before Clinton's first summit meeting with the new Russian president, Vladimir Putin, to see if an arms control deal on missile defense could be worked out. Such quiet diplomacy by the president's closest adviser can often help untie knotty problems. Scowcroft's quiet trip to Beijing in the aftermath of Tiananmen, designed to keep communications channels open, falls into the same category. So did Lake's trip to Europe in August 1995 to sell key allies on the president's new approach to end the Bosnian conflict. At the time, Lake considered continuing on to the Balkans to lead actual negotiations, but he rightly decided that this was not his job, which required him to coordinate matters from Washington rather than in the field. In each of these cases, the NSC adviser traveled abroad with the full knowledge of the secretary of state, and always in the company of senior State Department officials. And in each case, there was value in sending the unmistakable message of presidential concern or involvement.

In contrast, when Rice traveled to Moscow in July 2001 to discuss Bush's new approach on missile defenses, she went on a quite routine visit that would normally have been undertaken by the secretary of state. In fact, though Powell had met his Russian counterpart on earlier occasions, Rice's Moscow visit was the first by a senior official in the Bush administration. Kissinger went much further—his domination of the three primary Nixon administration negotiations (with the Soviet Union, the People's Republic of China, and North Vietnam) essentially neutered the secretary of state as a credible diplomat, and made it impossible for the national security adviser to fulfill his role of policy review and oversight.

The national security adviser should also limit his or her public profile. Short of the president, it is the secretary of state who must remain the administration's principal spokesperson on foreign affairs. This principle has admittedly become more difficult to follow in recent decades. As foreign policy has become more controversial politically, the number of news outlets has exploded, and the news cycle has shrunk from days to hours to minutes, the demands on administration officials to go out and make the case for policy have gone up noticeably. It is not surprising, therefore, that the NSC adviser has become an increasingly public figure. To use one telling indicator, during the last twenty years, the NSC adviser appeared on more than two hundred Sunday morning talk shows, an average of nearly once a month. For the twenty years before that, NSC advisers appeared just thirty-one times (though there were only three such shows in the 1970s and 1980s, compared to five in recent years). But even within the last three administrations, television appearances among the five advisers have differed markedly—from a low of five by Lake during his four-year tenure to a high of eighty-four by Rice. In her four years at the White House, Rice alone accounts for more than 40 percent of the total appearances by NSC advisers on the Sunday shows over the twenty-year period. The 9/11 attacks and the Iraq War are partly responsible; but there is no doubt that Rice was seen by the administration as its most effective defender of the president's policies (though Powell appeared even more often than Rice did in the same period).

Such activity by the national security adviser poses a serious problem of accountability. When taking on a public role, the adviser becomes not just a confidential counselor to the president and manager of the process but a public articulator and advocate for particular policies. This raises the obvious constitutional question: shouldn't a senior official with such a public role also be accountable to Congress? Responding to Brzezinski's high profile, Senator Edward Zorinsky introduced legislation in 1979 making the president's national security assistant subject to Senate confirmation. Successive presidents have resisted congressional attempts to make their personal White House staff accountable to Congress on the argument that their advice and activities are privileged. Moreover, a primary advantage of the position to presidents is that the incumbent is responsive to them alone. But a high public profile makes the argument hard to sustain. For example, Bush initially refused to let Rice testify before the congressionally mandated 9/11 Commission even as she was defending the administration's conduct prior to the attacks on the Sunday talk show circuit. The obvious discrepancy forced him to back down. Rice testified, publicly and under oath.

This raises the question of whether, in recognition of this growing public role, the position should be made statutory and subject to Senate confirmation. Frustrated by the widespread view that he had "usurped Vance's legitimate prerogatives," Brzezinski gave qualified support to this proposition in 1983 in his memoirs. He has since had second thoughts, and rightly so. It would fundamentally alter the unique relationship between the president and his NSC adviser, and would likely lead the president to turn elsewhere in the White

House for confidential assistance. The appropriate way to respond to pressure to make the position more accountable is for the adviser to take a less publicly prominent role than has become recent custom. In this position, less publicity translates into more effectiveness—and vice versa.

Finally, there is the issue of partisan politics. By its very nature, the White House stands at the center of the nation's political life. Its occupant is the only person to have been elected by the American people as a whole, and at least for the first four years, a key concern of any president is to secure his reelection. "Politics pervades the White House," Theodore Sorensen once noted, even when it does not prevail. It is therefore impossible for anyone who serves the president, including the NSC adviser, to escape politics completely. But though the adviser must be sensitive to political influences, he or she should eschew any direct, partisan political involvement—and certainly should strive to insulate their staff from political roles. Many on that staff will be career people, who are aware of what is appropriate in this regard. But many—including the adviser and most senior aides—are political supporters of the president, who enter the White House with the president after his election. All of them must understand that overt participation in politics undermines their ability to deal with those who may not share the president's partisan affiliation.

Establishing good and cordial relations with members of Congress on both sides of the aisle is often critical to getting the president's agenda enacted. Berger and Hadley were particularly good at this aspect of the job; both spent a lot of time working with congressional leaders on critical legislation. Such efforts are undercut if the NSC adviser takes on an overt political role—traveling on the campaign plane or giving speeches in key battleground states, as Rice did in 2004. But it is not possible for the assistant to separate himself completely from politics, as Lake tried to do. The adviser can—and should—defend the president and his policies, even in the heat of a campaign, provided he does so without questioning the policies and priorities of opposing candidates. Another appropriate role is to make sure that the party platform conforms with the administration's policies. These are political activities that advisers can perform without having to be partisan.

———

National security advisers have one tough job. They must serve the president, yet balance this primary allegiance with a commitment to manage an effective and efficient policy process. They must be forceful in driving that process forward to decisions, yet represent other agencies' views fully and faithfully. They must be simultaneously strong and collegial, able to enforce discipline across the government, yet engage senior officials and their agencies rather than exclude them. They must provide confidential advice to the president, yet establish a reputation as an honest broker of the conflicting officials and interests across the government. They must be indispensable to the process and the president, yet operate in the shadows to the maximum extent possible. They must do the heavy lifting, yet allow others to receive the glory. Above all, they must assure that the president and his senior advisers give the most thorough and careful consideration to that handful of critical issues that will make or break their administration; and they must handle all issues, large and small, in a manner that establishes and retains the trust of their senior administration colleagues.

It's a tall order. The failures of many previous advisers show the importance of getting the job right. Their successes offer hope that future national security advisers can do so. When they don't, the nation loses much. When they do, the nation stands much to gain.

Notes

―――――

1. "THE PRESIDENT NEEDS HELP"

Page

1 *"Some say it was"*: Alexander L. and Juliette L. George, *Woodrow Wilson and Colonel House: A Personality Study* (New York: John Day Co., 1956), xiii.

1 *"Or perhaps it"*: Bundy to John F. Kennedy, "The Use of the National Security Council," memorandum of January 24, 1961, in U.S. Department of State, *Foreign Relations of the United States, 1961–1963,* Vol. XXV, Document 4 (pp. 12–15).

2 *"Charles G. Dawes"*: Elliot Richardson and James Pfiffner, "Our Cabinet System Is a Charade," *New York Times,* May 28, 1989.

3 *"By 1963, leading"*: Richard E. Neustadt, "Approaches to Staffing the Presidency: Notes on FDR and JFK," *American Political Science Review,* vol. 57, no. 4 (December 1963), p. 855.

3 *"The big story"*: Bertram D. Hullen, "Unification Signed," *New York Times,* July 27, 1947, p. A1; http://select.nytimes.com/mem/archive/pdf?res=F1 0D15F7355A147B93C5AB178CD85F438485F9.

3 *"The Council,"*: David K. Hall, *Implementing Multiple Advocacy in the National Security Council,* PhD dissertation, Stanford University, 1982 (University Microfilms International), p. 150.

3 *"This bruising battle"*: Clark Clifford, with Richard Holbrooke, *Counsel to the President* (New York: Random House, 1991), p. 164.

4 *"Roosevelt's 'intimate, personalized'"*: Neustadt, "Approaches to Staffing the Presidency," p. 860.

4 *"He also insisted"*: Marshall to Truman, February 7, 1947, quoted in Hall, *Implementing Multiple Advocacy,* p. 151, and in Anna Kasten Nelson, "National Security I: Inventing a Process," in Hugh Heclo and Lester M. Salamon, eds., *The Illusion of Presidential Government* (San Francisco: West-

view Press, for the National Academy of Public Administration, 1981), p. 233.

4 *"Once the Council":* Nelson, "Inventing a Process," p. 245.

4 *"He did, however":* Ibid., pp. 234–35; Hall, *Implementing Multiple Advocacy,* pp. 157ff.

4 *"Souers defined his role":* Unsigned, undated document (apparently drafted by Souers) in Box 1, Souers Papers, Harry S. Truman Library.

4 *"With Truman's approval":* Harry S. Truman, *Memoirs. Vol. II: Years of Trial and Hope* (New York: Doubleday, 1956), p. 60.

5 *"To review and":* Data on NSC meetings available at www.brookings.edu/nsc.

5 *"The aim, in":* Andrew Goodpaster in *The Nixon Administration National Security Council,* Oral History Roundtable, National Security Council Project, Center for International and Security Studies at Maryland (CISSM) and the Brookings Institution, December 8, 1998, p. 2, www.brookings.edu/nsc/oralhistories/nixonnsc.

5 *"And Cutler lovingly":* Robert Cutler, "The Development of the National Security Council," *Foreign Affairs* (April 1956).

5 *"At the very":* Robert H. Johnson, "The National Security Council: The Relevance of Its Past to Its Future," *Orbis,* 13 (Fall 1969), p. 729.

6 *"Eisenhower liked to":* Goodpaster in *The Nixon Administration National Security Council,* p. 4.

7 *"This invited, in":* U.S. Senate, Committee on Government Operations, Subcommittee on National Policy Machinery (henceforth Jackson Subcommittee), *Organizing for National Security,* Vols. I–III (Washington, DC: GPO, 1961).

7 *"Their negative take":* This was the title of a June 7, 1959, *New York Times Magazine* article by Hans J. Morgenthau. This and other critiques, by such leading lights as George Kennan, are reprinted in Jackson Subcommittee, Vol. II.

7 *"But as the historian":* Nelson, "Inventing a Process," pp. 256, 255.

7 *"And, as two":* Robert R. Bowie and Richard H. Immerman, *Waging Peace: How Eisenhower Shaped an Enduring Cold War Strategy* (New York: Oxford University Press, 1998), p. 258.

7 *"In a December 1960":* Bromley K. Smith, "Organizational History of the National Security Council During the Kennedy and Johnson Administrations" (Washington, D. C., 1988), p. 3.

8 *"Brent Scowcroft was appalled":* George Bush and Brent Scowcroft, *A World Transformed* (New York: Alfred A. Knopf, 1998), pp. 317–18.

2. "YOU CAN'T BEAT BRAINS"

Page

12 *"'There's this job'":* Kai Bird, *The Color of Truth: McGeorge Bundy and William Bundy: Brothers in Arms* (New York: Simon & Schuster, 1998), pp. 152–53.

14 *"'And this is'"*: A famous toast by the poet John Collins Bossidy.

15 *"First rejected for"*: Bird, *The Color of Truth*, p. 79.

15 *"Bundy's public service"*: Henry L. Stimson and McGeorge Bundy, *On Active Service in Peace and War* (New York: Harper & Bros., 1948).

15 *"Then, after working"*: McGeorge Bundy, ed., *The Pattern of Responsibility: From the Records of Dean Acheson* (Boston: Houghton Mifflin, 1952).

15 *"Within four years"*: David Halberstam, *The Best and the Brightest* (New York: Random House, 1972), p. 44.

15 *"But this was balanced"*: Bird, *The Color of Truth*, p. 7.

16 *"Bundy, the Boston"*: Ibid., p. 134.

16 *"Both 'delighted in'"*: The phrase is from Richard E. Neustadt, "Kennedy in the Presidency: A Premature Appraisal," *Political Science Quarterly*, 79 (September 1964), p. 330.

16 *"Bundy came to"*: John Prados, *Keepers of the Keys: A History of the National Security Council from Truman to Bush* (New York: William Morrow, 1991), p. 97.

16 *"Senator Henry Jackson's"*: U.S. Senate Committee on Government Operations, Subcommittee on National Policy Machinery, "The National Security Council," in *Organizing for National Security*, Vol. III, 1961, p. 38.

17 *"When engaged by"*: "Memorandum on Staffing the President-Elect," October 30, 1960, John F. Kennedy Library, p. 20. This paragraph is edited out of the version of this memo in the excellent collection edited by Charles O. Jones, *Preparing to Be President: The Memos of Richard E. Neustadt* (Washington, D.C.: American Enterprise Institute, 2000).

18 *"Three months later"*: Interview with Carl Kaysen, May 18, 1982.

18 *"a 'new frontier'"*: This was how the administration labeled itself, following FDR's "New Deal" and Harry Truman's "Fair Deal" and preceding LBJ's "Great Society." The term "Camelot" was coined, in mournful retrospect, by Theodore H. White after the November 1963 assassination—"For President Kennedy: An Epilogue," *Life*, December 6, 1963, pp. 158–59.

19 *"'The currents of'"*: Arthur M. Schlesinger, Jr., *A Thousand Days: John F. Kennedy in the White House* (Boston: Houghton Mifflin, 1965), pp. 213–14.

19 *"When Rusk brought"*: Interview with Lucius Battle, August 12, 1982.

20 *"Eisenhower had stressed"*: Interview with Andrew Goodpaster, January 18, 1982.

20 *"But he recommended"*: Schlesinger, *A Thousand Days*, p. 164.

21 *"As Dean Acheson"*: Quoted in Bird, *The Color of Truth*, p. 198.

21 *"Neustadt remarked ruefully"*: Interview with Richard E. Neustadt, February 18, 1982.

22 *"He offered his"*: Bundy to Kennedy, handwritten note, n.d., John F. Kennedy Library, Presidential Office Files, Box 62.

22 *"'It's just like'"*: Schlesinger, *A Thousand Days*, p. 292.

22 *"As he told"*: Interview with Neustadt, February 18, 1982.

22 *"So, one day"*: Interview with Bromley Smith, July 30, 1981.

23 *"As Bundy explained"*: Interview with McGeorge Bundy, November 16, 1981.

23 *"'In the olden'"*: Bundy to O'Donnell, January 5, 1962, John F. Kennedy Library.

23 *"'Nothing propinks like'"*: George W. Ball, *The Past Has Another Pattern: Memoirs* (New York: W. W. Norton & Co., 1982), p. 458.

24 *"Bromley Smith was"*: These paragraphs rely substantially on interviews with Smith on January 21 and July 30, 1981, and February 2 and May 4, 1982.

24 *"Smith and his"*: The most substantial treatment of this facility and its evolution is Michael K. Bohn, *Nerve Center: Inside the White House Situation Room* (Washington, D.C.: Brassey's, 2003).

25 *"By June 22"*: "Current Organization of the White House and NSC for Dealing with International Matters," "Memorandum for the President," June 22, 1961, U.S. Department of State, *Foreign Relations of the United States, 1961–1963*, Vol. VIII, Document 31.

26 *"By summer 1961"*: The other two were Samuel Belk, who handled UN and Africa issues, and Harold Saunders, who assisted Komer on the Middle East and South Asia, and would rise to become a key Middle East player in subsequent administrations of both political parties. Henry Kissinger and Henry Owen served as consultants.

26 *"In his June 22"*: "Current Organization of the White House," *FRUS, 1961–1963*, Vol. VIII, Document 31.

27 *"And other presidential"*: Martin Hillenbrand, *Fragments of Our Time: Memoirs of a Diplomat* (Athens, GA: University of Georgia Press, 1998), p. 177.

27 *"The president's 'plain'"*: "Current Organization of the White House" (emphasis in the original).

27 *"As early as"*: "Memorandum for the President," February 25, 1961, John F. Kennedy Library.

27 *"Six months later"*: "Memorandum for Secretary of State," August 16, 1961, John F. Kennedy Library.

29 *"Partly for this reason"*: Theodore C. Sorensen, *Kennedy* (New York: Harper & Row, 1965), p. 588.

30 *"Indeed, in late 1962"*: Ted Sorensen, *Counselor: A Life at the Edge of History* (New York: HarperCollins, 2008), pp. 236–37.

30 *"The recruitment of Forrestal"*: Interview with Michael Forrestal, December 11, 1981.

31 *"Kennedy liked to"*: Interview with Bundy, November 16, 1981. This and the following paragraphs are based on an interview with Robert W. Komer, July 28, 1981.

32 *"For a time"*: Ethan Nadelmann, "Setting the Stage: American Policy Toward the Middle East, 1961–1966," *International Journal of Middle East Studies* (1982), p. 437.

32 *"Forrestal became a"*: Andrew Preston, *The War Council: McGeorge Bundy, the NSC, and Vietnam* (Cambridge, MA: Harvard University Press, 2006), chap. 5.

32 *"'I turned out'"*: Carl Kaysen in Ivo H. Daalder and I. M. Destler, *International Economic Policy and the National Security Council*, Oral History Roundtable, February 11, 1999, pp. 4–6; www.brookings.edu/nsc/oralhistories/internationaleconomics.

33 *"But as Komer"*: Oral history interview with Robert W. Komer, John F. Kennedy Library, October 31, 1964, pp. 20–22.

33 *"The press came"*: Cf. Andrew Preston, "The Little State Department: McGeorge Bundy and the National Security Council Staff, 1961–65," *Presidential Studies Quarterly*, 31 (December 2001), pp. 635–59.

33 *"There were also tasks"*: For one recent, detailed account, see Tim Weiner, *Legacy of Ashes: The History of the CIA* (New York: Doubleday, 2007), esp. chaps. 17 and 18.

33 *"'Week End Papers'"*: "Week End Papers for Hyannis Port," September 8, 1961, and "Week End Reading 9/13/63," all in John F. Kennedy Library. Alsop was an influential journalist; Ngo Dinh Diem and his brother, Ngo Dinh Nhu, were embattled Vietnamese leaders who would shortly be assassinated.

34 *"'I only hope'"*: *Newsweek*, March 4, 1963, quoted in Bird, *The Color of Truth*, p. 189.

34 *"Kennedy and Bundy"*: McGeorge Bundy, *Danger and Survival: Choices About the Bomb in the First Fifty Years* (New York: Random House, 1988), p. 391.

34 *"Kennedy had declared"*: News conference of September 4, 1962.

34 *"'I decided,' he"*: Memorandum for the President, March 4, 1963, reprinted in Bundy, *Danger and Survival*, pp. 684–85.

34 *"Policy was then"*: For full transcriptions and summaries of these meetings, see Ernest R. May and Philip Zelikow, *The Kennedy Tapes: Inside the White House During the Cuban Missile Crisis* (Cambridge, MA: Harvard University Press, 1997).

35 *"The secrecy held"*: The fifteen policy officials were George Ball, McGeorge Bundy, Douglas Dillon, Roswell Gilpatric, U. Alexis Johnson, Lyndon Johnson, Robert Kennedy, Edwin Martin, John McCone, Robert McNamara, Paul Nitze, Dean Rusk, Theodore Sorensen, Maxwell Taylor, and Llewellyn Thompson. Others involved included Dean Acheson, Robert Lovett, John McCloy, and Adlai Stevenson. For the full list, see Graham Allison and Philip Zelikow, *Essence of Decision: Explaining the Cuban Missile Crisis*, 2nd edn. (London: Longman, 1999), Figure 1: The Inner Circle: October 16–27, 1962, pp. 326–27.

35 *"Bundy found neither"*: "Straw boss" is Bundy's phrase, in *Danger and Sur-*

vival, p. 400. This account draws mainly on that source; on Allison and Zelikow, *Essence of Decision*; and on Bird, *The Color of Truth*, chap. 10.

35 *"the former thought"*: Arthur M. Schlesinger, Jr., *Robert Kennedy and His Times* (Boston: Houghton Mifflin, 1978), p. 507, quoting "handwritten notes" by RFK dated October 31, 1962.

35 *"the latter would"*: Bird, *The Color of Truth*, p. 232.

36 *"But the President"*: Bundy's oft-critical biographer, Kai Bird, reports a document discovered after Bundy's death recalling the president as "specifically instructing me—on Friday, I think it was—to keep that option open as best I could. I didn't succeed in keeping it very open because the only allies I got for an air strike were people who wanted to strike everything that could fly in Cuba, and that wasn't exactly what the President had in mind"—*The Color of Truth*, p. 234. See also Allison and Zelikow, *Essence of Decision*, p. 371, n.48. Francis M. Bator, who would later join Bundy's NSC staff, called the document to the attention of the authors of both works.

36 *"'I almost deliberately'"*: Quoted in Patrick Anderson, *The President's Men* (New York: Doubleday, 1968), p. 270.

36 *"Ernest May and"*: May and Zelikow, *The Kennedy Tapes*, p. 693.

36 *"Of course, few"*: Allison and Zelikow, *Essence of Decision*, pp. 346–47.

36 *"As David Hall"*: David Kent Hall, *Implementing Multiple Advocacy in the National Security Council*, PhD, diss., Stanford University, May 1982, pp. 532–33; Roger Hilsman, *To Move a Nation: The Politics of Foreign Policy in the Administration of John F. Kennedy* (New York: Doubleday, 1967), pp. 45–46.

37 *"Astonishing in retrospect"*: Bundy, *Danger and Survival*, p. 438.

37 *"Kennedy, though, did"*: May and Zelikow, *The Kennedy Tapes*, esp. pp. 173–88.

37 *"So anxious was"*: Dean Rusk, as told to Richard Rusk, *As I Saw It* (New York: Penguin Books, 1990), pp. 240–41. In *Danger and Survival*, Bundy declares that "the rest of us learned [this story] from Dean Rusk in 1987." In his 1981 interview with Destler, however, Bundy went out of his way to highlight Rusk's role on the Turkey missile issue. Here the secretary of state was "the most important person short of the president." But the details were "his secret," Bundy declared.

38 *"As Allison and"*: Allison and Zelikow, *Essence of Decision*, p. 363.

38 *"Or as John Lewis Gaddis"*: John Lewis Gaddis, *We Now Know: Rethinking Cold War History* (Oxford: Clarendon Press, 1997), p. 272.

38 *"The denouement came"*: Bundy, *Danger and Survival*, p. 406.

38 *"Carl Kaysen, deputy"*: Joseph Kraft, *Profiles in Power: A Washington Insight* (New York: New American Library, 1966), p. 174.

39 *"But with the newly arrived"*: Preston, *The War Council*, p. 123.

39 *"This despite the"*: Robert S. McNamara, *In Retrospect: The Tragedy and Lessons of Vietnam* (New York: Random House, 1995), p. 55.

39 *"'My God! My'"*: Preston, *The War Council*, p. 123.

40 *"Martin Hillenbrand, who"*: Hillenbrand, *Fragments of Our Time*, p. 212.

41 *"Kennedy had 'gathered'"*: Bird, *The Color of Truth*, p. 266.

42 *"'Johnson was a rough person'"*: McNamara, *In Retrospect*, p. 99.

42 *"On Bundy, he"*: Schlesinger, *Robert Kennedy and His Times*, p. 661.

43 *"Less than three hours"*: Cable traffic quoted in Daniel Ellsberg, *Secrets: A Memoir of Vietnam and the Pentagon Papers* (New York: Viking, 2002), pp. 9–10.

44 *"McNamara checked with"*: McNamara, *In Retrospect*, p. 134.

44 *"After hearing the"*: Bird interview of Bundy, Sept 19, 1995, quoted in *The Color of Truth*, p. 289.

44 *"When domestic aide"*: Halberstam, *The Best and the Brightest*, p. 414.

45 *"At a December 1964"*: John D. Steinbruner, *The Cybernetic Theory of Decisions: New Dimensions of Political Analysis* (Princeton: Princeton University Press, 1974), p. 332.

45 *"By early 1965"*: Preston, *The War Council*, p. 155.

45 *"'the serious and deteriorating'"*: The phrase is from Leslie H. Gelb, with Richard K. Betts, *The Irony of Vietnam: The System Worked* (Washington, DC: Brookings Institution, 1979), p. 327. The authors argue persuasively that it was the threat of collapse and loss, not hopes for victory, that drove U.S. decisions to escalate throughout the decades of involvement in Vietnam.

46 *"Before then, on"*: Preston, *The War Council*, pp. 165–67; Bird, *The Color of Truth*, pp. 304–05. For the full memo, see Memorandum from Bundy to Johnson, January 27, 1965, in U.S. Department of State, *Foreign Relations of the United States, 1964–1968*, Vol. II, *Vietnam January–June 1965*, Document 42.

46 *"A program of"*: The history of U.S. troop deployments in Vietnam is recounted in Bundy's memorandum for the President dated July 24, 1965, reprinted in Gelb, with Betts, *The Irony of Vietnam*, pp. 372–74.

47 *"Bundy did, on"*: McNamara, *In Retrospect*, pp. 196–99.

47 *"Later in July"*: Clark Clifford, with Richard Holbrooke, *Counsel to the President: A Memoir* (New York: Random House, 1991), pp. 410–22.

47 *"Bundy still accommodated"*: James C. Thomson, Jr., "A Memory of McGeorge Bundy," *New York Times*, September 22, 1996, p. 50.

48 *"What was 'the'"*: Hall, *Implementing Multiple Advocacy*, p. 606. It was this action, and not Vietnam, which precipitated Senator J. William Fulbright's first major break with Johnson and his administration.

48 *"As Larry Berman"*: Larry Berman, *Planning a Tragedy: The Americanization of the War in Vietnam* (New York: W. W. Norton & Co., 1982), p. 147. See also Lyndon Baines Johnson, *The Vantage Point: Perspectives of the Presidency, 1963–1969* (New York: Holt, Rinehart & Winston, 1971), pp. 322–24.

49 *"Bundy was relentless"*: Interview with Bundy, November 16, 1981; Bird, *The Color of Truth*, pp. 318–22.

49   *"But the assistant"*: Bird interview with Bundy, February 15, 1994, in Bird, *The Color of Truth*, p. 322.

49   *"Bundy knew he"*: Interview with Bundy, November 16, 1981.

50   *"He promoted two"*: Memorandum from Bundy to Johnson, September 14, 1965, in U.S. Department of State, *Foreign Relations of the United States, 1964–1968*, Vol. XXXIII, *Organization and Management of Foreign Policy. The National Security Council and the White House* (henceforth *FRUS, 1964–1968*, Vol. XXXIII), Document 156.

50   *"And he honored"*: Citation of award conveyed on June 7, 1964.

50   *"Komer never figured"*: Johnson, *The Vantage Point*, p. 245.

52   *"'It was not until'"*: Walt Whitman Rostow, *The Diffusion of Power 1957–1972: Men, Events, and Decisions That Shaped America's Role in the World—from Sputnik to Peking* (New York: Macmillan, 1972), p. 363.

52   *"Johnson was aware"*: Johnson-McNamara phone conversation, February 27, 1966, in *FRUS, 1964–1968*, Vol. XXXIII, Document 161.

52   *"As Bundy remarked"*: informal conversation, spring 1970.

53   *"Beginning sporadically in"*: Editorial Note, *FRUS, 1964–1968*, Vol. XXXIII, Document 142.

53   *"When notes were"*: Rostow, *The Diffusion of Power*, p. 359. For more on the Tuesday lunch, see Henry F. Graff's incorrectly titled *The Tuesday Cabinet: Deliberation and Decision on Peace and War Under Lyndon B. Johnson* (Englewood Cliffs, NJ: Prentice-Hall, 1970).

53   *"But when LBJ"*: Doris Kearns, *Lyndon Johnson and the American Dream* (New York: Harper & Row, 1976), p. 322.

54   *"As one academic"*: Hall, *Implementing Multiple Advocacy*, pp. 620–21.

55   *"He was backed"*: Quoted in Bird, *The Color of Truth*, p. 367.

55   *"As recalled by"*: Interview with Richard Holbrooke, June 19, 2008.

3. "YOU DON'T TELL ANYBODY"

Page

57   *"The most important"*: National Security Decision Memorandum (NSDM) 2. The NSDM series, established by NSDM 1, supplanted the series of National Security Action Memoranda (NSAMs) employed to convey presidential policy and operational decisions in the Kennedy and Johnson administrations. NSDM 3 reiterated the overseas coordination role of the Department of State. NSDM 4 mandated "program analyses for designated countries and regions." NSDMs 1–4 are reprinted in U.S. Department of State, *Foreign Relations of the United States, 1969–1976*, Vol. II, *Organization and Management of U.S. Foreign Policy, 1969–1976: The NSC System* (henceforth *FRUS, 1969–1976*, Vol. II), pp. 29–36.

57   *"Nixon presented the"*: "The Security Gap," Address by Richard M. Nixon

over the CBS Radio Network, October 24, 1968, released by Republican National Committee, October 25, 1968, mimeo.

58 *"He retained and"*: Henry Kissinger, *White House Years* (Boston: Little Brown, 1979), p. 29.

58 *"Heinz Alfred Kissinger"*: Walter Isaacson, *Kissinger: A Biography* (New York: Simon & Schuster, 1992), p. 98.

59 *"And while he asserts"*: Kissinger, *White House Years*, p. 8.

59 *"Even Nixon labeled"*: Richard M. Nixon, *RN: The Memoirs of Richard Nixon* (New York: Grosset & Dunlap, 1978), p. 340.

59 *"When 'the grocer's'"*: Nixon's words, ibid., p. 341.

60 *"Nixon asked Kissinger"*: This summary draws particularly on Halperin's unpublished paper, "The 1969 NSC System," circa 1974, which he wrote for the Commission on the Organization of the Government for the Conduct of Foreign Policy (the Murphy Commission). Goodpaster describes his role in "The Nixon Administration National Security Council," Oral History Roundtable, National Security Council Project, Center for International and Security Studies of Maryland (CISSM) and the Brookings Institution, December 8, 1988. The December 27 "Memorandum on a New NSC System" and other key documents appear in *FRUS, 1969–1976*, Vol. II, pp. 1–36.

60 *"Nixon was determined"*: Nixon, *RN*, p. 340.

60 *"Finally, Nixon reiterated"*: Memorandum from Nixon to Kissinger, *FRUS, 1969–1976*, Vol. II, pp. 25–26; Kissinger, *White House Years*, p. 46.

61 *"In his acerbic"*: Robert Dallek, *Nixon and Kissinger: Partners in Power* (New York: HarperCollins, 2007), p. 81.

61 *"To quote Dallek"*: Ibid., pp. 92–93.

61 *"During a brief"*: Kissinger, *White House Years*, p. 9.

61 *"From early on"*: Quoted in Roger Morris, *Uncertain Greatness: Henry Kissinger and American Foreign Policy* (New York: Harper & Row, 1977), p. 3; and in Isaacson, *Kissinger*, p. 145.

61 *"Nixon would bait"*: Isaacson, *Kissinger*, p. 148.

61 *"'For Kissinger,' recalled"*: Quoted in ibid., p. 561.

62 *"Indeed, in the"*: Comments in Ivo H. Daalder and I. M. Destler, *Nixon Administration National Security Council*, Oral History Roundtable, December 8, 1998, p. 11; www.brookings.edu/nsc/oralhistories/nixonnsc.

63 *"But, as Davidson"*: Davidson ibid., p. 11.

63 *"The National Security"*: Data on NSC meetings compiled by the authors are available at www.brookings.edu/nsc.

64 *"Nixon and Kissinger"*: Seymour Hersh, *The Price of Power: Kissinger in the Nixon White House* (New York: Summit Books, 1983), p. 40; Nixon, *RN*, p. 369; Kissinger, *White House Years*, p. 28.

64 *"'Then,' in Dobrynin's"*: Anatoly Dobrynin, *In Confidence: Moscow's Ambassa-*

dor to America's Six Cold War Presidents (New York: Times Books, 1995), p. 198. See also *FRUS, 1969–76*, Vol II, pp. 67–69.

65   *"At the senior level"*: Hersh, *The Price of Power*, p. 69.

65   *"So, Kissinger recalled"*: Quotes are from Kissinger, *White House Years*, pp. 320–21.

65   *"Somewhat implausibly, Nixon"*: Nixon, *RN*, p. 384.

65   *"Nixon was 'enraged'"*: Ibid., p. 388.

66   *"Before morning was out"*: Three memoranda by Hoover to his deputies, all dated May 9, 1969, reporting telephone conversations with Kissinger, and a memorandum by Assistant FBI director William Sullivan, dated May 11, reporting Haig's visit to him the previous day—*FRUS, 1969–1976*, Vol. II, pp. 94–100; Isaacson, *Kissinger*, p. 216; Hersh, *The Price of Power*, chap. 7.

66   *"Nixon concluded in"*: Nixon conversation with John Dean, February 28, 1973, quoted in Isaacson, *Kissinger*, p. 225. See also Nixon, *RN*, pp. 388–89.

66   *"The national security adviser"*: Hersh, *The Price of Power*, p. 86.

66   *"He also 'began'"*: Ibid.

66   *"Sonnenfeldt complained of"*: Sonnenfeldt to Kissinger, April 30, 1969, *FRUS, 1969–1976*, Vol. II, pp. 89, 90.

66   *"Nixon reinforced the"*: Memorandum, Haldeman to Kissinger, May 15, 1969, in ibid., p. 102.

67   *"'The NSC system'"*: Quoted in memorandum from Haig to Kissinger, June 25, 1969, ibid., p. 113.

67   *"'I am not volunteering'"*: Haig to Kissinger, February 7, 1969, ibid., p. 51.

67   *"Meanwhile, Kissinger—all"*: Assistant FBI director Sullivan to Hoover, May 20, 1969, ibid., p. 103.

67   *"Each time he"*: National Security Archive, interview with Winston Lord, available at www.gwu.edu/~nsarchiv/coldwar/interviews/episode-15/lord1.html.

67   *"Staff secretary William"*: Watts to Kissinger, December 1, 1969, in *FRUS 1969–1976*, Vol. II, pp. 192–93.

68   *"And two aides"*: Draft letter of resignation (not sent) by Anthony Lake and Roger Morris, late April 1970, in ibid., p. 233.

68   *"By April 1971"*: Data on staffing patterns and organizational changes compiled by the authors, available at www.brookings.edu/nsc.

68   *"'No more NSC meetings'"*: H. R. Haldeman, *The Haldeman Diaries: Inside the Nixon White House* (New York: G. P. Putnam's Sons, 1994), June 4, 1969, p. 63.

68   *"Haldeman's 'informal, handwritten'"*: *FRUS, 1969–1976*, Vol. II, p. 107.

68   *"Haldeman interpreted such outbursts"*: *Haldeman Diaries*, author's note, p. 63.

70   *"someone would penetrate"*: Hersh quotes Halperin's description of this phenomenon in *The Price of Power*, p. 104.

70 *"Hence, the frequency"*: Data on NSC meetings compiled by the authors, available at www.brookings.edu/nsc.

70 *"Nixon was forced"*: Kissinger, *White House Years*, p. 499.

71 *"Noting this decline"*: Donald Stukel to Richard T. Kennedy, December 26, 1972, in *FRUS, 1969–1976*, Vol. II, p. 358.

71 *"First to take form"*: Kissinger to Rogers, Laird, and Helms, May 16, 1969, ibid., pp. 102–03.

71 *"It was followed"*: Kissinger to Attorney General John Mitchell, Under Secretary of State Elliot Richardson, Deputy Secretary of Defense David Packard, Arms Control and Disarmament Agency director Gerard Smith, JCS chairman Earle Wheeler, and director of Central Intelligence Richard Helms, July 21, 1969, ibid., pp. 141–42. See also Lawrence Lynn to Kissinger, July 14, 1969, *ibid.*, pp. 139–41.

71 *"In September, the"*: NSDM 23, September 16, 1969, ibid., pp. 156–57.

71 *"In October was"*: NSDM 26, October 11, 1969, ibid., pp. 166–67.

72 *"They were of varying effectiveness"*: FRUS, 1969–1976, Vol. II, contains a plethora of memos highlighting Laird's resistance to the broad concept of the DPRC and NSC staff frustration at DoD's failure to cooperate. See, for example, Documents 84, 88–91, 100–02, and 171–72. See also the comments by Philip Odeen and other in "The Nixon Administration National Security Council," Oral History Roundtable, pp. 20–21.

72 *"But all five"*: Chester A. Crocker, "The Nixon-Kissinger National Security Council System, 1969–1972: A Study in Foreign Policy Management," in *Commission on the Organization of the Government for the Conduct of Foreign Policy* (June 1975), Appendix O, pp. 92–94.

72 *"Kissinger states that"*: See I.M. Destler, Haruhiro Fukui, and Hideo Sato, *The Textile Wrangle: Conflict in Japanese-American Relations 1969–1971* (Ithaca, NY: Cornell University Press, 1979), esp. chaps. 5 and 6; Kissinger, *White House Years*, pp. 330–40; Kei Wakaizumi, *The Best Course Available: A Personal Account of the Secret U.S.-Japan Okinawa Reversion Negotiations* (Honolulu: University of Hawaii, 1994); and "Telecoms Between Kissinger and Wakaizumi," comp. Takashi Shinobu from U.S. National Archives documents, Iwate Prefectural University, Working Papers Series, No. 22, August 11, 2004.

73 *"This led, in January"*: FRUS, 1969–1976, Vol. II, "Foreign Economic Policy," Nixon memo of January 18, 1971, pp. 811–12.

74 *"Lodge was not"*: See William Bundy, *A Tangled Web: The Making of Foreign Policy in the Nixon Administration* (New York: Hill & Wang, 1998), p. 61.

74 *"Meanwhile, Kissinger continued"*: Kissinger, *White House Years*, pp. 1043–44, and *passim*.

75 *"But Nixon didn't trust"*: Hersh, *The Price of Power*, p. 42.

75 *"'Kissinger confronted Dobrynin'"*: Isaacson, *Kissinger*, p. 325.

75 *"If the Russian"*: Kissinger, *White House Years*, p. 819.

75 *"Kissinger told Smith"*: *Haldeman Diaries*, pp. 288–29.

75 *"He shared William"*: Bundy, *A Tangled Web*, p. 253.

75 *"But he held"*: Gerard Smith, *Doubletalk* (New York: Doubleday, 1980).

75 *"The secretary of state"*: *Haldeman Diaries*, multimedia edition, entry for May 19, 1971, quoted in *FRUS, 1969–1976*, Vol. II, pp. 311–13.

76 *"Nonetheless, for Kissinger"*: Kissinger, *White House Years*, p. 822.

76 *"'relations between the'"*: Lake to Kissinger, November 14, 1969, in *FRUS, 1969–1976*, Vol. II, pp. 183–86.

77 *"Prior to that"*: Haig to Kissinger, July 12, 1969, ibid., p. 138.

77 *"Rogers's failure 'to'"*: Haig to Kissinger, October 29, 1969, ibid., pp. 177, 182.

77 *"In February 1970"*: Haig to Kissinger with attachment, February 21, 1970, ibid., pp. 213–16.

77 *"There is no"*: *Haldeman Diaries*, p. 131.

77 *"'Problem {with K}'"*: Ibid., October 15, 1969, p. 120.

77 *"'P . . . feels K'"*: Ibid., October 27, 1969, p. 124.

78 *"'P . . . knows what'"*: Ibid., July 16, 1970, multimedia edition.

78 *"'K called at'"*: Ibid., September 25, 26, and 27, 1970, multimedia edition.

78 *"'After K went'"*: Ibid., December 3, 1970, p. 256, and December 4, 1970, multimedia edition.

78 *"'We had a'"*: Ibid., January 20, 1971, pp. 284–85.

79 *"'I had a'"*: Ibid., February 22, 1971, p. 301.

79 *"The root problem"*: Transcript of Oval Office conversation between Nixon and Haldeman, June 12, 1971, in *FRUS, 1969–1976*, Vol. II, p. 321.

79 *"'We were on'"*: Comments in "The Nixon Administration National Security Council," Oral History Roundtable, p. 42.

80 *"Kissinger and his"*: So represented to the State Department—see Kissinger, *White House Years*, p. 728.

80 *"He then read"*: The full text is reprinted in Kissinger, *White House Years*, pp. 759–60.

81 *"The covertness was"*: Isaacson, *Kissinger*, p. 342.

81 *"During his first"*: Mentions in the *New York Times Index:* Bundy: 38 (1961), 15 (1962); Kissinger: 150 (1969), 145 (1970), 292 (1971), and 592 (1972). Data available at www.brookings.edu/nsc.

81 *"Thereafter, he ordered"*: Isaacson, *Kissinger*, p. 351.

82 *"'Power is the'"*: Ibid., p. 365.

82 *"While Kissinger, in"*: Henry Kissinger, *Years of Upheaval* (Boston: Little, Brown, 1982), p. 7.

83 *"Kissinger 'took this'"*: Kissinger, *White House Years*, p. 907.

83 *"Nixon then made"*: Ibid., pp. 910–11.

83 *"Throughout the crisis"*: Report of December 3, 1971, WSAG meeting, quoted in summary document prepared for Kissinger, available at www.gwu.edu/~nsarchiv/NSAEBB/NSAEBB79/BEBB45.pdf.

85 *"'The P was'"*: *Haldeman Diaries*, December 21, 1971, p. 386.

85 *"Three days later"*: Transcript of telephone conversation between Nixon and Haig, December 24, 1971, in *FRUS, 1969–1976*, Vol. II, p. 337.

85 *"'I tell you'"*: Transcript of Oval Office conversation between Nixon and Haldeman, December 22, 1971, in *ibid.*, p. 336.

85 *"Nixon was expressing"*: Kissinger paraphrased in *Haldeman Diaries*, January 10, 1972, p. 394.

85 *"'The policy became'"*: Kissinger, *White House Years*, p. 918.

87 *"Nonetheless, presented with"*: Ibid., p. 1360.

87 *"Kissinger now sought"*: Ibid., p. 1361.

87 *"Nixon was 'enraged'"*: Isaacson, *Kissinger*, pp. 458, 460.

88 *"Kissinger felt that"*: Kissinger, *White House Years*, p. 1409.

88 *"He exacerbated matters"*: "Kissinger: An Interview with Oriana Fallaci," *The New Republic*, December 16, 1972, p. 21.

88 *"So shaky was"*: Kissinger, *White House Years*, p. 1455.

89 *"Kissinger then offered"*: Isaacson, *Kissinger*, pp. 507–08.

89 *"Still, as 1973"*: Kissinger, *Years of Upheaval*, pp. 6–7.

89 *"In March, the"*: Carl Bernstein and Bob Woodward, *All the President's Men* (New York: Simon & Schuster, 1974), p. 275.

89 *"Early in the"*: Kissinger, *Years of Upheaval*, pp. 77–78.

90 *"When Kissinger's role"*: Isaacson, *Kissinger*, p. 499.

90 *"Nixon 'did not'"*: Ibid., p. 502.

90 *"Finally, in an"*: Kissinger, *Years of Upheaval*, pp. 3–4.

92 *"And most of"*: Crocker, "The Nixon-Kissinger System," p. 99.

93 *"It is no"*: Kissinger, *White House Years*, p. 47.

93 *"For he worked"*: Elizabeth Drew, *Richard M. Nixon* (New York: Times Books, 2007), pp. 151, 150.

4. "I WOULD NEVER BE BORED"

Page

94 *"In the words"*: Anatoly Dobrynin, *In Confidence: Moscow's Ambassador to America's Six Cold War Presidents* (New York: Times Books, 1995), p. 386.

95 *"Its report in"*: "Comments by Senator Mike Mansfield," in *Commission on the Organization of the Government for the Conduct of Foreign Policy, Report* (Washington, DC: GPO, 1975).

95 *"But the study"*: Graham Allison and Peter Szanton, *Remaking Foreign Policy: The Organizational Connection* (New York: Basic Books, 1976), pp. 81, 83, and 78.

96 *"'As far as'"*: Debate of October 6, 1976, available at www.debates.org/pages/trans76b.html.

96 *"He was determined"*: Jimmy Carter, *Keeping Faith: Memoirs of a President* (New York: Bantam Books, 1982), p. 52.

96 *"This was perhaps"*: Quoted in Cyrus Vance, *Hard Choices: Critical Years in America's Foreign Policy* (New York: Simon & Schuster, 1983), p. 30.

97 *"By October 1976,"*: Quoted in I. M. Destler, Leslie H. Gelb, and Anthony Lake, *Our Own Worst Enemy: The Unmaking of American Foreign Policy* (New York: Simon & Schuster, 1984), p. 216.

97 *"And 'it was'"*: Zbigniew Brzezinski, *Power and Principle: Memoirs of the National Security Adviser 1977–1981* (New York: Farrar, Straus & Giroux, 1983), p. 4.

97 *"When early returns"*: Conversation with Richard Gardner, August 1986.

97 *"Concern about Zbig"*: Dobrynin, *In Confidence*, p. 368; Patrick Tyler, *A Great Wall: Six Presidents and China* (Washington, DC: Public Affairs for the Century Foundation, 1999), pp. 234–35.

97 *"But, though the"*: Carter, *Keeping Faith*, p. 52.

98 *"But after the"*: Brzezinski, *Power and Principle*, p. 4.

98 *"A late 1950s"*: Story confirmed by Stanley Hoffmann, December 2007.

99 *"But Brzezinski persisted"*: Zbigniew Brzezinski, *The Soviet Bloc: Unity and Conflict* (Cambridge, MA: Harvard University Press, 1960).

99 *"Both men were"*: Elizabeth Drew, "A Reporter at Large: Brzezinski," *The New Yorker*, May 1, 1978, p. 95.

99 *"He was, in"*: Ibid.

100 *"Moreover, as one"*: Gary Sick, *All Fall Down: America's Tragic Encounter with Iran* (New York: Random House, 1985), p. 71.

100 *"And Brzezinski had"*: Carter, *Keeping Faith*, p. 54.

101 *"'Zbig, I prefer'"*: Handwritten response to memo of December 23, 1976, Brzezinski to the President-Elect," declassified by the NSC on January 15, 1981.

102 *"In his journal"*: Brzezinski, *Power and Principle*, p. 60.

102 *"He did declare"*: Ibid., p. 63.

102 *"'The national security'"*: Vance, *Hard Choices*, p. 37.

102 *"When his appointment"*: Leslie Gelb, "Brzezinski Says He'll Give Advice to Carter Only When He Asks for It," *New York Times*, December 17, 1976, p. 33.

102 *"An early Washington"*: Murrey Marder, "Carter and Brzezinski Stress What NSC Chief Will Not Do," *Washington Post*, January 24, 1977, p. A3.

103 *"Moreover, Carter's initial"*: Raymond L. Garthoff, *Détente and Confrontation: American-Soviet Relations from Nixon to Reagan* (Washington, DC: Brookings Institution, 1994), p. 625.

103 *"Brzezinski and his deputy"*: Data on staffing patterns and organizational changes compiled by the authors, available at: www.brookings.edu/nsc.

103 *"Brzezinski, observed Gary"*: Sick, *All Fall Down*, p. 120.

103 *"But if he"*: Drew, "A Reporter at Large: Brzezinski," p. 102.

104 *"However, the specific"*: U.S. Public Law 92–448, approving the Interim Agreement: 92nd Congress, Joint Resolution, approved September 30, 1972.

104 *"He had expressed"*: Jimmy Carter, Inaugural Address, January 20, 1977.

105 *"The president believed"*: Garthoff, *Détente and Confrontation*, pp. 633–34.

105 *"Carter, not wishing"*: Brzezinski, *Power and Principle*, p. 166.

106 *"Now, as Vance"*: Vance, *Hard Choices*, p. 55.

106 *"The United States"*: Garthoff, *Détente and Confrontation*, p. 713.

106 *"This was done"*: Brzezinski, *Power and Principle*, p. 180.

106 *"Vance demurred, seeing"*: Ibid., pp. 182–83; Vance, *Hard Choices*, p. 87.

107 *"As Brzezinski recalled"*: Brzezinski, *Power and Principle*, p. 179.

107 *"The adviser said"*: Vance, *Hard Choices*, pp. 87–88, Brzezinski, *Power and Principle*, p. 185; Bernard Gwertzman, "Top Carter Aides Seen in Discord on How to React to Soviet Actions," *New York Times*, March 31, 1978, p. A3.

107 *"To combat this"*: Vance, *Hard Choices*, p. 102.

108 *"The* Washington Post*"*: Murrey Marder, "Carter Challenges Soviet Leaders: Two Different Speeches," *Washington Post*, June 8, 1978, p. A1.

108 *"'Instead of combating'"*: Vance, *Hard Choices*, p. 102.

108 *"In seeking Carter's"*: Brzezinski, *Power and Principle*, p. 204.

108 *"Vance resisted, believing"*: Vance, *Hard Choices*, p. 114.

108 *"Brzezinski would later"*: Woodrow Wilson Center, "Forum on the Role of National Security Adviser," April 12, 2001, reprinted in Karl F. Inderfurth and Loch K. Johnson, *Fateful Decisions: Inside the National Security Council* (New York and London: Oxford University Press, 2004), p. 151.

108 *"During his touristic"*: Tyler, *A Great Wall*, p. 255.

108 *"This dismayed Vance"*: "Interview by Hedrick Smith of Dr. Brzezinski," January 16, 1981, copy in the Jimmy Carter Library.

108 *"Brzezinski didn't help"*: Tyler, *A Great Wall*, pp. 252–56.

108 *"He engaged in"*: Brzezinski, *Power and Principle*, p. 220.

108 *"The* Washington Post*"*: Murrey Marder, "Brzezinski Delivers Attack on Soviets: Draws Hard Line Against Kremlin 'Marauders,'" *Washington Post*, May 29, 1978, p. A1.

109 *"Carter chastised his"*: Quoted in Brzezinski, *Power and Principle*, pp. 220–21.

109 *"Then, in the"*: Authors' interviews with William Quandt, January 19, 1982, and October 28, 1999.

109 *"Peace hopes rose"*: This discussion draws upon the two interviews with Quandt and an interview with Harold Saunders, October 29, 1999.

110 *"'Of all the'"*: William B. Quandt, *Camp David: Peacemaking and Politics* (Washington, DC: Brookings Institution, 1986), p. 35.

110 *"Vance, Brzezinski wrote"*: Brzezinski, *Power and Principle*, p. 273.

110 *"Brzezinski characterized his"*: Ibid, p. 273.

110 *"Carter 'turned his'"*: William B. Quandt, *Peace Process: American Diplomacy*

and the Arab-Israeli Conflict Since 1967 (Washington, DC: Brookings and University of California, 1993), p. 329.

110 *"But, Quandt added":* Ibid., p. 330.

111 *"Carter minimized the":* Carter, *Keeping Faith*, p. 54.

111 *"The reason Carter":* Ibid., p. 199.

111 *"Brzezinski suggests another":* Brzezinski, *Power and Principle*, p. 230.

111 *"To minimize any":* Vance, *Hard Choices*, pp. 118–19.

112 *"Carter, though, was":* Brzezinski, *Power and Principle*, p. 233; Carter, *Keeping Faith*, pp. 198–200.

112 *"Brzezinski's triumph was":* Vance, *Hard Choices*, pp. 110, 112.

112 *"This was one":* Garthoff, *Détente and Confrontation*, esp. pp. 776–89.

112 *"Vance urged that":* Strobe Talbott, *Endgame: The Inside Story of SALT II* (New York: Harper Colophon, 1980), p. 243; Brzezinski, *Power and Principle*, pp. 329–30.

113 *"'The whole scene'":* Dobrynin, *In Confidence*, p. 414; see also Brzezinski, *Power and Principle*, p. 330, and Vance, *Hard Choices*, pp. 111–12.

113 *"Meanwhile, the Shah":* Sick, *All Fall Down*, pp. 68–71, 122.

113 *"In early November":* Ibid., pp. 109, 130–32; George Ball, *The Past Has Another Pattern* (New York: W. W. Norton & Co., 1982), pp. 458–61.

114 *"In retrospect, Vance":* Vance, *Hard Choices*, p. 347; Brzezinski, *Power and Principle*, p. 371.

114 *"To George Ball":* Ball, *The Past Has Another Pattern*, p. 462.

114 *"Brzezinski denied this":* Vance, *Hard Choices*, p. 328.

114 *"But from Carter's":* Carter, *Keeping Faith*, pp. 449–50. See also Sick, *All Fall Down*, p. 153.

114 *"For the president":* Sick, *All Fall Down*, p. 154.

114 *"And to balance":* Carter, *Keeping Faith*, p. 450.

115 *"So visible had":* John M. Goshko, "Senate Voice Sought on Brzezinski's Successors," *Washington Post*, May 11, 1979, p. A2.

115 *"Brzezinski does not":* Brzezinski, *Power and Principle*, p. 398.

116 *"'It's always more'":* Ivo H. Daalder and I. M. Destler, *The Role of the National Security Adviser*, Oral History Roundtable, National Security Council Project, Center for International and Security Studies at Maryland (CISSM) and the Brookings Institution, October 25, 1999, p. 2, www.brookings.edu/nsc/oralhistories/nationalsecurityadviser.

117 *"'I think that'":* Brzezinski, in Wilson Center Forum, reprinted in Inderfurth and Johnson, *Fateful Decisions*, p. 145.

118 *"Vance in particular":* Vance, *Hard Choices*, p. 37.

118 *"Broader inattention to":* Philip Odeen, "National Security Policy Integration: Report of a Study Prepared for the President Under the Auspices of the President's Reorganization Project," September 1979, reprinted in Senate Foreign Relations Committee, *The National Security Adviser*, p. 109.

118 *"By contrast, as"*: Brzezinski, *Power and Principle*, p. 30.

119 *"Vance did the"*: Brzezinski at Wilson Center Forum, in Inderfurth and Johnson, *Fateful Decisions*, p. 152.

119 *"'As a result,'"*: Odeen Report, p. 111.

119 *"The assistant himself"*: Brzezinski at Wilson Center Forum, in Inderfurth and Johnson, *Fateful Decisions*, p. 143.

120 *"Yet the shake-up"*: Richard Burt, "In the Washington Shake-Up, No Tremors for Brzezinski," *New York Times*, July 20, 1979, p. A2.

121 *"'This action of'"*: Carter statement to ABC-TV, December 31, 1979, quoted in the *New York Times*, January 1, 1980, p. 4.

121 *"And support of"*: Carter, *Keeping Faith*, p. 476.

121 *"Noting that Carter"*: Authors' interview with David Newsom, January 5, 1982.

122 *"As Schecter recalled"*: Jerrold and Leona Schecter, *Sacred Secrets: How Soviet Intelligence Operations Changed American History* (Washington, DC: Brassey's, 2003), p. 282.

122 *"Beginning in early"*: Sick, *All Fall Down*, pp. 207 and 210–11.

122 *"Sick's authoritative inside"*: Ibid., pp. 250–79.

123 *"On Friday, April"*: Vance, *Hard Choices*, p. 409.

123 *"The secretary's 'reaction'"*: Warren Christopher, *Chances of a Lifetime* (New York: Scribner, 2001), p. 100.

123 *"Vance argued that"*: Vance, *Hard Choices*, pp. 410–11; Carter, *Keeping Faith*, p. 513.

124 *"At the same"*: Brzezinski, *Power and Principle*, p. 502.

124 *"Carter, however, stuck"*: Christopher, *Chances of a Lifetime*, p. 107.

124 *"He 'let it'"*: Bernard Gwertzman, "Muskie Said to Want Major Shift in Management of Foreign Policy" *New York Times*, October 6, 1980, p. A1.

125 *"In his informative"*: Brzezinski, *Power and Principle*, pp. 32, 35.

125 *"'Next to members'"*: Carter, *Keeping Faith*, p. 54.

125 *"'Of all the'"*: Sick, *All Fall Down*, p. 290.

126 *"McGeorge Bundy, who"*: McGeorge Bundy, "Mr. Reagan's Security Aide," *New York Times*, November 16, 1980, p. D21.

126 *"Brzezinski himself recognized"*: Brzezinski, *Power and Principle*, p. 536.

126 *"His solution, interestingly"*: Ibid., pp. 536–37.

5. "SERIOUS MISTAKES WERE MADE"

Page

127 *"In one last speech"*: Address of October 19, 1980, reprinted in *New York Times*, October 20, 1980, p. D10.

128 *"From my point"*: Richard Allen in Ivo H. Daalder and I. M. Destler, *The Role of the National Security Adviser*, Oral History Roundtable, October 25,

1999, p. 3; www.brookings.edu/nsc/oralhistories/nationalsecurityadviser.

130 *"Leslie Gelb, a national security":* Leslie Gelb, "The Mind of the President," *New York Times Magazine,* October 6, 1985, p. 21.

130 *"One of Reagan's":* Lou Cannon, *Reagan* (New York: G. P. Putnam's Sons, 1982), p. 373.

130 *"In his eight":* Lou Cannon, *President Reagan: The Role of a Lifetime* (New York: Public Affairs, 2000), p. 117.

130 *"His was 'the'":* Ibid., chap. 22.

130 *"They would run":* Frances Fitzgerald, "A Critic at Large: Memoirs of the Reagan Era," *The New Yorker,* January 16, 1989, p. 87.

131 *"As one aide":* Quoted in George Church, "Business as Usual—Almost," *Time,* April 13, 1981, p. 23.

131 *"But Reagan followed":* I. M. Destler, Leslie H. Gelb, and Anthony Lake, *Our Own Worst Enemy* (New York: Simon & Schuster, 1984), p. 225.

132 *"When the president-elect":* Alexander Haig, *Caveat* (London: Weidenfeld & Nicolson, 1984), p. 12.

132 *"He would be":* "The Document That Sowed the Seed of Haig's Demise," *Washington Post,* July 11, 1982, p. C1.

132 *"In his memoirs":* Haig, *Caveat,* p. 58.

132 *"'The policy formulation'":* Richard Burt, "Reagan Aides Tell of Plans to Strengthen Secretary of State and Curb Security Adviser," *New York Times,* November 19, 1980, p. A28.

133 *"Yet even in":* Daalder and Destler, *The Role of the National Security Adviser,* p. 7.

133 *"The NSC adviser":* Don Oberdorfer, "A Low Profile Man for a Highly Sensitive Post," *Washington Post,* December 24, 1980, p. A4.

133 *"Allen tried to":* Hedrick Smith, "A Scaled-Down Version of Security Adviser's Task," *New York Times,* March 4, 1981, p. A28.

133 *"Allen, Haig later":* Haig, *Caveat,* p. 85.

134 *"Indeed, the White":* Allen in Daalder and Destler, *The Role of the National Security Adviser,* p. 7.

134 *"From the onset":* Cannon, *President Reagan,* p. 162.

134 *"Did he 'want'":* Haig, *Caveat,* p. 11.

134 *"'It was essential'":* David Gergen, *Eyewitness to Power* (New York: Simon & Schuster, 2000), p. 172.

135 *"Early on, for":* Don Oberdorfer and John M. Goshko, "U.S. Gives Warning on Cuba-Salvador Arms Flow," *Washington Post,* February 22, 1981, p. A1.

135 *"He would 'steal'":* Martin Schram, "Reagan Ends Daily Briefing with National Security Aide," *Washington Post,* July 12, 1981, p. A1.

136 *"Meese subjected the":* Hedrick Smith, *The Power Game* (New York: Random House, 1988), p. 309.

136 *"Meese, Baker, and":* Cannon, *President Reagan,* p. 161.

136 *"I left the'"*: Haig, *Caveat*, pp. 76–77.

136 *"Within weeks of"*: *Time*, March 16, 1981; Steven R. Weisman, "Bush Flies Back from Texas Set to Take Charge in Crisis," *New York Times*, March 31, 1981, p. A1; and Hedrick Smith, "Foreign Policy: Costly Feud," *New York Times*, March 26, 1981, p. A1.

137 *"I used to describe'"*: Deborah Hart Strober and Gerald S. Strober, *Reagan* (New York: Houghton Mifflin, 1998), p. 86.

137 *"And Weinberger, who"*: Caspar Weinberger, *Fighting for Peace* (New York: Grand Central Publ., 1990), p. 29.

137 *"'Robert Haldeman and'"*: Haig, *Caveat*, p. 80.

137 *"After Haig's initial"*: See "National Security Council Structure," NSDD 2, January 12, 1982, reprinted in Christopher Simpson, *National Security Directives of the Reagan and Bush Administrations* (San Francisco: Westview Press, 1995), pp. 20–26.

138 *"Unfortunately, no one"*: Martin Schram, "White House Revamps Top Policy Roles," *Washington Post*, March 22, 1981, p. A1; and Don Oberdorfer and Lee Lescaze, "Haig Loses Out in Dispute Over Key Policy Role," *Washington Post*, March 25, 1981, p. A1.

138 *"Baker and Meese"*: Statement by the Press Secretary, White House, Office of the Press Secretary, March 24, 1981 in *Public Papers of the President of the United States: Ronald Reagan, 1981* (Washington D. C.: GPO, 1982) (emphasis added).

138 *"Reagan, who thought"*: Ronald Reagan, *An American Life* (New York: Simon & Schuster, 1990), p. 256; Haig, *Caveat*, pp. 142–50.

139 *"'Even his friends'"*: James A. Baker III, *"Work Hard, Study . . . and Keep Out of Politics"* (New York: G. P. Putnam's Sons, 2006), p. 126.

139 *"Meese once slyly"*: Leslie Gelb, "Foreign Policy System Criticized by U.S. Aides," *New York Times*, October 19, 1981, p. A1.

139 *"'Instead of having'"*: Richard V. Allen in Daalder and Destler, *The Role of the National Security Adviser*, p. 7.

140 *"If Meese couldn't"*: Gelb, "Foreign Policy System Criticized by U.S. Aides."

140 *"The administration was"*: I. M. Destler, "Congress, Defense, and the Foreign Policy Process: The AWACS Sale to Saudi Arabia," in Robert E. Hunter, Wayne L. Berman, and John F. Kennedy, eds., *Making Government Work: From White House to Congress* (San Francisco: Westview Press for the Center for Strategic and International Studies, 1986), pp. 179–94.

141 *"Having learned how"*: Authors' interview with Richard Burt, March 31, 2000.

141 *"At times, he"*: Allen in Daalder and Destler, *The Role of the National Security Adviser*, p. 24.

141 *"Neither did it"*: Quoted in Gelb, "Foreign Policy System Criticized by U.S. Aides," p. A8.

142 *"On December 1"*: Bob Woodward, *Veil: The Secret Wars of the CIA* (New York:

Simon & Schuster, 1987), pp. 171–74; Cannon, *President Reagan*, pp. 308–9; Robert D. McFarlane and Zofia Smardz, *Special Trust* (New York: Padell & Davies, 1994), pp. 174–75.

142 *"He saw the"*: James Baker, *The Politics of Diplomacy* (New York: G. P. Putnam's Sons, 1995), p. 26.

143 *"A White House"*: Statement by the Press Secretary, January 4, 1982, in *Public Papers of the Presidents of the United States: Ronald Reagan, 1982* (Washington, D.C.: GPO, 1983).

143 *"'I'll be reviewing'"*: Cannon, *Reagan*, p. 400.

144 *"The number of"*: Details on staffing patterns, organizational changes, and directives compiled by the authors, available at www.brookings.edu/nsc.

144 *"In a rare"*: Dick Kirschten, "Clark Emerges as a Tough Manager," *National Journal*, July 17, 1982, p. 1244.

145 *"Clark convened an"*: Haig, *Caveat*, pp. 308–10, 312–13; George Shultz, *Turmoil and Triumph* (New York: Charles Scribner's Sons, 1993), pp. 135–36.

145 *"'You never shoot'"*: Quoted in Richard Reeves, *President Reagan: The Triumph of Imagination* (New York: Simon & Schuster, 2005), p. 117n.

145 *"But now he"*: Haig, *Caveat*, pp. 312, 314; Smith, *The Power Game*, pp. 310–11.

146 *"Clark continued to"*: Joseph Kraft, "Clark's Tenuous Takeover," *Washington Post*, August 7, 1983, p. A21; George J. Church, "A Big Stick Approach: U.S. Policy in Central America Becomes Tougher—and Harder to Sell," *Time*, August 8, 1983; and Steven R. Weisman, "The Influence of William Clark," *New York Times Magazine*, August 14, 1983; Destler, Gelb, and Lake, *Our Own Worst Enemy*, pp. 233–35.

146 *"'Clark simply didn't'"*: Shultz, *Turmoil and Triumph*, pp. 167, 305.

147 *"By summer 1983"*: James Reston, "Judge and President," *New York Times*, August 17, 1983, p. A2.

148 *"Shultz, 'increasingly convinced'"*: Shultz, *Turmoil and Triumph*, pp. 317–18.

148 *"He complained bitterly"*: Ibid., pp. 311–318, quote at p. 317. See also Don Oberdorfer, "'Disgrace': Shultz's Roar on Policy-Making Got Results," *Washington Post*, October 23, 1983, p. A1; Cannon, *President Reagan*, pp. 363–64.

148 *"In the end"*: David Abshire, *Saving the Reagan Presidency* (College Station, TX: Texas A&M University Press, 2005), p. 58.

149 *"Reagan would later"*: Reagan, *An American Life*, p. 448.

149 *"'I was not'"*: Jane Leavy, "McFarlane and the Taunting Glare of Truth," *Washington Post*, May 7, 1987, p. C1.

150 *"'When Weinberger learned'"*: Smith, *The Power Game*, p. 581.

150 *"In the words"*: Cannon, *President Reagan*, p. 353.

150 *"At bottom, though"*: See comments by Allen Holmes in Daalder and Destler,

Arms Control Policy and the National Security Council, Oral History Round-table, March 23, 2000, pp. 39–43; www.brookings.edu/nsc/oralhistories/nscandarmscontrol.

151 *"The two senior":* Caspar Weinberger, "The Uses of Military Power," Address at the National Press Club, November 28, 1984, reprinted in Weinberger, *Fighting for Peace* (New York: Warner Books, 1990), pp. 441–42.

151 *"Sitting in Foggy":* George Shultz, "Power and Diplomacy in the 1980s," Address to the Trilateral Commission, April 3, 1984, reprinted in *Department of State Bulletin*, vol. 84, no. 2086 (May 1984), pp. 12–15.

152 *"The Pentagon chief":* McFarlane, *Special Trust,* pp. 270–71.

152 *"'You have two'":* Phil McCombs, "McFarlane and the Web of Rumor," *Washington Post,* April 18, 1986, p. D1.

153 *"'They would say'":* Wil S. Hylton, "Casualty of War," *GQ* (June 2004); http://men.style.com/gq/features/full?id=content_5155&pageNum=4.

153 *"It was a venue":* Interview with Robert C. McFarlane, in Daalder and Destler, *The Role of the National Security Adviser,* November 1, 1999, p. 43.

153 *"If he kept":* Ibid., p. 42.

154 *"All of this":* Smith, *The Power Game,* p. 595.

154 *"Lou Cannon put":* Cannon, *President Reagan,* p. 295; Smith, *The Power Game,* pp. 599ff.

156 *"The idea was":* Lee H. Hamilton and Daniel K. Inouye, co-chairman, *Report of the Congressional Committee Investigating the Iran-Contra Affair,* 100th Cong. 2nd Sess., November 13, 1987, p. 165.

157 *"But apparently accepting":* Bernard Gwertzman, "McFarlane Took Cake and Bible to Tehran," *New York Times,* January 11, 1987; query.nytimes.com/gst/fullpage.html?res=9B0DE1D71539F932A25752C0A961948260.

158 *"'Established procedures for'":* John Tower, et al., *Report of the President's Special Review Board* (Washington, D.C.: GPO, 1987), pp. iv–1.

159 *"Too often, very":* Lou Cannon, "The White House Crisis; Why Reagan Is Finally Winning in Foreign Policy," *Washington Post,* March 27, 1988, p. C1.

160 *"In presenting his":* "Excerpts from the Tower Commission's News Conference," *New York Times,* February 27, 1987, p. A8.

160 *"'The sad, shared'":* Cannon, *President Reagan,* p. 374.

161 *"He ignored both":* Interview with John M. Poindexter, in Daalder and Destler, *The Role of the National Security Adviser,* March 29, 2000, p. 64.

161 *"'Need-to-know'":* Bob Woodward, "Tale of Two White House Aides," *Washington Post,* November 30, 1986, p. A1.

161 *"'I made a'":* Testimony of John M. Poindexter, *Joint Hearings before the House Select Committee to Investigate Covert Arms Transactions with Iran and the Senate Select Committee on Secret Military Assistance to Iran and the Nicaraguan Opposition,* 100 Cong., 1 sess. (Washington, D.C.: GPO, 1987), p. 37.

162 *"After Iran-Contra"*: Frank Carlucci in Daalder and Destler, *The Role of the National Security Adviser*, October 25, 1999, p. 2.

162 *"'The nation is'"*: James Schlesinger, "Reykjavik and Revelations," *Foreign Affairs: America and the World 1986*, vol. 65, no. 3 (1987), pp. 440–41.

164 *"'The NSC process'"*: *Report of the President's Special Review Board*, pp. iv–10.

164 *"'I didn't bother'"*: Quoted in Dick Kirschen, "Competent Manager," *The National Journal*, February 28, 1987, p. 468.

164 *"Carlucci insisted on"*: Carlucci in Daalder and Destler, *The Role of the National Security Adviser*, p. 12.

164 *"By mid-May"*: Shultz, *Turmoil and Triumph*, pp. 902, 877 (emphasis added).

165 *"A key recommendation"*: Ibid., pp. 903–04.

165 *"Shultz, however, resolved"*: Ibid., p. 907.

165 *"But Carlucci finessed"*: Carlucci in Daalder and Destler, *The Role of the National Security Adviser*, p. 12.

165 *"As his deputy"*: Interview with General Colin L. Powell, ibid., November 23, 1999, p. 56.

166 *"And when Weinberger"*: Shultz, *Turmoil and Triumph*, p. 991; Carlucci in Daalder and Destler, *The Role of the National Security Adviser*, p. 18.

166 *"Shultz invited Carlucci"*: Carlucci in Daalder and Destler, *The Role of the National Security Adviser*, p. 18.

166 *"With Carlucci now"*: Shultz, *Turmoil and Triumph*, p. 991.

166 *"'George would come'"*: Interview with General Colin L. Powell, in Daalder and Destler, *The Role of the National Security Adviser*, p. 54.

167 *"It proved a"*: Cannon, *President Reagan*.

6. "BRENT DOESN'T WANT ANYTHING"

Page

168 *"Bush clearly intended"*: George Bush and Brent Scowcroft, *A World Transformed* (New York: Alfred A. Knopf, 1998), p. 18; Bush press conference in *New York Times*, November 24, 1988, p. B12.

169 *"The national security"*: John Tower, et al., *Report of the President's Special Review Board* (Washington, D.C.: GPO, 1987), pp. v–3.

171 *"Kissinger, who had"*: Quoted in Jeffrey Goldberg, "Breaking Ranks," *The New Yorker*, October 31, 2005; www.newyorker.com/archive/2005/10/31/051031fa_fact2?currentPage=all.

172 *"Bush made clear"*: Bush and Scowcroft, *A World Transformed*, p. 17.

173 *"They would pursue"*: Don Oberdorfer, *The Turn: From the Cold War to a New Era* (New York: Touchstone Books, 1992), p. 329.

173 *"It would be"*: Larry Martz, "The Tough Tasks Ahead," *Newsweek*, November 21, 1988, p. 9.

173 *"They were small"*: David Hoffman, "On Panama, Bush Characteristically Cautious," *Washington Post*, October 15, 1989, p. A1.

173 *"'I don't want'"*: Charles-Phillipe David, "Who Was the Real George Bush? Foreign Policy Decision-Making Under the Bush Administration," *Diplomacy and Statecraft,* vol. 7, no. 1 (March 1996), p. 198.

174 *"They had regarded"*: Bob Woodward, *The Commanders* (New York: Simon & Schuster, 1991), p. 51; Oberdorfer, *The Turn*, p. 329.

174 *"Gorbachev, the new"*: Michael R. Beschloss and Strobe Talbott, *At the Highest Levels: The Inside Story of the End of the Cold War* (Boston: Little, Brown, 1994), p. 17.

174 *"Indeed, Scowcroft thought"*: Bush and Scowcroft, *A World Transformed*, p. 13.

175 *"Bush was determined"*: Ibid., p. 18.

175 *"'I would hate'"*: Maureen Dowd and Thomas L. Friedman, "The Fabulous Bush and Baker Boys," *New York Times Magazine*, May 27, 1990, p. 58.

175 *"It was no surprise"*: Michael Kramer, "Playing for the Edge," *Time*, February 13, 1989; Dowd and Friedman, "The Fabulous Bush and Baker Boys," 58; and James A. Baker III, *The Politics of Diplomacy* (New York: Putnam Adult, 1995), p. 17.

176 *"Word had it"*: Bernard Weinraub and Peter Kilborne, "Baker Will Wield Broad Influence, Aides to Bush Say," *New York Times*, November 13, 1988, p. A1.

176 *"'The trick is'"*: Kramer, "Playing for the Edge," *Time*, February 13, 1989, p. 26.

177 *"'There were a'"*: Interview with Richard Burt, March 31, 2000.

177 *"China after Tiananmen"*: David Rothkopf, *Running the World: The Inside Story of the National Security Council and the Architects of American Power* (New York: Public Affairs, 2005), p. 290.

177 *"Another was the"*: J. F. O. Mcallister, "Atrocity and Outrage; Specters of Barbarism in Bosnia Compel the U.S. and Europe to Ponder: Is it Time to Intervene?" *Time*, August 17, 1992, p. 20.

177 *"Brent Scowcroft not only"*: Bush and Scowcroft, *A World Transformed*, p. 22.

178 *"'Dick washes dishes'"*: Baker, *The Politics of Diplomacy*, p. 24.

179 *"At times, Bush"*: Owen Ullmann, "Bush's 'Inner Inner Circle' Is an Exclusive Club of 3," *Orange County Register*, January 16, 1991, p. A10.

179 *"For example, Cheney"*: Beschloss and Talbott, *At the Highest Levels*, p. 126; David, "Who Was the Real George Bush?" p. 204; Woodward, *The Commanders*, pp. 37, 168.

180 *"It is true"*: "Brent Scowcroft's Several Strengths," *New York Times*, November 24, 1988, p. A22.

181 *"'I think it is'"*: David Callahan, "The Honest Broker: Brent Scowcroft in the Bush White House," *Foreign Service Journal* (February 1992), p. 30.

181 *"'If you don't'"*: Brent Scowcroft in Ivo H. Daalder and I. M. Destler, *The*

Role of the National Security Adviser, Oral History Roundtable, National Security Council Project, October 25, 1999, p. 2; www.brookings.edu/nsc/oralhistories/nationalsecurityadvisers.

181 *"The first responsibility"*: Ibid.

182 *"Everybody knew they"*: Interview with Robert Gates, March 31, 2000.

182 *"The secretary of state"*: Brian Brumley, "Bush's National Security Adviser Says Foreign Policy Rests with President," *Associated Press Newswire*, January 22, 1989.

182 *"This was important"*: Scowcroft in Daalder and Destler, *The Role of the National Security Adviser*, p. 9.

183 *"I bent over"*: Ibid.

183 *"With few exceptions"*: Baker, *The Politics of Diplomacy*, p. 26.

183 *"This was a"*: Bush and Scowcroft, *A World Transformed*, p. 36.

183 *"The secretary of"*: Beschloss and Talbott, *At the Highest Level*, p. 146.

184 *"The coup failed"*: George F. Will, "An Unserious Presidency," *Washington Post*, October 12, 1989, p. A23.

184 *"Within the administration"*: Baker, *The Politics of Diplomacy*, p. 186.

184 *"Powell, who had"*: Colin Powell, *My American Journey* (New York: Random House, 1996), p. 418.

184 *"Baker concurred 'it's'"*: Baker, *The Politics of Diplomacy*, p. 186.

185 *"At 11 a.m., the"*: Robert Kimmitt in Ivo H. Daalder and I. M. Destler, *The Bush Administration National Security Council*, Oral History Roundtable, April 29, 1999, p. 33, www.brookings.edu/nsc/oralhistories.bushnsc.

185 *"It had to"*: Interview with Gates, March 31, 2000.

186 *"When I would"*: Ibid.

187 *"There was hostility"*: Philip Zelikow in Daalder and Destler, *The Bush Administration National Security Council*, p. 15.

187 *"When people saw"*: Dennis Ross in ibid.

188 *"The Steering Group"*: Robert M. Gates, *From the Shadows: The Ultimate Insider's Story of Five Presidents and How They Won the Cold War* (New York: Simon & Schuster, 1997), p. 494.

188 *"Indeed, his perspective"*: Bush and Scowcroft, *A World Transformed*, p. 19.

188 *"Since the deputies"*: Interview with Arnold Kanter, November 3, 1999; and Ivo H. Daalder and I. M. Destler, *Arms Control Policy and the National Security Council*, Oral History Roundtable, March 23, 2000, pp. 45–46; www.brookings.edu/nsc/oralhistories/nscandarmscontrol.

189 *"Though it differed"*: Arnold Kanter in Daalder and Destler, *The Bush Administration National Security Council*, p. 17.

190 *"You didn't get"*: Richard Haass in ibid., p. 5.

190 *"If there were"*: Interview with Gates, March 31, 2000.

190 *"Balding, gray-haired"*: John Judis, "Statecraft and Scowcroft," *The New Republic*, February 24, 1992, p. 18.

191 *"More, he was"*: Christian Alfonsi, *Circle in the Sand: Why We Went Back to Iraq* (New York: Doubleday, 2006), p. 88; Gates, *From the Shadows*, p. 458.

191 *"His self-effacement"*: David Lauter, "The Man Behind the President," *Los Angeles Times*, October 14, 1990, p. A1.

191 *"At times, one"*: Phil Zelikow in Daalder and Destler, *The Bush Administration National Security Council*, p. 5.

193 *"'There are those'"*: David Gergen, "Bush's Very Own Ford Foundation," *Washington Post*, April 2, 1989, p. C2.

193 *"'We've got to'"*: Beschloss and Talbott, *At the Highest Levels*, p. 51.

193 *"Scowcroft responded by"*: Ibid.

195 *"'Our policy has'"*: Ibid., p. 346.

195 *"'It's tempting to'"*: Ibid., p. 109.

195 *"And he traveled"*: William Safire, "Bush at the U.N.," *New York Times*, September 16, 1991, p. A19.

196 *"But Scowcroft, Bob"*: Andrew Rosenthal, "Bush's Modulator of the Gulf Policy," *New York Times*, October 1, 1990, p. A9.

196 *"In a photo-op"*: George H. W. Bush, "Remarks and an Exchange with Reporters on the Iraqi Invasion of Kuwait," Washington, D.C., August 2, 1990, available at bushlibrary.tamu.edu/research/public_papers.php?id= 2123&year=1990&month=8.

196 *"Bush's 'choice of'"*: Bush and Scowcroft, *A World Transformed*, p. 315; Woodward, *The Commanders*, p. 225.

197 *"'I was frankly'"*: Bush and Scowcroft, *A World Transformed*, p. 317.

197 *"'I am aware'"*: Ibid., p. 322.

197 *"Opening the NSC"*: "Meeting of the National Security Council," Washington, DC, August 3, 1990, available at www.margaretthatcher.org/docume nt/8FB156AB24994C20B249A3B7855A975D.pdf.

198 *"'This will not'"*: George H. W. Bush, "Remarks and an Exchange with Reporters on the Iraqi Invasion of Kuwait," Washington, D. C., August 5, 1990, available at bushlibrary.tamu.edu/research/public_papers.php?id= 2138&year=1990&month=8.

198 *"'I never had'"*: "Frontline: Oral History: Brent Scowcroft," available at www.pbs.org/wgbh/pages/frontline/gulf/oral/scowcroft/3.html.

198 *"He wanted to"*: Bush and Scowcroft, *A World Transformed*, p. 353.

198 *"Once a sufficient"*: Woodward, *The Commanders*, pp. 318–20.

199 *"'Saddam is irrational'"*: "Meeting of the National Security Council," Washington, DC, August 5, 1990, available at www.margaretthatcher.org/docu ment/1C30431F2B47466E8B54C611C31B518C.pdf.

199 *"He had been"*: George H. W. Bush, "Remarks at a Republican Fundraising Breakfast in Burlington, Vermont," Washington, DC, October 23, 1990, available at bushlibrary.tamu.edu/research/public_papers.php?id= 2351&year=1990&month=10.

199 *"Scowcroft was deeply"*: Bush and Scowcroft, *A World Transformed*, p. 389.

200 *"'Mr. President, I know'"*: Alfonsi, *Circle in the Sand*, p. 162.

200 *"To that end"*: National Security Directive 54, The White House, January 15, 1991, available at www.fas.org/irp/offdocs/nsd/nsd_54.htm.

201 *"According to Chas"*: Alfonsi, *Circle in the Sand*, p. 188.

201 *"'It was our'"*: Jeffrey Goldberg, "Breaking Ranks," *The New Yorker*, October 31, 2005; www.newyorker.com/archive/2005/10/31/051031fa_fact2.

202 *"'There is another'"*: George H. W. Bush, "Remarks to the American Association for the Advancement of Science," Washington, DC, February 15, 1991, available at bushlibrary.tamu.edu/research/public_papers.php?id=2709&year=1991&month=2.

202 *"Though Bush had"*: George H. W. Bush, "Exchange with Reporters on Aid to Iraqi Refugees," Washington, DC, April 11, 1991, available at bushlibrary.tamu.edu/research/public_papers.php?id=2863&year=1991&month=4.

202 *"'The U.S./international community'"*: Alfonsi, *Circle in the Sand*, p. 235.

203 *"'Bush wants twins'"*: Quoted in Dowd and Friedman, "The Fabulous Bush and Baker Boys," p. 36.

203 *"'By the midpoint'"*: Robert L. Hutchings, *American Diplomacy and the End of the Cold War: An Insider's Account of U.S. Diplomacy in Europe, 1989–1992* (Baltimore: Johns Hopkins University Press, 1998), p. 156.

204 *"When Scowcroft briefed"*: David Halberstam, *War in a Time of Peace: Bush, Clinton, and the Generals* (New York: Scribner, 2001), p. 44.

7. "YOU HAVE TO DRIVE THE PROCESS"

Page

205 *"Clinton promised to"*: Thomas Friedman, "Aides Say Clinton Will Swiftly Void GOP Initiatives," *New York Times*, November 6, 1992, p. A1.

206 *"'That's why he'"*: Thomas Friedman, "Clinton Keeping Foreign Policy on a Back Burner," *New York Times*, February 8, 1993, A9.

206 *"Instead, Clinton delegated"*: Interview with Anthony Lake, September 27, 2000.

207 *"'There was a'"*: James Steinberg in Ivo H. Daalder and I. M. Destler, *The Clinton Administration National Security Council*, Oral History Roundtable, September 27, 2000, p. 11; www.brookings.edu/nsc/oralhistories/clintonnsc.

208 *"In the end"*: Bill Clinton, *My Life* (New York: Alfred A. Knopf, 2004), pp. 455–56.

208 *"Initially, he thought"*: Interview with Lake, September 27, 2000.

208 *"'I remember thinking'"*: Jason DeParle, "The Man Inside Bill Clinton's Foreign Policy," *New York Times Magazine*, August 20, 1995, p. 35.

209 *"'No foreign service'"*: David Halberstam, *War in a Time of Peace: Bush, Clinton, and the Generals* (New York: Scribner, 2001), p. 182.

209 *"A decade later":* Interview with Lake, September 27, 2000.

210 *"When Clinton asked":* Elizabeth Drew, *On the Edge: The Clinton Presidency* (New York: Touchstone Books, 1995), p. 27.

210 *"'People ask me'":* Warren Christopher, *Chances of a Lifetime: A Memoir* (New York: Scribner, 2001), p. 176 (emphasis in the original).

210 *"'Dean Rusk without'":* Halberstam, *War in a Time of Peace*, p. 175; and Michael Elliott, "Damned Yankees," *Newsweek*, October 25, 1993, p. 21.

211 *"Instead of the":* Paul Y. Hammond, "Central Organization in the Transition from Bush to Clinton," in Charles A. Hermann, ed., *American Defense Annual* (New York: Lexington Books, 1994), pp. 169–72.

211 *"'Smart's not everything'":* Colin Powell, *My American Journey* (New York: Ballantine Books, 1996), p. 563.

211 *"'He lost the'":* David Rothkopf, *Running the World: The Inside Story of the National Security Council and the Architects of American Power* (New York: Public Affairs, 2005), p. 324.

212 *"David Gergen, who":* Halberstam, *War in a Time of Peace*, p. 242.

213 *"'My premise,' Clinton":* Ann Devroy and R. Jeffrey Smith, "Clinton Reexamines a Foreign Policy Under Siege," *Washington Post*, October 17, 1993, p A1.

213 *"At one point":* Doyle McManus and Art Pine, "Aspin's Foreign Policy Role Is Eclipsed by Christopher," *Los Angeles Times*, March 21, 1993, p. A1.

213 *"'This administration wanted'":* Vincent Auger, "The National Security Council System After the Cold War," in Randall B. Ripley and James M. Lindsay, eds., *U.S. Foreign Policy After the Cold War* (Pittsburgh: University of Pittsburgh Press, 1997), p. 43.

214 *"He also sought":* Anthony Lake, *6 Nightmares: The Real Threats to American Security* (Boston: Back Bay Books, 2001), p. 261.

214 *"It institutionalized the":* Rothkopf, *Running the World*, p. 313.

214 *"Neither Christopher nor":* Interview with Lake, September 27, 2000.

214 *"'Tony understood the'":* Rothkopf, *Running the World*, pp. 313–14.

214 *"In Our Own":* I. M. Destler, Leslie H. Gelb, and Anthony Lake, *Our Own Worst Enemy: The Unmaking of American Foreign Policy* (New York: Simon & Schuster, 1984), p. 279.

214 *"One of his":* Anthony Lake in Ivo H. Daalder and I. M. Destler, *The Role of the National Security Adviser*, Oral History Roundtable, October 25, 1999, p. 11; www.brookings.edu/nsc/oralhistories/nationalsecurityadvisers.

215 *"He had a":* Elizabeth Cohen, "On Campus with Eric Liu: Last Job? Speeches for Clinton," *New York Times*, September 15, 1994; query.nytimes.com/gst/fullpage.html?res=9C05E6DA123BF936A2575AC0A962958260.

215 *"Some referred to":* R. W. Apple, Jr., "A Domestic Sort with Global Worries," *New York Times*, August 25, 1999, p. A1; Ann Devroy and Daniel Wil-

liams, "New Face of Foreign Policy," *Washington Post*, December 3, 1993, p. A1.

215 *"Although the president"*: Interview with Lake, September 27, 2000.

215 *"In the early"*: Quoted in authors' interview with Robert Oakley, March 27, 2000. Renaissance Weekends were annual talk shops discussing all manner of policy and other issues, which the Clintons attended before they moved to the White House, and continued to do for some years thereafter.

215 *"'A very big'"*: Interview with Samuel R. Berger, April 13, 2001.

216 *"'What Clinton needed,'"*: John F. Harris, *The Survivor: Bill Clinton in the White House* (New York: Random House, 2005), p. 47.

216 *"Lake believed that"*: Interview with Lake, September 27, 2000.

217 *"It would take"*: Ruth Marcus, "Anthony Lake's Secretive Mission," *Washington Post*, December 20, 1993, p. A1.

217 *"Moreover, by his"*: Interview with Lake, September 27, 2000.

217 *"Elizabeth Drew notes"*: Drew, *On the Edge*, p. 140.

217 *"As for Lake"*: Quoted in ibid., p. 141.

217 *"A few weeks"*: George Stephanopoulos, *All Too Human: A Political Education* (New York: Little, Brown, 2000), p. 139; Interview with Lake, September 27, 2000.

218 *"He warned that"*: Jason DeParle, "The Man Inside Bill Clinton's Foreign Policy," *New York Times Magazine*, August 20, 1995, p. 35.

218 *"When Albright challenged"*: Powell, *My American Journey*, pp. 576–77.

219 *"Combat 'could be'"*: Nancy Soderberg, *The Superpower Myth: The Use and Misuse of American Might* (New York: John Wiley, 2005), pp. 36–37.

221 *"'You guys go'"*: Jeremy Rosner, *The New Tug-of-War: Congress, the Executive Branch, and National Security* (Pittsburgh: Carnegie Endowment for International Peace, 1995), p. 51; Strobe Talbott, *The Russia Hand: A Memoir of Presidential Diplomacy* (New York: Random House, 2003), pp. 54ff.

222 *"Complicating matters even"*: Soderberg, *The Superpower Myth*, p. 23; Stephanopoulos, *All Too Human*, p. 185.

222 *"At the last"*: Karen DeYoung, *Soldier: The Life of Colin Powell* (New York: Alfred A. Knopf, 2006), p. 239.

222 *"Powell appreciated the"*: Ibid., pp. 233–34.

222 *"'I always felt'"*: Powell, *My American Journey*, p. 577.

223 *"And Clinton delivered"*: President Clinton, Remarks by the President and Prime Minister Miyazawa in Joint Press Availability, April 16, 1993, available at www.clintonfoundation.org/legacy/041693-joint-press-conference-with-president-and-pm-miyazawa.htm.

224 *"Not a single"*: Soderberg, *The Superpower Myth*, p. 38.

224 *"'A total fuckup'"*: Quoted in Joe Klein, *The Natural: The Misunderstood Presidency of Bill Clinton* (New York: Broadway Books, 2003), p. 73.

225 *"Rather than insisting"*: Barton Gellman and R. Jeffrey Smith, "Hesitant by

Design: Aspin's Style at Pentagon Leaves Important Decisions in Hands of Others," *Washington Post*, November 14, 1993; Drew, *On the Edge*, p. 333.

226 *"Even before the"*: Stephanopoulos, *All Too Human*, p. 129.

226 *"Now, nearly two"*: Halberstam, *War in a Time of Peace*, p. 299.

226 *"Powell told Jordan"*: Powell, *My American Journey*, p. 603.

227 *"'After Black Hawk'"*: Clinton, *My Life*, p. 554.

227 *"He told Stephanopoulos"*: Stephanopoulos, *All Too Human*, p. 140.

228 *"'I had admired'"*: Lake, *6 Nightmares*, p. 262.

228 *"Clinton was, as"*: Drew, *On the Edge*, p. 357.

229 *"The Clinton team"*: Thomas Friedman, "Clinton's Foreign Policy: Top Adviser Speaks Up," *New York Times,* October 31, 1993, p. 8.

229 *"'I remember Colin'"*: Lake in Daalder and Destler, *The Role of the National Security Adviser*, p. 5; Colin Powell in ibid., p. 58.

229 *"'There are very'"*: DeParle, "The Man Inside Bill Clinton's Foreign Policy," p. 34.

229 *"He would remain"*: Lake, *6 Nightmares*, p. 132.

230 *"There was one"*: Ann Devroy and Daniel Williams, "New Face of Foreign Policy," *Washington Post,* December 3, 1993, p. A1.

230 *"The model was"*: Clinton, *My Life,* p. 504.

231 *"'It didn't arise'"*: "Frontline: Interview Anthony Lake," available at www. pbs.org/wgbh/pages/frontline/shows/ghosts/interviews/lake.html.

231 *"But, Lake adds"*: Interview with Lake, September 27, 2000.

231 *"'Western Europe is'"*: Thomas Friedman, "Bright Sun of Trade Rising in the East," *New York Times*, November 19, 1993, p. A6.

232 *"Working with a"*: James M. Goldgeier, *Not Whether But When: The U.S. Decision to Enlarge NATO* (Washington: D.C.: Brookings Institution Press, 1999), p. 57. Goldgeier's book is the definitive treatment of decisions to enlarge NATO.

232 *"'Never again,' Sandy"*: Ann Devroy, "Debate Over Risks Split Administration," *Washington Post*, September 25, 1994, p. A1.

232 *"The NSC adviser"*: Lake, *6 Nightmares*, p. 133.

232 *"'I know we'"*: Quoted by Richard Clarke, who was present at the meeting. Interview with Clarke, March 30, 2000.

233 *"In what John"*: Harris, *The Survivor*, p. 199. For details on Lake's Bosnia policy, see Ivo H. Daalder, *Getting to Dayton: The Making of America's Bosnia Policy* (Washington, D.C.: Brookings Institution Press, 2000).

234 *"The economic agencies"*: Robert L. Suettinger, *Beyond Tiananmen: The Politics of U.S.-China Relations* (Washington, D.C.: Brookings Institution Press, 2003), p. 192.

234 *"'It was in'"*: Barton Gellman, "Reappraisal Led to New China Policy," *Washington Post*, June 22, 1998, p. A1.

234 *"He had become"*: Lake, *6 Nightmares*, p. 144.

236 *"He understood my'"*: Clinton, *My Life*, p. 738.

237 *"Of Haiti's junta"*: Thomas W. Lippman, *Madeleine Albright and the New American Diplomacy* (San Francisco: Westview Press, 2004), pp. 14–15.

237 *"'Clinton,' one biographer"*: Harris, *The Survivor*, p. 369.

237 *"At one point"*: Halberstam, *War in a Time of Peace*, p. 440.

237 *"'I voted against'"*: Ibid., p. 441.

238 *"He was, Albright"*: Elaine Sciolino, "Berger Manages a Welter of Crisis in the Post-Cold-War White House," *New York Times*, May 18, 1998, p. A9.

238 *"And his policy"*: R. W. Apple, Jr., "A Domestic Sort with Global Worries," *New York Times*, August 25, 1999, p. A1; Harris, *The Survivor*, p. 371.

238 *"'He was the'"*: Jacob Heilbrun, "Mr. Nice Guy," *The New Republic*, April 13, 1998, p. 19.

238 *"'Very few important'"*: Interview with Berger, April 13, 2001.

238 *"'Talk to the'"*: Ibid.

239 *"At the ABC"*: Tyler Marshall, "Mutual Loyalty Helps Clinton's 'ABC' Team Tackle ABC's of Foreign Policy," *Los Angeles Times*, March 1, 1998, p. A8.

239 *"'People get a'"*: Interview with Berger, April 13, 2001.

239 *"'Problems arose when'"*: Madeleine Albright, *Madame Secretary: A Memoir* (New York: Miramax Books, 2005), p. 348.

239 *"For his part"*: Harris, *The Survivor*, pp. 369–70.

239 *"To help smooth"*: Sciolino, "Berger Manages a Welter of Crisis in the Post-Cold-War White House," p. A9.

240 *"At the outset"*: Samuel Berger, "A Foreign Policy Agenda for the Second Term," Remarks at the Center for Strategic and International Studies, Washington, DC, March 27, 1997; available at www.clintonpresidential-center.org/legacy/032797-remarks-by-berger-speech-on-foreign-policy-at-csis.htm.

241 *"'The secretary of'"*: Interview with Berger, April 13, 2001.

241 *"He would also"*: Ibid.

241 *"'Part of my'"*: Frank Ahrens, "The Reluctant Warrior," *Washington Post*, February 24, 1998, p. C1.

241 *"As a result"*: Data on television appearances compiled by the authors, available at www.brookings.edu/nsc.

242 *"'Since so many'"*: James Steinberg in Daalder and Destler, *The Clinton Administration National Security Council*, p. 29.

243 *"'We would not'"*: Interview with Sandy Berger, February 9, 2000, cited in Ivo H. Daalder and Michael O'Hanlon, *Winning Ugly: Nato's War to Save Kosovo* (Washington, DC: Brookings Institution Press, 2001), p. 97.

243 *"Indeed, it was"*: See Daalder and O'Hanlon, *Winning Ugly*, pp. 96–100, 184–92, and 203–04.

244 *"From the start"*: Interview with Lake, September 27, 2000.

244 *"'It was always'"*: Interview with Berger, April 13, 2001.

245   *"However, 'many in'"*: James B. Steinberg, "Foreign Policy: Time to Regroup," *Washington Post*, January 2, 2001, p. A15.

245   *"As Lake told"*: Poneman, quoting Lake, in Daalder and Destler, *The Clinton Administration National Security Council*, p. 3.

245   *"Since traditional national"*: Data on staffing patterns and organizational changes compiled by the authors, available at www.brookings.edu/nsc.

246   *"'Get me the'"*: Richard A. Clarke, *Against all Enemies: Inside America's War on Terror* (New York: Free Press, 2004), p. 93.

246   *"For nearly fifty"*: *National Security Act of 1947*, Title I, sec. 101 (a); Interview with Clarke, March 30, 2000.

247   *"'My job,' Clarke"*: Interview with Clarke, March 30, 2000.

248   *"'We now have'"*: Ibid.

249   *"'I think you'"*: Quoted in *9/11 Commission Report: Final Report of the National Commission on Terrorist Attacks Upon the United States* (New York: W. W. Norton & Co., 2004), p. 199.

249   *"'I'm here because'"*: Daniel Benjamin and Steven Simon, *The Age of Sacred Terror* (New York: Random House, 2002), p. 328.

249   *"'Terrorism,' he said"*: Interview with Berger, April 13, 2001.

8. "I'M A GUT PLAYER"

Page

250   *"George W. Bush"*: Bob Woodward, *State of Denial: Bush at War, Part III* (New York: Simon & Schuster, 2006), p. 3.

250   *"After winning reelection"*: James Mann, *Rise of the Vulcans: The History of Bush's War Cabinet* (New York: Penguin Press, 2004), 253.

251   *"'I may not'"*: Maureen Dowd, "Freudian Face-Off," *New York Times*, June 16, 1999; http://query.nytimes.com/gst/fullpage.html?res=9405E1DB1E 38F935A25755C0A96F958260.

251   *"'His basic instincts'"*: Craig Unger, *The Fall of the House of Bush* (New York: Scribner, 2007), p. 161.

252   *"'This is a'"*: Ivo H. Daalder and James M. Lindsay, *America Unbound: The Bush Revolution in Foreign Policy* (New York: John Wiley, 2005), pp. 18–19.

252   *"'If I have'"*: Bob Woodward, *Bush at War* (New York: Simon & Schuster, 2002), p. 74.

252   *"'You know,' Bush"*: Stephen F. Hayes, *Cheney: The Untold Story of America's Most Powerful and Controversial Vice President* (New York: HarperCollins, 2007), p. 281.

252   *"'I have a'"*: Barton Gelman and Jo Becker, "A Different Understanding with the President'," *Washington Post*, June 24, 2007, p. A1.

253   *"Two days into"*: Charles L. Pritchard, *Failed Diplomacy: The Tragic Story of*

How North Korea Got the Bomb (Washington, D.C.: Brookings Institution Press, 2007), p. 50.

253 *"It soon turned":* Dana Priest and Robin Wright, "Cheney Fights for Detainee Policy," *Washington Post*, November 7, 2005, p. A1.

254 *"Bush gushed about":* "Remarks at the Announcement of Powell's Nomination as Secretary of State," *New York Times*, December 17, 2000, p. A51.

254 *"'Powell seemed to'":* Dana Milbank and Mike Allen, "Powell Is Named Secretary of State," *Washington Post*, December 17, 2000, p. A1.

255 *"'At times General'":* Alison Mitchell, "Powell to Head State Dept. as Bush's First Cabinet Pick," *New York Times*, December 17, 2000, p. A1.

255 *"And the columnist":* Thomas Friedman, "The Powell Perplex," *New York Times*, December 19, 2000, p. A35.

255 *"Cheney, always wary":* Johanna McGreary, "Odd Man Out," *Time*, September 10, 2001, p. 28.

255 *"'We're screwed,' he":* Interview with Richard Armitage, January 15, 2008.

255 *"At one point":* Mann, *Rise of the Vulcans*, p. 267.

255 *"Nixon had called":* "President Nixon and Bob Haldeman Discuss Donald Rumsfeld," March 9, 1971; tapes.millercenter.virginia.edu/clips/rmn_rumsfeld.html.

255 *"Kissinger, who had":* Henry Kissinger, *Years of Renewal* (New York: Simon & Schuster, 1999), pp. 175–76.

256 *"'I see this'":* Ibid., p. 842.

256 *"When the younger":* Robert Draper, *Dead Certain: The Presidency of George W. Bush* (New York: Free Press, 2007), p. 282.

256 *"Neither Bush nor":* Eric Schmitt and Elaine Sciolino, "To Run Pentagon, Bush Sought Proven Manager with Muscle," *New York Times*, January 1, 2001, p. A8.

256 *"He had no":* Sebastian Mallaby, "The Character Question," *Washington Post*, August 30, 2004, p. A26.

257 *"'One of the'":* "Transcript of President-elect Bush's News Conference Naming Donald Rumsfeld as His Nominee to Be Secretary of Defense," December 28, 2000; www.washingtonpost.com/wp-srv/onpolitics/elections/bush text122800.htm.

257 *"'I'm a gut'":* Woodward, *Bush at War*, p. 342.

257 *"'My job,' Rice":* Barbara Slavin and Judy Keen, "Bush Trusts Foreign Policy Tutor with World," *USA Today*, June 11, 2001, p. 7.

257 *"'I'm by far'":* David J. Rothkopf, *Running the World: The Inside Story of the National Security Council and the Architects of American Power* (New York: Public Affairs, 2005), p. 406.

257 *"He regarded her":* Bill Keller, "The World According to Powell," *New York Times*, November 25, 2001, p. 65; and Karen DeYoung, *Soldier: The Life of Colin Powell* (New York: Vintage Books, 2007), p. 287.

258 *"He was, Andrew"*: Elisabeth Bumiller, *Condoleezza Rice: An American Life: A Biography* (New York: Random House, 2007), p. 178.

258 *"'I report to'"*: Draper, *Dead Certain*, p. 284.

258 *"He ordered that"*: Anne Plummer, "DOD Staff Ordered to Pre-Report Interaction with Congress, Press," *Inside the Pentagon*, February 8, 2001, p. 13.

258 *"Rice strongly objected"*: Bumiller, *Condoleezza Rice*, p. 137.

258 *"'Condi will run'"*: Ron Suskind, *The Price of Loyalty: George W. Bush, the White House, and the Education of Paul O'Neill* (New York: Simon & Schuster, 2004), p. 70.

258 *"Even so, when"*: "Organization of the National Security Council System," National Security Presidential Directive 1, The White House, February 13, 2001; www.fas.org/irp/offdocs/nspd/nspd-1.htm.

259 *"'I wish you'"*: Mike Allen, "Next Question," *Washington Post*, December 1, 2004, p. C1.

259 *"As for Rice"*: Marcus Mabry, *Twice as Good: Condoleezza Rice and Her Path to Power* (New York: Modern Times, 2007), p. 210.

259 *"The president often"*: Glenn Kessler, *The Confidante: Condoleezza Rice and the Creation of the Bush Legacy* (New York: St. Martin's Press, 2007), p. 5.

259 *"She was the"*: Elaine Sciolino, "Compulsion to Achieve," *New York Times*, December 18, 2000, p. A1.

259 *"Her model, naturally"*: Rothkopf, *Running the World*, 405.

260 *"'I'm the National'"*: Condoleezza Rice, Preview of the President's Trip to Asia and Australia, White House Press Briefing, Washington, D.C., October 14, 2003; www.whitehouse.gov/news/releases/2003/10/print/20031014-4.html.

260 *"Rice and Hadley"*: Joshua Kulantzick, "The Rice Capades," *American Prospect* (May 2004), p. 19.

260 *"'We don't implement,'"*: Woodward, *State of Denial*, p. 318.

260 *"'I'm not saying'"*: Rothkopf, *Running the World*, p. 405.

261 *"'I'm really a'"*: Elaine Sciolino, "Bush's Foreign Policy Tutor: An Academic in the Public Eye," *New York Times*, June 16, 2000, p. A1.

262 *"'The NSC looks'"*: Richard Clarke, *Against All Enemies: Inside America's War on Terror* (New York: Free Press, 2004), p. 229.

262 *"Four days after"*: Richard A. Clarke, "Presidential Policy Initiative/Review—The Al Qida Network," Memorandum to Condoleezza Rice, National Security Council, Washington, D.C., January 25, 2001 (emphases in original). The strategy document can be accessed at www.gwu.edu/~nsarchiv/NSAEBB/NSAEBB147/clarke%20attachment.pdf.

263 *"Indeed, when she"*: The *9/11 Commission Report: Final Report of the National Commission on Terrorist Attacks Upon the United States* (New York: W. W. Norton & Co., 2004), p. 200; Clarke, *Against All Enemies*, p. 230.

263 *"The principals' first"*: Clarke, *Against All Enemies*, p. 26.

263 *"That may explain"*: Draper, *Dead Certain*, pp. 145–46.

263 *"'Al Qida is'"*: Clarke, "Presidential Policy Initiative/Review—The *Al Qida* Network."

263 *"'There are others'"*: Clarke, *Against All Enemies*, p. 231.

263 *"'We weren't going'"*: Richard Armitage in *The 9/11 Commission Report*, p. 205.

264 *"In March 2001"*: George Tenet, *At the Center of the Storm: My Years at the CIA* (New York: HarperCollins, 2007), pp. 143–44, 154.

264 *"The assessment, Tenet"*: Ibid., p. 151.

264 *"The CIA director"*: Ibid., pp. 151–52.

264 *"'This country needs'"*: Ibid., p. 153 (emphasis in the original).

265 *"Bob Woodward was"*: See Woodward, *State of Denial*, pp. 49–52.

265 *"Once Tenet had"*: Bob Woodward, "Reaping the Whirlwind: A Review of George Tenet's *At the Center of the Storm*," *Washington Post Book World*, May 6, 2007, p. 3.

265 *"'I remember directors'"*: Jeffrey Goldberg, "Woodward vs. Tenet," *The New Yorker*, May 21, 2007; www.newyorker.com/reporting/2007/05/21/070521fa_fact_goldberg.

265 *"Rice later suggested"*: Tenet, *At the Center of the Storm*, p. 151.

265 *"The meeting came"*: Bumiller, *Condoleezza Rice*, p. 157.

266 *"Prepared in answer"*: The declassified portions of the paper are reprinted in *The 9/11 Commission Report*, pp. 261–62.

266 *"'All right,' Bush"*: Ron Suskind, *The One Percent Doctrine: Deep Inside America's Pursuit of Its Enemies Since 9/11* (New York: Simon & Schuster, 2007), p. 2.

266 *"After 9/11, Bush"*: *The 9/11 Commission Report*, p. 261.

266 *"'This was not'"*: "Testimony of Condoleezza Rice Before the National Commission on the Terrorist Attacks on the United States," Washington, D.C., April 8, 2004; http://govinfo.library.unt.edu/911/archive/hearing9/9-11Commission_Hearing_2004-04-08.htm.

266 *"Instead, she looked"*: *The 9/11 Commission Report*, p. 263.

266 *"In the end"*: Mabry, *Twice as Good*, p. 222.

267 *"Indeed, Rice had"*: Condoleezza Rice, "National Security Challenges for the New Administration," in *Passing the Baton: Challenges of Statecraft for the New Administration*, Peaceworks No. 40 (Washington, D.C.: U.S. Institute of Peace, May 2001), p. 61.

268 *"And all of"*: *The 9/11 Commission Report*, chap. 8, p. 359.

268 *"And there, Tenet"*: Tenet, *At the Center of the Storm*, p. 139.

268 *"'I didn't feel'"*: Woodward, *Bush at War*, p. 39.

268 *"'My impression at'"*: Hayes, *Cheney*, p. 323.

268 *"Up to that"*: David Frum, *The Right Man* (New York: Random House, 2003), p. 272.

268 *"'I am here'"*: Woodward, *Bush at War*, pp. 205, 281–82.

269 *"Our responsibility to'"*: George W. Bush, "President's Remarks at National Day of Prayer and Remembrance," National Cathedral, Washington, DC, September 14, 2001; www.whitehouse.gov/news/releases/2001/09/20010914-2. html/.

269 *"At a meeting"*: One of us was present at this meeting in Washington, D.C., February 5, 2003.

269 *"In an interview"*: Bumiller, *Condoleezza Rice*, 168.

269 *"If there's a'"*: Suskind, *The One Percent Doctrine*, p. 62.

270 *"We will make'"*: George W. Bush, "Address to the Nation," The White House, September 11, 2001; www.whitehouse.gov/news/releases/2001/09/20010911-16.html.

270 *"The president made"*: Woodward, *Bush at War*, p. 30.

270 *"Days before the"*: Ibid., p. 195.

270 *"Rice had scoffed"*: Michael R. Gordon, "Bush Would Stop U.S. Peacekeeping in Balkan Fights," *New York Times*, October 21, 2000, p. A1.

270 *"I don't think'"*: Donald Rumsfeld, Press Briefing on Afghanistan, The Pentagon, October 9, 2001; www.defenselink.mil/news/Oct2001/t10092001_t1009sd.html.

271 *"It would be'"*: George W. Bush, Prime Time News Conference, October 11, 2001.

271 *"For hundreds of'"*: George W. Bush, Address on the End of Major Combat Operations in Iraq, Remarks from the USS *Abraham Lincoln* at Sea off the Coast of San Diego, California, May 1, 2003; www.whitehouse.gov/news/releases/2003/05/20030501-15.html. The context of Bush's statement here is Iraq, but it proved more valid in the case of Afghanistan.

271 *"Prior to Afghanistan"*: The 9/11 *Commission Report*, p. 336.

271 *"On November 21"*: Bob Woodward, *Plan of Attack* (New York: Simon & Schuster, 2004), p. 4; Bumiller, *Condoleezza Rice*, p. 171.

271 *"Indeed, a few"*: Bill Keller, "The World According to Powell," *New York Times*, November 25, 2001, p. 63.

272 *"As it was"*: Richard Haass was the first to characterize the Iraq War as a "war of choice"—Richard N. Haass, "Wars of Choice," *Washington Post*, November 23, 2003, B7.

272 *"In terms of"*: Bill Sammon, *Misunderestimated: The President Battles Terrorism, Media Bias, and Bush Haters* (New York HarperCollins, 2004), p. 145.

272 *"The president, Powell"*: Rothkopf, *Running the World*, p. 401.

272 *"That perspective became"*: Woodward, *Bush at War*, p. 332.

272 *"You are going'"*: Woodward, *Plan of Attack*, pp. 150–52, 274.

273 *"He would read"*: Bumiller, *Condoleezza Rice*, p. 178.

273 *"He would come"*: Woodward, *State of Denial*, pp. 316–17.

273 *"In early 2004"*: Barton Gellman, *Angler: The Cheney Vice Presidency* (New York: Penguin Press, 2008), 340–42.

273 *"Steve Herbits, one"*: Ibid., pp. 116–170.

274 *"General Richard Myers"*: Quoted in Woodward, *State of Denial*, p. 72.

274 *"Asked by Bush"*: Quoted in Woodward, *Bush at War*, p. 251.

274 *"'There is only'"*: Memorandum from Rumsfeld to Rice, November 1, 2001, reprinted in Roman Scarborough, *Rumsfeld's War: The Untold Story of America's Anti-Terrorism Commander* (New York: Regency Publishing, 2004), p. 193.

274 *"'You're not in'"*: Woodward, *State of Denial*, p. 109.

275 *"He was, as"*: Andrew Cockburn, *Rumsfeld: His Rise, Fall, and Catastrophic Legacy*: (New York: Scribner, 2007), p. 98.

275 *"'Bush rather enjoyed'"*: Draper, *Dead Certain*, p. 283.

275 *"'When I look'"*: Rothkopf, *Running the World*, p. 412.

275 *"His participation in"*: Tenet, *At the Center of the Storm*, p. 138.

275 *"More worrisome was"*: Karen DeYoung, *Soldier: The Life of Colin Powell* (New York: Vintage Books, 2007), pp. 326–29; Bumiller, *Condoleezza Rice*, pp. 148–50.

275 *"On November 13"*: "Executive Order on Detention, Treatment, and Trial of Certain Non-Citizens in the War Against Terrorism," Washington, The White House, November 13, 2001; www.whitehouse.gov/news/releases/2001/11/20011113-27.html. See also Tim Golden, "After Terror, A Secret Rewriting of Military Law," *New York Times*, October 24, 2004, p. A1.

276 *"'That shouldn't have'"*: Bumiller, *Condoleezza Rice*, p. 171.

276 *"She once dressed"*: Barton Gellman and Jo Becker, "Pushing the Envelope on Presidential Power," *Washington Post*, June 25, 2007, p. A1.

276 *"Early on, she"*: Bumiller, *Condoleezza Rice*, p. 150.

276 *"Henry Kissinger once"*: Stephen R. Weisman, "What Rift? Top Aides Deny State Dept.–Pentagon Chasm," *New York Times*, May 31, 2003, p. A1.

277 *"Often, once the"*: Interview with Armitage, January 15, 2008; DeYoung, *Soldier*, p. 518.

277 *"'There was not'"*: Rothkopf, *Running the World*, p. 408.

277 *"Two-plus years"*: DeYoung, *Soldier*, p. 477.

277 *"'We'd get on'"*: Bumiller, *Condoleezza Rice*, p. 217.

277 *"The problem, Armitage"*: Interview with Armitage, January 15, 2008.

277 *"'We are not'"*: Woodward, *Plan of Attack*, p. 415.

277 *"'People generally think'"*: Mabry, *Twice as Good*, p. 212.

278 *"'I don't talk'"*: Elisabeth Bumiller, "A Partner in Shaping an Assertive Foreign Policy," *New York Times*, January 7, 2004, p. A6.

278 *"'I've been tremendously'"*: James Harding, " 'Weakness' in the White House," *Financial Times*, September 15, 2003, p. 13.

278 *"'People don't understand,'"*: Draper, *Dead Certain*, p. 286.

278 *"'One of the'"*: Tenet, *At the Center of the Storm*, p. 301.

278 *"In the sixteen"*: DeYoung, *Soldier*, p. 429.

279 *"By spring 2002":* Bumiller, *Condoleezza Rice,* p. 171.

279 *"'In none of'":* Tenet, *At the Center of the Storm,* p. 308.

279 *"After visiting Washington":* See "The Downing Street Memo," July 23, 2002; www.pbs.org/newshour/bb/middle_east/jan-june05/memo; sf6-16.html.

279 *"'Don't waste your'":* Nicholas Lemann, "How It Came to War," *The New Yorker,* March 31, 2003; www.newyorker.com/archive/2003/03/31/030331fa_fact?currentPage=2.

279 *"Haass was stunned":* Interview with Richard Haass, January 17, 2008.

280 *"The result was":* Daalder and Lindsay, *America Unbound,* pp. 133ff.

280 *"Throughout these many":* Bumiller, *Condoleezza Rice,* p. 184.

280 *"'How could you'":* Jeffrey Goldberg, "Breaking Ranks," *The New Yorker,* October 31, 2005; www.newyorker.com/archive/2005/10/31/051031fa_fact2.

281 *"'Anytime someone wasn't'":* Woodward, *State of Denial,* p. 100.

281 *"The national security":* Data on television appearances compiled by the authors, available at at www.brookings.edu/nsc.

281 *"'The initial response'":* Richard Berke, "White House Aides Trying to Balance Attention on Terrorism, the Economy and Politics," *New York Times,* December 26, 2001, p. A14.

281 *"Cheney had said":* "Vice President Speaks at VFW 103rd National Convention," Remarks by the Vice President to the Veterans of Foreign Wars 103rd National Convention, August 26, 2002; www.whitehouse.gov/news/releases/2002/08/20020826.html; Bumiller, *Condoleezza Rice,* pp. 189–90.

282 *"'As a student'":* Nicholas Lemann, "Without a Doubt," *The New Yorker,* October 14–21, 2002, p. 176.

282 *"'We have experts'":* Dana Milbank and Mike Allen, "Iraq Flap Shakes Rice's Image," *Washington Post,* July 27, 2003, p. A18.

282 *"Some of the":* Tenet, *At the Center of the Storm,* p. 370.

283 *"'Can't you make'":* Bumiller, *Condoleezza Rice,* p. 199.

283 *"Before the war":* Donald Rumsfeld, "Beyond Nation Building," Remarks at the 11th Annual Salute to Freedom, Intrepid Sea-Air-Space Museum, New York, February 14, 2003; www.defenselink.mil/speeches/2003/sp20030214-secdef0024.html.

283 *"'The concept was'":* Michael R. Gordon and Bernard E. Trainor, *Cobra II: The Inside Story of the Invasion and Occupation of Iraq* (New York: Vintage Books, 2007), p. 142.

284 *"In other words":* Michael Gordon and Eric Schmitt, "U.S. Plans to Reduce Forces in Iraq, with Help of Allies," *New York Times,* May 3, 2003, p. A1.

284 *"Someone had to":* Interview with Armitage, January 15, 2008; Woodward, *Plan of Attack,* p. 282.

284 *"'It was not'":* Bumiller, *Condoleezza Rice,* p. 195.

284 *"After repeated ad hoc":* "Managing Complex Contingency Operations," Presidential Decision Directive 56, The White House, May 1997. A declassi-

fied version of the directive is available at clinton4.nara.gov/textonly/WH/
EOP/NSC/html/documents/NSCDoc2.html.

285 *"And so, on"*: Woodward, *State of Denial*, p. 112.

285 *"First, the range"*: Ibid.

285 *"Amazingly, Rumsfeld had"*: Ibid., pp. 109–10; Bumiller, *Condoleezza Rice*, p. 203.

286 *"Once the war"*: Thomas E. Ricks, *Fiasco: The American Military Adventure in Iraq* (New York: Penguin Press, 2006), p. 255.

286 *"He completely ignored"*: James Fallows, "Blind into Baghdad," *The Atlantic* (January–February 2004); www.theatlantic.com/doc/200401/fallows.

286 *"'I think we'"*: Quoted in Ricks, *Fiasco*, p. 105; Gordon and Trainor, *Cobra II*, p. 159.

286 *"And he later"*: Gordon and Trainor, *Cobra II*, pp. 162, 483; Michael R. Gordon, "Fateful Choice on Iraq Army Bypassed Debate," *New York Times*, March 17, 2008, p. A1.

286 *"'Well, the policy'"*: Draper, *Dead Certain*, p. 211.

286 *"'The whole structure'"*: Michael R. Gordon, "Debate Lingering on Decision to Dissolve Iraqi Military," *New York Times*, October 21, 2004, p. A1; Woodward, *State of Denial*, p. 197.

286 *"She did so"*: David Sanger, "White House to Overhaul Iraq and Afghan Missions," *New York Times*, October 6, 2003, p. A1.

287 *"'Condi has taken'"*: L. Paul Bremer, *My Year in Iraq: The Struggle to Build a Future of Hope* (New York: Threshold Editions, 2006), p. 245.

287 *"Rice, in contrast"*: Elisabeth Bumiller, "A Partner in Shaping an Assertive Foreign Policy," *New York Times*, January 7, 2004, p. A6.

288 *"'You can't make'"*: Carl Cannon, "Memory and More in the Mideast," *National Journal*, June 7, 2003, p. 1780.

288 *"'I'm not going'"*: Kessler, *The Confidante*, p. 124.

288 *"Peace could come"*: "President Bush Calls for New Palestinian Leadership," The White House, June 24, 2002; www.whitehouse.gov/news/releases/2002/06/20020624-3.html.

289 *"'The United States'"*: Kessler, *The Confidante*, pp. 125–26.

290 *"This group, which"*: Pritchard, *Failed Diplomacy*, p. 50.

291 *"As a result"*: Kessler, *The Confidante*, p. 70; Michael Mazarr, "The Long Road to Pyongyang," *Foreign Affairs*, 86 (September–October 2007), pp. 75–94.

291 *"'I don't know.'"*: Bumiller, *Condoleezza Rice*, p. 310.

291 *"'If that's the'"*: Helene Cooper, "As Her Star Wanes, Rice Tries to Reshape Legacy," *New York Times*, September 1, 2007, p. A1.

292 *"'Ultimately,' Kissinger observed"*: Henry Kissinger, "Condoleezza Rice: A New Panache in Foreign Affairs," *Time, Special Issue: The Time 100*, April 25, 2005; www.time.com/time/subscriber/2005/time100/leaders/100rice.html.

293 *"Early on in"*: Carla Anne Robbins, "New Security Post Lifts Hadley Profile," *Wall Street Journal*, January 13, 2005, p. A4; Tumbler, "Washington Watch," *Prospect* (July 2005); Kessler, *The Confidante*, p. 36.

293 *"For example, the"*: David Sanger and Thom Shanker, "Rice Is Said to Have Speeded North Korea Deal," *New York Times*, February 15, 2007; www.nytimes.com/2007/02/16/washington/16korea.html; Kessler, *The Confidante*, pp. 238–39.

293 *"'I give us'"*: Woodward, *State of Denial*, p. 384.

293 *"'We need to'"*: David Ignatius, "Bush's Clark Kent," *Washington Post*, February 11, 2005, p. A25.

293 *"The NSC would"*: Carla Anne Robbins, "New Security Post Lifts Hadley Profile," *Wall Street Journal*, January 13, 2005, p. A4.

293 *"A new office"*: Interview with Peter Feaver, January 29, 2008.

293 *"After trying for"*: David Sanger, "4 Years On, the Gap Between Iraq Policy and Practice Is Wide," *New York Times*, April 12, 2007, p. A12; Peter Baker and Thomas E. Ricks, "In White House Plan, 'War Czar' Would Cut Through Bureaucracy," *Washington Post*, April 13, 2007, p. A13.

294 *"'This is what'"*: "DoD News Briefing with Secretary Gates and General Pace," The Pentagon, April 11, 2007; www.defenselink.mil/transcripts/transcript.aspx?transcriptid=3928.

294 *"In fact, the"*: Interview with Feaver, January 29, 2008; the chart accompanying Baker and Ricks, "In White House Plan, 'War Czar' Would Cut Through Bureaucracy," p. A13.

294 *"'I was worried,'"*: Stephanie Smith and Nitya Venkataraman, "Exclusive: Bush Says Petraeus' Timeline for Troops Not Open Ended," ABC News, April 11, 2008; abcnews.go.com/WN/Politics/story?id=4633561&page=1.

295 *"'He knew my'"*: Fred Barnes, "How Bush Decided on the Surge," *Weekly Standard*, February 4, 2008, p. 22; Interview with Jeff Kojac, January 3, 2008; Interview with Feaver, January 29, 2008.

295 *"Meanwhile, a bipartisan"*: *The Iraq Study Group Report* (New York: Vintage Books, 2006), p. xvi.

296 *"'If the bicycle'"*: Bumiller, *Condoleezza Rice*, pp. 299–300.

296 *"As his successor"*: Barnes, "How Bush Decided on the Surge," p. 22.

296 *"Though Cheney didn't"*: Hayes, *Cheney*, p. 515.

298 *"'Hadley drove a'"*: Bob Woodward, *The War Within* (New York: Simon & Schuster, 2008), p. 177.

9. "TRUST IS THE COIN OF THE REALM"

Page

305 *"And some even"*: Among them was one of the co-authors—see I. M. Destler, "A Job That Doesn't Work," *Foreign Policy* (Spring 1980), pp. 80–88.

311 *"Bush had no"*: Robert Draper, *Dead Certain: The Presidency of George W. Bush* (New York: Free Press), p. 282.

313 *"Decades later, his"*: Robert S. McNamara, *In Retrospect: The Tragedy and Lessons of Vietnam* (New York: Random House, 1995), p. 95.

314 *"The national security"*: Brent Scowcroft, "Passing the Baton: The Challenges of Statecraft for the New Administration," presentation at the U.S. Institute of Peace Conference; Washington, D.C., January 17, 2001; www.usip.org/events/pre2002/presents/baton_presents.html.

322 *"Bundy put it"*: McGeorge Bundy, "Mr. Reagan's Security Aide," *New York Times*, November 16, 1980, p. D21.

324 *"To use one"*: Data on television appearances compiled by the authors, available at www.brookings.edu/nsc.

325 *"Frustrated by the"*: Zbigniew Brzezinski, *Power and Principle: Memoirs of the National Security Adviser, 1977–1981* (New York: Farrar, Straus & Giroux, 1983), pp. 536–37.

326 *"'Politics pervades the'"*: Theodore C. Sorensen, *Decision-Making in the White House: The Olive Branch or the Arrows* (New York: Columbia University Press, 1963), p. 44.

Acknowledgments

This book has been long in the making. In an official sense, it began twelve years ago when, as faculty colleagues, we launched the National Security Council Project at the University of Maryland's Center for International and Security Studies. We used some of our earlier research in a course we co-taught on American Foreign Policymaking. The project continued when Daalder moved to the Brookings Institution, with the two organizations co-sponsoring a series of seven Oral History roundtables where former officials discussed the role of the national security adviser, the conduct of the NSC in the Nixon, Bush (41), and Clinton administrations, and how the Council operated across administrations on international economic policy, arms control, and U.S. relations with China.

This book draws substantially on those roundtables. But its roots lie deeper—in Destler's early research on foreign policymaking and the NSC, in Daalder's service on the NSC staff in 1995–96, and in interviews and related research conducted by one or both of us over more than three decades. And as we reflected on a half century of experience, we recognized that each administration's NSC was indelibly shaped by its top official, the national security adviser, and by the presidents they served. Hence we decided to center our book explicitly on these advisers: who they were, what roles they played, how they worked with their presidents, and whether and how they engaged (or excluded) the rest of the government.

In the process of research and writing, we accumulated many debts. First we must mention the organizations where we work: the Brookings Institution and the Maryland School of Public Policy, and the colleagues who encouraged us in our efforts, foremost amongst them Michael Armacost, Carlos Pascual, Steve Fetter, Richard Haass, Susan Schwab,

James Steinberg, and Strobe Talbott. Both institutions have provided congenial homes and financial support. The book further draws on literally hundreds of interviews and informal conversations with officials engaged in U.S. foreign policy, including the preponderant majority of those who have served as national security adviser since 1961. Some are directly quoted. All are deeply appreciated.

Over the course of our project we have engaged a number of able research assistants: Justin De Rise, Shakira Edwards, Alexandra Kahan, Anne Kramers Larson, Erik Leklem, Brett Marvin, Holly Plank, Josh Pollack, and Maranda Sorrels all gave time and talent in support of the book and the Oral History Roundtables that preceded it. Toby Shepard and Ian Livingston helped create the Web site—www.brookings.edu/nsc—where we posted much of the data and information that we have collected over the years. There the reader can also find additional facts about particular presidential administrations that may be helpful for university courses and other purposes. We owe a special debt to Jeffrey Gelman, whose indefatigable research especially on the later years was indispensable, and to Karla Nieting, who organized all of the Oral History workshops, oversaw their publication, and helped set up numerous interviews that informed much of this book.

In our quest for a publisher, we are grateful to Andrew Stuart, who connected us to Simon & Schuster and its legendary editor, Alice Mayhew. She, in turn, offered criticism that was both tough and sympathetic. The book is the better for it. We received helpful comments and suggestions from others who read the manuscript in whole or in part—including James Goldgeier, Karl F. Inderfurth, Catherine Kelleher, Glenn Kessler, Roger Labrie, James Lindsay, and Strobe Talbott.

On the home front, we have both profited immensely from moral support and substantive conversations with our spouses, Harriett Destler and Elisa Harris, each of whom continues to pursue a notable professional career in matters international. It is to them that we dedicate this book.

Our greatest debts, however, are to one another. We have enjoyed and learned much from our collaboration. We hope that it shows. And while we each drafted separate chapters, reflecting our respective comparative advantages, we are jointly responsible for every word.

Index

About the Authors

Ivo H. Daalder served on the National Security Council staff in the Clinton administration, and is now a senior fellow at the Brookings Institution. He is the co-author (with James M. Lindsay) of *America Unbound: The Bush Revolution in Foreign Policy*, which won the 2003 Lionel Gelber Prize. He lives in Vienna, Virginia.

I. M. (Mac) Destler is Saul I. Stern professor at the School of Public Policy at the University of Maryland. He is the author of numerous books, including *American Trade Politics* and (with Leslie Gelb and Anthony Lake) *Our Own Worst Enemy: The Unmaking of American Foreign Policy*. He lives in Great Falls, Virginia.